David Dalton

THE UKRAINIAN OLIGARCHY AFTER THE EUROMAIDAN

How Ukraine's Political Economy Regime Survived the Crisis

With a foreword by Andrew Wilson

Bibliografische Information der Deutschen Nationalbibliothek

Die Deutsche Nationalbibliothek verzeichnet diese Publikation in der Deutschen Nationalbibliografie; detaillierte bibliografische Daten sind im Internet über http://dnb.d-nb.de abrufbar.

Bibliographic information published by the Deutsche Nationalbibliothek

Die Deutsche Nationalbibliothek lists this publication in the Deutsche Nationalbibliografie; detailed bibliographic data are available in the Internet at http://dnb.d-nb.de.

Cover illustration: European Square, Kyiv, seen from the Dnipro Hotel, 2017. Picture taken by Dave Dalton. © copyright 2017 Dave Dalton

ISBN-13: 978-3-8382-1740-6
© *ibidem*-Verlag, Stuttgart 2023
Alle Rechte vorbehalten

Das Werk einschließlich aller seiner Teile ist urheberrechtlich geschützt. Jede Verwertung außerhalb der engen Grenzen des Urheberrechtsgesetzes ist ohne Zustimmung des Verlages unzulässig und strafbar. Dies gilt insbesondere für Vervielfältigungen, Übersetzungen, Mikroverfilmungen und elektronische Speicherformen sowie die Einspeicherung und Verarbeitung in elektronischen Systemen.

All rights reserved. No part of this publication may be reproduced, stored in or introduced into a retrieval system, or transmitted, in any form, or by any means (electronical, mechanical, photocopying, recording or otherwise) without the prior written permission of the publisher. Any person who does any unauthorized act in relation to this publication may be liable to criminal prosecution and civil claims for damages.

Printed in the EU

Soviet and Post-Soviet Politics and Society (SPPS) Vol. 260
ISSN 1614-3515

General Editor: Andreas Umland,
Stockholm Centre for Eastern European Studies, andreas.umland@ui.se

Commissioning Editor: Max Jakob Horstmann,
London, mjh@ibidem.eu

EDITORIAL COMMITTEE*

DOMESTIC & COMPARATIVE POLITICS
Prof. **Ellen Bos**, *Andrássy University of Budapest*
Dr. **Gergana Dimova**, *University of Winchester*
Dr. **Andrey Kazantsev**, *MGIMO (U) MID RF, Moscow*
Prof. **Heiko Pleines**, *University of Bremen*
Prof. **Richard Sakwa**, *University of Kent at Canterbury*
Dr. **Sarah Whitmore**, *Oxford Brookes University*
Dr. **Harald Wydra**, *University of Cambridge*

SOCIETY, CLASS & ETHNICITY
Col. **David Glantz**, *"Journal of Slavic Military Studies"*
Dr. **Marlène Laruelle**, *George Washington University*
Dr. **Stephen Shulman**, *Southern Illinois University*
Prof. **Stefan Troebst**, *University of Leipzig*

POLITICAL ECONOMY & PUBLIC POLICY
Dr. **Andreas Goldthau**, *Central European University*
Dr. **Robert Kravchuk**, *University of North Carolina*
Dr. **David Lane**, *University of Cambridge*
Dr. **Carol Leonard**, *Higher School of Economics, Moscow*
Dr. **Maria Popova**, *McGill University, Montreal*

FOREIGN POLICY & INTERNATIONAL AFFAIRS
Dr. **Peter Duncan**, *University College London*
Prof. **Andreas Heinemann-Grüder**, *University of Bonn*
Prof. **Gerhard Mangott**, *University of Innsbruck*
Dr. **Diana Schmidt-Pfister**, *University of Konstanz*
Dr. **Lisbeth Tarlow**, *Harvard University, Cambridge*
Dr. **Christian Wipperfürth**, *N-Ost Network, Berlin*
Dr. **William Zimmerman**, *University of Michigan*

HISTORY, CULTURE & THOUGHT
Dr. **Catherine Andreyev**, *University of Oxford*
Prof. **Mark Bassin**, *Södertörn University*
Prof. **Karsten Brüggemann**, *Tallinn University*
Dr. **Alexander Etkind**, *University of Cambridge*
Dr. **Gasan Gusejnov**, *Moscow State University*
Prof. **Leonid Luks**, *Catholic University of Eichstaett*
Dr. **Olga Malinova**, *Russian Academy of Sciences*
Dr. **Richard Mole**, *University College London*
Prof. **Andrei Rogatchevski**, *University of Tromsø*
Dr. **Mark Tauger**, *West Virginia University*

ADVISORY BOARD*

Prof. **Dominique Arel**, *University of Ottawa*
Prof. **Jörg Baberowski**, *Humboldt University of Berlin*
Prof. **Margarita Balmaceda**, *Seton Hall University*
Dr. **John Barber**, *University of Cambridge*
Prof. **Timm Beichelt**, *European University Viadrina*
Dr. **Katrin Boeckh**, *University of Munich*
Prof. em. **Archie Brown**, *University of Oxford*
Dr. **Vyacheslav Bryukhovetsky**, *Kyiv-Mohyla Academy*
Prof. **Timothy Colton**, *Harvard University, Cambridge*
Prof. **Paul D'Anieri**, *University of Florida*
Dr. **Heike Dörrenbächer**, *Friedrich Naumann Foundation*
Dr. **John Dunlop**, *Hoover Institution, Stanford, California*
Dr. **Sabine Fischer**, *SWP, Berlin*
Dr. **Geir Flikke**, *NUPI, Oslo*
Prof. **David Galbreath**, *University of Aberdeen*
Prof. **Alexander Galkin**, *Russian Academy of Sciences*
Prof. **Frank Golczewski**, *University of Hamburg*
Dr. **Nikolas Gvosdev**, *Naval War College, Newport, RI*
Prof. **Mark von Hagen**, *Arizona State University*
Dr. **Guido Hausmann**, *University of Munich*
Prof. **Dale Herspring**, *Kansas State University*
Dr. **Stefani Hoffman**, *Hebrew University of Jerusalem*
Prof. **Mikhail Ilyin**, *MGIMO (U) MID RF, Moscow*
Prof. **Vladimir Kantor**, *Higher School of Economics*
Dr. **Ivan Katchanovski**, *University of Ottawa*
Prof. em. **Andrzej Korbonski**, *University of California*
Dr. **Iris Kempe**, *"Caucasus Analytical Digest"*
Prof. **Herbert Küpper**, *Institut für Ostrecht Regensburg*
Dr. **Rainer Lindner**, *CEEER, Berlin*
Dr. **Vladimir Malakhov**, *Russian Academy of Sciences*

Dr. **Luke March**, *University of Edinburgh*
Prof. **Michael McFaul**, *Stanford University, Palo Alto*
Prof. **Birgit Menzel**, *University of Mainz-Germersheim*
Prof. **Valery Mikhailenko**, *The Urals State University*
Prof. **Emil Pain**, *Higher School of Economics, Moscow*
Dr. **Oleg Podvintsev**, *Russian Academy of Sciences*
Prof. **Olga Popova**, *St. Petersburg State University*
Dr. **Alex Pravda**, *University of Oxford*
Dr. **Erik van Ree**, *University of Amsterdam*
Dr. **Joachim Rogall**, *Robert Bosch Foundation Stuttgart*
Prof. **Peter Rutland**, *Wesleyan University, Middletown*
Prof. **Marat Salikov**, *The Urals State Law Academy*
Dr. **Gwendolyn Sasse**, *University of Oxford*
Prof. **Jutta Scherrer**, *EHESS, Paris*
Prof. **Robert Service**, *University of Oxford*
Mr. **James Sherr**, *RIIA Chatham House London*
Dr. **Oxana Shevel**, *Tufts University, Medford*
Prof. **Eberhard Schneider**, *University of Siegen*
Prof. **Olexander Shnyrkov**, *Shevchenko University, Kyiv*
Prof. **Hans-Henning Schröder**, *SWP, Berlin*
Dr. **Yuri Shapoval**, *Ukrainian Academy of Sciences*
Prof. **Viktor Shnirelman**, *Russian Academy of Sciences*
Dr. **Lisa Sundstrom**, *University of British Columbia*
Dr. **Philip Walters**, *"Religion, State and Society"*, *Oxford*
Prof. **Zenon Wasyliw**, *Ithaca College, New York State*
Dr. **Lucan Way**, *University of Toronto*
Dr. **Markus Wehner**, *"Frankfurter Allgemeine Zeitung"*
Dr. **Andrew Wilson**, *University College London*
Prof. **Jan Zielonka**, *University of Oxford*
Prof. **Andrei Zorin**, *University of Oxford*

* While the Editorial Committee and Advisory Board support the General Editor in the choice and improvement of manuscripts for publication, responsibility for remaining errors and misinterpretations in the series' volumes lies with the books' authors.

Soviet and Post-Soviet Politics and Society (SPPS)
ISSN 1614-3515

Founded in 2004 and refereed since 2007, SPPS makes available affordable English-, German-, and Russian-language studies on the history of the countries of the former Soviet bloc from the late Tsarist period to today. It publishes between 5 and 20 volumes per year and focuses on issues in transitions to and from democracy such as economic crisis, identity formation, civil society development, and constitutional reform in CEE and the NIS. SPPS also aims to highlight so far understudied themes in East European studies such as right-wing radicalism, religious life, higher education, or human rights protection. The authors and titles of all previously published volumes are listed at the end of this book. For a full description of the series and reviews of its books, see www.ibidem-verlag.de/red/spps.

Editorial correspondence & manuscripts should be sent to: Dr. Andreas Umland, Department of Political Science, Kyiv-Mohyla Academy, vul. Voloska 8/5, UA-04070 Kyiv, UKRAINE; andreas.umland@cantab.net

Business correspondence & review copy requests should be sent to: *ibidem* Press, Leuschnerstr. 40, 30457 Hannover, Germany; tel.: +49 511 2622200; fax: +49 511 2622201; spps@ibidem.eu.

Authors, reviewers, referees, and editors for (as well as all other persons sympathetic to) SPPS are invited to join its networks at www.facebook.com/group.php?gid=52638198614 www.linkedin.com/groups?about=&gid=103012 www.xing.com/net/spps-ibidem-verlag/

Recent Volumes

251 *Marc Dietrich*
A Cosmopolitan Model for Peacebuilding
The Ukrainian Cases of Crimea and the Donbas
ISBN 978-3-8382-1687-4

252 *Eduard Baidaus*
An Unsettled Nation
State-Building, Identity, and Separatism in Post-Soviet Moldova
With forewords by John-Paul Himka and David R. Marples
ISBN 978-3-8382-1582-2

253 *Igor Okunev, Petr Oskolkov (Eds.)*
Transforming the Administrative Matryoshka
The Reform of Autonomous Okrugs in the Russian Federation, 2003–2008
With a foreword by Vladimir Zorin
ISBN 978-3-8382-1721-5

254 *Winfried Schneider-Deters*
Ukraine's Fateful Years 2013–2019
Vol. I: The Popular Uprising in Winter 2013/2014
ISBN 978-3-8382-1725-3

255 *Winfried Schneider-Deters*
Ukraine's Fateful Years 2013–2019
Vol. II: The Annexation of Crimea and the War in Donbas
ISBN 978-3-8382-1726-0

256 *Robert M. Cutler*
Soviet and Post-Soviet Russian Foreign Policies II
East-West Relations in Europe and the Political Economy of the Communist Bloc, 1971–1991
With a foreword by Roger E. Kanet
ISBN 978-3-8382-1727-7

257 *Robert M. Cutler*
Soviet and Post-Soviet Russian Foreign Policies III
East-West Relations in Europe and Eurasia in the Post-Cold War Transition, 1991–2001
With a foreword by Roger E. Kanet
ISBN 978-3-8382-1728-4

258 *Pawel Kowal, Iwona Reichardt, Kateryna Pryshchepa (Eds.)*
Three Revolutions: Mobilization and Change in Contemporary Ukraine III
Archival Records and Historical Sources on the 1990 Revolution on Granite
ISBN 978-3-8382-1376-7

259 *Mikhail Minakov (Ed.)*
Philosophy Unchained.
Developments in Post-Soviet Philosophical Thought.
With a foreword by Christopher Donohue
ISBN 978-3-8382-1768-0

Contents

List of Figures 7
List of Tables 9
Abstract 11
Acknowledgements 12
Foreword 13
1 Introduction 15
   1.1 Topic, basic definitions and approach 15
   1.2 What is the link between regime resilience and low standards of living? 16
   1.3 What explains Ukraine's poor record on economic growth, other than oligarchy? 22
   1.4 Thesis, "national" scope and book structure 27
   1.5 Contribution and wider implications 31
   1.6 Methodology, methods and "research journey" 33
2 Wealth defence and prosperity institutions 39
   2.1 Introduction and "rational actors" approach 39
   2.2 The theories of wealth defence and institutional prosperity, and their relevance to Ukraine 41
   2.3 The two theories conjoined 58
   2.4 Institutional economics, old and new 59
3 The origins, operations, resilience and evolution of the Ukrainian oligarchy 63
   3.1 Outline and aims 63
   3.2 Ukrainian oligarchs and the oligarchic system 64
   3.3 Evolution of the Ukrainian oligarchy 83
4 The wealth of the very rich in modern Ukraine 99
   4.1 Preliminaries 99
   4.2 Patterns of elite wealth distribution and dynamics in contemporary Ukraine 118
   4.3 Chapter summary and conclusions 148

5	Voting on institutional prosperity bills in the Verkhovna Rada, 2014-17	155
	5.1 Preliminaries	155
	5.2 Voting patterns in the Rada on "prosperity" legislation: three analyses	174
	5.3 Chapter findings and conclusions	215
6	Post-Euromaidan energy rent-extraction schemes, amid energy-sector reforms	221
	6.1 Introduction and approach	221
	6.2 Contextualising tools	224
	6.3 Rent-extraction schemes in the Ukrainian energy sector, post-Euromaidan: three case studies	241
	6.4 Chapter findings and conclusions	270
7	Conclusion	275
	7.1 What kind of institution is the Ukrainian oligarchy? How did it survive the Euromaidan?	275
	7.2 A "currency flow" model	278
	7.3 The Ukrainian oligarchy as a process	283
	7.4 Economic side-effects of institutional reproduction	286
	7.5 Suggestions for further research	290
References		293

List of Figures

Figure 1.1:	Real GDP per head index for selected east European countries, 2017	18
Figure 1.2:	Human Development Index (HDI) for some east European countries & China, 1991-2017	22
Figure 1.3:	Currency flows of the Ukrainian oligarchy	28
Figure 2.1:	Winters' "Oligarchies and wealth defense"	47
Figure 3.1:	Konończuk's "Links of the main oligarchic groups in Ukraine"	79
Figure 3.2:	Political rights scores for Ukraine, Russia & Belarus, 1991-2017	87
Figure 4.1:	Estimated wealth-income ratios for Ukraine & Russia, 2008-17	117
Figure 4.2:	Wealth & income Ginis for selected countries, 2016-17	121
Figure 4.3:	Ukraine & Russia: Forbes' billionaires vs per head GDP, 2017	124
Figure 4.4:	Focus-100 domestic business wealth vs national wealth, 2006-17	131
Figure 4.5:	Focus-100 business wealth as a share of national wealth: median & IQR, 2006-17	134
Figure 4.6:	Domestic material power of the Ukrainian economic elite vs PFTS stock index, 2006-17	136
Figures 4.7 & 4.8:	Business wealth of the rich as a share of national wealth vs years on the rich list, 2006-17 (top chart); zoomed-in version of the same (bottom chart)	142
Figure 4.9:	Changing share of domestic business wealth of the "core" rich in national wealth, 2013 vs 2017	150
Figure 4.10:	Dynamics of domestic & external material resource power of the Ukrainian economic elite, 2006-17	153
Figure 5.1:	Formal factional dynamics in the 7th convocation of the Rada, 2012-14	176
Figure 5.2:	Share of formal Rada factions voting "for" business environment laws, Feb-Nov 2014	188

Figure 5.3:	Contribution of "for" votes of formal Rada factions on business environment laws, Feb-Nov 2014	190
Figure 5.4:	Factional shares of 5-party coalition voting "for" prosperity bills, Dec 2014-Apr 2016	194
Figures 5.5 & 5.6:	Associated "for" votes of core coalition with PW & the FLB group (top chart); & of the Opposition Bloc with Akhmetov & Medvedchuk groups (bottom chart), period 2	196
Figure 5.7:	"For" votes of formal Rada factions on prosperity laws, Dec 2014-Mar 2016	198
Figure 5.8:	Change in formal Rada faction shares voting "for" prosperity laws, periods 2 & 3	202
Figure 5.9:	Changing shares of "old" oligarch groups voting "for" prosperity bills, period 2 & 3	203
Figures 5.10 & 5.11:	Associated "for" votes of core coalition parties & FLB group (top chart); & of post-PoR parties & informal factions (bottom chart), period 3	204
Figure 5.12:	Change in average contribution of small Rada parties to "for" votes, periods 2 & 3	206
Figure 5.13:	"For" votes of formal Rada factions on prosperity laws, Apr 2016-Dec 2017	207
Figures 6.1 & 6.2:	Ukraine's gas & heat tariffs in east European comparison, 2013 (top chart); retail gas tariffs for different users in Ukraine, 2013 (bottom chart)	227
Figure 6.3:	Volumes of production, import & use of natural gas in Ukraine, 2010-17	231
Figure 6.4:	Naftogaz & main subsidiaries: structure & functions	234
Figure 6.5:	Convergence & re-divergence of gas tariffs for household & industrial users, 2013-17	264
Figure 7.1:	Currency flows of the Ukrainian oligarchy	281
Figure 7.2:	Institutional recreation of the Ukrainian oligarchy sets up a negative economic feedback loop	289

List of Tables

Table 1.1:	Stock of inward FDI for selected east European countries by 2017	21
Table 3.1:	GFI estimates for illicit capital outflows from Ukraine, 2004-13; US$ bn, unless otherwise stated	67
Table 3.2:	Extractive practices of political influence of the Ukrainian oligarchy	83
Table 4.1:	Ukraine's "experimental" balance sheet of non-financial assets (excl housing), 2014; UAH bn	112
Table 4.2:	Ukraine's "experimental" balance sheet of financial assets & liabilities, 2014; UAH bn	113
Table 4.3:	Ukraine: the share of non-financial assets in household wealth, 2008-17	114
Table 4.4:	National wealth estimates for Ukraine & Russia from national accounts, 2008-17	115
Table 4.5:	Comparison of national wealth estimates for Ukraine & Russia, 2014	116
Table 4.6:	Forbes' estimates of the private wealth of Ukrainian & Russian billionaires, 2013 & 2017	120
Table 4.7:	Wealth concentration in Ukraine & Russia in international comparison, 2017	123
Table 4.8:	Focus-100 domestic business wealth & Ukraine's estimated national wealth, 2006-17; US$ bn, unless otherwise stated	129
Table 4.9:	Distribution of Focus-100 domestic business wealth: 5 number summary & IQR, 2006-17; US$ m	133
Table 4.10:	Individual longevity on Focus-100 rich list, 2006-17	139
Table 4.11:	Average annual business wealth of individuals on the Focus-100 rich list, 2006-17	140
Table 4.12:	Ukraine's "core" rich, 2006-17	146
Table 5.1:	Deputies in the 8th convocation of the Verkhovna Rada by "old" oligarch group & formal faction	171

Table 5.2:	Results of Rada elections in Ukraine for parties taking seats in the national vote, 2012 & 2014	178
Table 5.3:	The changing formal factional allegiances between Radas of re-elected deputies, 2014-15	181
Table 5.4:	People's deputies of the 7th & 8th convocations who appear on Focus-100 rich list, 2006-17	183
Table 5.5:	Voting results on 23 "institutional prosperity" bills, Feb 2014-Dec 2017	186
Table 5.6:	Do "old" oligarch groups tend to vote against prosperity bills in period 2? (%)	211
Table 5.7:	Chi-square test & Cramér's V measure for voting of "old" oligarch groups on prosperity laws, 2014-17	213
Table 5.8:	Distribution of "old" oligarch Rada MPs by simplified formal faction, Dec 2014-Dec 2017; (no.)	214
Table 6.1:	Ukraine's public finances, 2010-17; % of GDP	230
Table 6.2:	Value of the Svistunkivsko-Chervonolutsk gas deposit, by contrasting reserve estimates	245
Table 6.3:	Estimated value of volumes of gas involved in regional "manipulations"	266
Table 6.4:	Key features of elite rent-extraction schemes in the Ukrainian gas sector, 1995-2017	272

Abstract

This book examines the process of reproduction of the modern Ukrainian oligarchy, and its survival as an evolving political economy institution across the "critical juncture" of the Euromaidan revolt of 2013/14 by way of its "extractive" political and economic practices, focusing on the role played by material resource power (wealth). Covering capacities and practices central to the reproduction process, the empirical chapters describe, analyse and explain the dynamics of the wealth of the Ukrainian super-rich in relation to Ukrainian society in 2006-17, and its political implications; the conversion of wealth into political influence through vote-buying in the Ukrainian parliament; and elite rent-extraction schemes in the Ukrainian gas sector, illustrating one means of conversion of political influence back into wealth. A key argument is that continuity in informal practices between the Yanukovych and Poroshenko presidencies, and of the elite political-economic networks that conduct them, signals continuity in the dominant political economy regime across the two periods. The main economic effects of the continuation of the informal practices of the Ukrainian oligarchy since its inception in the 1990s have been to undermine state capacity and investment, helping to explain Ukraine's perennially poor economic performance and low average income. Although this will not surprise close observers of Ukraine's post-Soviet economic development, what is new in this study is that it shows concretely some ways in which poor national economic outcomes can be connected to specific political-material processes of reproduction of Ukraine's governance structures. Based on the empirical investigations, the book proposes a novel way of envisaging the interconnection between the capacities, practices and processes of the Ukrainian oligarchy at a more general level, represented as a "currency flow", or circuit, of wealth and power. To the academic literature on the dynamics of informally dominated post-communist political and political economy regimes, the study adds, therefore, a detailed, integrated, and internally comparative case study of Ukraine.

Acknowledgements

The first people I have to thank are my PhD supervisors, Professor Andrew Wilson and Dr Peter Duncan, not only for their invaluable guidance, support and feedback while I was doing the research for this book, but also for letting me onto the PhD programme at UCL SSEES in the first place. Also, Joan Hoey of the EIU and the late Professor Alan Smith, who gave me references.

Of the many other UCL SSEES academics who helped me along the way, I'd like to thank Dr Randolph Bruno, Dr Svetlana Makarova, Marta Jenkala, Professor Richard Mole and Dr Uilleam Blacker, whose courses I attended; Dr Ben Noble, who read my upgrade report in detail, offering much useful advice; Dr Elodie Douarin, Professor Nauro Campos and Dr Benjamin Abrams, on whose courses I taught; Dr Felix Ciută, who ran a very useful PhD evening class on social research; and Dr Seth Graham, whose PhD writing class on Teams was a lifeline during lockdown. Among my *odnoklasnyky*, I thank Bohdana Kurylo, Dr Yuliya Klimova and Dr Jakob Hauter for their companionship and support. Thanks also to my PhD examiners, Dr Sarah Whitmore and Dr Rasmus Nilsson, who suggested many improvements to the text, as well as to Irina Voitusik in Kyiv, who tried to teach me Ukrainian. Of the "Twitter" academics who gave me suggestions and encouragement, I want to thank Dr Alexander Clarkson, who is usually right on Ukraine, and Professor Jeremy Morris, who is usually right on Russia.

Most of all, in lieu of a dedication, I want to thank and acknowledge the contribution of my wife, Inna, who strongly encouraged me to return to study for a doctorate — which is considerable income foregone, as an economist might say. She helped me to put together the thesis at the end, and undertook most of the proofreading for this book. It's a lot to ask. Before the onset of the war with Russia in early 2014, we spent many happy holidays in Ukraine, especially in Donetsk and Crimea; and, after that, more often in Kyiv and Poltava. May it soon be so again. So, to all of the above, and to others whom I have failed to mention, I say: До зустрічі на морі в Криму!

Foreword

David Dalton's excellent book advances research in four key areas. First, it builds on the analysis of Oleh Havrylyshyn (2017) and others that has shown how slow or partial economic reform after communism was not only less successful, but created cycles of self-perpetuation. Since the 1990s, Ukraine has been stuck in the "post-Soviet" condition; not just as a label for neo-colonialism and Russian influence, but as a unique sub-type of political economy and politics that proved resistant to reform. Dalton explains that this was why Ukraine's attempts so far at catch-up reform had only limited effects. Certainly, before the Russian invasion of February 2022, Ukraine's main problem was oligarchy and corruption.

Dalton's second key area of focus is on comparative oligarchy. He looks at oligarchy in the West and in the developing world, drawing on the work of Jeffrey A. Winters (2011). But the post-Soviet region is where oligarchy is such a key term and problem. Dalton produces key insights in comparative oligarchy studies: on Alena Ledeneva's work on informal politics (2013), on what Henry Hale (2015) calls single versus competitive pyramids (networks of influence), on the role of the state and key actors like the president. Dalton shows both what Ukrainian oligarchy shares with oligarchy in other post-Soviet states, and what is distinct.

Third, Dalton's most original contribution is his detailed examination of oligarchs' self-defence mechanisms, looking at the way in which Ukrainian oligarchs have proven adept at surviving, shape-shifting and defending their interests—despite two would-be revolutions. A Marxist analysis might look only at oligarchs' material wealth. Dalton provides the data on this, but also shows how this wealth is then used to own media, to use that media to sell parties and politicians, and to penetrate state institutions like parliament to defend their interests. There is an abundance of empirical detail in the book looking at how modes of influence in parliament work, and how legislation and financial flows are shaped to serve oligarchic interests. Dalton's case studies also show how oligarchs buy influence and fight each other in the courts.

Fourth, Dalton looks at oligarchy as a key reason for Ukraine's economic underperformance since 1991. A famous Deutsche Bank report on the eve of Ukrainian independence argued it was one of the best-placed Soviet Republics for future growth. Although Ukraine and Poland started in roughly the same place, the Polish economy is now three times as big. Dalton shows how oligarchy is not just a symptom and general cause of lower growth; he explains exactly how this works. Oligarchic networks weaken the state institutionally; so it is less able to collect tax, spend and administer effectively. Oligarchic wealth leads to offshorisation, which weakens the state financially. Offshorisation means there is less fixed capital investment; so Ukraine remains stuck in a low-wage, low-productivity economy. The final indirect stage in what Dalton calls this "negative feedback loop" is that low living standards encourage migration, weighing on Ukraine's long-term growth.

Finally, Dalton's book is an invaluable guide to what might happen next. What effect will the latest phase of the war with Russia have on Ukraine's oligarchy? It may provide a shock to the system stronger than the Revolution of Dignity of 2013/14. Most oligarchs have lost wealth and physical assets. Their media is now part of the state-supervised wartime "United News Marathon". The president, Volodymyr Zelenskyi, who came to office in 2019, is much more his own man now than when his government's "de-oligarchisation" law was passed in 2021. Parliament sits, but sessions are necessarily minimal and business-like. State power is stronger in the regions, where oligarchs used to build local fiefdoms. As well as being a highly informative study of independent Ukraine's first thirty years of economics and politics, therefore, Dalton's book is an invaluable guide to how these factors might affect oligarchy's future in Ukraine.

Andrew Wilson, Professor of Ukrainian Studies, UCL SSEES.

1 Introduction

1.1 Topic, basic definitions and approach

This book is about the contemporary Ukrainian oligarchy. It sets out some of the main political and economic capacities and practices by which the oligarchy is reproduced as an institution, drawing attention also to key economic outcomes of this process. My use of the term "oligarchy" for this institution reflects local convention, but also aims to underline a focus on the material dimension of its reproduction. With modern Ukraine as a detailed case study of a post-communist political economy regime dominated by informal modes of operation, the framework developed here offers a fresh angle on the development problems of countries in which the economic and political realms of social life have not undergone the same process of separation as in the liberal democratic West (Magyar and Madlovics, 2020, p. 8).

But who counts as an oligarch, and what is an oligarchy? In *The Politics*, Aristotle defines oligarchs as the wealthy few and oligarchy as the self-interested form of their rule, reserving the term "aristocracy" for the version of minority rule of the rich that is better able to balance the interests of all social groups (Aristotle, 1996, pp. 71-72). In modern Ukraine, oligarchs may be described, adapting the definitions of Winters (2011) and Pleines (2016a), as the very rich heads of business conglomerates who are involved in national politics to protect and augment wealth, their characteristic "resource power". But they are only one set of actors in a larger institutional structure to which their group lends its name, with "structure" here indicating a repeating pattern of group activity, somewhat independent of its individual membership, that is relatively stable over time. As a first step, therefore, I will define the Ukrainian oligarchy relationally, as a system of elite rule that links oligarchs and their business networks in a sometimes rivalrous, but often mutually beneficial relationship with electorally successful politicians and their networks in the state apparatus.

Mainly a work of political economy, this book draws also on the disciplines of politics, political sociology, economic sociology and macroeconomics. Political economy can be distinguished by its adoption of a social science approach to the study of economics (Stilwell, 2012, p. 8), as opposed to attempting to emulate the natural sciences. But if political economy is the study of the relation of the political and economic realms of social life to one another, it is also the study of how different schools of thought have conceived of this. Although the approach of this book is somewhat eclectic in this respect, it is closest to the institutional school. That is, my investigation takes as one of its starting points a "new" institutional theory of economic development. In the final empirical chapter, however, on elite rent-extraction schemes in the Ukrainian energy sector, my approach takes its cue more from "old" institutionalism, with its concepts of habit and evolution, and an emphasis on descriptive contextualisation. One reason for this is that "old" institutionalism better aligns with the "informality" approach to political analysis outlined in my examination of voting patterns in the Verkhovna Rada, Ukraine's parliament (chapter 5).

1.2 What is the link between regime resilience and low standards of living?

1.2.1 Origin and resilience of the Ukrainian oligarchy vs Ukraine's chronic economic underperformance

The essential components of the oligarchy as a political economy institution emerged in Ukraine in the early to mid-1990s, following its declaration of independence in 1991 from an ailing Soviet Union, and crystallised towards the end of the same decade. Since then, it has come through two major domestic political upheavals (the Orange Revolution of 2004/05 and the Euromaidan Revolution of 2013/14), as well as military conflict with Russia, more or less intact. Early on in my research, therefore, it became apparent that the Ukrainian oligarchy is a resilient institution which, following a number of episodes of serious political disjuncture, has so far been able to pick itself up and carry on much as before.

The original motivation for this project, however, was Ukraine's chronic macroeconomic underperformance in the independence era. A basic stylisation of regional economic development since the early 1990s is that the former communist countries of central eastern Europe (and the Baltic states) generally did much better than those of the former Soviet Union (excluding the Baltic states). In particular, economies in the first group tended to record shallower and shorter "transition" recessions, and to recover more quickly (Turley and Luke, 2011, pp. 72-74; Douarin and Mickiewicz, 2017, pp. 5-6; Roaf et al, 2014).

In Ukraine, by contrast, economic performance has been weak even by the standards of other former Soviet economies, so that by 2017 Ukraine's real GDP per head, as a general measure of living standards, was still 20% below its level at the time of the break-up of the Soviet Union in 1991, according to IMF data. This is shown in Figure 1.1 below, which uses simple indices of real GDP per head, with 1991 as the base year. Ukraine's real output per head in 2017 is represented by the height of darker grey bar on the right-hand side of the chart relative to a 1991 starting level of 100, represented by the dashed, grey horizontal line. The use of a real purchasing power parity (PPP) measure allows comparison of living standards between countries over time by taking into account the differential rates of change in living costs. The better economic performance of some of Ukraine's former communist neighbours is indicated by the height of their 2017 output bars relative to the starting line in 1991. On this measure, therefore, while Ukraine's output per person remained below the starting line, the average standard of living in Poland rose almost threefold over the interim, and more than doubled in Romania and Belarus. Even for Russia, annual output in 2017 was 27% higher than in 1991. The difference in economic performance is more striking because the starting points for Poland and Romania in 1991 were similar to that of Ukraine, while for Belarus, real GDP per head was a little lower. As a result, Ukraine in 2017 found itself close to the bottom of the European income rankings, alongside Moldova and Kosovo, when measured by GNI (gross national income) per head (World Bank DataBank).

Figure 1.1: Real GDP per head index for selected east European countries, 2017

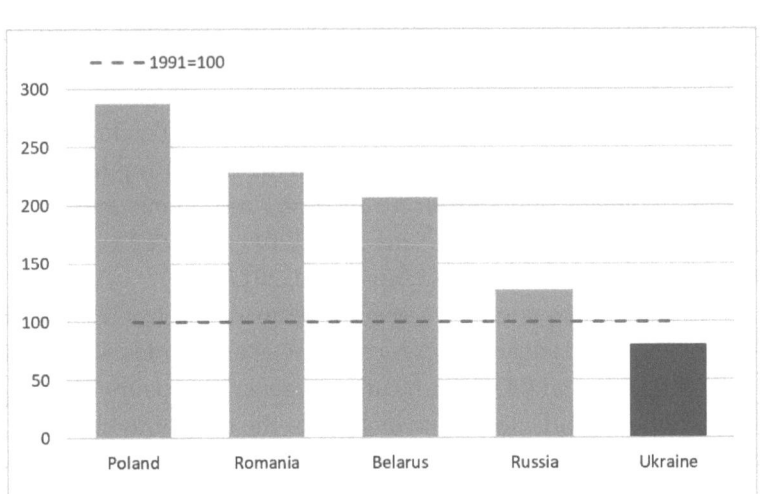

Sources: IMF, World Economic Outlook (WEO) Database, October 2019. Available: https://www.imf.org/en/Publications/WEO/weo-database/2019/October.
Note: Own calculations, based on data in 2011 US dollars, PPP.

1.2.2 Was Ukraine's GDP growth really so poor?

There has been much dispute about the veracity of east European economic growth data, especially regarding the scale of the falls in officially recorded output in the 1990s. Anders Aslund (2001) brings together a number of such concerns, including over conceptual and measurement problems, as well as a failure to take into account the size of the informal economy, which is the part of economic activity that goes on, untaxed, beneath the authorities' radar.

In Ukraine, the informal economy ballooned in this period. Based on an IMF report, Marko Bojcun suggests that, by 1995, it may have accounted for up to half of all Ukrainian economic activity (Bojcun, 2020, p. 187), higher than for Russia or Lithuania, where it is estimated to have peaked at around 40% of official GDP. The country's informal economy remains substantial, according to the Ministry of Economic Development, at an estimated 33% of official GDP in the first nine months of 2017 (Burakovsky et al, 2018, p. 15).

Taking into account the range of flaws in official statistics that he notes, Aslund re-estimates real GDP (rather than real GDP per head) for the transition economies at the end of the 1990s, concluding that only the war-torn former Soviet republics, such as Georgia or Tajikistan, really suffered very large production losses. For the economies of central eastern Europe and the Baltics, he argues, no real drop in output occurred. In the case of Ukraine, rather than falling by more than half, as official statistics indicate, he estimates a fall in real output of just 15% from 1991 to its nadir towards the end of that decade (Aslund, 2001, p. 15).

Some of these data criticisms appear valid, especially those concerning the change of reporting incentives, with overreporting encouraged during the socialist era by production targets, and underreporting since the move towards a market-based system linked both to the desire to avoid paying taxes to enrich corrupt state elites and to the failure to capture the growth of new private businesses (Havrylyshyn et al, 2016).

Nevertheless, the scale of Aslund's proposed readjustment of the official numbers is problematic. In Ukraine's case, for example, if output had declined by just 15% cumulatively in the 1990s, or about the same as in 2009 owing to the global financial crisis, then it might be expected that the impact on indicators of life expectancy and poverty would be similar. So, by the middle of the 1990s average life expectancy at birth in Ukraine had dropped by 1.7 years for women, to 72.5 years, and by 3.4 years for men, to 61.2, both compared with 1991 (World Bank DataBank, *World Development Indicators*). Over the same period, the share of Ukrainians living on less than US$3.90 per day — a measure of the incidence of poverty — peaked at just over one-fifth of the population. Towards the end of the first decade of the current century, by contrast, no such sharp deteriorations were recorded. Even on Aslund's revised GDP estimates, however, Ukraine's performance remains very poor in regional comparison, and it is this relatively worse position that is one of the two main research puzzles behind my investigation.

INTRODUCTION

1.2.3 Ukraine's socio-economic performance in wider comparative perspective

Taking a wider view of Ukraine's economic and social development over the past three decades, following Oleh Havrylyshyn (2017, pp. 35-60), only confirms this picture of Ukraine's relatively worse performance, even in post-Soviet comparison.

Table 1.1 below shows 2017 World Bank data for the stock of inward foreign direct investment (FDI) for some east European countries. Inward FDI is investment into domestic companies from abroad, usually implying a degree of enterprise control. Its economic significance is not only that it provides additional demand for home-produced goods and services, but that it also tends to raise production and export capacity over the longer term, without adding to foreign debt, as would borrowing from abroad. A notable feature of the data is the large absolute volume of investment accumulated in Russia (US$400bn) and Poland (US$240bn) since the onset of economic transition (World Bank DataBank, *World Development Indicators*). However, both as a share of 2017 GDP and by head of population, the stock of inward FDI is considerably lower for the eastern Slavic countries (Russia, Ukraine and Belarus) than for the former centrally planned economies to their west (Poland, Slovakia and Estonia). In the first group, accumulated inward FDI was equal to 20-40% of 2017 GDP, or US$1,000-3,000 per head; in the second group, it was equal to 45-90% of GDP, or US$6,000-18,000 per head. A common explanation for this is the differences in investment climate, or how welcoming, in terms of policy and regulation, each economy is perceived to be by foreign investors. By 2017 Ukraine's total FDI stock, of US$43bn, was relatively high as a share of its 2017 GDP, following the battering of the Ukrainian economy by war and recession in 2014-15. Its stock of inward FDI per head, however, at less than US$1,000 per person over 26 years, was below even that of Belarus, which did not really begin to consider significant market reforms until 2014 (IMF, 2016b; Dalton, 2016).

Table 1.1: Stock of inward FDI for selected east European countries by 2017

	FDI (US$ bn)	Share 2017 GDP (%)	FDI per head (US$)
Ukraine	43.3	38.6	972
Russia	441.1	27.9	3,031
Belarus	12.8	23.4	1,358
Poland	238.5	45.3	6,284
Slovakia	59.5	62.3	10,923
Estonia	23.9	89.1	18,135

Source: World Bank DataBank, *World Development Indicators*. Available: https://databank.worldbank.org/source/world-development-indicators.

Finally, the UN's Human Development Index (HDI) endeavours to produce a more rounded indicator of socio-economic progress and well-being than given by GDP alone (UNDP, Human Development Data Center). It combines assessments of levels of income (GNI per head), education (adult literacy rates and enrolment ratios) and heath (life expectancy at birth) into a single number between 0 and 1, with 1 as the best outcome. Figure 1.2 below shows the change in the HDI index number for several east European countries (and China) between 1991 and 2017, presented alongside the average change in the HDI across the world over the same period, depicted as the two bars on the right-hand side of the chart.

Reading these bars against the left-hand scale, the world average index number rose from 0.6 in 1991 to just above 0.7 in 2017, or by about 20%. This is indicated on the chart by a black dot between the bars, to be read against the right-hand scale. In eastern Europe, while the pace of improvement for Poland is a little above the world average, it is considerably below this for Russia and Moldova.

In contrast to Russia and Poland, but in common with Moldova, by 2017 Ukraine remained among the countries considered to be of "medium" level in terms of human development (that is, with scores of 0.5-0.8), its index number rising to just 0.747, from 0.701 in 1991. The improvement over this period in Ukraine, of just 6.6%, is therefore the least impressive of the countries shown here. By

INTRODUCTION

contrast, the index number for China shot up by close to 50% over the same quarter of a century.

Figure 1.2: Human Development Index (HDI) for some east European countries & China, 1991-2017

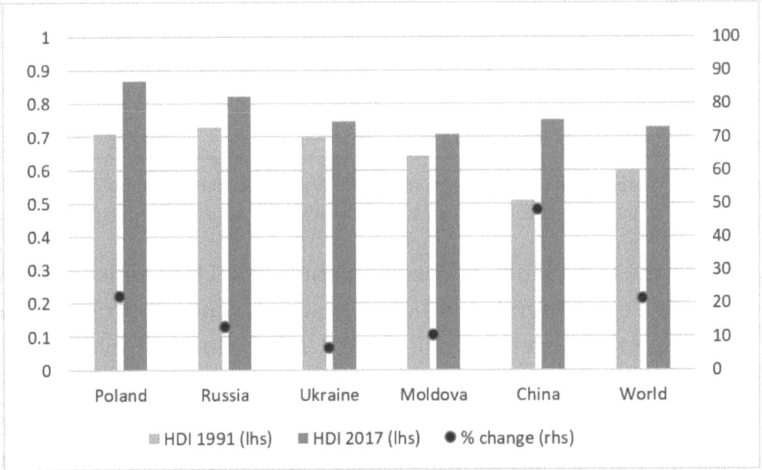

[Bar chart showing HDI 1991 (lhs), HDI 2017 (lhs), and % change (rhs) for Poland, Russia, Ukraine, Moldova, China, and World]

Sources: United Nations Development Programme (UNDP), Human Development Data Center. UNDP, *Human Development Reports*. Available: http://www.hdr.undp.org/en/data. Own calculations.

On all these counts, therefore — standard of living, foreign investment, life expectancy and educational levels — Ukraine's socio-economic performance in the post-communist era has been worse than most of its near neighbours, while its sub-optimal political economy regime has nonetheless remained intact.

1.3 What explains Ukraine's poor record on economic growth, other than oligarchy?

1.3.1 Initial conditions, macroeconomic stabilisation, market reforms and institution-building

Over the past three decades, a large body of economic research has been developed to account for the marked variation in the patterns of income growth among the post-communist economies of eastern

Europe, proposing numerous explanations for this other than oligarchy. The following thumbnail sketch of these explanations is based mainly on Turley and Luke (2011, pp. 225-264).

One approach has been to distinguish explanations that focus on the unexpectedly severe recessions of the 1990s from those that try to identify the main determinants of growth in transition economies over the longer term. This reflects concerns about the applicability of traditional neoclassical theories of long-term economic growth, based on the accumulation of production factors, such as physical and human capital, and technological change (Douarin and Mickiewicz, 2017, p. 147), to the transition recessions of the 1990s, when issues of resource reallocation by way of systemic transformation came more to the fore.

Two key factors behind the transition recessions of the 1990s are economic shocks from the disintegration of trade links and the disorganisation of supply chains. The disruption of trade was due primarily to the break-up of the CMEA (the Council of Mutual Economic Assistance, a trading bloc dominated by the Soviet Union) and the Soviet rouble zone. On the disordering of supply links between firms, it is argued, most prominently by Oliver Blanchard, that liberalisation offered firms previously locked into planned production relationships the room to bargain with a wider range of buyers on price. With one party in the transaction (the producer) having better information about the product, however, there was no guarantee that the bargaining process would succeed, so that old production relationships broke down, but without new ones taking their place (Turley and Luke, 2011, p. 243).

By now, however, the core economic explanations for the cross-country variations in growth over the long term have been identified by way of a large number of econometric studies and, in particular, of "meta-analyses" of them (for example, Turley and Luke, 2011, pp. 248-260), the aim of which is to iron out methodological errors and inconsistencies between studies and, in light of this, identify valid common patterns and trends. Chief among the determinants of growth so identified are initial conditions, macroeconomic stabilisation, market reforms and institution-building.

Initial conditions include the institutional inheritances carried over from both the communist and pre-communist eras, with institutions understood broadly as sets of socially transmitted rules guiding and constraining individual action. Of the factors carried over from the communist era can be included industrial structure, the degree of trade integration with the CMEA, the extent of macroeconomic imbalance at the start of transition, and length of time under communist rule.

In the post-communist period, dissimilar initial conditions are found to affect the tendency of the different economies to adopt the policies required both to achieve macroeconomic stabilisation and to embed the rules needed for a market economy to work. According to these studies, the length and depth of the 1990s recessions is linked with the timing of adoption of liberalising reforms, which centrally involved the removal of administrative price controls; and on macroeconomic stabilisation, which usually aimed to bring down the high post-communist inflation triggered by price liberalisation, including through control of budget deficits. The message of this is that rapid reformers tended to suffer the least. Alongside structural market reforms, over the longer term, the pace of economic recovery and growth is found to correlate with the adoption of institutional reforms, such as on property rights and the development of appropriate regulatory bodies. Although these were usually politically more difficult everywhere, countries that moved fastest on the first set of liberalising reforms tended to do so also on the second institutional ones.

Two other factors are frequently mentioned in the literature as distinguishing the best east European post-communist economic performers from the worst. These are, respectively, EU membership and regional conflict, under the reasoning that qualification for EU membership imposed an additional degree of reform discipline, whereas war destroyed parts of the labour force, physical assets and the confidence needed among economic actors to drive a sustained expansion in output.

1.3.2 Lagging reform was central in Ukraine's case

Reform lags shown by EBRD transition indicators

Just as macroeconomic stabilisation and the introduction of market reforms are conceived to have set the groundwork for sustained economic growth, so the lag in the introduction of such reforms in Ukraine is frequently identified as a key reason for the depth and duration of the country's transition slump in 1991-98, when output volume fell by 53% from peak to trough (calculated using same IMF data as for Figure 1.1), and for its generally poor economic outcomes since then.

In his overview of the economic growth record of Ukraine, Havrylyshyn, for example, reproduces Ukraine's EBRD "transition indicator" scores on two sets of market economy reforms, liberalisation and institutional development, in regional context up until 2010 (Havrylyshyn, 2017, pp. 39-40). The combined scores for economic liberalisation measures show that Ukraine lagged behind not just the leading reformers such as Poland and other central European states, but, until 2010, other former Soviet countries also. Institutional reforms were often delayed for political reasons across the region. In Ukraine, however, they did not make much headway until the end of the 1990s, with the reforming government of Viktor Yushchenko. In the following decade, although Ukraine overtook other former Soviet states on this indicator, it remained far behind the region's leading reformers.

Why did reforms lag in Ukraine?

This raises questions, however, not only of why progress on the transformation of economic institutions has been slow in Ukraine, even compared with some countries with similar starting conditions, but also of who has been doing the slowing, and how, so that the issue of reform lags appears as an explanation in need of an explanation. This is where a political economy approach — examining the changing incentive structures that face social actors as a result of the evolving relations of political and economic power — comes into its own. Here, we may start with two proximate causes for the delay in reforms. The first is that towards the end of the Soviet era, nascent reformist elements in Ukraine, gathered in the Rukh movement but aware of their own weakness as a national political force, made a "Grand Bargain" with the "nationalising" nomenklatura (the communist-party-controlled political and state economic elite) led by Leonid Kravchuk, Ukraine's first post-Soviet president, allowing them to remain in power in return for their support for Ukrainian independence (Wilson, 2015, pp. 174-175). Kravchuk, in turn, focused on nation-building, neglecting urgent economic reforms, which did not really begin to get under way until 1994. Second, for well-connected actors, the combination of limited property rights introduced in the late Soviet era and the lag in market economic reforms in the early post-communist period produced opportunities for significant wealth accumulation (chapter 3). The most successful of them, dubbed "oligarchs", used the political power conferred by their newfound wealth both to tip the privatisation process in their favour, so boosting the process of wealth concentration still further (chapter 4), and to perpetuate the conditions of incomplete political and economic reform, of which they were the main beneficiaries (Hellman, 1998).

Rather than examining again the impact on Ukraine's economic performance of its institutional inheritance, or of economic shocks from the break-up of the Soviet Union, therefore, the focus of this book is on the establishment of a new kind of post-communist political economy regime—the modern Ukrainian oligarchy—and the ways in which the means of its constitution, regeneration and survival across crises have contributed to the country's perennially poor economic performance. The basic relations of post-communist political-economic power in Ukraine were established during the presidency of Leonid Kuchma in the late 1990s (chapter 3). Although these relations have evolved under successive leaderships, the fundamental modes of operation have remained the same (Matsiyevsky, 2018; Dalton, 2021), which is what I mean here by "regime". It is not, then, just a question of economic winners and losers from the transition process, but more of the kind of resilient institutional structures the winners created that have helped to perpetuate their winning, at the expense of Ukrainian society as a whole.

1.4 Thesis, "national" scope and book structure

1.4.1 Thesis

On this basis, and drawing also on a theory of oligarchy as the politics of wealth defence (chapter 2), I arrived at the central thesis of my investigation. This is that **the process of reproduction of the contemporary Ukrainian political economy model – popularly referred to as the oligarchy – has economic side-effects that help to explain Ukraine's perennially poor economic performance**. One way of putting this is that the means of political influence that the very rich use in Ukraine to protect and enhance their wealth encourages the persistence of institutional norms and behaviours that inhibit the development of economic institutions associated with broad economic prosperity. Seen this way, my two research problems – Ukraine's poor post-independence economic performance, and the resilience of the oligarchy as an institution – appear as two sides of the same research problem.

1.4.2 The national level of institutional reproduction in its broader context

To show how the Ukrainian oligarchy managed to keep going after the Euromaidan Revolution – the most serious domestic "critical juncture" in modern Ukrainian history – the body of my investigation, designed around a comparison of the post-Euromaidan and Yanukovych eras, is organised into three empirical chapters. Each chapter examines a capacity, or political-economic practice, as an exemplifying element in the process of institutional reproduction of the Ukrainian oligarchy at the national level. In turn, an understanding of how these national-level processes fit in with lower-level (regional) and higher-level (international) processes is one of the outcomes of my research. This is depicted in Figure 1.3, below, as a "currency flow" of wealth and power at different planes of institutional reproduction or support to situate my national-level empirical chapters within this broader "process" conception of institutional reproduction. The conception itself, however, is discussed in more detail in the conclusion to this study (chapter 7).

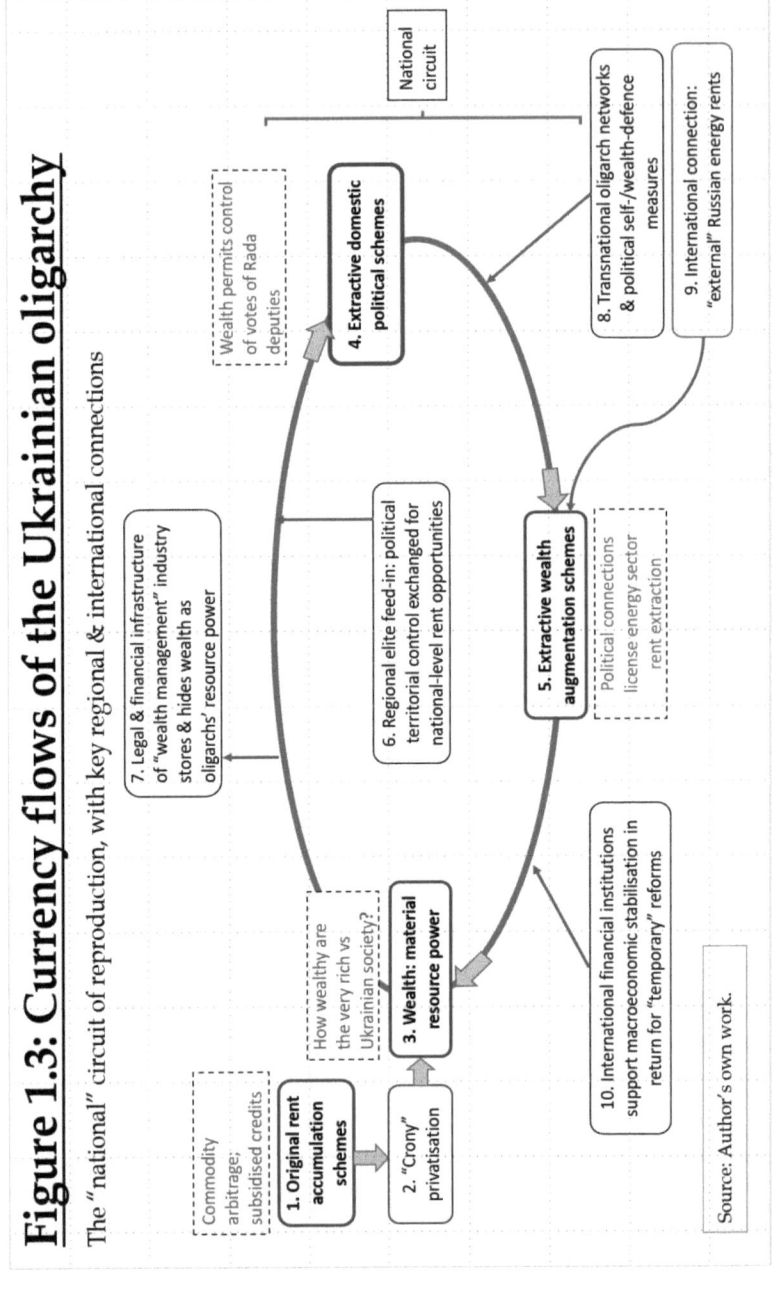

Figure 1.3: Currency flows of the Ukrainian oligarchy

The "national" circuit of reproduction, with key regional & international connections

Source: Author's own work.

1.4.3 Book structure

The first empirical chapter (chapter 4) examines the patterns of wealth concentration and dynamics of Ukraine's economic elite. It addresses the question: Has the wealth of Ukrainian oligarchs since 2014 remained sufficiently concentrated, relative to Ukrainian society, for it still to be considered a major "material resource power" in national politics? The central finding is that in 2010-17 the domestic business wealth of the economic elite fell by half as a share of national wealth. This need not, it is argued, imply a decline of elite, and especially of oligarchic, potential political power. One reason for this is that a steep drop in the hryvnya exchange rate in the economic crisis of 2014-15 is likely to have amplified the material resource power at home of wealth already held abroad.

A second empirical investigation (chapter 5) asks whether voting patterns in the Rada in 2014-17 support the idea that politically active business network leaders (oligarchs) have continued to use their wealth to influence the outcome of political economy reforms. Although the evidence for such a direct relationship proved less robust than it first appeared, this result in itself may express something more basic about the operation of politics in the Rada, as well as about its role in Ukraine's political economy system more widely. This is that a certain "fuzziness" of the organisational forms within parliament and the relative looseness of alignments between them are not incidental features of the operation of the Ukrainian legislature, but rather necessary ones to enable the flexible process of deal negotiation between leaders of business-political networks that is at the heart of contemporary Ukrainian elite politics. A break of factional voting patterns in the Rada in April 2016, a key finding of the chapter, is a striking example of this flexible process in action, appearing to mark the full recreation of the oligarchy as a transactional relation between elites (Dalton, 2021).

The third empirical investigation (chapter 6) examines the adaptation of elite rent-extraction schemes in the energy sector—a traditional source of oligarchs' wealth—to changing political and economic conditions, and energy policy, in the post-Euromaidan period, comparing these with "historical" energy intermediary schemes. The chapter finds that, with opportunities greatly reduced for the operation of traditional gas rent schemes, in the early post-Euromaidan years, the schemes examined tended to become smaller and more regionally confined, but that opportunities for rent extraction began to open up again once the worst of the crisis had passed, and especially following the reintegration of leading "old" oligarchs into post-revolutionary politics from 2016.

Chapter 3 gives a critical account of the political and economic literature on the genesis and operation of the contemporary Ukrainian oligarchy, producing also a synthesised overview of its evolution. Chapter 2, meanwhile, outlines a theoretical framework for conceptualising the links between economic and political power in Ukraine. The choice and ordering of the topics of the empirical chapters are thus conditioned by the theoretical framework of chapter 2, as well as the "currency flow" model depicted in Figure 1.3 above. Specifically, they are conditioned by the ideas of the primacy of political institutions, of political rules affecting economic ones, and of wealth—the power resource characteristic of oligarchs, conceived as the driver and end-goal of the cycle of institutional reproduction—as the concept that, running through the empirical chapters, threads them together. More concretely, a link between the Rada and energy chapters is the implied exchange of a widening of politically licensed rent-extraction opportunities (chapter 6) in return for increased support in the legislature from MPs assumed to be materially linked to leading oligarchs, following the disintegration of the five-party governing coalition in 2015-16 (chapter 5).

The first half of the empirical chapters aims not only to develop the data and make explicit the sources and methods used, but also to situate the analyses of the second half of each in their appropriate intellectual context, indicating thereby the broader academic conversations to which my investigations add. One purpose, therefore, of the brief assessment of Thomas Piketty's *Capital in the Twenty First Century* (2014) early on in chapter 4 is to align my analysis of the wealth of the richest Ukrainians with the relatively recent re-emergence of wealth as a topic of academic study, connected in part to the international success of Piketty's book. In chapter 5, an account of the position of Rada within the Ukrainian political system performs a similar role for my examination of material power as an informal mode of political influence. A brief outline of "old" institutional economics, originally written for chapter 6 with the same goal in mind, was relocated to chapter 2 in order to follow my exposition of a "new" institutionalist theory of prosperity. At the end of each empirical chapter, on the basis of its main findings, I answer the corresponding research question and derive some broader conclusions about the operation of the Ukrainian oligarchy and its economic side-effects.

Concluding that the main economic effect of the institutional production of Ukrainian oligarchy is through the establishment of a persistent negative feedback loop between low state capacity and low investment, the final chapter of the book (chapter 7) depicts and explicates a proposed schematic "model" of the interconnection between the capacities, practices and processes of Ukraine's political economy regime, envisaged as a "currency flow", or circuit, of wealth and power (as in Figure 1.3). A recap and synthesis of the main findings of my research paves the way for a revised definition of the Ukrainian oligarchy as **an institution habitually reproduced by its informal extractive political and economic practices, interconnecting at regional, national and international levels, motivated and facilitated by wealth.** This alternative definition of the oligarchy as a process rather than a relational structure (as at the start of this chapter) is a key result and contribution of this study. At the end of this concluding chapter, I make some suggestions for further research.

1.5 Contribution and wider implications

Overall, to the academic literature on the dynamics of informally dominated post-communist political economy regimes, this monograph adds a detailed, integrated, and internally comparative case study of Ukraine. Individually, the empirical chapters contribute useful original findings and perspectives to the literatures on:

- comparative international wealth inequality;
- the politics of extreme wealth inequality, using the Ukrainian elite as an illustration;
- the operation of parliaments in post-communist regimes, and their systemic role, with the Rada as an example;
- informal economic practices, by way of a detailed, contextualised comparative analysis and taxonomy of rent-extraction schemes in the Ukrainian gas sector.

The cyclical, or "process" conception of institutional reproduction developed here, and represented in the diagram above, offers a fresh angle — of "political" materialism — on the problems of economic and democratic development in societies dominated by wealthy elites, where economic and political activities overlap more extensively than in the liberal democratic West. From a development perspective, an original feature of my analysis is not so much the identification of a negative feedback loop between low state capacity and low investment, as to connect this to key elements of the process of reproduction of Ukraine's dominant political economy governance institution, "the oligarchy". My book suggests that, just as the continuance of the Ukrainian oligarchy is not mainly the outcome of the individual moral failings of its leading beneficiaries, so the inability of successive "de-oligarchisation" drives to dismantle the oligarchy as a ruling institution in Ukraine is not mainly explained by an absence of political will on the part of political leaders, but is rather the outgrowth of long-established elite and societal norms and values that have become institutionalised, habitual, ingrained. This has implications for the formulation and adaptation of reform policy, post-war, especially for reform policy on governance institutions, on which the success of other reconstruction goals will depend. The "combined" theory of oligarchy and institutional prosperity proposed in chapter 2, meanwhile, suggests a possible way of linking this mode of politics to Ukraine's low living standards, by way of the poor economic outcomes that it tends to foster.

Outside of Ukraine and eastern Europe, my study has broader relevance to the study of the interaction of politics and economics.

This is because the kinds of materially driven informal political and economic practices that go on relatively openly in Ukraine may be better hidden elsewhere. Study of the operations of the Ukrainian oligarchy therefore offers a guide to the kinds of practices to look out for elsewhere. Examples from the experience of contemporary Britain might be the award of government contracts to ministers' personal or business acquaintances for the supply of personal protective equipment (PPE) during the Covid-19 pandemic (Kinder et al, 2020), or the role of large private media organisations in converting wealth into political influence.

1.6 Methodology, methods and "research journey"

1.6.1 Methodology, theory and epistemology

In terms of methodology, the approach I adopted was conditioned by the subject matter (an alliance of power arising from structured economic inequality and positional power in the state) and by my attempt to combine two theories into a "tailor-made" framework for examining the political economy of contemporary Ukraine (chapter 2). In the first theory, oligarchs are conceived as wielders of material resource power (wealth), whose politics are based on wealth defence. The second is a general theory of prosperity in which economic rules are conditioned by political institutions. Both can be considered as "rational actors" approaches to social explanation, in which people are assumed to pursue the course of action that they believe will benefit them most, given their environmental and institutional settings. The shared approach renders the two parts of the joint theory compatible conceptually, and fits with a broadly realist epistemology, as well as the data-based methods of analysis that I use.

1.6.2 Data sources and methods

Data collection and methods

One of the main methods used in my research is simple **statistics**. This required the collection of economic, political and financial data from a variety of international and Ukrainian sources. For many of the analyses, I used Stata, a statistical software package widely used in social science research. Alongside statistics, I also employ **document analysis** of official, journalistic and think-tank materials. In the final empirical chapter on energy rent schemes, I use contextualised **case studies**.

How were the sources and case studies chosen?

The documentary sources that I used were chosen on two main criteria. The first was their provision of sufficiently detailed coverage of the topic of interest. A second was the reputation for reliability of the reporting organisation. For example, as an organisation set up following the Euromaidan Revolution, the National Anti-Corruption Bureau of Ukraine (NABU), whose reports are the main source for one of my post-Euromaidan gas sector case studies, has a better reputation for integrity than most other Ukrainian law-enforcement bodies.

While similar criteria were applied to my selection of post-Euromaidan rent-extraction case studies, additional ones were also used. Most obviously, each scheme had to have been run in the gas sector, in order to make it comparable with the earlier, large-scale, gas intermediary schemes. Second, schemes were chosen to illustrate different modes of the operation of energy rent-extraction by Ukrainian elites, so that, between them, the case studies might produce a more rounded picture of the rent-extraction process. Lastly, the reappearance between chapters of key figures working in Ukraine's political economy system—most clearly, in the persons of Oleksandr Onyshchenko and Oleksiy Malovatskyi—was an additional attractive feature in my choice of schemes, as long as the other criteria were met. This is because, by drawing attention to individual personnel links between extractive political practices in the Rada and extractive economic practices in the energy sector, they exemplify at the micro-level the connecting sinews of the oligarchy as a political economy institution across more than one of its dimensions—specifically, between political or judicial influence and links on the one hand and access to gas rents on the other.

Alongside the comparison of the operational and institutional features of historical and post-Euromaidan gas rent-extraction schemes of chapter 6, a second internally **comparative organisational element**, built into the design of the study, is structured around a contrast between the four years of the presidency of Viktor Yanukovych (2010-13) with the four years following his political downfall (2014-17).

Possible pitfalls

When using official statistics and publicly available documents, it is important to be aware of the pitfalls. This means approaching data sources critically, in at least two senses. First, the researcher should check not just the broad reliability of the sources and data they plan to use, but also ask themselves whether an indicator is the right one to measure the concept in question (in my case, for example, business wealth as material resource power), or whether it needs to be transformed first to do the conceptual work required (Henn, Weinstein and Foard, 2009, p. 58). Second, it means being aware that documents and statistics are not "neutral" facts unproblematically corresponding to, and revealing, a true picture of the social world. Rather, they are themselves an outcome of social processes, in definite societies, mediated and made by social actors for their own purposes. These purposes are unlikely to align perfectly with those of the social researcher (Henn, Weinstein and Foard, 2009, p. 124).

In the political context of document production in Ukraine, for example, when attempting to trace the reconstruction of elite networks following the Euromaidan events, what should the researcher do to ensure that business-political links reported in local media outlets are not themselves "political technology"? That is, that they are not disinformation, or partial information, placed by one political actor to discredit another?[1] One way to try to address this is to verify (or "triangulate") information using a second source, as I do, where possible, for key aspects of the "synthetic" accounts I produce from a critical reading of my main sources for the energy case studies of chapter 6. Although the effectiveness of

---

[1] This is a point I make in relation to the release of parts of Yanukovych's "black ledger" accounts in the opening section of chapter 5.

this approach may be compromised to some extent in the age of the internet and 24-hour news — that is, with many outlets reproducing from one another the same mistaken reports, unchecked, for example — it does not mean that the method cannot be used. Rather, it calls for a degree of consideration about the possible implications of the changing social-technical context for its effectiveness as a verification technique.

More broadly, I am aware of the many criticisms of the "rational actors" approach to social explanation emanating from rival traditions of social theory. For interpretivists, for example, rational choice theories fail to produce sufficiently meaningful explanations of social action (Little, 1991, p. 41). For structuration theorists, the rational choice approach overemphasises the role of conscious intention in the completion of day-to-day social routines (Inglis and Thorpe, 2019, p. 136). My sympathy with such criticisms, already present, only grew in the course of my research. By including document analysis using local sources, alongside case study elements, I aimed to address these issues to some degree.

1.6.3 Research journey

How, then, within a framework of analysis broadly informed by a "rational actors" approach to social explanation, do I make use of the qualitative materials selected, alongside some of the quantitative, statistical analyses? Also, how does the use of these materials affect my analysis? What do they add?

First, the deployment of local documentary materials can add — from the inside, so to speak — useful insights on the meaning and interpretation of the results of statistical analyses. An example in my investigation is the use of elements of the analysis of journalists from *Ukrayinska Pravda*, an online news outlet, on the composition and workings of parties in the Rada (Romanyuk and Kravets, 2016a, 2016b, 2016c, 2017a, 2017b, 2017c, 2018) in elucidating aspects of the voting patterns described statistically in chapter 5. Sometimes, however, the contribution of such materials can be more substantial. This is the case with my use of the editorials for the annual Focus Ratings (*Reytingi Fokusa*) rich lists, which suggest a range of international and domestic developments as the plausible causal factors behind the "dilution" of the wealth of the very rich, relative to Ukrainian society, in 2010-17 — one of the main findings of chapter 4 (Focus Ratings, 2007-18).

While the process of investigation of the first two empirical chapters, on wealth and Rada voting, brought home to me the power of even the simple statistical methods that I use, it also underscored some limitations. Probably the most important is that the discovery of a pattern in the data, or of a relationship between variables, is not in itself an explanation, in the absence of the provision of a plausible causal mechanism, which other techniques, such as a comparative method or contextualised case studies, can help to suggest (Little, 1991, Kindle location 4,891).

It was my experience of researching the first two empirical chapters, therefore, that encouraged a more thoroughgoing change in approach to the more contextualised, case study investigation of chapter 6, influenced also by my reading on "old" institutional economics (see chapter 2). This change of direction had a crucial effect on the overall conclusions of my book. In particular, the shift in approach, informed by the concepts of evolution and habit from "old" institutional economics, permitted the development of both a "process" re-definition of the Ukrainian oligarchy and a "thickening" of the "rational actors" concept of wealth defence. By "thickening", I mean a re-conceptualisation of the Ukrainian oligarchy as an evolving political economy institution, motivated and facilitated by the control and accumulation of wealth — not in the abstract, but rather as mediated through local, historically developed, shared cultural-institutional understandings, which are manifested as, and reproduced by, a relatively restricted range of routine, reusable political and economic practices. This is probably not too far from Winters' original intent, when he describes oligarchy as the way in which wealth defence works within a specific political-institutional setting (Winters, 2011, pp. 6-7). One of the things I do in this book, then, is to show some aspects of what the specific institutional context of wealth defence looks like in today's Ukraine. In turn, this re-conceptualisation allows, I argue in chapter 7, a more convincing explanation of certain developmental conundrums — namely, why

INTRODUCTION

Ukraine since independence has failed to develop a fully-fledged rule-of-law state.

Despite the advantages of this "institutionally thickened" notion of rational action, and the value of the concept of habit—one of the keys to understanding the institutional resilience of the Ukrainian oligarchy—the qualitive methods that I use in my study also have limitations. In contrast to results of inferential statistics, their results may not be applicable in other settings—in other words, they are not "generalisable". This means that the results of rent-extraction case studies cannot be assumed, without further investigation, to hold for patterns of operation of rent-seeking schemes elsewhere, or in other sectors. More broadly, if my study as a whole is taken, as I intend, as a case study of a post-communist political economy regime dominated by informal practices, the findings cannot be assumed to apply outside of Ukraine. This could be scrutinised, of course, through international comparison—probably most instructively with contemporary Russia.

It can be seen from this account that, in the course of my study, I moved more in the direction of a mixed methods approach than I had originally intended, as new questions and new problems arose, with this outcome driven largely by the topics and the problems encountered as the research developed.

2 Wealth defence and prosperity institutions

2.1 Introduction and "rational actors" approach

What is the connection between oligarchs' wealth and the failure of reforms in modern Ukraine to develop the political and economic institutions associated with prosperity? As an aid to answering this question, I propose in this chapter an alignment of two theoretical frameworks. The first outlines a distinctive politics of oligarchy (wealth defence) arising from minority material power (Winters, 2011). The essential idea is that extreme wealth offers the super-rich capacities to deal with the special threats they face and that, in interaction with political institutions, this produces characteristic forms of political rule. The second is a general theory of economic prosperity in which political institutions have primacy (Acemoglu and Robinson, 2012). As with the concept of wealth defence, the institutional theory of prosperity provides a general framework for interpreting patterns of behaviour based on the "logic" of the incentive structures that political and economic actors face.

One approach to political economy is by way of the different schools of thought that comprise it, of which classical, neo-classical, Keynesian, institutional, Marxist and, more recently, heterodox, are the most well-known. Each school offers a distinctive account of what politics and economics is, and of how the relationship between them is best understood at a general level. Seen in this way, the idea of the primacy of political rules in the development theory of Daron Acemoglu and James Robinson could be seen as a reversal of a central motif of classical economics, which, rising in tandem with European capitalism of the eighteenth and nineteenth centuries, tended to view social development and social order less as a result of political decisions, as with the earlier mercantilist school, than as an unintended outcome of the interaction of private interests (Caporaso and Levine, 1992, p. 26). Specifically, the *Why Nations Fail* approach of Acemoglu and Robinson is closest to "new" institutional economics, which emphasises the operation of guiding and constraining organisational rules and norms, in line with "old" institutionalism, but with assumptions about individual motivation drawn from neo-classicism (Stilwell, 2012, pp. 226-227). The distinction between "new" and "old" institutional economics is elaborated further towards the end of this chapter.

Both the theory of wealth defence and the institutional theory of prosperity, then, are species of the "rational actors" approach to social explanation, in which the actions of goal-seeking individuals, conditioned by their natural and institutional settings, are conceived to produce recurring outcomes at the aggregate, social level (Little, 1991, pp. 39-44; Inglis and Thorpe, 2019, pp. 119-122, 136-138). This way of thinking is most closely linked with neo-classical microeconomics. However, its roots stretch back at least to Thomas Hobbes in the seventeenth century, in whose political philosophy social relations are conceived — in the absence of the elective, externally imposed order he proposes — as a perpetual struggle over scarce resources (Inglis and Thorpe, 2019, pp. 120-121). Moreover, it is the methodological strategy adopted by other branches of social enquiry, such as collective action theory, as well as certain readings of Marxism — sometimes called "analytical" Marxism — that prospered for a time from the late 1970s. In the case at hand, the commonality of approach renders the theories of oligarchic politics and "new" institutional economics compatible.

In combination, the theories encourage greater precision in the formulation of key concepts, questions and hypotheses. They shed light on the possible mechanics, or links in the chain, by which oligarchic politics in Ukraine might affect economic outcomes. While one part of the joint theory sets out some channels through which the material resource power of oligarchs might be translated into political-institutional influence, the other traces the process by which self-interested minority politics fosters rules and behaviours that lead to poor national economic policies and growth outcomes. The two theories fit together for research purposes if the modern Ukrainian oligarchy is conceived as being constituted by the "extractive" political and economic operations that it runs.

The "rational actors" approach is not unproblematic, however. A persistent criticism of it is that, by abstracting from cultural specifics, it fails to produce sufficiently meaningful explanations of social action. For this reason, rational choice models are sometimes disparaged by critics as "thin" social theories, where "thick" implies "detailed accounts of norms and values, cultural assumptions, metaphors, religious beliefs and practices" (Little, 1991, p. 41). My goal has been to address this criticism, at least in part, by drawing on the reports of local journalists and think-tanks to "flesh out", concretise, contextualise — and so help to explain — the results of statistical analyses, while a case study approach drawing on these contextualising practices is adopted for the analysis of chapter 6.

2.2 The theories of wealth defence and institutional prosperity, and their relevance to Ukraine

2.2.1 Winters' theory of oligarchy

Against the "Italian school"
The theorisation of oligarchs and oligarchies as a distinct mode of minority political rule based on concentrated wealth has undergone a revival in recent years, a number of such studies developing out of the analysis of Suharto's Indonesia. Jeffrey Winters (2011), for example, attempts to elaborate a theory of oligarchy of this kind that is applicable across historical periods and political systems. He sees elite theories of the early 20th century — associated with the "Italian school" of Vilfredo Pareto, Gaetano Mosca and Robert Michels — as having blurred the distinction between oligarchies and other kinds of minority rule. Thus, he argues, Michels' "iron law of oligarchy" is not about a wealth-defined oligarchy, but rather the tendency of any large organisation to evolve towards minority rule (Winters, 2011, p. 6). In response, Winters proposes to distinguish oligarchs from elites by means of the different kinds of "power resource" on which their social and political influence depends, and which condition the strategies that minority political actors can pursue.

Power resources theory and the concept of power
In political sociology, power resources theory comes under the rubric of a "conflict theory". The implied contrast is with the "consensus" models, primarily functionalism, which, drawing on ideas

of biological evolution, tend to stress the necessity of the separation of social roles in achieving social order (Inglis and Thorpe, 2019, p. 35). As developed by Walter Korpi and Michael Shalev, power resources theory looks at the ability of the working class in advanced capitalist societies to offset through collective action some of the impact of structurally generated economic resource inequality. In particular, the strength of the organised working class, relative to organised business, is held to explain variations in "welfare state regimes" and patterns of income redistribution (van den Berg and Janoski, 2005, pp. 78-81).

For his analysis of oligarchy, Winters adapts this broad approach in the following way. "A power resources approach," he writes, "emphasises particular capacities, instruments or positions that individuals hold…and use for social and political influence" (Winters, 2011, p. 13). Although power resources theory is relatively recent in origin, the concept of power involved in Winters' account of it is a straightforward and traditional one of the ability to realise a desired outcome, of power over others. In large part, the notion of power employed is dictated by the subject matter, which concerns differential political influence based on extreme material inequality. This is a notion of concentrated wealth as an individually exercised political capacity arising from hierarchical socio-economic structures. An implied contrast is with the idea, pioneered by Michel Foucault, a French social theorist, of power embedded in identity-shaping cultural practices and products, and especially authoritative bodies of knowledge (such as medicine), that generate restrictive expectations, and self-understandings, of behavioural norms (Drake, 2010, pp. 41-43).

From this contrast it can be seen that the concept of power is a central but contested one in politics and political sociology. Its place in political economy is perhaps more controversial, however. Most obviously, a structural conception of class conflict and class power rooted in the unequal ownership of productive capacities, and the clashing material interests that these confer, is at the heart of Karl Marx's theory of social change (eg Marx, 1994, pp. 107-112). From a more social democratic perspective, JK Galbraith, a US institutional economist, saw the operation of power in the ability of large corporations to "transcend" the constraints of market forces that smaller firms remain subject to, through their influence on the prices and costs of their products, on consumer tastes and on government policy (Galbraith, 1973, pp. 4-5). Neo-classical economics, in contrast, tends to resist the notion that market exchange, as voluntary because mutually beneficial, could involve power relations (Caporaso and Levine, 1992, pp. 151-152, p. 171).

The contribution of Steven Lukes to the debate on the nature of power has proven influential. Expanding on an earlier view that the operation of differential societal power could only be examined in observable open conflict, he develops conceptually two additional dimensions, of hidden and latent conflict, as ways for understanding the operation of power unseen. On the second dimension, of hidden conflict, power may take the form of agenda-setting, or the capacity to exclude some issues from consideration. The third, latent dimension involves the powerful "getting others to want what they want them to want, shaping their perceptions, cognitions and thus preferences" (Lukes, 2013, p. 749), attaching to power a meaning close to the concepts of ideology and discourse, in which individuals internalise beliefs, norms and narratives that run against their own interests, perhaps ensuring that no conflict occurs.

For Korpi, power is a relational concept, so that the deployment of a power resource, viewed as a capacity, is what permits one social actor to affect the behaviour of another through the application of penalties or rewards (Korpi, 1998, p. 42). While a focus on the open, observable exercise of power in decision-making invites a causal mode of explanation, Korpi argues, an analysis that starts from a consideration of actors' power resources supplements this with an intentional, or future-oriented means of explanation more appropriate for underpinning Lukes' hidden and latent dimensions of power. More precisely, he suggests, a consideration by rational social actors, not only of their rivals' possible goals and expectations, but also of the power resources at their disposal, can lead to strategic decisions to avoid direct conflict (Korpi, 1998, p. 41, 45). Korpi therefore sees power resources theory as coming to the explanatory aid of Lukes' supplementary dimensions of conflict by adding motivational and strategic modes of explanation to the causal approach appropriate for explaining open, visible conflict. (In Winters' theory of oligarchy, it is the motivation of wealth defence, therefore, that offers a possible explanation for outcomes of the operation of hidden and latent power.)

Oligarchy as the politics of wealth defence

Great wealth, Winters argues, is the power resource on which oligarchs characteristically depend, while wealth defence is both the distinctive motivation behind oligarchs' political activity and the "objective" basis of their common interest. On Winters' definition, oligarchs are "actors who command and control massive concentrations of material resources that can be deployed to defend or enhance their personal wealth" (Winters, 2011, p. 6). He defines oligarchy as "the politics of wealth defence by materially endowed actors" (p. 7). The definition of oligarchs is fixed — that is, it is independent of historical or political context. In contrast, the definition of oligarchy allows for variation, as the form that the process of wealth defence takes can change, depending on kind of threats faced and the political-institutional context.

As with other holders of concentrated societal power, oligarchs comprise a small minority of a society's population. However, because of their wealth, and the marked socio-economic stratification that it implies, they face specific threats, which emanate from different positions in the social structure. Specifically, concentrated wealth tends to generate social and political conflict with those further down the socio-economic structure and to attract the unwanted attentions of more powerful actors. "Vertical" threats can come from below, "as when the poor attack the rich... and redistribute their property" (p. 23), or from above, in the form of actors more powerful than individual oligarchs, such as the state or a ruling autocrat. "Lateral" threats come from rival wealth holders, if "one oligarch encroaches on the holdings of another" (p. 23).

From this continual exposure to property contestation arises the need for enforcement of property claims. Although the concentration of wealth brings with it specific challenges, it also affords its holders specific capacities to meet these challenges — namely, the ability to buy security or other kinds of defensive services. This makes wealth a power resource that is uniquely resistant to confiscation or redistribution. The quantitative material basis of oligarchic behaviour and influence constitutes a qualitative difference that distinguishes oligarchs from the holders of other types of power resource, some of which help to define the social and political elite. Winters lists other power resources that individuals might possess as follows.

- Coercive power. Force has traditionally been central to maintaining both property claims and systems of minority political rule, while a legitimate monopoly on the means of coercion is an essential feature of the modern nation state on the influential definition of Max Weber, a founding figure in modern sociology (Giddens, 1971, p. 156).
- Official position. This offers leading office holders decision-making power over the resources and actions of large institutions, such as government, the civil service, big business and labour organisations.
- Mobilisational power. An individual's capacity to "shape the attitude and sway the actions of actors far beyond their circle of personal associates" (Winters, 2011, p. 7). It seems to overlap with Weber's idea of the charismatic leader, able to secure political consent because of the special qualities they are perceived to possess (Giddens, 1971, p. 160).
- The right of political participation. This can take the forms of universal suffrage and liberal political freedoms (such as the right to vote or to express political opinions). However, Winters argues that, historically, the social and political power of this resource was greatly enhanced by exclusionary mechanisms. For the individual political actor, it is a power resource that is of less significance the more socially dispersed it is.

Winters conceives of his theory as reconnecting with an older tradition that focuses on the problems of oligarchs and oligarchy as materially founded. However, the definition of oligarchy as the "rule of the few" — still widely deployed in the academic literature (Orum and Dale, 2009, p. 102; Havrylyshyn, 2017, p. 203) — is a misconstrual of the analytical basis of Aristotle's typology of government constitutions, Winters contends. This is because Aristotle makes clear that the distinction between the few and the many is itself materially determined, as "the number of the governing body...is an accident due to the fact that the rich everywhere are few and the poor numerous" (Winters, 2011, p. 7).

Moreover, Winters shows, a range of seventeenth and eighteenth century political thinkers and practitioners grappled with the problem of reconciling rising aspirations for formal political equality with the potential threat to private property that this was thought to entail. An explanation for the rise of the modern state, characterised by the concentration of society's coercive means, is seen in part in its role as guarantor of property rights amid the development of political movements and regimes based on ideals of popular sovereignty. On this, Winters quotes Adam Smith, the foundational figure in classical economics: "Civil government, so far as it is instituted for the security of property, is in reality instituted for the defence of the rich against the poor" (p. 29).

From two further distinctions linked to the concept of wealth defence, and a stylisation of two dimensions of oligarchic political activity stemming from it, Winters constructs a typology of oligarchy in general. The first distinction is between property claims and property rights. While individual oligarchs are obliged to enforce their property claims personally against rival claims arising from within the community, property rights are enforced impersonally on behalf of the community. The second distinction is made within the concept of wealth defence between property defence (actions to secure property claims) and income defence (actions to maintain revenue accruing from wealth holdings). A facsimile of Winters' chart illustrating these ideas is reproduced below.

On this chart, the horizontal dimension depicts the extent of oligarchs' direct involvement in coercive activities to secure property claims. The gradation runs from fully armed to fully disarmed, with partial oligarch disarmament and the hiring of coercive force distributed along the conceptual line between. The vertical dimension looks at the transition from individual to collective forms of political rule that oligarchs might adopt to defend their property claims. From the possible combinations along these dimensions, four distinct types of oligarchy are identified (warring, ruling, sultanistic and civil), corresponding to positions along the two dimensions represented by the four corners of Figure 2.1.

Figure 2.1: Winters' "Oligarchies and wealth defense"

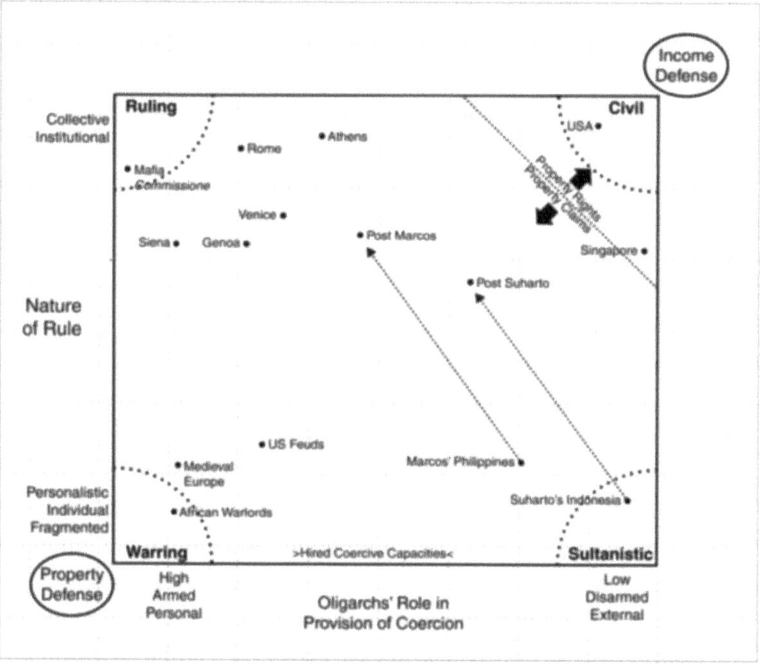

Source: Winters (2011, p. 34). Title adapted in order to make attribution clear.
© Jeffrey A. Winters, 2011.

Oligarchies can be described as warring when oligarchic political power is fragmented and each individual armed oligarch takes a direct, personal role in coercive defence of the property they claim. The examples that Winters gives are of warlords in contemporary Africa and of feudal lords in medieval Europe (bottom left corner in Figure 2.1).

In ruling oligarchies, by contrast, defence of property claims is more collective and institutional. In the less stable varieties — such as the mafia "commissions" initiated by Lucky Luciano, an American crime boss—institutional remits may be limited, perhaps aiming only to keep in check conflicts between rival mafia gangs. The institution for co-ordinating collective rules may not command any permanent coercive capacity of its own (pp. 69-72). In its more stable forms, the organisations and rules of oligarchic control are more extensive, with the oligarchs perhaps disarming partially and pooling some resources to fund public coercive bodies for common property defence. Winters offers as examples classical Athenian citizen democracy in the 5th-4th centuries BCE (pp. 77-90), and Republican Rome, which lasted for about 500 years until 27 BCE (pp. 90-121). These appear towards the top left of Winters' chart.

A sultanistic oligarchy, such as Suharto's Indonesia (1966-98), is one in which a single wealth-holder monopolises the means of coercion, with their survival in this role depending on success in enforcing the property claims of the super-rich as a whole (bottom right corner in Figure 2.1).

The final form of rule, depicted in the top right corner of Winters' typology, is civil oligarchy. Under this arrangement, the switch to an impersonal, institutional property rights regime—represented by the movement across the straight dotted line drawn diagonally towards the upper right corner of the chart—changes the balance of threats and incentives facing individual wealth holders, so that the nature of their political engagement evolves. Direct oligarchic rule becomes unnecessary for wealth defence. With the transition from property claims to property rights, taxation becomes the main threat to the holders of concentrated wealth, encouraging a shift from property defence to income defence. Oligarchs' operational emphasis changes from avoiding confiscation to avoiding redistribution, shifting the burden of property defence—of which oligarchs are the main beneficiaries—to those further down the wealth-income hierarchy. Rather than focusing on procuring coercion and payments to a network of officials, as when the rule of law and property rights are weak, the emphasis shifts to obtaining the services of specialised professionals[2]. The rise of civil

---

[2] Such as lawyers, accountants and lobbyists, who are able to lighten their clients' tax burden.

oligarchy is a relatively recent historical development, occurring alongside the rise of the modern nation state, and especially the liberal democratic state, in the course of the past 200 years or so. Winters' example is the modern-day US.

A final complicating element in Winters' analytical framework relates to the ability of collective bodies of oligarchic rule to restrain their strongest members. That is, whether they are able to ensure effectively that all members follow the collective rules, or whether some actors are able to defy and disrupt them. He describes this as the difference between "tame" and "wild" oligarchs (pp. 36-38). Following his Enlightenment-era forerunners, Winters argues that the placing of property rights at the heart of representative polities has generally prevented oligarchy and democracy from clashing. However, in the transition from authoritarian rule, he suggests, when legal systems are likely to be weak or underdeveloped, a lack of focus on oligarchy as a distinct phenomenon, based on financial power and the politics of wealth defence, has blurred understanding of how "wild" oligarchs can disrupt the democratisation process. This insight has the potential to bring a fresh perspective to the practical problems faced by some east European countries, and especially former Soviet countries, in the building of enduring democratic institutions since the fall of communism.

2.2.2 Oligarchic theory and Ukrainian politics

On Winters' analytical framework, modern Ukraine could be described as a ruling oligarchy, albeit with some caveats. That is, some institutions of collective oligarchic rule, including informally understood behavioural norms, operate alongside personal and hired coercion of individual oligarch's property claims, especially in the regions; and with the rule of law underdeveloped and sometimes selectively and politically applied. At the same time, democratic developments affect the political process through regular elections, which oligarchs must take into account, whether by attempting to sway the outcomes in their favour, or by adapting to unexpected results. Moreover, the mode of political action of the very rich in Ukraine has shifted from more direct to more indirect means of influence as the institution of the Ukrainian oligarchy has evolved (Markus and Charnysh, 2017). Potentially instructive historical analogies for Ukraine's system of informal political rule might include classical Greece, as well as Great Britain and the US in the eighteenth and nineteenth centuries, respectively. Nonetheless, in any analysis, key features of the informally dominated political system specific to contemporary Ukraine should be taken into account. Some that might be considered are as follows.

- Aside from reports of occasional, ad hoc meetings in the wake of a significant crisis (Matsiyevsky, 2018, p. 351), Ukraine's oligarchs do not seem to have established a special-purpose, overarching, national standing committee for the realisation of their collective interests. Rather, a range of pre-existing state bodies in combination perform the function of an institution of collective rule (perhaps reflecting a statist political culture inherited from the Soviet and Tsarist eras), or venue for contestation, agreement and troubleshooting. This includes Ukraine's parliament, the Verkhovna Rada (the focus of chapter 5), the presidential administration (Minakov, 2019, p. 232), and even Naftogaz, the national oil and gas firm, set up in the late 1990s to regulate and distribute energy rents between the main business-political networks (Balmaceda, 2013, p. 113).
- The distinctive structures of political power in contemporary Ukraine, described as an oligarchy after the strongest component, tend to fuse official elite politics with big business, formal with informal codes of operation. In terms of Winters' "power resources", its institutions bring together those with material power (oligarchs), proven mobilisational power (successful political leaders) and positional power (the holders of administrative office), with a considerable overlap between the three in practice.
- The wealthiest business leaders achieve political influence through a combination of sponsored representation in state bodies; alliances with the currently most electorally successful political leaders, whose associates occupy important positions in the state apparatus (since

important state posts may be treated as one of the spoils of political victory); and media dominance.
- The "Azarovshchina" of the Yanukovych presidency — or period in public office of Mykola Azarov, associated with the use of state financial institutions to extort private business — was unstable because it represented an attempt by a group within a group (Yanukovych's "family" within the Donetsk business-political group) to monopolise collective institutions as a means of augmenting the wealth of his personal, developing network base. This could be read as a failed attempt to move from a "ruling" towards a more "sultanistic" mode of oligarchic rule.
- Popular political participation, in the form of regular elections and civil society activity (the socially disbursed power of formal political rights, on Winters' list), must also be reckoned with, even if this means attempting to subvert or soften its practical political force. This helps to explain the extraordinary lengths, and expense, to which prominent oligarchs can go to defray potential electoral risks to their political influence (and so their ability to protect their wealth). This includes backing multiple candidates and setting up fake parties to confuse voters in order to draw support away from candidates backed by business rivals, for example. It also helps to account for the limitations on oligarchs' political influence, which encourage them into alliances with political winners. In short, the Ukrainian oligarchy has to take voters into account, albeit with parliamentary politics as one medium through which informal deals may be struck. This points to the Verkhovna Rada (parliament) as a central institution for the operational intertwining of formal and informal politics in Ukraine.

But what is of value in oligarchic theory for the study of politics in Ukraine, other than bringing to light some family resemblances? First, by honing in on wealth as the distinctive source of oligarchic power, the theory offers guidance on the sorts of behaviour that might be researched, as well as the institutional locations in which they might take place. In particular, it helps to focus enquiry on the possible financial mechanisms and strategies that the very rich use to exert political influence. In modern Ukraine, such mechanisms could include:

- Network payments by oligarchs to officials, perhaps to influence judicial decisions or voting outcomes in the Rada.
- Electoral expenses, such as in the 2014 presidential and parliamentary campaigns.
- Oligarchs' media dominance, especially of TV.
- Offloading of the cost of collective security. This could be seen as a public good from which oligarchs benefit but do not pay (ie, through pooling of their own resources).
- The hiring of private coercive force, often from sports clubs, as well as nationalist and Cossack groups.
- The funnelling of oligarchs' wealth to tax havens abroad.

Second, oligarchic theory provides a framework for interpreting the mechanisms of political influence of the rich as means of wealth defence when the rule of law, and so property rights, are weak.

Third, the theory raises interesting questions about the self-perpetuation of the Ukrainian oligarchy in its current "ruling" form. What is it in Ukraine's political practice, for example, that hinders the transition to a fully operational rule-of-law state, and so to an impersonally enforced property rights regime from which the oligarchs as a group would benefit? (I offer an answer to this in the concluding chapter of the book.) Might there be useful lessons for Ukraine from the historical experience of counties, such as Great Britain and the US, that have already made the transition from ruling to civil oligarchy?

A final attraction of the application of oligarchic theory to Ukraine is that it prevents the treatment of oligarchy as something unusually dysfunctional or abnormal, so helping to guard against the "orientalisation" of Ukrainian politics. Rather, it shows oligarchy as one of the historical and contemporary norms of minority political power, from which liberal democracy is a quite recent, and perhaps temporary, deviation, within which forms of oligarchy, as the conversion of wealth into political influence to defend wealth, continue to thrive, albeit in a less obtrusive "civil" political form, reflecting a reduced necessity for big property owners to become personally involved in the coercion required for wealth defence (Winters, 2011, p. 24).

2.2.3 *Why Nations Fail*: Acemoglu and Robinson's institutional theory of prosperity

Winters' oligarchic theory brings fresh focus to the distinctive politics of minority holders of concentrated material power. However, to turn its political sociology into a useful political economy for understanding contemporary Ukraine, the assumed causal connections between oligarchs' political practices and the expected economic effects should be made explicit. The institutional theory of prosperity of Acemoglu and Robinson (2012) provides such a link. Drawing on a wide range of historical and contemporary examples to illustrate its propositions, the theory presents a relatively conventional set of rules and practices said to provide the economic incentives by which countries become rich. While making use of some of the assumptions, tools and terminology of neo-classical economics, the institutional theory of prosperity is more eclectic, promoting a model of economic development based on an institutionally embedded, dynamic market economy in which the primacy of politics is emphasised. "Political institutions determine economic institutions and, through these, the economic incentives and the scope for economic growth," the authors write (Acemoglu and Robinson, 2012, p. 91). Alongside the mainstream neo-classical school, then, this framework appears to show the influence of the ideas of Karl Polanyi, a Hungarian economic sociologist (institutionally embedded markets) and Joseph Schumpeter, an Austrian economist (creative destruction).

The institutional theory of prosperity is an attempt to provide a general theory to explain why some countries have become rich and others remain poor. The cases of the town of Nogales, which straddles the US-Mexican border, and of North and South Korea, divided by civil war since the 1950s, are used to refute some explanations for the persistent large disparity in per head national incomes globally. This includes geographical explanations, such as differences in resource endowment or climate; cultural explanations, such as the existence or absence of a strong work ethic; and the supposed ignorance of political leaders about the appropriate development policies (pp. 48-69). Rather, the authors propose an institutional explanation for the income divergence in the two parts of Nogales and Korea, with institutions conceived as the rules, practices and norms that inform political and economic motives and behaviour. They propose an "inclusive" combination of political and economic institutions to account for sustained economic growth and relatively high average incomes, contrasting this with an "extractive" institutional combination which, they argue, stands behind persistent poverty.

What is the difference between inclusive and extractive institutions? On political institutions, the authors draw the distinction based on the extent of participation and the existence of a functioning central state. In inclusive political institutions, power is relatively broadly spread and formally constrained (pluralism), while in extractive institutions it is narrowly held and unrestricted (absolutism). On its own, however, relatively socially dispersed power is an insufficient condition for an inclusive polity. For this, a central state performing a range of stabilising functions is required. The US is offered as a case of a country with such political institutions, but the designation seems to refer to liberal democratic polities in general. The authors summarise as follows: "We will refer to institutions that are sufficiently centralised and pluralistic as inclusive political institutions. When either of these conditions fails, we will refer to the institutions as extractive political institutions" (p. 81). Extractive political institutions "enable the elites controlling political power to choose economic institutions with few constraints or opposing forces" (p. 81). Examples cited of extractive political systems include the Soviet Union and the rudimentary coercive structures established by European colonists in Barbados in the seventeenth century.

Correspondingly, inclusive economic institutions, such as those in the US and South Korea, "allow and encourage participation by the great mass of the people in economic activities that make the best use of their talents and skills, and that enable individuals to make the choices they wish" (p. 81). To achieve this, several interlinked organisations and conditions must be in place, as follows.

- Secure private property rights, including even-handed contract enforcement by way of an unbiased legal system.
- "Inclusive" markets with low barriers to entry, in which economic opportunities are realised through the right to choose a career or start a business.
- Entrepreneurial initiative is supported by the financial sector and domestic firms are allowed to join forces with foreign ones.

Between them, these rules establish the microeconomic incentives needed to set off the process of "creative destruction", or dynamic and innovative macroeconomic growth, by which investment, invention and innovation drive productivity (yielding more output from the same or fewer inputs) and income growth. Invention and innovation are distinguished as the practical creation, as against the commercial application, of new devices, techniques and processes (Dadkhah, 2009, p. 224). Investment is related to the production of new technology, which boosts productivity across production inputs (land, labour and capital). Education, which adds skills and brings out talents, allows individuals to generate, adopt and operate new technology. Alongside inclusive markets, technology and education are among the "engines of prosperity" (Acemoglu and Robinson, 2012, p. 81) that are fostered by inclusive institutions.

Without such inclusive institutions, however, amid fears of property theft, expropriation or high taxes, the incentives to work hard, invest or adopt new technology are absent. Rather, political elites are able to tilt the economic rules in their own favour, at the expense of society as a whole. Methods of doing this could include raising of barriers to market entry to limit competition, or expropriation of resources. These are described as extractive economic institutions because they are "designed to extract incomes and wealth from one subset of society to benefit a different subset" (p. 76). The process of anti-social minority enrichment in turn provides elites with the resources to consolidate their political hold.

Alongside "pluralistic" institutions, the role of a strong central state is emphasised. It is viewed as crucial, not only as an enforcer of basic law and order, and property rights, needed for commercial contracts to operate; or as a provider of public services, including education, necessary for economic opportunities to be grasped; but also as an economic regulator, and an economic actor in its own right (p. 76). This view of the positive potential of the state contrasts sharply with the market-constraining role attributed to government by some strands of neo-liberal thought from the 1970s, while sharing assumptions on individual motivation.

On the relations between kinds of institution, the authors stress the primacy of politics. This is because politics determines the political and economic rules that take hold. But while jointly inclusive or jointly extractive political and economic structures reinforce one another, tending to system stability, a mix of inclusive and extractive institutions will be less sturdy. Thus, the drive for pluralistic polities will undermine extractive economic practices, while permitting and encouraging the development of competitive and accessible markets which set off dynamic economic development. However, economic change — and especially the characteristically modern, growth-sustaining "creative destruction" unleashed by systematic incentives to innovate — threatens elite economic interests, social status and political power. Social groups that benefit from "extractive" practices therefore often take pre-emptive political action to block change, although with varying results. An example is the opposition to early industrialisation among Europe's landed aristocracy, in which the political struggle of the Russian and Hungarian upper classes was more successful — at least for a time — than their British counterparts (p. 85).

In conclusion, the authors state that "nations fail when they have extractive economic institutions supported by extractive political institutions that impede or even block economic growth" (p. 83). To escape such a situation, it would seem, forceful political activity promoting the development of political pluralism and state centralism is required.

2.2.4 The institutional theory of prosperity and contemporary Ukraine

Many of the patterns of political and economic behaviour still prevalent in Ukraine can be cast in terms of the "extractive" institutional behaviours described by Acemoglu and Robinson. Examples of this might include the following.

- The persistent blocking of economic and state institutional reforms thought to impinge on oligarchs' business interests in order to protect "extractive" economic interests against the encroachment of more "inclusive" and competitive economic rules championed by some domestic political forces, civil society and international institutions.
- The use of political influence and connections to push economic practices favourable to political insiders. Examples would be the under-priced sale of the Kryvorizhstal steel plant in 2004 (Havrylyshyn, 2017, p. 117), and of domestic energy infrastructure in 2012.
- The intra-elite struggle for control of state institutions, and especially state enterprises such as Naftogaz, not just as a means of setting political and economic rules, but also of controlling their income flows.

The "extractive" character of the economic schemes associated with the Ukrainian oligarchy (some of which are outlined in the next chapter) may have peaked during the presidency of Viktor Yanukovych in 2010-14, but continued and evolved in the wake of the Euromaidan protests. As with Winters' concept of wealth defence, the institutional theory of prosperity provides a framework for interpreting patterns of political and economic behaviour based on the "logic" of the incentive structures faced. Ukraine's oligarchs and political elite may be understood as being enmeshed in the intertwining norms of political and economic behaviour from which they not only benefit, but are also accustomed. That is, not only do material interests motivate their actions, and so the reproduction of the oligarchy as an informal political economy structure, but so does habit, or the repeated re-enactment of social-institutional identities, once formed.

In the context of Ukraine's business-political networks and the linked issue of the relative weakness of the state, the emphasis of prosperity theory on the vital developmental role of an effective central state is relevant to a consideration of both the resilience of the oligarchy and the country's poor economic record, the two-sides of my research puzzle. The financial and political strength of the oligarchs and the financial and organisational weakness of the central Ukrainian state may thus be manifestations of the same process. In particular, the phenomena of private armies and privately funded battalions challenge the state's monopoly of legitimate force, and so perhaps also the consolidation of a central state capable of upholding impersonally a property rights regime, while the institutionalisation of state-centred rent-extraction schemes routinely drains the state of financial resources. A factor that favours the development of an effective central state, according to Acemoglu and Robinson, is when a single group is able to muster sufficient power relative to others. In post-independence Ukraine, this has rarely been the case for any length of time, in part owing to persistent rivalry between originally regionally located business organisations and political elites. According to the historical sociologist Charles Tilly, however, the crucial stimulus to national state development in Europe over a millennium has been the preparation and execution of war (Tilly, 1992). Whether there is any evidence that Ukraine's war with Russia, ongoing since 2014, but greatly intensified since February 2022, has had any positive "spill-over" effects on the efficiency of state institutions other than the army, would be a promising line of research.

2.3 The two theories conjoined

2.3.1 A distinctive perspective on the problems of political and economic development

The distinctiveness of the institutional theory of prosperity, and its usefulness as a framework for analysis, is that it ties the development of "prosperous" economic practices to political institutions, which it views as constitutive of economic institutions. Aligning oligarchic and prosperity theories, Ukraine's ruling oligarchy can be interpreted as an "extractive" political institution that encourages and supports "extractive" economic practices. This could provide a means of showing systematically how specific mechanisms of oligarchic political influence map onto expected negative economic outcomes.

This alignment of theoretical frameworks also suggests a possible novel solution to the problem of Ukraine's perennially poor economic performance. Envisaging economic reform on its own as an insufficient measure, this solution would be for Ukraine to set as a key developmental goal the construction of a civil oligarchy, alongside a more inclusive or plural political system and a more effective central state, as the means of fostering the kinds of economic behaviour associated with prosperity. As with oligarchic theory, the application of Acemoglu and Robinson's theoretical framework could offer to Ukraine some practical lessons from the historical experience of counties, such as the US and the UK, that have already gone through this kind of transition.

2.4 Institutional economics, old and new

In recent decades, institutionalism as an approach to economic analysis has made something of a comeback. Originally, it was associated with the economic sociology of Thorstein Veblen, best-known for his work on the consumption patterns of the US *nouveaux riche* of the 1890s and the distortion of the potential of industrial society by the profit motive (Stilwell, 2012, pp. 215-218). At the level of theory, Veblen argues that, because it eschews the influence of culture and institutions, the goal-seeking logic of "hedonistic calculus" (his term for marginal utility theory) is unable to grasp vital issues of the modern world, such as technological change and economic growth, but that these influences fall below the attention of neo-classical economists precisely because they have become customary (Veblen, 1909). Following Veblen, an institutionalist tradition developed in North America in the first half of the twentieth century. However, this tradition lost ground with the mathematisation of economics as a subject after the second world war (Backhouse, 2002, pp. 237-240).

A "new" or reconfigured institutionalism has been in the ascent since perhaps the 1980s, in some ways rivalling, but in other ways overlapping with neo-classical assumptions, techniques and themes (Stilwell, 2012, pp. 226-227). For the earlier version, we may take Veblen's definition of institutions as "settled habits of thought common to the generality of men", including "usage, customs, canons of conduct, principles of right and propriety" (quoted in Sowell, 1967, p. 189). For the later version, we can use Douglas North's tighter definition of institutions as the formal and informal rules governing individual behaviour, but aiding co-operation (Douarin and Mickiewicz, 2017, p. 13). Examples of institutions include markets, firms and states, but also money, language and traffic rules. With its emphasis on the centrality of the rules of political behaviour conditioning economic growth outcomes, the theory of Acemoglu and Robinson, outlined above, can be identified as belonging to the school of "new" institutional economics.

While both "old" and "new" versions adopt a rather broad view of institutions, subsuming within them organisations and social norms, they are not exactly the same. For instance, "new" institutionalism incorporates into its analytical framework a key assumption of neo-classicism — namely, the figure of the rational, utility-maximising individual with fixed consumption preferences — that the older version explicitly rejects (Stilwell, 2012, p. 226). Instead of explaining the emergence of institutions from the interactions of rational individuals, therefore, "old" institutionalism envisages a more circular process, centred on the concept of habit, which Geoffrey Hodgson defines as "self-sustaining, non-reflective behaviour that arises in repetitive situations" (Hodgson, 1998, p. 179). In this process, the actions of individuals, informed by habit, cohere through imitation into routines and social customs, and then into larger, evolving institutional structures, which in turn feed into individuals' habit formation, including of intellectual habits, such as the process of rational calculation. This means that for "old" institutionalism: i) individuals' habits and institutions are "mutually constitutive"; and ii) that the rational actor is an outcome of institutional development, rather than an assumption leading to institutional emergence, as for the "new" school. From this perspective, for example, although consumer tastes may be subject to inertia—that is, people tend to buy products that they have bought before—individual tastes are not assumed to be innate, but rather moulded by socioeconomic conditions, corporate advertising among them (Hodgson, 2019, pp. 129-30, 139).

In contrast, neo-classicism proper, while placing "consumer sovereignty" at the heart of its theory, does not usually consider the process of formation of consumer tastes as falling within the remit of economics. Rather, as the "science of rational choice", it focuses on what happens once consumers' tastes have been formed. This is similar to a point made later in my analysis of wealth (chapter 4), that the focus of neo-classicism on factors affecting the allocation of capital assumes that the process of wealth distribution has already happened, somewhere off stage. This reflects the (very successful) hegemonising strategy of this school of economics of presenting its own approach to the study of the economy as "economics" *per se* (Hodgson, 1998, p. 189).

It can be seen from this account that institutional economics offers a specific take on the "agent-structure" problem, with which social theory has been wrestling since its inception, in an attempt to develop a credibly balanced general understanding of social reproduction and social change in the two-way relation between the conditioning of individuals by economic and cultural factors on the one hand, and individual volition and creativity on the other. As such, institutionalism is reminiscent of certain ideas still current in social theory—namely, the structuration theory of Pierre Bourdieu and some aspects of the ideas of Michel Foucault. In particular, Bourdieu finds in the notion of social practices the necessary unity between social structure and social action as two dimensions of a single process, since social practices are everyday activities that have become routine, while, in combination, sets of practices that have become routine are what is meant by "social structure" (Inglis and Thorpe, 2019, p. 196). Moreover, Bourdieu's concept of practical consciousness as governing the performance of everyday actions of which the individual may only be intermittently aware (Inglis and Thorpe, 2019, p. 202) comes close to the institutionalist concept of habit. Lastly, institutionalism's emphasis on the constitution of individuals' mental framework by institutional structures recalls, but perhaps does not go as far as, Foucault's take on the relationship of discourses of knowledge to identity formation in the creation and recreation of how social individuals understand and perceive themselves (Drake, 2010, pp. 38-51).

The key concepts of "old" institutionalism (emulation, habit, customs, routines, institutions, evolution, action-information loops, inertia, cumulative causation) are thus quite different from those of neo-classicism (subjective preference, utility, profit maximisation, market equilibrium, marginal and diminishing factor returns) familiar from microeconomics. It follows from this, therefore, that its methods of analysis are different too. In brief, these methods stress concrete detail, context, as well as historical, geographical and cultural specificity. An advantage of the approach of "old" institutionalism, moreover, is that it aligns better with notions of informality as implicitly understood customary political behaviours outlined in my examination of the Rada (chapter 5), pointing to a possible bridge between political and economic approaches to the study of informality at the theoretical level.

The relevance of this brief excursus on the difference between old and new institutionalism, and on certain conceptual similarities with other branches of social theory, is that the variety of perspectives offer more diverse points of reference on which to draw – in my case, to aid in the description and analysis of the origin, workings, reproduction and development of the Ukrainian oligarchy, which is the focus of the next chapter. It will be especially helpful in informing my account of the institutional evolution of Ukraine's modern political economy regime (chapter 3) and in the case studies of energy rent-extraction schemes (chapter 6).

3 The origins, operations, resilience and evolution of the Ukrainian oligarchy

3.1 Outline and aims

A variety of factors have been advanced to explain Ukraine's poor economic showing since independence, as outlined in the first chapter. The line of enquiry that I will take, however, focuses on delays in market economic reform following independence in 1991 creating the conditions for the formation of the oligarchy — the fusion of big business and state authority — as Ukraine's dominant political economy institution. As such, it has weighed heavily on the country's political and economic development ever since, as oligarchs, it is often argued, routinely obstruct economic reforms that may impinge on their business interests. In an influential paper from 1998, Joel Hellman describes this as a situation of "partial reform equilibrium" (p. 228).

In this chapter, I first explore the political and political economy literature for accounts of the genesis, socio-economic character, economic operations, modes of political influence and institutional reproduction of the Ukrainian oligarchy following political crises, both after independence and in the wake of the Euromaidan anti-government protests of 2013/14. The conclusions I arrive at here form the foundation on which both the lines of research and argument of this study are built. The final part of the chapter synthesises an overarching narrative of the post-communist development of the Ukrainian oligarchy as an institution constituted by the evolving relation of leading business-political networks to formal politics, focusing on changes between the presidencies of Viktor Yanukovych and Petro Poroshenko. This establishes a narrative backdrop that informs the analyses of subsequent chapters.

3.2 Ukrainian oligarchs and the oligarchic system

3.2.1 Key definitions and estimates of wealth

What is an oligarch and what is the Ukrainian oligarchy? In the literature on the politics and political economy of modern Ukraine, a variety of definitions of oligarchs and oligarchy are offered. Oleh Havrylyshyn, for example, starts with a traditional one, taken from Aristotle, of oligarchy as "rule by the few" (2017, p. 203). In Aristotle's analysis of political constitutions, however, there are two kinds of "rule by the few" — oligarchy and aristocracy. The first he contrasts unfavourably with the second as the self-interested rule of the rich versus the even-handed rule of the best. Here, "best" implies natural governing talent, and so the ability to balance competing social interests (Kenny, 2010, pp. 69-71).

The "self-interested rule of the rich" may be a reasonable starting point for examining the informal elite politics of contemporary Ukraine. However, it captures only one dimension, or one set of actors, of Ukraine's oligarchic political economy system. In practice, in the literature, definitions tend to focus on one of the two lines of movement between great wealth and political influence, which may be thought of as a basic feature of the Ukrainian oligarchy as a system. This means that although oligarchs' wealth can be seen as a way of influencing political outcomes, political office can be used as a means of accumulating wealth. The first direction of travel is usually described as "state capture", while the second is termed "business capture" (Markus and Charnysh, 2017, p. 1,641). At the same time, the purpose of oligarchs' involvement in politics, it is recognised, is not just to protect, but also to expand, their economic holdings (Pleines, 2016a, p. 112).

Anders Aslund describes Ukraine's oligarchs as very wealthy, politically connected businessmen, who lead large, vertically integrated industrial conglomerates (2009, p. 107), while Wojciech Konończuk extends this to "big entrepreneurs, who have been able to turn their business prowess into powerful political influence" (2016, p. 5). In contrast, Turchynov contends that "the [traditional] formula of 'capital forms power'... has been completely inverted into its opposite—'power forms capital'" (quoted in Havrylyshyn, 2017, pp. 206-207). Havrylyshyn defines the "oligarchate", or the informally dominated political system of rule as a whole, as one in which "the establishment players are oligarchs, politicians and high-level officials" (2017, p. 201). This last is probably the most succinct starting point for a definition of the three main kinds of political economy actors of which the contemporary Ukrainian oligarchy is composed at the national level.

However, in the literature the terms "oligarch" and "oligarchy", along with those of "rent-seeker", "capitalist" and "entrepreneur", can be used interchangeably—that is to say, somewhat imprecisely. Havrylyshyn, for example, refers to oligarchs as both rent-seekers and capitalists, even though profit-seeking is usually the characteristic motivation ascribed to the capitalist entrepreneur in competitive markets[3]. Thus, he views oligarchs as the most successful of the "new capitalists" who accumulated their original stock of wealth amid delayed reform in the early 1990s, a consequence of which was the "embryonic start of a rent-seeking capitalist class later called the oligarchy" (2017, p. 306). Aslund, in contrast, tends to describe oligarchs either as entrepreneurs, owner-managers, or as the heads of "industrial groups" (2009, pp. 107-113), but to use the term "capitalist" less frequently. Rather than "capitalism", he prefers the term "market economy", although he defines it not in its own terms, but by way of contrast, as "the opposite of a socialist economy" (2009, p. 5).

These definitional questions can affect research outcomes. For example, Stanislav Markus and Volha Charnysh adopt a wide, relative definition of the "super-rich" as "being among the 200 richest persons in the country" (2017, p. 1,638). Heiko Pleines, in contrast, begins by describing oligarchs as "entrepreneurs who use their wealth to exert political influence" (2016a, p. 106). He goes on to add a number of qualifications—including involvement in national politics and the pursuit of business interests as the core activity—in order to distinguish oligarchs analytically from either "pure" apolitical business people or professional politicians (2016, p. 114). As a result,

---

[3] The two are related, however, as described in section 3.2.3 below.

the number of "unique plutocrats" included in the first study comes to 177 for 2006-12 (Markus and Charnysh, 2017, p. 1,637), but to only 29 "oligarchs" for the second, longer period of 2000-15 (Pleines, 2016a, p. 116).

How rich are Ukrainian oligarchs?

For oligarchs, the possession of great wealth may be seen a defining feature, as their characteristic source of power. In the literature, the high level of wealth of the Ukrainian oligarchy tends to be shown by reference to the individual fortunes of its leading members. This is sometimes justified by reference to the rivalry between wealthy business leaders, which can make it hard for them to work together (Markus and Charnysh, 2017, pp. 1,635-1,636).

Havrylyshyn, for example, shows that by 2005-06 the incidence of Ukrainian billionaires was high in relation to the country's GDP in international comparison. He does this by calculating: i) the share of each country's billionaires in the billionaire total on Forbes' List for 2006; ii) each country's economic output as a share of the global economy in 2005; then iii) dividing the first figure by the second. For Kazakhstan, Russia and Ukraine, this produces ratios of between two and three, which are higher than those for much richer economies (2017, pp. 42-43). All the same, the number of Ukrainian billionaires in 2006 cited by Havrylyshyn, of three, is much lower than other estimates from around the same time. So, from an article in *Korrespondent*, a Ukrainian weekly, Aslund cites a figure of 23 Ukrainian billionaires in spring 2008 (Aslund, 2009, p. 110). Forbes' List, a US business publication, counts just seven the same year (Forbes' List, 2008). Such wide variation in numbers, as well as a lack of clarity on differences in methodologies, can produce an incomplete, anecdotal impression to such exercises.

Andrew Wilson estimates the assets of the 50 richest Ukrainians at almost 46% of the country's GDP in 2010 (that is, their stock of wealth was equal to almost half of the country's annual income flow), compared with around 20% for Russia and 10% for the US (2013, pp. 187-189). Markus and Charnysh estimate the total as higher still. Using a large, detailed data set, they calculate that their sample of 177 individuals in 2006-12 controlled an annual average of US$85.9bn, equal to 60% of GDP over this period (2017, p. 1,638). Viewing the issue through the lens of international financial movements, Taras Kuzio cites a study by Global Financial Integrity (GFI), a US think-tank, which estimates illicit capital outflows from developing countries in 2004-13 (Kuzio, 2016, p. 133). The estimates for Ukraine are reproduced in the second column of Table 3.1; in the fourth column, I have scaled these flows to Ukraine's annual GDP (the third column). On this data, then, such financial outflows from Ukraine averaged US$11.7bn per year over the decade, equivalent to an average of 8.5% of annual nominal GDP.

Table 3.1: GFI estimates for illicit capital outflows from Ukraine, 2004-13; US$ bn, unless otherwise stated

	Outflows (GFI)	GDP (IMF)	Outflows/GDP (%)
2004	4.4	67.2	6.5
2005	5.6	89.3	6.3
2006	5.4	111.9	4.8
2007	7.2	148.7	4.8
2008	16.9	188.2	9.0
2009	10.6	121.6	8.7
2010	13.8	136.0	10.2
2011	17.9	163.2	11.0
2012	21.0	175.7	12.0
2013	13.9	179.6	7.7

Sources: Kar & Spanjers (2015), *Global Financial Integrity* (GFI) report, cited in Kuzio (2016); IMF, World Economic Outlook (WEO) Database, October 2017; available: https://bit.ly/3i3ME46. Own calculations for ratio of outflows to GDP.

3.2.2 Origins of oligarchs and the oligarchic system

Two key structural economic conditions

On the formation of the modern Ukrainian oligarchy, the narratives of several commentators (Aslund, 2009; Havrylyshyn, 2017; and Yurchenko, 2018) are quite similar. All draw attention to the preparatory role played by the economic reforms brought in under Mikhail Gorbachev's policy of *perestroika* (reconstruction), and especially a law on co-operatives, which introduced rudimentary private property rights into the late Soviet economy. Here, Yuliya Yurchenko's account is the most detailed and instructive (2018, pp. 25-41). She shows that *perestroika* was a response to the accumulated failures in the Soviet economy, which appeared as a progressive slowdown in output growth. The reforms of Gorbachev and his team were designed, therefore, to boost economic efficiency and the pace of output growth by introducing limited elements of market pricing and competition. Alongside a degree of price deregulation, plans were developed to permit new kinds of ownership (shareholding and leasing, as well as a renewed emphasis on cooperatives) and an increased role for financial intermediation. Most importantly, the aim was to devolve to enterprises greater responsibility for decisions on financing, purchasing, sales, wages and accounting, with an emphasis on balancing the books. Although cooperatives quickly increased their share of Soviet output and employment, the reforms had multiple unintended consequences, Yurchenko argues. One was that the changes "threw out of balance the whole system of economic management" (Yurchenko, 2018, p. 28), exacerbating pre-existing co-ordination problems and fractious rivalries within the late Soviet state apparatus.

The political rise of the Ukrainian oligarchy is customarily dated to the second half of the 1990s, during the first presidency of Leonid Kuchma. However, both Havrylyshyn and Aslund point to the earlier delay in economic reforms during the presidency of his predecessor, Leonid Kravchuk, as a second crucial factor behind oligarchic formation. Havrylyshyn argues that the former Soviet nomenklatura (the politically vetted holders of state office in the Soviet system) delayed market economic reforms to give themselves time to transform themselves into the new property-owning class (2017, pp. 77-78). However, this may project back onto members of the old Soviet bureaucracy more foresight, as well as greater powers to realise their plans, than they are likely to have had. More persuasive, I think, is the argument that, in contrast to nearby countries such as Poland and Estonia, a "new", multi-ethnic state like Ukraine did not at the time possess the necessary social and political cohesion to undertake rapid market reforms. In part, this may have been owing to the relatively passive way in which Ukrainian independence was achieved—that is, "partly through its own efforts, but primarily because the Soviet order imploded" (Wilson, 2013, p. 182).

Common socio-political backgrounds

Alongside these two structural economic conditions—the partial introduction of market-style reforms, but the delay of full-scale ones heralding a switch in economic systems—the active ingredient in the process of formation of the oligarchy is to be found in the socio-political inheritance from the late Soviet period. On this, too, there is surprisingly broad agreement. Havrylyshyn, for example, runs through the biographies of prominent, named oligarchs, from the early phase of their emergence to the present day, sifting out common sociological characteristics in their backgrounds (2017, pp. 202-207). He shows that the first Ukrainian oligarchs had their origins in the former Soviet nomenklatura, either from within the party-state apparatus, or as managers of large industrial concerns, the so-called red directors. Also, many new oligarchs were relatively young in the 1990s, having founded their first businesses early, in the late 1980s or early 1990s, making commercial progress, it is implied, either by capitalising on political connections linked to their privileged positions (as members of the Komsomol, the key Soviet political youth organisation, or as students at prestigious institutions of higher education), or as political outsiders able to develop relationships with public officials to their mutual benefit. Yurchenko argues that the roots of this connection between high state officials and the underworld, for which she borrows the term "political-criminal nexus" and which was crucial to the formation of the oligarchy in the decade after independence, can be traced back to the 1960s and to the structural deficiencies of the Soviet economy—namely, an overemphasis on military production at the expense of consumer goods (2018, pp. 29-34).

Between them, the combination of limited private property rights and the delayed introduction of liberalisation and market competition created opportunities for arbitrage (making money on price differences between markets). From such opportunities, privileged political insiders, or those with good connections to public officials, were able to build their initial capital. The wealth so gained was used in part to develop sufficient political influence to allow the oligarchs to perpetuate the "partial reform equilibrium" from which they continued to benefit financially. This mode of analysis, as indicated above, comes from Hellman's 1998 paper, in which he contends that, in the transition from east European centrally planned economies, the early winners of reform often proved to be the main political actors blocking the development of fully functioning market economies, rather than the short-term losers of the reform process, as was the conventional wisdom at the start of the transition process.

A recent quantitative study by Markus and Charnysh (2017) chimes with the above account in confirming red directorships and (insider?) privatisations as two important original sources of the wealth of the rich in Ukraine. At the same time, the study demonstrates two further "wealth origin stories" among the Ukrainian super-rich, one linked to the holding of executive posts in big corporations and another generated "from scratch" — in other words, through entrepreneurial activity. This may tie in with the view, considered below, on the development of "normal" capitalist modes of wealth accumulation in Ukraine after the 1990s.

Two "classic" arbitrage schemes

Despite a proliferation of corrupt economic schemes, two kinds of "classic" arbitrage scheme stand out as characteristic, the first of the early 1990s and the second of the mid-1990s on.

In the first, while price liberalisation had already occurred by 1992-93 in neighbouring countries such as Poland and Russia, in Ukraine the prices of many tradable commodities were still state-controlled or subsidised. This meant that those with insider connections — for example, to officials in charge of issuing export licences — were able to buy goods cheaply at home and sell them abroad at higher prices. Aslund estimates "export rents" generated in this way at US$4.1bn in 1992, or the equivalent of about 20% of that year's GDP (2009, p. 55).

In the second kind of scheme, natural gas was imported from Russia at low or subsidised Russian prices by private Ukrainian intermediaries, but under Ukrainian state-guarantee. In Ukraine, the gas was sold at higher domestic prices, but with the Ukrainian state footing the bill for unpaid private gas debts upon default, including by ceding to Gazprom, the Russian state gas supplier, ownership in energy infrastructure (Havrylyshyn, 2017, p. 209; pp. 227-228). Aslund describes the gas trade the "greatest source of rent-seeking" in the second half of the 1990s (Aslund, 2009, p. 105). For Havrylyshyn, the long-term political impact of these gas-trading schemes with Russia has been more harmful still than the earlier, more indigenous arbitrage schemes, first by boosting the wealth of corrupt local business elements, so accelerating the formation of the oligarchy; and, second, by handing Russia an additional means of coercing Ukraine politically in line with its own strategic interests (Havrylyshyn, 2017, p. 229).

3.2.3 What is the Ukrainian oligarchy and how does it work?

Oligarchs as operators of state-centred rent-extraction schemes

Perhaps again following Hellman (1998, p. 219), the term "rent-seeking" is liberally used in the literature to describe the economic practices characteristic of the Ukrainian oligarchy. "The theory of rent-seeking provides the simplest explanation of oligarchic formation," writes Havrylyshyn (2017, p. 207). Referring to the 1990s, Aslund notes that "since the most successful businessmen made their money rent-seeking, they ignored production" (Aslund, 2009, p. 4). Neither offers a definition of the phenomenon, however.

Nonetheless, from the range of lucrative schemes that they outline, it is possible to discern a common link. This might be termed the acquisition of something for nothing. Alongside the two "classic" arbitrage schemes referred to above, economic mechanisms of this kind that have operated in post-independence Ukraine include:

- subsidised credits, with cheap loans offered to politically connected businesses;
- transfer pricing, in which, for example, the manager of a state enterprise sells its products at low cost to a private

firm owned by the manager or a family member, but with any losses incurred at the state enterprise covered from the public purse (Havrylyshyn, 2017, p. 210);
- insider privatisations, in which, for instance, eligibility criteria for possible new owners have been tailored in advance to fit a specific, favoured business;
- the padding of state procurement contracts, alongside the avoidance or abolition of oversight controls; and
- hostile business takeovers, either by means of institutional intimidation (such as threatening to conduct official inspections), or the threat or use of physical force (such as the so-called *reiderstvo*).

A feature of these enrichment schemes is that some endure and evolve, whereas others arise and are prominent for a time but then fade, to be replaced by new ones. For example, large-scale schemes in the energy sector have been a staple of post-independence elite enrichment from at least the mid-1990s, proving resilient and adaptable in the face of periodic anti-corruption drives. An example of a "fleeting" scheme might be the issue by the National Bank of Ukraine (NBU, the central bank) of cheap credits to favoured sectors and actors in the early 1990s. This scheme was fleeting in the sense that it was quickly made untenable by the economic phenomenon—of fast-rising prices—that it helped to fuel. By means of this scheme, Aslund writes, "A small group of privileged insiders usurped a huge share of GDP". He estimates the total value as equal to 65% of GDP in 1992 and 47% in 1993 (2009, pp. 55-56).

More formally, the concept of rent-seeking is understood in relation to the theory of income distribution associated with neo-classical microeconomics (Stilwell, 2012, pp. 191-199). According to this theory, patterns of income distribution in a market economy are explained by the relative prices of factor services—that is, for the use of land, labour and capital—which are determined by market forces (that is, by supply and demand). From this perspective, then, a capitalist is someone who derives income from the market-determined value of the wealth-contributing capital services they provide. (This, then, is both a theory of income distribution and an implicit justification for it.) On the one hand, according to the influential account of Friedrich Hayek, an Austrian economist, of the dynamic nature of competition (1948), temporary economic rents are an essential part of the process of both innovation and adjustment by which market economies direct investment and rebalance themselves following economic shocks, since in competitive conditions, price movements provide the correct signals for resource reallocation. It is only when this mechanism is prevented from working that rent-seeking opportunities become more persistent and so problematic (Sethi et al, 2017), allowing some actors to gain access to wealth-enhancing income, but without participating in wealth-creating economic activities.

The changing role and relative strength of oligarchs in the system
Views of the Ukrainian oligarchs in the academic literature differ on at least two issues. The first is over their status as capitalists – in particular, whether some were able to transform themselves from rent-seekers in the 1990s into productive business owners by the early 2000s. The second is over the relative strength of the very rich in the informal system of political economy rule as a whole, which I am calling "the oligarchy" after its strongest part. (My view is that Ukrainian oligarchs can be capitalists, but are better distinguished by their extractive schemes, permitted by political connections, and that oligarchs are a powerful group within a system they do not fully control.)

Oligarchs as emergent capitalists
On the first issue, the accounts that diverge most sharply from the mainstream view of the oligarchy as made up of anti-competitive rent-seekers are those of Aslund, and of Adam Swain and Vlad Mykhnenko. Both make the case that industrial restructuring undertaken by home-grown capitalists played a significant role in Ukraine's economic recovery after 1999.

Aslund argues that the economic reforms undertaken in 1999-2001 by Viktor Yushchenko as prime minister "created a market economy and went far enough to become irreversible" (2009, p. 6). Alongside the development of a "competitive oligarchy", he says, this drove rapid economic growth and the political pluralism that led to the "democratic breakthrough" of the Orange Revolution in 2004/05 (2009, p. 6; pp. 107-113). Most striking is his argument that some talented local entrepreneurs were able to restructure successfully Ukraine's large, failing heavy industrial concerns owing to superior knowledge of local political and work-place practices, in this way contributing significantly to the 2000-07 boom, when the country's real GDP per head grew at an average annual rate of 7% (IMF, 2019b). Summing up the presumed underlying shift in the way in which big business operates, he writes that "the country had traversed the crucial hurdle from arbitrage to export production" (2009, p. 6). Later stepping back from this upbeat assessment, however, the author recognises that the rent-seeking system continued to predominate under the "predatory" rule of Viktor Yanukovych, in large part, he thinks, because the "old Soviet state system continues in a rudimentary market economy" (2014, p. 240).

Swain and Mykhnenko tell a similar story, even if, like Yurchenko, their main purpose is to criticise the orthodox transition economics of which Aslund is an exponent. But their criticism is from a "varieties of capitalism" perspective rather than an anti-capitalist one like Yurchenko, so that their target is not capitalism *per se*, but rather the wholesale transplantation of Western-style capitalism into Ukraine — that is to say, capitalism in its "transition" guise. They perceive in Ukraine, and wish to defend, the rise of "indigenous capitalism, involving local accumulation" (Swain and Mykhnenko, 2007, p. 41), at least in the Donbas, the region in eastern Ukraine on which they focus. "It is our contention," they write, "that the economic growth between 1999 and 2004 was in part linked to the revival of the economy in the Ukrainian Donbas". Chiming with Aslund's account, the main factor explaining this is industrial restructuring (Swain and Mykhnenko, 2007, p. 7).

On the one hand, they try to open up a way of thinking about the process of economic and political development in "peripheral" countries like Ukraine that moves away from the "one size fits all" model frequently promoted by international (that is, Western-dominated) financial institutions since the 1980s. On the other hand, they seem to conflate the interests of the business-political groups that came to dominate the Donbas economically and politically after 1991 with those of Donbas population as a whole.

A common problem with these arguments is that, by focusing on the issue of supposed industrial restructuring, these authors seem to ignore or downplay other, more obvious factors behind Ukraine's 2000-07 economic boom. Chief among these are the low base of comparison created by the output slump of the 1990s; the global economic boom of 2000-07, which boosted world commodity prices (Turley and Luke, 2011, p. 226), including for Ukrainian steel; the rise in foreign borrowing, which, as elsewhere in eastern Europe at the time, helped to fuel a domestic credit boom; and a boost to domestic demand from a phase of fiscal loosening undertaken in 2002-04. More damaging still, perhaps, for the thesis of "indigenous capitalism, involving local accumulation" is the charge that by minimising oligarchs' production costs, the extensive use of transfer pricing in this period was perhaps responsible for boosting the profits of oligarchs' large industrial concerns, creating the appearance that successful industrial turnarounds had taken place, but with the state budget footing the bill.

How politically powerful are the oligarchs?
A second important issue on which views concerning the Ukrainian oligarchs diverge is over the degree of political and policy-making power that they exert. At one end of the scale, Havrylyshyn conceives of oligarchic power as extensive. He writes that "oligarchs [have enough power to] not only influence specific policies to favour themselves...they may in fact be powerful enough in collusion with each other to 'capture the state' in the sense of virtually controlling the direction of general policy or even election outcomes" (2017, p. 203). It is this high degree of direct control over policy direction that he sees as distinguishing the position of Ukraine's oligarchs from the system of special interest lobbying that routinely takes place in the liberal democratic West.

Pleines (2016a), in contrast, sees the typical *modus operandi* of the oligarchs as more reactive, with them hedging their bets and adapting to the realities of unpredictable political and electoral outcomes. He argues that, despite undergoing compositional changes, the position of a "core" of oligarchs has remained quite stable, and their political influence reliably strong, by means of a consistent strategy of informal manipulation. Like Markus and Charnysh, he links the strategies of successful oligarchs to a willingness to adopt a flexible approach to politics. Of Pleines' sample of 29 oligarchs, half are found to have held formal political posts during all four presidencies in 2000-15, so supporting the notion of "state capture" associated with Hellman (1998). However, he also concludes that oligarchs' use of their parliamentary and media influence has helped to create an uneven political playing field that favours political incumbents, in line with the concept of "competitive authoritarianism" of Steven Levitsky and Lucan Way. "At the same time," Pleines writes, "the oligarchs are not the major power brokers in Ukrainian politics", but rather have always tried to "seek accommodation with those having or gaining political power" (2016, p. 126). This is a crucial insight in understanding that oligarchs, with their financial power and business networks, are only one part of the informal, oligarchic system of political rule as a whole, in which successful politicians and the holders of important state offices are the other essential elements. This explains why, in the face of uncertain political outcomes, Pleines concludes, oligarchs tend to adopt a "wait and see" approach, supporting rival candidates and parties in elections, but often falling in behind the likely winner in any critical contest as soon as this becomes clear. This tallies with Henry Hale's thesis on the operation of "patronal politics" in many of the countries of the former Soviet Union (Hale, 2015), which I analyse below. In this way, Pleines seeks to show three theoretical approaches to the political sociology of post-Soviet polities as distinct, but not necessarily contradictory, perspectives.

3.2.4 Continuity of the oligarchic system

Following the dramatic flight of Viktor Yanukovych and his coterie from Kyiv, the Ukrainian capital, at the end of February 2014, the position of the oligarchs looked weakened and uncertain. This was especially so for those, such as Rinat Akhmetov and Dmytro Firtash, who had been among the leading backers and main beneficiaries of the Yanukovych presidency. The impression was accentuated by the rhetoric of "de-oligarchisation" coming from politicians in the interim government, in place from late February 2014, driven by popular expectations that the way of doing politics would change (Umland, 2017).

However, some studies suggest that, despite the erosion of the wealth and power of leading oligarchs, and an alteration in their relative positions, the oligarchic system itself remained intact. So Konończuk writes that "The oligarchic system, which intrinsically involves corruption and informal ties between the oligarchs and the top tier of government, did not disappear after the Euromaidan, it merely evolved slightly to adapt to the new political situation" (Konończuk, 2016, p. 35). Similarly, Wilson notes that, "For many, 'reform' in Ukraine has been synonymous with dismantling the ruling oligarchy", but that in the Ukrainian parliament in the post-Euromaidan era, "oligarchs dominate the old parties as well as the new ones" (Wilson, 2014, pp. 144-160).

Survival of the "old" oligarchs

On the reasons for the survival of the oligarchy through another period of momentous political turmoil, Konończuk argues that "the main cause...has been the decision, taken by some of the post-Euromaidan elite, to enter into informal alliances with the oligarchs" (Konończuk, 2016, p. 5). He sees two key moments in the re-establishment of this tactical, symbiotic alliance between the main pre-Euromaidan oligarchs[4] and new political leaders[5]. On Konończuk's analysis, instability is built into the relationship by the oligarchs' overriding rationale, which is to protect their business interests (this point echoes both Hale's analysis, which I outline below, and the logic of Winters' theory).

The first such moment was the election to the Verkhovna Rada (parliament) of October 2014. Konończuk argues that, with great wealth at their disposal and dominating the TV market, the

---

[4] Including Rinat Akhmetov, Dmytro Firtash and Ihor Kolomoyskyi.
[5] Primarily, Petro Poroshenko, elected president in May 2014, and Arseniy Yatsenyuk, who was prime minister from February 2014 until mid-April 2016.

oligarchs were able to offer financial and media backing to politicians, paving the way for the reaffirmation of their central role in the political process. Konończuk and Wilson (2016) concur that Ukraine's elections are unusually expensive in relation to its economic size. Wilson shows that the cost of recent Ukrainian elections extends beyond media advertising because of the extensive use of unscrupulous machine politics (2016, p. 5).

For Konończuk, the second moment in the practical political rehabilitation of the oligarchy was the departure of two parties (Self-Reliance and Fatherland) from the governing coalition in 2016, which left it with a slim parliamentary majority. In response, he argues, the government parties — the Petro Poroshenko Bloc (PPB) and Yatsenyuk's People's Front (PF) — entered into informal legislative alliance with oligarch-influenced parliamentary groups, accepting political support on key laws in return for deflecting or postponing reforms that would impinge on oligarchs' interests. (My empirical findings in chapter 5 are in line with this analysis.)

On Konończuk's account, the evidence for this is shown by an analysis of parliamentary activities. This includes an absence of prosecutions of figures from the Yanukovych government; the failure to reverse any of the Yanukovych era insider privatisations; efforts to delay in parliament the removal of electricity export subsidies, apparently to aid the business interests of Akhmetov; the blocking of a law on joint-stock companies that would have impinged on the interests of Kolomoyskyi; and the postponement of legislation on the public financing of political parties, designed to break their reliance on oligarch funding.

Emergence of the "new" oligarchs

Alongside these developments, Konończuk outlines the emergence of influential figures around key post-Euromaidan political leaders, whose *modus operandi* was to use their close personal connection to political leaders to gain control of profitable state-owned enterprises, and their revenues, to build their own business bases. He calls this group "new oligarchs". It includes Ihor Kononenko, a long-term business partner of Poroshenko. Around Yatsenyuk, profiles are sketched of Andriy Ivanchuck, the chair of the economics committee of the Rada, and of Mykola Martynenko, who chaired the energy committee[6]. Konończuk's chart (Figure 3.1), reproduced below, summarises his understanding on the main links of new and old oligarchs in the "orbits" around the president and prime minister at this time (2016, p. 34).

Figure 3.1: Konończuk's "Links of the main oligarchic groups in Ukraine"

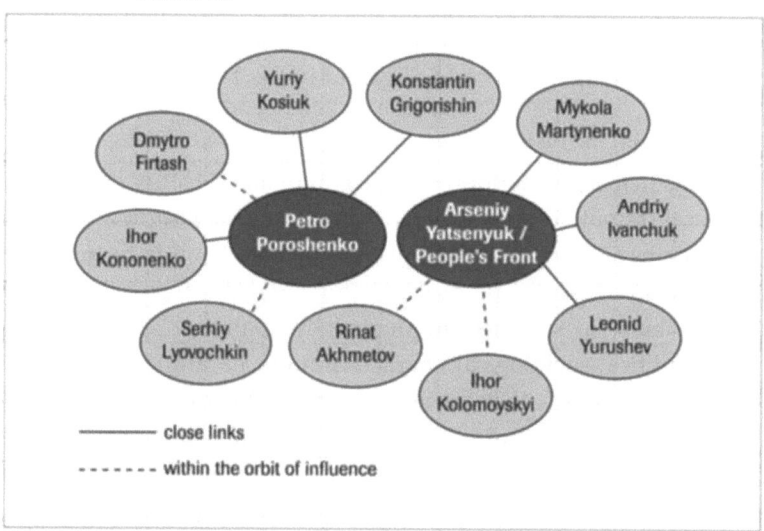

Source: Konończuk, 2016, p. 34. Title adapted in order make attribution clear. Available: https://bit.ly/3k2DaYL. © Copyright by Ośrodek Studiów Wschodnich im. Marka Karpia/Centre for Eastern Studies.

Looking at a similar phenomenon in somewhat wider focus, Wilson uses of the term "watchers" (*smotriashchi*) for the "network of placemen bureaucrats and state enterprise bosses, appointed by politicians in exchange for then funnelling public money into their election campaigns" (2016, p. 6). This is a good example of the "politics to riches" direction of movement on the oligarchic system's two-way street, or "business capture". It also suggests that, for the

---

[6] For profiles of these figures, see Konończuk (2016, pp. 22-33); also Zinets and Polityuk (2017).

elite, political power is conceived to depend not just on office but also on the control of economic assets.

That the influence of such new groups grew after the fall of Yanukovych, Konończuk suggests, is shown in their open clash with reformists in the administration, culminating in the resignation of the economy minister, Aivaras Abromavičius, and his team, in February 2016. Nevertheless, he suggests, the "new" oligarchs were weaker than the "old" ones because of the relative insecurity implied by control as against ownership of assets, as well as the continuing dominance by the old oligarchs of the TV market.

What is behind the institutional resilience of the Ukrainian oligarchy?
Drawing on local perceptions of political practice, Henry Hale offers a general framework for understanding the reconstitution of informal systems of rule, following episodes of disruption, in terms of the incentive structures faced by key actors, and the expectations that they develop, in societies dominated by "patronal" politics. This broad political-sociological characterisation, he argues, applies to Ukraine and many other former Soviet republics of Eurasia (Hale, 2015, p. 2). In a patronal political system, power, envisaged as the distribution of rewards and punishments, is organised through hierarchical networks of personal acquaintance (Hale, 2015, p. 9). Patron-client networks tend to form in three main milieus – regional politics, with bosses at the top; big business, headed by oligarchs; and national politics, with political leaders and state officials in charge (Hale, 2015, p. 29).

An important implication is that "patronal" regimes are more stable than they appear. That is, Hale argues, the periodic political disjunctures in post-Soviet politics might best be understood not as revolutions, nor as instances of democratic breakthrough or backsliding, but rather as cycles of adaptation and reconstruction of informal network "pyramids", as they interact with key elements of formal politics. These elements condition actors' expectations about the prospects for leadership change, and so too about the future ability of existing patrons to continue to perform effectively their reward and punishment functions. This means that, in the wake of significant political shift, network leaders have a strong incentive to fall in behind the political winners, and especially the chief political "patron", to protect their position and access to resources. However, Hale also stresses the overall informal institutional continuity that this helps to preserve. He recommends the "reorientation of scholarship from the logic of regime change to a logic of regime dynamics" in order to "capture how the moving parts of highly patronalistic polities (such as oligarchic networks or regional political machines) arrange and rearrange themselves in regular... ways that might on the surface look like regime 'change'" (Hale, 2015, p. 15).

From a different perspective, Markus and Charnysh (2017) use a quantitative approach to test the relative effectiveness of different wealth-protection strategies of the Ukrainian oligarchs in 2006-12. Chiming with the findings of Pleines (2016a), they find evidence that indirect strategies, including the financing of political parties and media ownership, have been more successful in defending oligarchs' wealth than direct ones (mainly holding government jobs or parliamentary seats). They explain this by means of the greater effectiveness of a political "logic of flexibility" — as against a "logic of commitment" — in conditions where the rule of law is weak but politics remains competitive. This means that, in the face of unpredictable political outcomes, which could be catastrophic from the point of view of wealth protection, very rich political actors have an incentive to exert political influence "at a distance", to avoid becoming too strongly identified with any one political force.

What is to be done?

Kończuk and Wilson both see the reconstitution of the relationships, processes and mechanisms of the oligarchic system following the Euromaidan revolt as a major obstacle to reform. This has significant implications not only for Ukraine's economic outlook, but also for its defence capacity, since economic competition, technological development and economic growth are linked. But whereas Kończuk sees a strengthening of state institutions as the crucial remedy (Kończuk, 2016. pp. 6-7), Wilson argues that breaking the links between big business and politicians, while allowing oligarchs to hold on to the assets they already have, would be less disruptive and quicker than either attempting to dismantle the oligarchy directly or cutting it off from all of its corrupt money-making schemes (Wilson, 2016, p. 4). Wilson adds that the survival of the oligarchic system post-Euromaidan may have been enabled in part by the failure of different reformist actors, both from inside and outside Ukraine, to act in concert (Wilson, 2015, p. 10).

Aslund's main suggestion for the post-Euromaidan authorities is the need to break the power of the old system, which is the source of growth-supressing corruption. By this, he seems to mean only those figures and officials most closely associated with the presidency of Viktor Yanukovych, and looks forward to the results of the law on lustration (a purge of politically tainted public officials) of September 2014. However, as several studies discussed so far in this chapter have implied, the system is wider and more ubiquitous than just the former president's main supporters and entourage. Nevertheless, this approach fits with the author's view that the presidential and parliamentary elections of 2014 had "put in place political leaders who want to save the country rather than themselves and their families" (Aslund, 2014, p. 243). It points to a more individualistic mode of explanation of the problem (the moral failings of top politicians), rather than a social-structural one (that the "new" successful politicians are part of a system that they promised to dismantle). It also chimes with the author's earlier optimistic judgement on the "market completing" and democratic breakthroughs he thought had been achieved by the Orange Revolution (Aslund, 2009), which soon appeared premature.

Table 3.2: Extractive practices of political influence of the Ukrainian oligarchy

Oligarchs dominate strategically important economic sectors
Oligarchs hold government posts
Oligarchs hold seats in parliament
Oligarchs pay for representatives to get onto party lists
Oligarchs "sponsor" deputies to gain legislative influence
Oligarchs' deputies sit on or chair parliamentary committees
Oligarchs fund politicians' election campaigns
Oligarchs dominate TV channels which support or undermine politicians
Politicians need political support of local big business in frontline areas
Politicians ensure associates are appointed to committees, state enterprises, top posts in the state administration (especially those of financial or coercive significance)

Sources: Own compilation from the various authors cited in this chapter.

3.3 Evolution of the Ukrainian oligarchy

3.3.1 Ukraine-Russia energy politics

Margarita Balmaceda offers a detailed comparative account of how post-Soviet political elites dealt with the political consequences of their dependence on energy imports from Russia in the first decades after the Soviet Union collapsed. Although described as "energy poor", Ukraine's reliance on Russia for energy imports (excluding of nuclear fuel) was considerably lower than for Belarus or Lithuania (Balmaceda, 2013, p. 93, 317). Nevertheless, the relationship led periodically to serious bilateral strains.

Rather than straightforward energy dependence, however, Ukraine's basic energy relation with Russia is better understood as one of "asymmetric interdependence", Balmaceda contends. By this she means that post-Soviet Ukraine had significant energy assets with which it could have mitigated the effects of its reliance on energy supplies from Russia. Chief among these she counts the Ukrainian gas transit system.

Her main argument, however, is that Ukrainian elites mismanaged this hand, so that valuable national energy assets were not used to further Ukraine's long-term national interests, such as energy diversification and security. One reason for this is that powerful individuals and networks in Russia and Ukraine prioritised their private, rent-seeking goals over the public interest. The author describes this "transborder sharing" as one of the main mechanisms for the management of energy conflict in this period. In Ukraine, these flows of energy rents formed a focal point of rivalry and co-operation around which the Ukrainian political and economic elites have cohered in the independence era, at the same time defining an uneasy relationship with their Russian counterparts — that is to say, tying the Ukrainian elite materially to the Russian elite, while subordinating them to it (Balmaceda and Rutland, 2014). A second, related reason for Ukraine's poor management of its asymmetric energy interdependence is the political influence that the main beneficiaries of the joint energy rent schemes were able to exert, not just on energy policy, but also on aspects of state formation. As a result, Ukraine was unable to adopt a strong, unified stance on energy policy, or to respond effectively to developments such as Russia's long-term plans to construct energy pipelines to Europe around Ukraine (Balmaceda, 2013, p. 150).

Ukraine's basic energy relation with Russia, at least until 2005, was one of gas imports bartered for transit services, but at a preferential price — in effect, a significant energy subsidy. While Russian subsidies afforded both Belarus and Ukraine substantial "external" rent-extraction opportunities, Ukraine also generated the "largest range of domestic rent-acquisition opportunities" (Balmaceda, 2013, p. 95). A distinguishing feature of Ukraine's energy relation with Russia, then, was the size of the energy rents available.

An especially useful aspect of Balmaceda's study, from the perspective of this book, is that, in showing how energy rent-extraction operations dovetail into the wider institutional political economy frameworks of the Kuchma and Yushchenko presidencies, she offers a practical example of how to portray the evolving relation between formal politics and business networks as means of analysing the changing political and policy conditions of rent-extraction schemes (the subject of chapter 6). It is to an account of the broad evolution of this relation that we now turn.

3.3.2 Ukraine's evolving political economy governance regime

In independent Ukraine, the basic understanding of the relations of power between the central state and the emergent regional business-political groups was established and began to be institutionalised during the first Kuchma presidency, in 1994-99, following a period of uncertainty and flux under Leonid Kravchuk. This is what is meant here by "political economy governance regime" — the evolving relation between political actors holding high public office in the main institutions of the state on the one hand, and the largest and most influential business-economic networks, usually led by oligarchs, on the other, as well as the intertwining of the formal and informal rules and practices[7] that permeate and blur the lines between them. What follows is a stylised account of the evolution of Ukraine's dominant political and economic institutions, and of the shifting relations between them in the independence era. Its purpose is to provide a backdrop against which the subsequent empirical investigations — on wealth, the Rada and the energy sector — can be read, helping to make sense of them. Although the focus of the following account is on the institutional contrasts between the Yanukovych and Poroshenko presidencies — the main comparative framework built into this study — it is useful to add some information on the structures and events from which they arose. Along with my own observations based on the research of this and other chapters, this narrative draws in particular on the studies of Avioutskii (2010), Balmaceda (2013), Hale (2015), Matsiyevsky (2018), Minakov (2019) and Whitmore (2019).

The Kuchma era

A strong presidency was a key institutional feature of the new understanding of the relation of formal and informal political and economic power forged under Kuchma. This was achieved through the passage of a new constitution in 1996, which Kuchma strong-armed the Rada into accepting (Hale, 2015, p. 146). Bolstered by these

---

[7] By "practice", I mean the routinised actions of individuals that mediate and recreate the social-institutional environment of which they are an active, somewhat creative element.

powers, Kuchma was able to balance the interests of the strongest "in-system" regional business-political groups, originally based in Dnipropetrovsk, Donetsk and Kyiv (Balmaceda, 2013, p. 98). They gained economic (rent-seeking) opportunities in return for political support, while Kuchma established a more stable support base for his presidency within big business. Hale describes this as "patronal presidentialism", resulting in single dominant "pyramid" of economic and political power, with the head of state at its pinnacle (Hale, 2015, pp. 82-83).

At around this time, in 1998, Naftogaz was established by Kuchma as the national energy company as a way to centralise the distribution of energy rents, apparently in response to the destabilising impact on the "balancing" system of the activities of one of its constituent networks, that of Pavlo Lazarenko from Kuchma's home region of Dnipropetrovsk (Balmaceda, 2013, p. 113).

The "Orange" era and the Yushchenko presidency

In comparison with the Kuchma era, the presidency of Viktor Yushchenko in 2005-10 is usually characterised as marking a phase of "democratic advance", leading to a more competitive political environment. Hale describes this as a switch from a more closed to a more open form of politics, which, he thinks, can be visualised using a country's political rights score in the index produced by Freedom House, a US-funded non-governmental organisation/NGO (Hale, 2015, p. 177; Freedom House, 2021). On this account, the scoring criteria for political rights combine elements of traditional and more modern interpretations of liberal democratic ideals. On the first, the index checks the extent to which policy-making governments have been selected in free and fair elections, underpinned by competitive popular political participation; on the second, it grades countries on whether they have safeguards in place against both public corruption and the exclusion of historically disempowered social groups. In this index, a score of 1 represents the highest level of provision of political rights and 7 the lowest. For comparison, Figure 3.2 below shows a steep deterioration in the situation on political rights in Belarus from the mid-1990s (the dotted grey line on the chart), corresponding to the rise to power of Alyaksander Lukashenka, and in

Russia from the late 1990s (the dashed grey line). In Ukraine, by contrast, in the post-independence period this alternates between a score of 4 and 3 (the solid grey line), corresponding roughly to phases of greater authoritarianism of the second Kuchma and Yanukovych presidencies, and the return to more open and democratic situations under Yushchenko and Poroshenko, respectively.

Figure 3.2: Political rights scores for Ukraine, Russia & Belarus, 1991-2017

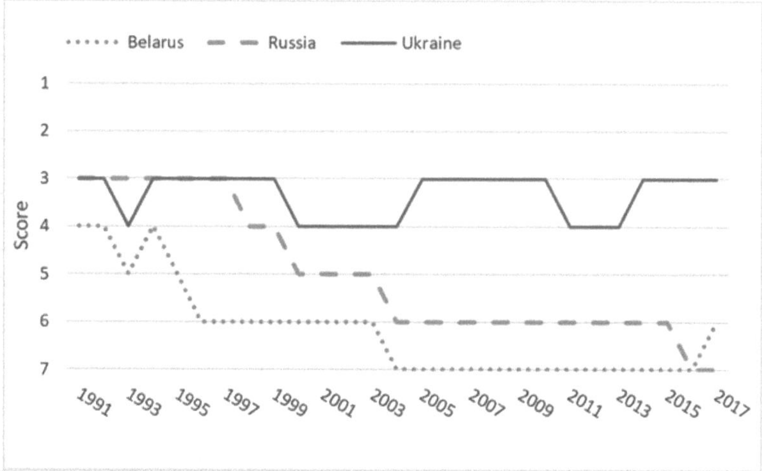

Source: Freedom House (2021). Freedom in the World: All Data, FIW 2013-21. Available: https://bit.ly/3zHrvUp.

Such indexes are not unproblematic, however. They can, for example, smuggle in unexamined or contested assumptions, while the presentation of results as numbers can lend a misleading air of scientific objectivity to analysts' inevitably somewhat subjective judgements in matching developments to scoring criteria. More seriously, perhaps, they can be accused of the basic sociological error of attempting to describe one set of societies (those in eastern Europe, in this case, which have arrived at modernity through their own specific paths) in terms of the political categories, concepts and institutions developed out of the historical experience of another set of societies (that is, of the liberal democratic market societies of northwestern Europe and the United States), so setting benchmarks for political and economic development that they may be unsuited to achieve (Magyar and Madlovics, 2020, pp. 1-3).

Under Yushchenko, greater political openness was facilitated by the appearance of multiple nodes of political power, itself partly a response to the switch to a constitution — written in 2004, but only introduced at the start of 2006 — in which the powers of the president and prime minister were more evenly dispersed[8]. Acute political rivalry went on not just within the winning "Orange" camp, however, between the business-political networks aligned to President Yushchenko and those around Yuliya Tymoshenko as prime minister, but also included the "blue" camp, temporarily defeated by the Orange Revolution, for which Yanukovych was the leading political representative. In particular, the RosUkrEnergo (RUE) gas intermediary scheme, which ran throughout this period, became a focal point of contestation between the network clusters. Despite the widespread use of informal methods in the tightly run 2010 presidential campaign, electoral integrity and media freedom were maintained, Hale argues (Hale, 2015, p. 336).

The Yushchenko presidency also saw the rise to political prominence of the leaders of networks — such as that of Petro Poroshenko, centred on his Ukrprominvest holding company, or of Kostyantyn Zhevaho, at the head of Finances and Credit — that had been more on the periphery of the Kuchma system (Balmaceda, 2013, p. 101). While the changed political situation gave business-political groups greater room for manoeuvre, it brought about institutional deadlock, hindering economic reform (Balmaceda, 2013, pp. 96-97), as rival network "pyramids" around the three political poles fought one another, unsuccessfully, for pre-eminence.

The Yanukovych presidency

Following his victory in the 2010 presidential contest, Viktor Yanukovych moved quickly to construct a more unified power structure reminiscent of the Kuchma years. In Hale's terminology, he moved to re-establish a "single pyramid" network structure.

---

[8] See chapter 5 for a discussion of the difference between the two constitutions.

A crucial early step in this process was the appointment of a prime minister, Mykola Azarov, from among Yanukovych's close associates, so securing control for his group, linked centrally with the Donbas region, of the two leading state executive posts while the 2004 premier-presidential constitution was still in place. This was aided by the co-option of Volodymyr Lytvyn, the speaker of the Rada, who had been part of Tymoshenko's parliamentary coalition (Hale, 2015, p. 343). Arguably, the most important step, however, involved engineering a restoration of the 1996 "Kuchma" constitution, which returned to the presidency some of the formal powers that had devolved to the prime minister following the Orange Revolution. When blocked on this in the Rada, Yanukovych side-stepped the legislature by packing the Constitutional Court, which subsequently rescinded the 2004 constitution on the grounds that the correct procedures for its introduction had not been followed (Hale, 2015, p. 345; Minakov and Rojansky, 2021, p. 324), so restoring stronger powers to the presidency.

During the Yanukovych presidency, the Rada was dominated by a single political machine, the Party of Regions (PoR), originally created by the leading business-political networks of the Donetsk region in the late 1990s. Other means used to control legislative outcomes included the financial inducement of deputy defections (recorded in the PoR's "black ledger", as is noted in chapter 5), as well as the manipulation of voting rules in time for the 2012 parliamentary election to sustain the PoR's Rada representation (Hale, 2015, p. 349). With his presidential powers strengthened, and in control of the executive and legislative branches of government, Yanukovych and his team were able to extend their control over other state institutions, including the judiciary.

Yanukovych's presidency has often been characterised as a period of "democratic backsliding" or increased authoritarianism, owing mainly to his jailing of prominent opposition politicians (Tymoshenko and Lutsenko), and to an increase in harassment of media outlets (Hale, 2015, p. 346, 348). Given the rapid fall in Yanukovych's poll ratings following his electoral win in 2010, the purpose is assumed to have been to create the conditions for him to retain the presidency in the election then planned for 2015.

Moreover, Yanukovych based his political economy governance system on a narrower range of business networks — primarily the Donetsk network of Rinat Akhmetov, for which Yanukovych had been for some time the main political figure, and that of Dmytro Firtash, another key financer of his 2010 presidential campaign — while building a (nepotistic) network of his own, dubbed "the family" (Wilson, 2015, p. 345). On way in which "the family" was built up economically was by using state institutions, especially the tax authority, to predate the businesses and income flows of actors lower down the pecking order (Tkach and Dalton, 2013, p. 5).

But for a series of blunders by his government, which each time re-stoked the Euromaidan protests just as they appeared to flag (Hale, 2015, pp. 235), Yanukovych's "power vertical" might well have survived the wave of anti-government protests triggered from late 2013 by his refusal, under pressure from Russia, to sign the long-planned association agreement (AA) with the EU. However, it was the sharp escalation of political violence towards the end of February 2014, leaving scores of dead, that saw the networks of support around Yanukovych first fray, and then abandon him *en masse*, in what scholars of revolutions would describe as a classic "central collapse" scenario of state breakdown (Goldstone, 2014a, pp. 27-28; 2014b).

Post-Euromaidan: the interim government
Immediately after the collapse of Yanukovych's "power vertical", leaders of the parliamentary opposition who had been among the most visible supporters of the Euromaidan protests came to the fore politically at the head of an interim administration. Of these, Arseniy Yatsenyuk, as interim prime minister, and Oleksandr Turchynov, taking on the roles of interim president and Rada speaker, emerged as the central figures, holding between them the three most powerful formal state posts. As regards changes to formal political institutions, perhaps the most crucial phase of their "duumvirate" involved the passing in March 2014 of legislation ejecting Yanukovych from the presidency for desertion, laying the groundwork for a pre-term presidential election later that year, and restoring the 2004 "premier-president" constitution (Matsiyevsky, 2018, p. 352). These decisions

were made not just with the backing of the pro-Euromaidan Rada parties, but also of some former PoR MPs keen to distance themselves from Yanukovych (see chapter 5).

The period of rule of the interim government coincides with the rise to its high watermark of the political influence and prestige of Kolomoyskyi's Privat business-political network[9]. Its early alignment with the Yatsenyuk-Turchynov team is suggested not only by Kolomoyskyi's appointment as governor of Dnipropetrovsk in March 2014, but also by the apparent protection of his economic interests by their parliamentary vehicle, the People's Front, into the eighth convocation of the Rada, after December 2014 (Konończuk, 2016, p. 18). Kolomoyskyi's association with the politicians around Fatherland (as well as its forerunners and offshoot parties), and especially with Tymoshenko, can be traced back considerably further (Avioutskii, 2010, p. 123).

Post-Euromaidan: the Poroshenko presidency

Continuity of practices

Between the Yanukovych and the Poroshenko presidencies, writes Matsiyevsky, "the leadership changed, but the regime remains the same" (Matsiyevsky, 2018, p. 350). His article covers a number of the topics that are central to this book, including on the continuity of the political regime between the pre- and post-Euromaidan periods. In particular, he stresses the carryover of informal political practices, including secret deals between elite actors, as well as the operation of quotas for government posts. In his estimation, Ukraine's political regime has changed only once in its modern history — specifically, from the set-up of the Soviet era to the one established in the years following the Soviet Union's demise (Matsiyevsky, 2018, p. 349). The latter he describes as "hybrid", because, despite the maintenance of democratic structures, informal rules and practices have continued to dominate, so preventing the development and acculturation of rule-of-law norms (Matsiyevsky, 2018, p. 350).

---

[9] That is, until its re-emergence with the victory of Volodymyr Zelenskyi in the presidential election of 2019, which is outside the timeframe of this study.

Election and biography

Following the reversion to the 2004 constitution with its reduced presidential powers, but with the war with Russia still in its somewhat clandestine early stages, Petro Poroshenko won a convincing first-round victory in a hastily prepared presidential contest at the end of May 2014 (Wilson, 2014, pp. 151-152). After this, he and Yatsenyuk, as president and prime minister, became the two main political focal points around which competing business-political networks would align, in keeping with Hale's broad prediction about elite politics in a patronal society under a "divided executive" constitution, in which the prime minister is chosen by parliament (Hale, 2015, p. 77, 80).

According to Havrylyshyn, Poroshenko's higher education was at the Institute of International Relations in Kyiv in the early 1990s, when he seems to have put to good use the knowledge and connections developed there to start a business importing cocoa beans, which grew eventually into his Roshen confectionery business (Havrylyshyn, 2017, p. 205). By the time of the Euromaidan in 2013/14, however, he had built up a large business empire gathered (until 2012) under the Ukrprominvest holding company[10], which included interests in vehicle and boat production, as well as banking. According to Focus Ratings, Poroshenko's domestic business wealth by this time was estimated at more than US$900m, placing him sixteenth on its rich list. Although this sum had fallen in US dollar terms by 2017, linked to steep depreciation of the hryvnya, it rose slightly as a share of national wealth, and his ranking crept up to 11th place (Focus Ratings, 2014, 2018). With the release of the Panama Papers, Poroshenko, already believed to have considerable financial wealth abroad, was shown adding to this after he had become president, appearing to take time in August 2014 to attend to the issue just as the disastrous battle of Ilovaisk was taking place (Garside et al, 2016). Moreover, by the onset of the Euromaidan mass protests, Poroshenko had built up considerable political and administrative experience, having held high-level public positions

---

[10] Holding, that is, shares in a number of subsidiary businesses.

under Yushchenko, first as the head of the National Security and Defence Council, Ukraine's main organ of security policy, then as chair of the National Bank of Ukraine (NBU; the central bank) and foreign minister. He also served briefly as minister of economic development and trade under Yanukovych.

Although Poroshenko qualifies amply, therefore, as an oligarch on the definition used in this book—that is, of a very wealthy business leader involved in national politics—he was, up to that point, a rather "second tier" figure. It was his early backing of the Euromaidan protests, as well as his image as a "safe pair of hands" following Russia's annexation of Crimea and its stoking of armed insurrection in the Donbas, that propelled him to the front rank of the country's political-economic actors.

The Vinnytsya group

A notable feature of political economy governance structures under Poroshenko was the deployment to key institutions of the state apparatus (such as the Rada, public enterprises, judicial bodies and the general prosecutor's office) of personnel from Poroshenko's own business-political network, the so-called Vinnytsya group, previously a relatively minor network based on Poroshenko's home region in central Ukraine (Andrusiv et al, 2018, pp. 65-66). From this set of connections was later drawn not only an "in-group" prime minister, Volodymyr Hroysman, but also parliamentary fixers (such as Serhiy Berezenko), as well as "overseers" of state-owned enterprises[11], some of whom became the "new oligarchs" that Konończuk refers to above, based on the wealth they were able to accumulate from these official positions.

Link up with the Firtash network

Moreover, by the time of the 2014 presidential election, Poroshenko appears already to have come to an arrangement with at least one of the major oligarchic blocs. Specifically, the network alliance centred on the Group DF businesses of Dmytro Firtash, with its economic base in gas, chemicals and the media, but also including the

---

[11] Ihor Kononenko, for example, is reported to have been Poroshenko's overseer for the energy sector (Andrusiv et al, 2018, p. 15).

distinct but aligned networks of Serhiy Lyovochkin and Yuriy Boyko, was reported to have struck a deal with Poroshenko ahead of the campaign. This view is supported, for example, by reports of a covert meeting of Poroshenko and Vitaliy Klychko with Firtash in March 2014 in Vienna, ahead of the 2014 presidential election, apparently to gain his blessing for their plan for Poroshenko to run for the presidency and Klychko for mayor of Kyiv, the Ukrainian capital. Allegedly, in return for support for their political ticket, immunity from prosecution was offered to Firtash associates still in Ukraine (Francis, 2016, p. 7). Lyovochkin had been head of the presidential administration under Yanukovych, while Boyko was energy minister. This arrangement may also have paved the way for the later merger of Klychko's Ukrainian Democratic Alliance for Reform (UDAR) political group with the president's parliamentary party, the PPB, set up to support his administration in parliament after his presidential win.

Matsiyevsky sees the meeting with Firtash as an example of the continuation of the political practice of the "secret" elite deal, echoing back to late Soviet times at least (Matsiyevsky, 2018, p. 351). Moreover, in Konończuk's analysis, it is worth recalling, the expensive election campaigns of 2014 should be counted among the key "moments" in which the "old" oligarchs, temporarily on the back-foot after the Euromaidan, again began in stages to step back into their customary roles in the political process, as political candidates and parties drew on their funding and media backing (Konończuk, 2016, pp. 15-16).

The Rada

If under the Yanukovych system a single political machine dominated the legislature, the political scene in eighth convocation of the Rada, after December 2014, by contrast, appears more fragmented organisationally. As a result, broader and more fractious coalitions of parties and factions were required to pass government legislation. As shown in chapter 5, there is a break in the pattern of alignment of elite political and economic forces in parliament between the second Yatsenyuk government, in office from December 2014, and the premiership of Volodymyr Hroysman, from mid-April 2016. Throughout this period, up until the end of 2017, the political vehicles of Poroshenko and Yatsenyuk—the PPB and PF—remained the principal means for supporting the passage of government bills. The necessary auxiliary support, however, came from different political sources during the Yatsenyuk and Hroysman administrations—that is, from the pro-Euromaidan parties in the first case, but with increased reliance on backing from the post-PoR parties and MPs associated with "old" oligarchs under the second.

The rehabilitation of Akhmetov's SCM network

This break coincides with the "rehabilitation" of Akhmetov and his System Capital Management (SCM) business-political network. As a leading backer of the Yanukovych presidency, tarnished both by his association with Yanukovych and his ambiguous dealings with Russian-backed separatists in the Donbas in 2014 before he fled west, Akhmetov's public image and prestige had plummeted in the immediate aftermath of Yanukovych's abscondment from the capital. According to Matsiyevsky, the parliamentary realignment of forces in 2016 under Hroysman again reflected a secret agreement between sections of the political and economic elite (2018, p. 353). In particular, the authorities—at least those in the orbit of Poroshenko—may have enlisted the support of Akhmetov and his group to counterbalance the ambitions of Kolomoyskyi and his Privat network, with which the "pyramid" of networks around the president had been engaged in protracted struggle from relatively early on in the Poroshenko presidency (this conflict is detailed in chapter 6). The shift in the pattern of parliamentary support and the rehabilitation of Akhmetov makes sense in context of this tussle with Kolomoyskyi, who aligned his group and resources behind the rival political node around Yatsenyuk.

These movements in the relative position to political authority of the leading business-political groups are a feature of the first two or three years of the post-Euromaidan era. In this sense, the political fortunes of Akhmetov and Kolomoyskyi in this period were on opposite trajectories, while the ongoing struggle between them is an additional underlying dimension of the behind-the-scenes politics of the period.

Formation of the Hroysman government

At the formal political level, this struggle of rival networks concluded, at least temporarily, with the removal of Yatsenyuk as prime minister in 2016 and his replacement with Hroysman, a close associate of the president from Vinnytsya, at once securing for the alliance around Poroshenko control of the two key state executive positions, so echoing Yanukovych's placement of Azarov into the post six years earlier. In the wake of this victory for his "pyramid" in the executive and legislative branches, Poroshenko moved to bolster his position further by extending his control of other strategic institutions in the state apparatus, despite his reduced presidential powers. In May, for example, taking advantage of the wide-spread public criticism of the prosecutor general, Viktor Shokin, over his failure to prosecute any high-profile corruption cases from the Yanukovych era, Poroshenko was able to replace him with another loyalist, Yuriy Lutsenko, despite the latter's lack of legal qualifications (Polityuk, 2016). Moreover, at the end of 2017 Poroshenko re-acquired the right to nominate regional governors (Matsiyevsky, 2017, p. 354), a crucial mechanism of the maintenance of the "power verticals" in both Russia and Belarus also (Savchenko, 2009, p. 187).

Economic recovery encourages reform slowdown

While the switch from the Yatsenyuk to the Hroysman premiership corresponds to a re-incorporation of some of the Yanukovych elites into the formal political process, it also seems to correspond to a slowdown in the pace of economic (and other) reforms. Alongside the realignment of parties and networks in parliament, this may be linked also to the onset of modest economic recovery, following implementation of a largely successful, albeit socially painful, macroeconomic stabilisation programme. As in earlier phases of reform in Ukraine, economic stabilisation and recovery seems to have led elements within the governing elite to conclude that post-Euromaidan economic reforms had gone far enough, triggering in February 2016 the resignation of the reformist economy minister, Aivaras Abromavičius, and his team (Havrylyshyn, 2017, p. 173).

Why was Poroshenko more successful than Yushchenko?

One question that arises from this overarching narrative is why Poroshenko proved more successful as head of state than Yushchenko in turning himself into the pre-eminent national political figure, even though both operated under constitutions with weaker formal presidential powers.

A possible answer lies in the elements of Poroshenko's personal biography, sketched above. In particular, owing to his wide and varied experience working within constituent parts of the oligarchic system — both in government and business, and at the regional, national and international levels — Poroshenko had equipped himself to become a more adept operator within its very specific institutional constraints. In short, more familiar with more of its subsystems, he was better able to make use of the fluidity of movement that oligarchic institutional structures afford to the heads of the most powerful business-political networks, so enabling the making and breaking of deals and alliances on an ad hoc basis — which the system requires to function — especially for those with access to both formal and informal levers of power. This is why, contrary to more individualistic modes of explanation, the perennial failure of reform in Ukraine is not mainly a question of the absence of "political will", but of a specific kind of institutional logic, informing and constraining the actions of individuals, so that, by conditioning their understanding of what politics is, they internalise and reproduce its behavioural norms in their actions.

Political economy governance under Poroshenko

Overall, the mode of alignment of elite political and economic power post-Euromaidan can be described as a return to greater network rivalry around the two main political leaders — Turchynov and Yatsenyuk first, then Poroshenko and Yatsenyuk, but with Poroshenko eventually displacing his rival and exerting more control over key areas of the state, while attracting the support of a wider range of business groups than under Yanukovych. Such an arrangement was perhaps more unstable, because informal, than it might have been under a more presidential constitution.

This creates the impression of a shifting pattern of alignment of business networks undergirding the mode of political economy governance of the Poroshenko presidency, which was both more successful in centralising authority than under Yushchenko, but also based more pragmatically on a wider range of business-political groups. It was not a single pyramid system, as under Yanukovych, but, after the side-lining of Yatsenyuk, it developed into something more resembling Kuchma's "balancing" system.

While it is vital to understand how elite political and economic alignments change the overall institutional architecture of a period, it is also important to stress, as does Matsiyevsky, that despite changes in institutional personnel (in the government, the Rada, at the top of state enterprises and the civil service), and despite the flight of Yanukovych's inner circle, the continuation of an informal mode of activity signals the continuity of political economy regimes between the Yanukovych and the Poroshenko periods, showing that although the Euromaidan can be described as a political revolution, it was not a social one touching on basic relations of ownership and power (Matsiyevsky, 2018, p. 350).

4 The wealth of the very rich in modern Ukraine

4.1 Preliminaries

4.1.1 Introduction

Aims and basic definitions

The aim of this chapter is to investigate whether wealth remained sufficiently concentrated within Ukraine's post-Euromaidan economic elites, and especially the oligarchs among them, for it still to be considered a source of significant potential political power. To recap, concentrated material resource power (wealth) is what allows its holders (oligarchs) to achieve their political ends, of protecting and augmenting their economic and social positions, by hiring coercive and professional services. It allows them "to purchase the sustained engagement of others who require no personal commitment to the goals of the oligarchs they serve" (Winters, 2011, p. 18). An investigation of elite wealth in Ukraine has been placed first of my empirical chapters to reflect the thinking behind the "currency flow" model, outlined in the opening chapter. In this model, accumulated wealth is viewed as both the facilitator and end-goal of an ongoing process of wealth concentration, which is also the cycle of reproduction of the Ukrainian oligarchy as a political economy institution. If wealth is conceptualised as a material resource power, however, as a basic operational definition, corresponding to data about the real world, it can be described as the combined value of physical and financial assets, minus debt (Stillwell, 2019, pp. 18-19).

Topic, research design and approach

In this chapter I assess the level of wealth of the richest Ukrainians in international comparison and relative to Ukrainian society, showing how these have changed between the 2010-13 and 2014-17 periods. In the first half of the chapter, the data sets necessary to measure the wealth of the very rich relative to Ukrainian society are developed. The periods of 2010-13 and 2014-17 were chosen for comparison because they lead up to, and follow on from, the Euromaidan protests of late 2013 and early 2014, corresponding to the first four years of the presidencies of Viktor Yanukovych and Petro Poroshenko, respectively. The reason that the Euromaidan was chosen as the dividing line between periods is because it appeared as a "critical juncture" (Hale, 2015, p. 67), or moment when Ukraine's existing political order found itself in disarray. For a short time, this seemed to open up the prospect of radical overhaul of Ukraine's political institutions.

The approach I use to investigate the Ukrainian oligarchy in this chapter is to examine how the relative material resource power (domestic business wealth) of key individuals changed between the Yanukovych and Poroshenko presidencies. This focus on the material power of oligarchs need not equate to methodological individualism, which stresses the role of individual action in explaining social phenomena, rather than larger-scale group dynamics (Inglis and Thorpe, 2018, p. 121; Little, 1991, p. 183). Instead, it is a special take on the problem of collective action that might better be termed "institutional individualism" (Rutherford, 1996, p. 38). That is, it is justified by the social character of the Ukrainian oligarchy itself — not just by the position of oligarchs as leaders of hierarchical business networks that enable and magnify their power as individual actors, but also by the shifting position of the networks, both to one another and to the state (chapter 3). This, in turn, points to a situation, in the absence of a fully effective rule-of-law state capable of protecting property claims even-handedly, in which rivalry between the very wealthy can make it difficult for them to work as a group, other than when the group's existence is threatened.

Statistics and levels of measurement
The main method of analysis in this chapter is simple statistics, supplemented by document analysis, which entails close reading of the reports of local journalists, think-tanks and public institutions, and of international bodies and corporations. The choice of statistical method depends on the data being examined or compared — specifically, on their "levels of measurement". Roughly, this boils down

to whether a variable is composed of categories or numbers, and whether the comparison is between variables of the same or a different type. The four levels of measurement — covering nominal, ordinal, interval and ratio variables — permit the use of increasingly sophisticated analytical techniques.

Chapter structure and main argument
The rest of this chapter is divided into three sections. The first is a brief assessment of Thomas Piketty's *Capital in the Twenty First Century* (2014). The aim is to place my research on the Ukrainian super-rich in the context of the relatively recent re-emergence of wealth inequality as a subject of academic enquiry. In the second section, I develop the two main data series used in this chapter, one on the domestic business wealth of the Ukrainian super-rich (Focus-100), and the other an estimate of the national wealth of modern Ukraine, calculated from national accounts.

The third section is where the original empirical analysis, using these two main data sets, gets under way. This section is composed of three related analyses, of the wealth concentration of the Ukrainian elite in an international context; of the dynamics of the domestic business wealth of the top 100 Ukrainians in 2006-17, relative to national wealth; and of the longevity of individuals on the Focus-100 rich list, leading to an identification of a stable "core" of the economic elite.

The chapter ends with a recap of its main findings and some conclusions. In answer to the research question for this chapter, my argument is that, although in 2010-17 the domestic business wealth of the Focus-100 economic elite is found to have fallen by half as a share of national wealth, this need not imply a decline of elite, and especially of oligarchic, capacity to influence political and policy outcomes. One reason for this is that the financial crisis of 2014-15 will have magnified the potential domestic political impact of wealth already held abroad. Another is that the informal business-political networks through which wealth is transformed into political influence in Ukraine survived the political disjuncture of the Euromaidan more or less intact.

4.1.2 Re-emergence of wealth as a subject of study

Until quite recently, wealth and its social distribution did not tend to receive an extended treatment in economics. One factor behind this is that, for the dominant neo-classical school, the main business of analysing the logical outcomes of the interaction of the constrained choices of individuals starts after the distribution of wealth has taken place, with the prior allocation of "resource endowments" considered "exogenous" (Caporaso and Levine, 1992, p. 89; Stilwell, 2019, p. 96). This contrasts with the case before the rise of the neo-classical paradigm from the 1870s, when issues of wealth, social class and the distribution of the economic surplus were more central to political-economic analysis (Stilwell, 2012, p. 152).

In the past decade, however, wealth as a subject of academic investigation has re-emerged, boosted in part by the worldwide success of Thomas Piketty's *Capital in the Twenty-First Century*, which investigates the changing patterns of economic inequality in western Europe and the US over the long term. Piketty pioneers an approach to the measurement of economic inequality based on reconciling information from different sources—of tax returns with asset values from national accounts, for example. He couples this with a mode of presentation of national wealth as a developing multiple "of the number of years of national income required to amass it" (Piketty, 2014, p. 19).

Since two of Piketty's basic definitions are central to the concerns of this chapter, I reproduce them here. The first is of national income, a "flow" concept, or measure of change over time. This he describes as "the sum of all income available to the residents of a given country in a given year, regardless of the legal classification of that income" (Piketty, 2014, p. 43). The second definition is of national wealth, a "stock" concept, or measure of accumulation. Piketty describes it as the "total market value of everything owned by the residents and government of a given country at a given point in time" (Piketty, 2014, p. 48). For analytical purposes, this is divided into financial and non-financial assets. Whether these assets are owned by individuals or by the government gives rise to a distinction between private and public wealth, which is central to

Piketty's descriptive analysis of the broad developments of national wealth-income ratios over time.

Traditionally, economics students are warned against comparing a stock with a flow, but in this instance, the scaling of wealth in terms of income is useful in two ways. First, it aids an intuitive grasp of international comparisons of wealth dynamics. Second, it brings out an important two-way relation, of wealth as the accumulation of property bought with income, and of the generation of income as depending on the level of (productive) wealth.

The "major findings" for the advanced economies that Piketty covers are of a resurgence in wealth concentration since the 1980s, following a long period of decline in the wake of the first world war (Piketty, 2014, p. 20), which he thinks could destabilise liberal democratic capitalism. He proposes two main explanations for this trend. The "fundamental force of divergence", he suggests, is "the accumulation and concentration of wealth when growth is weak and the return of capital is high" (Piketty, 2014, p. 23). A second important mechanism for the rise in wealth inequality, he suggests, is an increase in income inequality linked to the growing power of corporate executives to set their own pay (Piketty, 2014, p. 24).

Piketty addresses a significant omission in mainstream economics — the study of changing patterns of wealth distribution over the long term, and their social and political implications — while developing a detailed, followable and checkable empirical method to do so. At the same time, some criticisms present themselves. "To simplify the text," Piketty writes, "I use the words 'capital' and 'wealth' interchangeably" (2014, p. 47). This could be problematic in two ways. First, at the level of accounting categorisation, it may lead to misattribution of the main sources of wealth concentration, and so to misdiagnosis of the causes behind it. Joseph Stiglitz argues, for example, that a large part of the increase in wealth that Piketty observes is down to rising land values, rather than to returns of productive capital (Parramore, 2015). Second, at the level of theory, wealth held is not distinguished from wealth in use. This is a vital distinction in Marx's political economy of capitalism, in which capital is understood as "self-expanding value", or financial wealth invested for the purpose of increasing its value, an apparently "occult quality" (Heinrich, pp. 86-90, 2004) that is explained by the separation of production and exchange in conditions in which commodity production has become widespread. This means that, while surplus extraction takes place at the level of production — where the cost of the capacity to labour bought from the worker tends to be lower than the price of the goods or services they produce — it is only realised in exchange. This is what Marx means when he says that capital is not a thing, such as a machine, as in mainstream economics, but an extractive social relation between classes (Marx, 1976, pp. 1,005-1,006; Mohun, 1985, p. 60). From this perspective, then, an elision of "wealth" and "capital" loses the valuable analytical link between the quantitative economic and qualitative social-structural dimensions.

From this, it can be seen that Piketty in this book is no would-be tearer down of the established economic order. Rather, his use of pre-existing concepts and categories of neo-classical economics and conventional national accounting shows that his approach remains firmly within the framework of a long-established economic world view. Piketty's intervention therefore more recalls that of John Maynard Keynes, a British economist, in the global crisis of the 1930s than of Marx in the mid-nineteenth century, and should perhaps best be seen as a call for renewal and protection of liberal democratic capitalism by raising awareness of trends in economic inequality that could undermine it from within.

4.1.3 Which wealth data?

Focus Ratings: the richest people in Ukraine by domestic business wealth

Methodology of the "Focus-100" data set

For Ukraine, the ratings data produced by Focus, a local Russian-language online news magazine, offers perhaps the most comprehensive available picture of the level and evolution of wealth at the top end of the ownership scale for the contemporary period.

Each year, the magazine compiles from open sources a ranking of the individuals with the largest holdings of domestic business assets. The Focus rankings measure the market value of an individual's business enterprises and commercial property. Sources include the stock exchange, government, the courts, firms, press reports and statements of business owners. It supplements these with its own research, as well as the input of "expert" consultants (Focus Ratings, 2007). For publicly traded firms, valuation is by market capitalisation, based on the average value of the stock over the year. For private firms, the value is calculated according to an assessment of "fair value" — that is, by reference to the market price of publicly traded east European firms showing a comparable financial performance. The complexity of business structures deployed can prevent the inclusion in Focus' calculations of the debts of some large enterprises (Focus Ratings, 2008).

The first of the Focus "richest Ukrainians" rankings, for 2006, was published in 2007. At the time of conducting my research in 2019, it ran up until 2017, with the results published the following year. It therefore covers the main 2010-17 timeframe of this study.

For this investigation, I collated the Focus annual holdings of domestic business wealth for the richest 100 individuals into a full series for 2006-17, from which it is possible to sum annual totals. These are set out in the second column of Table 4.8 later in the chapter. As far as I know, at the time it was gathered, this was the most complete version of this data available. It will be central to the analysis of the chapter.

Pros and cons of the Focus rankings

The Focus series is, it proclaims in its inaugural edition, both the first large-scale and the most comprehensive wealth ranking conducted for Ukraine (Focus Ratings, 2007). It sets out a clear and defensible method for the direct calculation of business wealth from local sources. Some problematic aspects of the methodology, however, are as follows.

- Based on business assets held in Ukraine, the Focus ranking includes a number of non-Ukrainians who have accumulated the bulk of their wealth in the country (such as Vadym Novynskyi, who is from Russia), but excludes some wealthy Ukrainians who hold significant assets abroad, such as Boris Fuksman (Focus Ratings, 2009).

- The general lack of transparency in Ukraine's business environment, the magazine recognises, can create notable absences from, and distortions in, its rich list evaluations. An example given for the 2007 ranking is that of Privat Group, controlled by Ihor Kolomoyskyi and his business partner Hennadiy Boholyubov. According to the write-up, experts assessed the assets of Privat Group to be "at least US$13bn", but were unable to link all of these to the main owners of the holding company because of complex property structures (Focus Ratings, 2008). In an interview with *Novoye Vremya*, a Russian-language Ukrainian weekly, he claimed assets of at least US$7.5bn-8bn (Berdinskikh, 2019a). According to the Focus-100 ranking, in contrast, the domestic business assets of both Kolomoyskyi and Boholyubov averaged about US$3bn each in 2006-17.
- The wealth ranking has undergone periodic tweaks to its methodology. One example is the inconsistent treatment of sibling or husband-and-wife business partnerships, with the individuals sometimes counted separately and sometimes together. A second inconsistency relates to business debt. For the 2009 ranking, the magazine announced that business debt had been included in its wealth calculations (Focus Ratings, 2010), but in the 2010 ranking, reported that this decision had been reversed (Focus Ratings, 2011).
- Finally, in the most recent years of the ranking, corresponding to a period of marked instability, some individuals have been assigned levels of domestic business wealth that do not seem to change from year to year. So, for example, the wealth of Mykola Yankovskyi, whose main assets are in the east Ukrainian chemicals sector, are recorded at US$240m for 2015, 2016 and 2017 (Focus Ratings, 2016, 2017, 2018).

These shortcomings raise concerns about the internal consistency and comparability of the Focus wealth estimates across years. Nevertheless, the Focus rankings are still the best and longest-running source of information available on the domestic wealth of the contemporary Ukrainian super-rich, and of the subgroup of them, the Ukrainian oligarchs, on which this book focuses.

Recent estimates of national wealth for Ukraine and Russia

To assess changes in the material resource power of the very rich in relation to Ukrainian society, a measure of the wealth of society as a whole is needed, permitting the comparison of one stock (the Focus-100 domestic business wealth) to another (the wealth of the country). To aid international comparison, a measure of national wealth compatible with the procedures and categories of national accounting is also desirable. The most recent international version, used here, is the System of National Accounts 2008 (SNA 2008), produced jointly by several leading international organisations.

Three recent large-scale projects to estimate national and global wealth have culminated in the following publications.

- *The Changing Wealth of Nations 2018* (Lange et al, 2018), from the World Bank, an international financial institution (IFI) focusing on economic development;
- *Global Wealth Report 2018* (Shorrocks et al, 2018a), published by the Credit Suisse Research Institute, the "in-house think-tank" of the Swiss bank of the same name; and
- the *World Inequality Report 2018* (Alvaredo et al, 2018), produced by the World Inequality Lab (WIL), a group of academic researchers associated with Thomas Piketty.

Each report has its own data set. The first and third are interactive, while the second comes as a separate volume, the *Global Wealth Databook 2018* (Shorrocks et al, 2018b). However, as each report has been produced for a different purpose, using somewhat different wealth-accounting methods, their results diverge. It is important to be clear, therefore, about what is included and excluded from each of the measures of wealth.

Changing Wealth of Nations

Of these reports, *The Changing Wealth of Nations 2018* (CWN) is the most comprehensive, offering a measure of wealth that takes in the widest range of asset categories (human, financial, produced and natural capital) across all economic sectors (households, corporations, government, and "other").

In 2014, the most recent year for which estimates are produced, the World Bank reports global wealth at US$1,143trn (Lange et al, 2018, p. 8). Ukraine's total wealth was US$2.54trn, while Russia's was US$27.14trn (World Bank, 2018, Country Tool). These figures correspond to 0.2% and 2.4% of global wealth, respectively.

The World Bank's measure of national wealth is widest as it includes estimates for "human capital", comprised of the skills, knowledge and know-how of the labour force. Based on the discounted present value of expected future labour earnings, human capital comprised almost two-thirds of global wealth in 2014 (Lange et al, 2018, p. 8). The other approaches discussed below exclude this, which is why their wealth estimates are much smaller.

Alongside the more conventional assessment of the value of produced non-financial assets (including machinery, buildings and urban land) and of financial assets (such as bank deposits and securities) for 141 of the world's economies, CWN makes estimates for natural resource wealth ("non-produced non-financial assets", covering energy deposits and agricultural land, for example). The worth of a country's natural resources is calculated using the net present value of the estimated lifetime rent. Here, "rent" is the difference between the cost of extracting a resource and its market price (Lange et al, 2018, p. 22). This focus on estimating natural resource value separately reflects one of the aims of the study, which is to promote environmentally sustainable development.

Although the World Bank's wealth estimates stretch back to 1995, however, they do not make up a continuous annual series, whereas a goal of this chapter is to compare the annual stock of business wealth to an estimated stock of Ukraine's societal wealth for each of the 12 years for which data for the Focus rich list exists.

Global Wealth Report

The two Credit Suisse documents — a report outlining key findings, and booklet of methods, sources and data — comprise an extensive study of the levels and distribution of household wealth across the world, which the bank has produced annually since 2000. Household wealth is defined as "the marketable value of financial assets plus non-financial assets (principally housing and land) less debts" (Shorrocks et al, 2018b, p. 4).

The core method of wealth estimation is based on data of household balance sheets for the relatively small number of countries (49) that produce them. Household wealth distributions are adjusted, the authors report, by reference to Forbes' *World's Billionaires* list to take account of underreporting at the top end of the wealth spectrum. For countries with no direct wealth data, estimates are made by imputation, according to a country's region and income group. This is the approach used for Ukraine, with "regression" listed as the method of estimation (Shorrocks et al, 2018b, p. 33), but with no further details. Much of the variation in Credit Suisse's wealth estimates for Ukraine across time—from close to US$160bn before 2013 to half that or lower afterwards—appears linked to the researchers' decision to use current market exchange rates to convert household wealth into US dollars, rather than purchasing power parity (PPP) rates. They justify this as follows: "in all countries a large share of wealth is owned by households in the top few percentiles of the distribution, who tend to be internationally mobile and to move their assets across borders with significant frequency" (Shorrocks et al, 2018b, pp. 4-5). This may reflect the underlying business interest of the company producing the report, which is to estimate the amount of wealth potentially available worldwide for its "wealth management" services. However, the line of reasoning does not sit easily with the claim, made a little further up the report, that residential buildings or land— which are not easily movable—tend to make up the bulk of household non-financial assets (Shorrocks et al, 2018b, p. 4).

In 2014—the year that is used in Table 4.5 below to compare the results of the different wealth estimation methods for Ukraine and Russia—Credit Suisse estimates global household wealth at US$278trn. For Ukraine and Russia, the figures are US$80bn (Shorrocks et al, 2018b, p. 90) and US$2,280bn (Shorrocks et al, 2018b, p. 89), or just 0.03% and 0.82% of the global total, respectively—that is, very much lower, both as national totals and as shares of the global total, than those estimated by the World Bank.

A key point about the Credit Suisse study is that the conception of wealth it aims to measure is quite restrictive, appearing to cover just two wealth categories (financial and non-financial assets) for one economic sector (households). This means that the estimates produced by Credit Suisse represent only a fraction of total national and global wealth. Moreover, in Ukraine's case, household wealth is estimated at just US$50bn-80bn in 2014-17, equal to just 50-70% of net national income, which is low. For my purposes, then, the Credit Suisse data are problematic, since they do not appear to represent estimates of national wealth across the economy as a whole.

World Inequality Report

Perhaps the most promising of the three wealth-assessment reports I examined is the *World Inequality Report 2018* (WIR), and the World Inequality Database (WID) that goes with it, both building on Piketty's earlier work. The WID estimates of national wealth make use of the same two wealth categories as Credit Suisse, of physical and financial capital, but for all economic sectors. This is why their estimates of national wealth are bigger than those of Credit Suisse but smaller than the World Bank's.

Whereas the explicit theme of the World Bank study is sustainable development, and the implicit one of Credit Suisse may be an estimation of the global market for wealth-management services, the intention of the WIR authors is to inform public debate about rising global economic inequality.

The WIR presents its findings on the evolution of net national wealth — the sum of private and public wealth, minus debt — as a multiple of national income. Expanding the country coverage, the WIR brings up to date main findings of Piketty's book. The report notes that the share of wealth held by the top 1% across Europe, the US and China rose from 28% in 1990 to 33% in 2015 (Alvaredo et al, 2018, p. 19). In broad terms, they put this down to the "very large transfers of public to private wealth" (Alvaredo et al, 2018, p. 14) — that is, to privatisation. In a separate paper on the development of private property in Russia since the fall of communism (Novokmet et al, 2017), the WIR team has produced a series of wealth-income estimates for Russia. However, they have yet to do so for Ukraine.

The national wealth balance sheets of the SSSU and Rosstat
The above three reports aid understanding of wealth accounts and how they are produced, but do not provide a ready-made, internationally comparable national wealth series for Ukraine, against which to scale domestic business wealth. For this, we must turn to the "experimental" wealth balance sheets produced since 2011 by the State Statistical Service of Ukraine (SSSU).

At the time of my investigation (2019), the SSSU wealth balance sheets ran from 2009 to 2017 (SSSU, 2019a, 2019b). Because the end-2008 data form the "initial balance" for the 2009 balance sheets, it is possible to add a figure for the stock of national wealth in 2008, so extending the series back by one year. Using modern national accounting conventions, the balance sheets between them quantify the value of Ukraine's produced non-financial assets, as well as financial assets, minus financial debt, across the Ukrainian economy. The national wealth series for Russia, from the State Federal Statistics Service (Rosstat), are similarly laid out, but proved hard to find for the period before 2011. Both are most akin to the WIR in approach. There is no separate assessment of the value of natural capital, which, according to SNA 2008 methodology can be grouped, along with produced physical assets, under the single category of "non-financial assets". In practice, however, estimates of "non-produced" non-financial wealth do not appear to be included in the balance sheets of either statistics agency. Finally, the SSSU (but not Rosstat) explicitly excludes the domestic residential housing stock, on the grounds of insufficient information on prices and quality, while the housing stock typically comprises a significant proportion of national and especially household wealth.

Taking the SSSU's two sets of balance sheets for 2014 as an example, the first, presented in Table 4.1 below, shows that, at the end of 2013, Ukraine's produced non-financial assets (excluding housing) were valued at UAH4,714bn (US$589.7bn at the end-2013 average exchange rate). Owing to a small fall in the capital stock, alongside a rise in "other changes in assets", by the end of 2014 this had climbed modestly, to UAH4,734bn. In the intervening year, however, as the Ukrainian hryvnya had depreciated steeply, the US dollar value of Ukraine's non-financial assets fell to US$303bn.

According to SNA 2008 methodology, capital accumulation encompasses capital transfers plus new investment and changes in stocks, while "other changes in assets" account for variations in asset prices (revaluation) and in asset volumes not linked to economic transactions (because of natural disaster or war, for example). All the "action", therefore, is on this third row of accounts for fixed assets and inventories, showing a drop in the former of UAH153bn (presumably reflecting an assessment of the destruction of physical assets owing to war), masked by a sharper rise still in the value of unsold stocks, of more than UAH170bn (probably linked to sharp downturn in domestic and global demand).

Table 4.1: Ukraine's "experimental" balance sheet of non-financial assets (excl housing), 2014; UAH bn

	Produced	Fixed	Intangible	Inventories
Initial balance	4,713.5	4,122.4	39.1	552.0
Capital account	-3.2	11.3	-2.5	-12.1
Other changes	23.8	-152.9	3.5	173.2
Final balance	4,734.0	3,980.7	40.1	713.2

Source: State Statistical Service of Ukraine (SSSU; 2019a), experimental balance of non-financial assets in 2017 and archive. Available: https://bit.ly/3ltmrz0.

Similarly, Table 4.2 shows that, at the end of 2013, although the combined value of Ukraine's financial assets came to UAH7,396bn (US$925bn), liabilities were larger by almost UAH600bn (US$74bn). By the end of 2014, however, the shortfall on net financial assets had widened to more than UAH1,000bn. Subtracting this from the 2014 year-end total for produced non-financial assets generates an estimate of national wealth (minus housing) of UAH3,724bn, down from UAH4,120bn a year earlier. At the average official market exchange rate to the US dollar for December 2017, this was equal to US$238.5bn — a sharp drop from US$515.4bn at the end of 2013.

Table 4.2: Ukraine's "experimental" balance sheet of financial assets & liabilities, 2014; UAH bn

	Assets	Liabilities
Start of period	7,395.6	7,989.4
Monetary gold & SDRs	13.2	
Currency & deposits	1,822.9	1,019.6
Securities other than shares	592.2	736.9
Loans	1,083.9	1,595.8
Shares & other equity	966.3	1,538.4
Insurance technical reserves	21.8	21.7
Financial derivatives & stock options	2.2	1.2
Other accounts receivable/payable	2,893.1	3,075.8
Financial net worth at the start of the period		-593.8
Financial account	691.9	741.8
Other changes in assets & liabilities	1,240.2	1,606.2
End of period	9,327.7	10,337.3
Financial net worth, end of period		-1,009.6

Source: State Statistical Service of Ukraine (SSSU; 2019b), experimental balance sheets of financial assets and liabilities in 2017 and archive. Available: https://bit.ly/3rQGrN6.

Estimating the value of Ukraine's housing stock

The absence of housing stock in the SSSU's calculations makes it difficult to compare its measure of Ukraine's national wealth with that of Rosstat for Russia. To address this, an estimate for the value of Ukraine's housing stock is required. Although the SSSU produces data for the volume of the housing stock, it only began to produce an index of the changes in house prices nationwide from 2016. I have turned, therefore, to Credit Suisse's wealth series for assistance. In particular, to the SSSU's national wealth calculations, I have added 80% of Credit Suisse's estimates for Ukraine's household wealth for 2008-17.

My rationale is as follows. In its methodology, Credit Suisse, as we have seen, measures household wealth, composed by adding the value of household financial and non-financial assets, while subtracting financial debts. In the *Global Wealth Databook 2018* (GWD; Shorrocks et al, 2018b), US dollar sums per adult are estimated for each of these, allowing the calculation of the average annual share of each in total household wealth. In more advanced economies, according to this data, the non-financial component — the bulk of which was housing — is equal to 50-60% of overall household wealth in 2000-18 (Shorrocks et al, 2018b, p. 156). The figure for Ukraine averages 86% in 2008-17 (see Table 4.3).

Table 4.3: Ukraine: the share of non-financial assets in household wealth, 2008-17

	Household wealth per adult (US$)	Of which: non-financial (US$)	% household wealth
2008	3,964	3,256	82.1
2009	2,967	2,437	82.1
2010	3,522	2,893	82.1
2011	4,319	4,150	96.1
2012	4,335	4,369	100.8
2013	4,277	4,442	103.9
2014	794	410	51.6
2015	1,590	1,675	105.3
2016	1,407	1,550	110.2
2017	755	353	46.8
2008-17, av	**2,793**	**2,554**	**86.1**

Source: Shorrocks et al (2018b), Table 2.4, pp. 66-102 & Table 6.4, p. 156.

On the assumption that most of the non-financial component of household wealth is accounted for by housing, I arrive at the figure of 80%. In 2014, this values Ukraine's housing stock at US$64bn. Added to the SSSU's national wealth estimate for the year, of US$238.5bn, this produces a working estimate for Ukraine's stock of wealth of just over US$300bn. Following this procedure for other years, it is possible to produce a series of "full" estimates of Ukraine's national wealth (the third column in Table 4.4 below) that is comparable with the Rosstat series for Russia (the fifth column). It can be seen from the table that an exchange-rate effect takes hold from 2014, depressing the value of national wealth in US dollar terms, strongly for Ukraine and more mildly for Russia — although Ukraine's national wealth also fell in nominal hryvnya terms.

Table 4.4: National wealth estimates for Ukraine & Russia from national accounts, 2008-17

	Ukraine (SSSU + 80% of Credit Suisse household wealth)		Russia (Rosstat)	
	UAH bn	US$ bn	Rb bn	US$ bn
2008	3,839.3	507.5	n/a	n/a
2009	3,403.4	426.6	n/a	n/a
2010	3,885.7	488.4	n/a	n/a
2011	4,563.7	571.2	228,902	7,268.8
2012	5,169.5	646.7	260,585	8,477.8
2013	5,110.8	639.4	280,273	8,523.9
2014	4,723.9	302.5	320,245	5,742.2
2015	6,141.8	261.7	364,656	5,231.4
2016	6,654.5	253.7	374,901	6,037.9
2017	7,959.7	288.9	426,697	7,538.8

Sources: Shorrocks et al (2018b), Table 2.4, pp. 66-102. SSSU (2019a), experimental balance of non-financial assets in 2017 and archive. Available: https://bit.ly/3ltmrz0. SSSU (2019b), experimental balance sheets of financial assets and liabilities in 2017 and archive. Available: https://bit.ly/3rQGrN6. Rosstat (2020), *Statistical Yearbook 2020*, Table 13.23, p. 284. Available: https://bit.ly/2TZ8sWo. Note: Conversion at December exchange rates.

Comparison of wealth estimates for Ukraine and Russia in 2014

All of the estimates for the national wealth of Ukraine and Russia in 2014 from the different approaches are brought together in Table 4.5 below. To recap, the WID team, as well as the statistics agencies of Ukraine and Russia, all appear to produce estimates of national wealth using the categories of produced physical assets and net financial assets across economic sectors. By excluding natural and human capital from the World Bank's calculations, we can arrive at estimates more comparable with these. Nevertheless, the variations in the values of national wealth produced by the different methods remain wide. The range of estimates for Russia in 2014 is between US$5.7trn (Rosstat) and US$7.3trn (World Bank), with that of the WID in between, at US$6.2trn. As the Credit Suisse approach uses the same two wealth categories, but only for households, its estimate is correspondingly smaller, at US$2.3trn. For Ukraine, while my "augmented" estimate of US$300bn in 2014 is larger than that of Credit Suisse, it is less than one-third of the produced and net financial capital estimate of the World Bank, of US$1.1trn.

Table 4.5: Comparison of national wealth estimates for Ukraine & Russia, 2014

	US$ bn			% global wealth	
	Ukraine	Russia	World	Ukraine	Russia
World Bank					
Total wealth (human, natural, produced & net financial)	2,538	27,141	1,143,249	0.22	2.37
Total wealth, excl human & natural	1,075	7,332	298,967	0.36	2.45
Credit Suisse					
Household wealth	80	2,278	277,938	0.03	0.82
World Inequality Database					
Net national wealth	n/a	6,200	n/a	n/a	n/a
State Statistical Service of Ukraine (SSSU)					
National wealth (net financial + non-financial, + 80% of Credit Suisse total as "housing")	302	n/a	n/a	n/a	n/a
Russian Federal State Statistical Service (RFSSS)					
National wealth (net financial + non-financial)	n/a	5,742	n/a	n/a	n/a

Sources: World Bank (2018), *The Changing Wealth of Nations 2018*: Country Tool. Available: https://bit.ly/3jzLEp5; second tab, Data & Resources. Shorrocks et al (2018b), Table 2.4, pp. 89-90. World Inequality Lab, World Inequality Database (WID). Available: https://wid.world/data. SSSU (2019a), experimental balance of non-financial assets in 2017 and archive. Available: https://bit.ly/3ltmrz0. SSSU (2019b), experimental balance sheets of financial assets and liabilities in 2017 and archive. Available: https://bit.ly/3rQGrN6. Rosstat (2020), *Statistical Yearbook 2020*, Table 13.23, p. 284. Available: https://bit.ly/2TZ8sWo.

Looking, however, at my "synthetic" estimate for Ukrainian national wealth in 2008-17 in relation to the SSSU's estimates for net national income (NNI) over the same period, to produce a Piketty-style wealth-income ratio, these are in 400-450% range for Ukraine before 2014, falling to 300-350% after. These ratios can be seen as a broad measure of the development of the economic basis upon which the production of future income flows depend. Figure 4.1 below depicts their recent dynamics for Ukraine and Russia.

Figure 4.1: Estimated wealth-income ratios for Ukraine & Russia, 2008-17

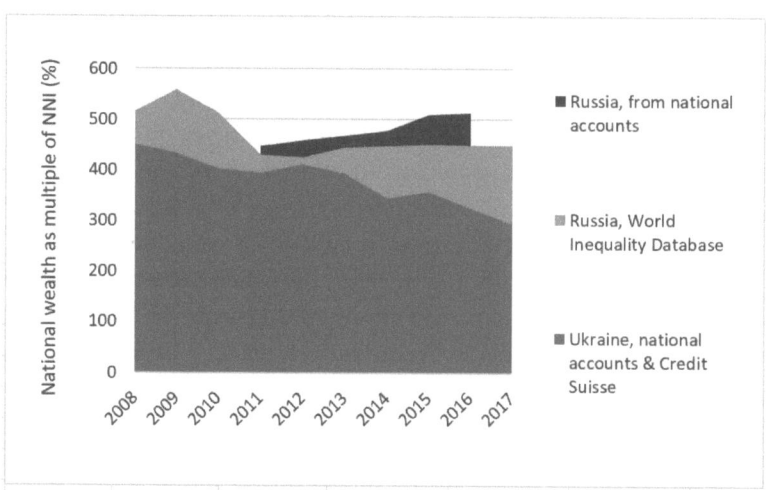

Sources: SSSU (2019a), experimental balance of non-financial assets in 2017 and archive. Available: https://bit.ly/3ltmrz0. SSSU (2019b), experimental balance sheets of financial assets and liabilities in 2017 and archive. Available: https://bit.ly/3rQGrN6. Shorrocks et al (2018b), Table 2.4, pp. 66-102. Rosstat (2020), *Statistical Yearbook 2020*, Table 13.23, p. 284. Available: https://bit.ly/2TZ8sWo. World Inequality Lab, World Inequality Database (WID). Available: https://wid.world/data.

Although Russia's national wealth is much larger than Ukraine's, Figure 4.1 shows that, before the onset of the Russo-Ukrainian war in 2014, Ukraine's wealth-income ratios (the medium grey, downward-sloping area in the foreground) were roughly in line with those for Russia on Rosstat data (the darkest grey, upward-sloping block). In turn, ratios from Rosstat data are in line with the WID estimates for Russia's wealth-income ratio (the light grey block), offering some assurance that the synthetic estimate for Ukraine is in the right ballpark, since it would make sense for countries sharing a Soviet economic-institutional inheritance to display similar levels of productivity at the macroeconomic level.

4.2 Patterns of elite wealth distribution and dynamics in contemporary Ukraine

4.2.1 Outline of wealth analyses

With the necessary data sets collected and prepared, it is possible to proceed with a statistical analysis of the scale and dynamics of the business wealth of the very rich in contemporary Ukraine, and what this says about the evolution of their material resource power relative to Ukrainian society. The three analyses on wealth have been positioned in this book ahead of my research on Rada voting and energy-sector rent-extraction schemes of chapters 5 and 6, since wealth as material power is conceived as a conceptual and motivational thread running through the other two investigations. The ordering of the empirical chapters thus aims to show a complete sequence of concrete, materially focused political and economic practices through which the Ukrainian oligarchy is reconstituted institutionally.

In this chapter, the first analysis investigates the degree of concentration of Ukraine's wealth in international comparison. It compares estimates for the wealth of the richest individuals in Ukraine and Russia in 2013 and in 2017, using Forbes' *World's Billionaires*. This is followed by an examination of the distributions of income and wealth in Ukraine and Russia, and then of the incidence of Forbes' billionaires, relative to population and economic output. The second analysis describes and explains the dynamics of the Focus-100 data for 2006-17, first at the overall level, and then by examining wealth levels and trends for the typical rich-list member. A third analysis examines the relationship between wealth and longevity on the rich list, drawing from this a shortlist of the "core" rich— those in the top quartile in terms of both average domestic business wealth and years on the rich list. The most prominent Ukrainian oligarchs dominate this group.

4.2.2 Wealth concentration in Ukraine and Russia in international comparison

Forbes: the private wealth of Ukrainian and Russian billionaires

Table 4.6 below shows the change in the combined private wealth of Ukrainian and Russian billionaires on the Forbes' *World's Billionaires* list between 2013 and 2017. While indicating high levels of wealth concentration in both countries, it shows the incidence of billionaires lower in Ukraine than in Russia, and that the wealth of the Ukrainian ultra-rich was harder hit by the crisis of 2014-15.

In 2013 the combined private wealth of Ukrainian and Russian Forbes' billionaires — of US$32bn and US$427bn, respectively — equalled 5% of each country's estimated national wealth. On average, Ukrainian billionaires were poorer than their Russian counterparts. Moreover, in Ukraine, the incidence of billionaires was much lower, both in terms of absolute numbers and relative to its population. So, while there were just ten Ukrainian billionaires in 2013, according to Forbes, in Russia, the figure was 110[12]; and while the ratio of Forbes' billionaires per million population was 0.22 for Ukraine, it was considerably higher for Russia, at 0.77, indicating the greater capacity of the Russian economy to generate very rich individuals. This may be connected with the disparity in natural resource endowments between the two economies, as well as with the high rents that can be realised, and relatively easily collected, in the energy sector by rentier elites.

By 2017 the number of billionaires had fallen in each country. In the interim, there had been serious domestic political instability in Ukraine, followed by geopolitical and military confrontation with Russia and, as a consequence, the imposition of international sanctions on Russia. At the same time, plummeting global prices for key export commodities, connected in part to fears about China's growth prospects (Noble and Wildau, 2014), undercut both countries' exchange rates, in Ukraine exacerbating tendencies towards financial destabilisation. These developments damaged not only

---

[12] Eduardo Casais junior and senior keep a full "list of lists" of Forbes' billionaires on their areppim website. Available: https://bit.ly/2XeK841.

incomes, but also asset valuations. However, the reduction in the number of Russian billionaires, from 110 in 2013 to 96 four years later—a drop of 13%—was less drastic than for their Ukrainian counterparts, whose numbers fell by 40%, from ten to six. Moreover, by 2017 although the wealth of the Russian super-rich had risen modestly, to an average of US$4bn each, from US$3.9bn each in 2013, in Ukraine, average wealth per billionaire fell to US$1.8bn, from US$3.2bn in 2013, a decline of 44%. While the combined wealth of fewer Russian billionaires remained relatively constant as a share of Russia's national wealth, at 5.1%, for the remaining Ukrainian tycoons, it fell to 3.7%.

Table 4.6: Forbes' estimates of the private wealth of Ukrainian & Russian billionaires, 2013 & 2017

	Ukraine		Russia	
	2013	2017	2013	2017
US dollar billionaires (no.)	10	6	110	96
Billionaires' combined wealth (US$ bn)	32.1	10.6	427.1	387.1
Wealth per billionaire (US$ bn; av)	3.2	1.8	3.9	4.0
National wealth (US$ bn, Dec exchange rates)	639.4	288.9	8,523.9	7,538.8
Ratio of billionaires' wealth to national wealth (%)	5.0	3.7	5.0	5.1
Population (World Bank; m)	45.5	44.8	143.5	144.5
Billionaires per million population	0.22	0.13	0.77	0.66

Sources: Forbes, Billionaires, 2008. Available: https://bit.ly/3CRGn3Q. Eduardo Casais Jr & Eduardo Casais Sr. The Complete World Billionaire Lists. areppim website. Available: https://bit.ly/2XeK841. World Bank DataBank, Health, Nutrition and Population Statistics. Available: https://bit.ly/3sLfX1G. SSSU (2019a), experimental balance of non-financial assets in 2017 and archive. Available: https://bit.ly/3ltmrz0. SSSU (2019b), experimental balance sheets of financial assets and liabilities in 2017 and archive. Available: https://bit.ly/3rQGrN6. Shorrocks et al (2018b), Table 2.4, pp. 66-102. Available: https://bit.ly/3775cuU. Rosstat (2020), *Statistical Yearbook 2020*, Table 13.23, p. 284. Available: https://bit.ly/2TZ8sWo.

Ginis for Ukraine and Russia in international comparison

Next, some recent wealth and income Ginis for Ukraine and Russia are presented in Figure 4.2 below, alongside those for a selection of

European countries and the US. A Gini coefficient offers in a single number, graded zero to 100, a way of assessing the degree of dispersion of a distribution—in this case, of how equally a country's income or wealth is divided among its population. A lower number indicates a more even spread; a higher number denotes that income or wealth is more restrictively concentrated. The income Ginis, taken from the World Bank's *World Development Indicators,* are produced from household survey data. Those for household wealth were calculated by Credit Suisse for its *Global Wealth Databook 2017.*

Figure 4.2: Wealth & income Ginis for selected countries, 2016-17

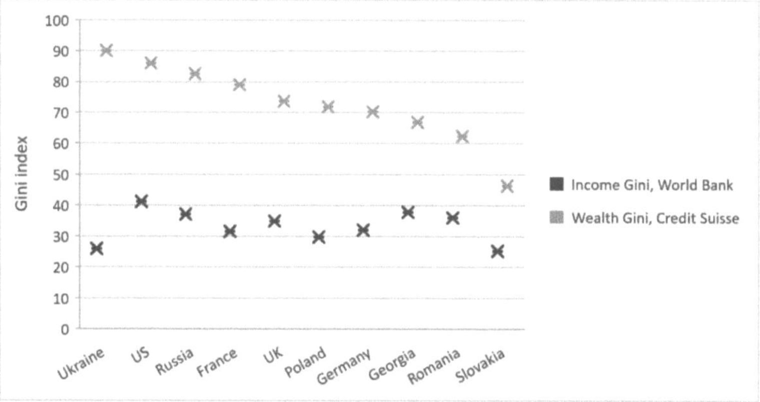

Sources: World Bank DataBank, *World Development Indicators* (for income Ginis). Shorrocks et al (2017), *Global Wealth Databook 2017,* Credit Suisse (for household wealth Ginis), Table 3.1, pp. 211-215.

A striking feature of this data is that household wealth is much more socially concentrated than income. This is often remarked upon in the economic inequality literature (Stillwell, 2019, p. 19). It is shown in Figure 4.2 above by the size of the vertical gap between the lower, darker crosses, indicating the degree of spread of income distributions within each country, and the higher, light grey crosses, representing their Ginis for the distribution of household wealth. The gap between the two tapers from left to right, as the countries are arranged across the chart by wealth Gini, from high to low. The gap is narrowest for Slovakia, and widest for Ukraine. While Ukraine's income Gini is 26—a relatively even distribution, comparable with those of Slovakia and Poland, the two countries shown here with the most equal income distributions — its wealth Gini of 90 suggests that household wealth concentration in Ukraine is higher still than for Russia and the US, the two countries in this group with the next-highest concentrations of household wealth.

The size of the gap in Ukraine's case is puzzling, but may reflect an especially marked example of the broader criticism, mentioned above, that the use of household surveys for collecting income data, upon which the World Bank's Gini calculations are based, can lead to underreporting of capital and business income (Alvaredo et al, 2018, p. 29). Moreover, a criticism of the Gini index is that it is less sensitive to capturing the lower and higher "tails" of a distribution than its mid-portion, which is a particular problem when distributions are highly skewed (Stilwell, 2019, p. 24), as is likely to be the case for incomes in Ukraine. This line of thinking, however, does not explain why the indicator of income distribution is (more plausibly) so much higher for Russia. Thus, Russia, in common with the US, has unusually high Gini coefficients for both income and wealth (38 and 83, versus 42 and 86, respectively), placing them both among the most highly economically stratified countries in the world. However, this makes more sense than the divergence in Gini indices for Ukraine, as you might expect the owners of substantial income-producing wealth to receive a correspondingly large share of the income produced.

A second feature of the statistics shown in Figure 4.2 is that the range of Gini scores is narrower for income than for wealth, indicating that household wealth distributions between these countries vary more than for income. So, for the income series, the range is between Slovakia, on 25, and the US, on 41, or 16 points on the 100-point scale. Comparing the World Bank's income Ginis with those of the OECD, it can be deduced that these are for income distributions after tax and transfers, which tend to make the distributions flatter. For the wealth Ginis, however, the range is much wider, from Slovakia on 46 to Ukraine on 90, or 44 points. Ukraine's very high coefficient here implies that, in international comparison, Ukraine's household assets are extremely highly concentrated among an unusually small portion of its population.

Incidence of billionaires in Ukraine and Russia in international comparison

The picture of Ukraine and Russia as economies in which wealth is highly concentrated is further supported by examining the number of Forbes' billionaires in relation to economic output and population. For the same countries as above, Table 4.7 below places these indicators alongside their household wealth Ginis in 2017.

Table 4.7: Wealth concentration in Ukraine & Russia in international comparison, 2017

	Household wealth Gini	Billionaires (no.)	GDP per head (PPP; 2017 US$)	Billionaires per million pop
Ukraine	90.1	6	11,871	0.13
US	85.9	565	60,062	1.74
Russia	82.6	96	26,006	0.66
France	79.1	38	44,755	0.57
UK	73.5	54	45,955	0.82
Poland	71.7	4	30,160	0.11
Germany	70.2	114	53,122	1.38
Georgia	66.8	1	13,590	0.27
Romania	62.3	1	27,231	0.05
Slovakia	46.3	1	30,189	0.18

Sources: Shorrocks et al (2017), Table 3.1, pp. 112-115. Eduardo Casais Jr & Eduardo Casais Sr. The Complete World Billionaire Lists. areppim website. Available: https://bit.ly/2XeK841. World Bank DataBank, *World Development Indicators*. Available: https://bit.ly/3l83fF9. World Bank DataBank, Health, Nutrition and Population Statistics. Available: https://bit.ly/3sLfX1G. Own calculations.

For Russia in 2017 there were 0.66 Forbes' billionaires per million population. Although this was lower than for most of the advanced capitalist democracies referenced here (the US, Germany and the UK), it was well above that of the other east European countries, and higher than for France, a considerably richer country with a larger economy. For Ukraine, although its ratio of 0.13 billionaires per million population is not high in comparison with the other east European countries viewed here, it is higher than for Poland, which is widely considered, unlike Ukraine, to have been one of the economic success stories of the transition from central planning.

Figure 4.3: Ukraine & Russia: Forbes' billionaires vs per head GDP, 2017

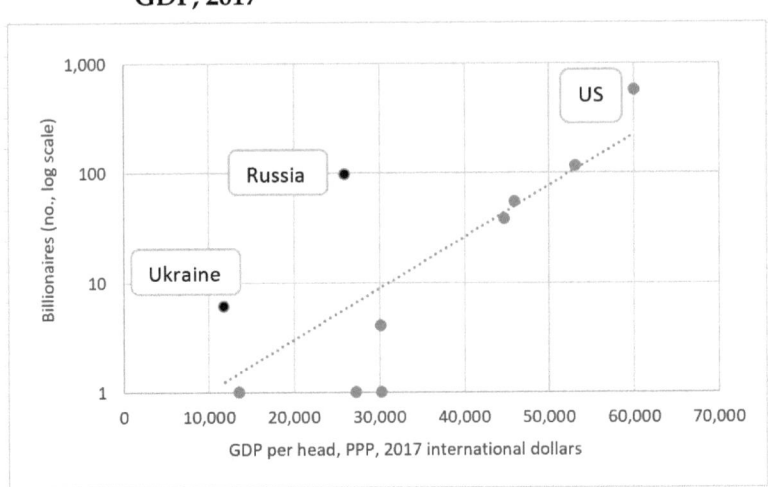

Sources: For Forbes' List, Eduardo Casais Jr and Eduardo Casais Sr. The Complete World Billionaire Lists, areppim website. Available: https://bit.ly/2XeK841. World Bank DataBank, *World Development Indicators*. Available: https://bit.ly/3l83fF9.

Figure 4.3 above shows the number of billionaires in Ukraine and Russia high relative to their GDP per head[13]. The use of a log scale for the vertical axis (number of billionaires) brings this out visually, by the distance of Ukraine and Russia above the trend line (the US, too, has more billionaires than you would expect for its income level). In 2017, Russia, with a GDP per head of US$26,000, had 96 billionaires on the Forbes' List, whereas Romania, with comparable average purchasing power, had just one. In the same year, Ukraine had an average income of less than US$12,000, but still had six billionaires, compared with one for Georgia, whose economy generated higher output on average. What is remarkable is that a country such as Ukraine, which usually comes close to bottom in European income rankings, makes it onto the Forbes' billionaires list at all. That is, in terms of production of very rich individuals, Ukraine and Russia punch above their economic weight.

---

[13] A purchasing power parity (PPP) series from the World Bank is used here to aid the validity of the comparison between countries.

Main "takeaways" on wealth concentration in Ukraine and Russia

Bringing together the evidence of the high absolute and relative wealth of the super-rich, the high estimates for household wealth concentration, and the high incidence of billionaires in relation to production and the population, it is possible to conclude that, in international comparison, an unusually small number of people in contemporary Ukraine and Russia control an unusually large proportion of each society's income-generating assets. In Ukraine, in contrast to Russia, the degree of concentration appears to have diminished between 2013 and 2017 as a result of a severe bout of political, geopolitical and financial instability. Meanwhile, the very high concentration of business wealth indicated by the Focus data — analysed later in this chapter — supports the picture of extreme economic stratification described here.

In Ukraine, privatisation was behind both wealth concentration and the crystallisation of the oligarchy

A global policy adapted by local elites

How, then, was it that wealth became so highly concentrated in post-communist Ukraine? The most straightforward answer is that it is the result of the large-scale transfer of state property into private hands, or privatisation.

Privatisation in Ukraine should be seen in the context of a resurgence of free-market ideology internationally, leading by the early 1980s to a swing in the policy "pendulum" away from public ownership (Douarin and Mickiewicz, 2017, pp. 177-178). However, it should not be understood simply as the passive local adoption of a central tenet of a globally ascendant economic ideology, but also as the adaptation by local elites of the formal rhetoric of privatisation for their own informal ends, where this proved possible. Stylising the process of wealth concentration in post-communist Ukraine somewhat, it can be seen as composed of four main interlinked moments.

The first is the original rent accumulation schemes of politically connected insiders of the early 1990s, examined in the previous chapter. This gave the new wealth-holders, the oligarchs who emerged out of regional business-political networks, the material resource power and political access to skew the privatisation process in their favour. In turn, the increase in wealth from skewed privatisations helped to crystallise, stabilise and institutionalise the dominant form of relations between emerging big business networks and the state. It is this new institutional relation of formal political and informal economic forces, "the oligarchy", which has licensed the routine proliferation of elite rent-extraction schemes ever since, through which the wealth holdings of elite participants have been continually replenished, albeit at the expense of public finances. In Ukraine, therefore, the process of privatisation as wealth concentration and the process of formation of the oligarchy as the dominant political economy regime are inseparable.

Rising wealth inequality as part of a global pattern
Just as privatisation in eastern Europe in the 1990s was in part an outcome of a global shift in the policy consensus, so rising wealth inequality in Ukraine and Russia is part of a wider global pattern. For example, in the 20 years from 1995, the share of personal wealth held by the top 1% rose sharply in both Russia and the US, to 43% and 39% of the national total, respectively, according to the *World Inequality Report 2018* (Alvarado et al, 2018, p. 16). In Russia, these researchers find an "extreme case" (p. 174) of the general rise in private wealth linked to privatisation. In the US, by contrast, they suggest that whereas in the 1980s and 1990s rising income inequality, in part linked to fast-rising CEO pay, was the dominant factor behind the further concentration of wealth at the high end of the ownership scale, by the 2000s, an increase in earnings from wealth had become the driving factor (p. 173), corresponding to the main explanations offered by Piketty in his earlier work (Piketty, 2014).

Privatisation in Ukraine benefited emergent elites...
In Ukraine's case, the explanatory story is of course closer to that of Russia. That is, the process of privatisation played a central role in the development of its highly stratified pattern of wealth distribution, albeit without appearing to contribute greatly to economic growth — as may have happened elsewhere in eastern Europe — because of the form which privatisation took.

Privatisation in Ukraine took place in waves, and in such a way as to mainly benefit well-connected members of the emerging post-communist business-political elite. In the first wave, in 1992-94, for example, although around 12,000 state-owned enterprises were sold off, these were mostly buyouts by the incumbent management (Boytsun, 2019, p. 112). The focus of the second wave in 1994-98 was on mass privatisation through vouchers. Although shares were sold in up to 50,000 publicly owned firms, there was a *de facto* change of ownership in only one-third of these cases. Amid the economic slump of the 1990s, many Ukrainians converted their ownership vouchers into ready cash, so that the bulk ended up in the hands of intermediaries and Soviet-era factory bosses, the so-called "red directors". In this way, the privatisations of the 1990s "cemented the position of the 'red directors', provided politically connected individuals access to the state assets and...laid the foundation of the oligarchy in Ukraine" (Boytsun, 2019, p. 112). A third phase of "insider privatisation" followed in the 2000s, and a fourth during the presidency of Yanukovych.

...and is associated with corruption rather than growth
Alongside liberalisation and macroeconomic stabilisation, privatisation was one of the "holy trinity" of marketising, globalising policies usually recommended by the international financial institutions (IFIs), such as the IMF and the EBRD, for the transformation of planned into market economies. From this perspective, the main justification for privatisation, drawn from the central theoretical propositions of neo-classical political economy, is an argument for economic efficiency. That is, it was expected that by retying asset control to asset returns, profit maximisation could be re-introduced as a central tenet of economic life, with competition between producers raising innovation and productivity growth systematically (Douarin and Mickiewicz, 2017, pp. 181-184). Whereas there is some evidence that privatisation helped to boost firms' performance in central Europe and the Baltics, outcomes have been more ambiguous for privatised enterprises in former Soviet countries, such as Ukraine, especially where assets were sold to domestic buyers (Estrin et al, 2009).

Rather than boosting economic growth, one of the most significant economic effects of privatisation-driven wealth concentration in Ukraine has been wealth "offshorisation", itself reflecting the failure of the Ukrainian state to develop the capacity to enforce property claims impersonally, while the state's ability to develop such capacity was itself undercut by the implied tax losses. The likely impact on levels of investment in post-communist Ukraine, and through this on its perennially poor growth rates, may be one of the key economic side effects of the dominance of the Ukrainian oligarchy as a self-reproducing set of political and economic rules.

As a result of an inequitable privatisation process, alongside disappointment over the unrealised promises made about its economic outcomes, in Ukraine, privatisation has become widely discredited (Boytsun, 2019, pp. 113-114).

4.2.3 Dynamics of domestic business wealth in Ukraine, 2006-17

How did the business wealth of the Focus-100 evolve?

A time series for domestic material resource power
Shifting down from the international to the national level, the second analysis focuses on the two sets of time series data developed in the first half of this chapter to examine the development of the relative wealth of Ukraine's economic elite. These series are summarised in Table 4.8 below. The second column sets out the Focus-100 annual totals of domestic business wealth. The third column adds my estimates of Ukraine's national wealth based on national accounts. Both are in billions of current US dollars. By treating business wealth as a ratio of national wealth, it is possible to produce an indicator of the scale and dynamics of the potential (domestic) material resource power of the very rich in Ukraine in 2006-17. This series is shown in the final column of Table 4.8.

The following section describes how this indicator changed over time, for the 100 rich-list members taken together, and for the representative individual. It explains the fall in domestic material power across the Yanukovych and Poroshenko presidencies, one of the key findings.

Estimates for national wealth have been projected backwards for 2006 and 2007 by assuming wealth-income ratios similar to that for 2008. This provides a figure for the multiple of national income from which to derive the national wealth estimates for 2006-07, which are the underlined numbers in the table.

Table 4.8: Focus-100 domestic business wealth & Ukraine's estimated national wealth, 2006-17; US$ bn, unless otherwise stated

	Focus-100 domestic business wealth	National wealth (SSSU + 80% of Credit Suisse)	Net national income (SSSU)	Wealth-income ratio	Focus-100 wealth as % of national wealth
2006	71.0	422.1	93.8	450	16.8
2007	101.4	565.7	125.7	450	17.9
2008	31.6	507.5	112.6	451	6.2
2009	45.9	426.6	98.7	432	10.8
2010	86.9	488.4	121.1	403	17.8
2011	79.5	571.2	144.8	394	13.9
2012	77.8	646.7	157.3	411	12.0
2013	69.0	639.4	162.6	393	10.8
2014	37.0	302.5	87.9	344	12.2
2015	23.8	261.7	73.2	358	9.1
2016	24.1	253.7	78.1	325	9.5
2017	27.0	288.9	97.7	296	9.3

Sources: Focus.ua. The Focus Ratings archive for 2006-17 data (published the following year) is available at: https://focus.ua/rating/archive. State Statistical Service of Ukraine (SSSU; 2019a), experimental balance of non-financial assets in 2017 and archive. Available: https://bit.ly/3ltmrz0. SSSU (2019b), experimental balance sheets of financial assets and liabilities in 2017 and archive. Available: https://bit.ly/3rQGrN6. Shorrocks et al (2018b), Table 2.4, pp. 66-102. Own calculations.

Focus-100 business wealth: US dollar series

Examining the US dollar series for the Focus-100 wealth (the second column of Table 4.8), some observations suggest themselves. The first is that there is considerable variation over time. The annual value of domestic business wealth of the richest 100 Ukrainians peaked at just over US$100bn in 2007, at the tail end of a global boom that began in the early 2000s, but fell to a low of less than one-quarter of that, or around US$24bn, in 2015-16, in the aftermath of the flight of Yanukovych and his inner circle, the onset of war with Russia, and steep declines in global commodity prices, epitomised by a fall in world oil prices to a 20-year low. The highest individual domestic business wealth, of US$18.7bn, was recorded in 2011 for Rinat Akhmetov, the pre-eminent Donetsk oligarch who held first place on the Focus-100 rich list for all 12 years of the series analysed here. The least wealthy individual to qualify for the list was Vladimir Tsoi, who heads MTI group, a distributor of electronic products. He was positioned in 100th place in 2015, with domestic business wealth of just US$26m (Focus Ratings, 2016).

While the patterns of change of national wealth and national income follow one another quite closely in US dollar terms in 2006-17, the totals for business wealth tend to diverge around periods of crisis. So, whereas the value of domestic business wealth dropped much more steeply than national wealth and income with the onset of the global financial crisis of 2008, it also recovered more rapidly in its wake, touching almost US$87bn by 2010, the first year of the Yanukovych presidency. Thereafter, business wealth began to fall, despite the growth in national income and national wealth, with the pace of decline accelerating from 2013. Amid mass protests, war, the onset of recession and financial destabilisation, the scale of the drop in domestic business wealth in 2014-15 was, perhaps surprisingly, less steep than in 2008 and more in tune with the size of the economic impact more broadly—although the effect was more drawn out, and the ensuing recovery of business wealth weaker.

Focus-100 business wealth as a share of national wealth

On their own, the nominal US dollar data do not tell us what we want to know, which is the pattern of change in the potential material resource power of the economic elite to Ukrainian society. The way I decided to operationalise this concept was to relativise domestic business wealth to national wealth. This is shown in the final column of Table 4.8. The same series is presented graphically in Figure 4.4 below as an undulating black line, to be read against the right-hand scale, as share of estimated national wealth. The data from which this ratio was calculated are also shown in the chart. These are the Focus-100 annual domestic business wealth totals (represented as dark grey bars for each year) and estimates for national wealth (the backgrounded, lighter grey blocked area), both to be read against the left-hand scale, in billions of US dollars.

Figure 4.4: Focus-100 domestic business wealth vs national wealth, 2006-17

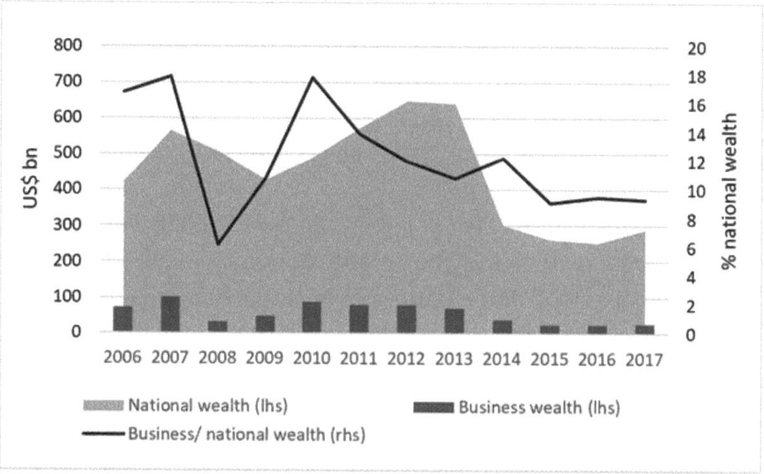

Sources: Focus.ua. Archive for 2006-17 data (published the following year) is available at: https://focus.ua/rating/archive. SSSU (2019a), experimental balance of non-financial assets in 2017 and archive. Available: https://bit.ly/3ltmrz0. SSSU (2019b), experimental balance sheets of financial assets and liabilities in 2017 and archive. Available: https://bit.ly/3rQGrN6. Shorrocks et al (2018b), Table 2.4, pp. 66-102. Available: https://bit.ly/3775cuU.

From Figure 4.4, a number of observations can be made.

- Most strikingly, on this measure, the observable, domestically held business wealth of the richest 100 Ukrainians peaked as a share of national wealth at almost 18% just before and immediately after the 2008-09 financial crisis, but was hit hard by the financial and economic turmoil in between, so that the black horizontal line in the chart dips steeply in 2008.
- After peaking again in 2010, the broad trend is downward. Consequently, between 2010 and 2017, the business wealth of the very rich roughly halved as a share of national wealth, from 18% to 9%. This is one of the chapter's key empirical findings.

- Surprisingly, relative to national wealth, domestic business wealth fell more markedly in the Yanukovych presidency, by 7 percentage points between 2010 and 2013, than during the following 4 years, amid domestic political turmoil and war, when it dropped by about 3 percentage points.
- Even after their relative wealth had fallen by half, however, the 100 richest Ukrainians between them, out of a total population of 44.8m in 2017 on World Bank data, still had domestic business assets worth just over 9% of the value of all of the financial and physical assets of the country.

How did business wealth change for the "typical" wealthy individual?

Another way of viewing the wealth dynamics of the Ukrainian super-rich is to look at the pattern of business holdings for the typical group member and representative distribution of the Focus-100 series — that is, through statistical measures of central tendency and dispersion. But which ones?

Because of the preponderance of outliers, using the mean would exaggerate the typical level of wealth among the richest Ukrainians. As such, median values are a better indicator of the data's central tendency, or point around which the rest of the observations are distributed. Similarly, although the standard deviation is the most common measure of dispersion, one of the inputs for its calculation is the mean. Alongside the median, I will therefore use the inter-quartile range (IQR) as the appropriate measure of dispersion to examine the dynamics of the wealth for the typical individual of the Focus-100 group in 2006-17.

Focus-100 business wealth: medians and IQRs

Table 4.9 below presents a "five number summary" of the Focus-100 data. In line with the overall figures, it shows the median domestic business wealth of group members — the fourth column in the table — peaking at US$522m in 2007, but recording a low of US$99m in 2015. The middle value was most consistently high in 2010-13, during the Yanukovych presidency, when it averaged US$326m. In 2014-17 the median business wealth of the very rich fell by about three-fifths in nominal US dollar terms, to US$123m.

Table 4.9: Distribution of Focus-100 domestic business wealth: 5 number summary & IQR, 2006-17; US$ m

	Min	25th percentile	Median	75th percentile	Max	IQR
2006	100	201	341	640	12,000	439
2007	207	292	522	915	14,620	623
2008	56	74	121	290	3,683	216
2009	68	115	229	380	7,520	265
2010	121	199	365	897	15,590	698
2011	105	161	284	781	18,659	621
2012	127	198	346	751	16,830	553
2013	74	201	311	546	14,871	346
2014	40	90	128	333	7,700	243
2015	26	62	99	184	3,100	123
2016	34	67	133	239	2,200	172
2017	41	71	133	268	3,100	197

Sources: Focus.ua. The Focus Ratings archive for 2006-17 data (published the following year) is available at: https://focus.ua/rating/archive. Own calculations. Note: For each year of the ratings, the relevant web page on wealth is usually titled "100 samykh bogatykh lyudey Ukrainy", "Ukraine's 100 richest people".

In 2010 the middle 50% of those on the Focus-100 list owned business assets worth between US$200m and US$900m, an IQR of US$700m. By 2017, the middle 50% of individuals held between US$70m and US$270m in business wealth, reducing the IQR to just US$200m as the ceiling and floor of the IQR began to converge more closely on the (declining) median values.

As with the Focus-100 annual totals, it is more useful for the aims of this study — looking at wealth as potential political power — to examine the dynamics of the wealth of the typical individual (the median) and the representative distribution pattern (the interquartile range) as a ratio of estimated national wealth. While this offers a better indication of the changing material power of the representative rich-list member, the results — the value of individual business assets as a share of all of Ukraine's assets — are less easy to grasp than their corresponding US dollar values because of the small scale. The information is therefore presented visually in the Figure 4.5 below.

Figure 4.5: Focus-100 business wealth as a share of national wealth: median & IQR, 2006-17

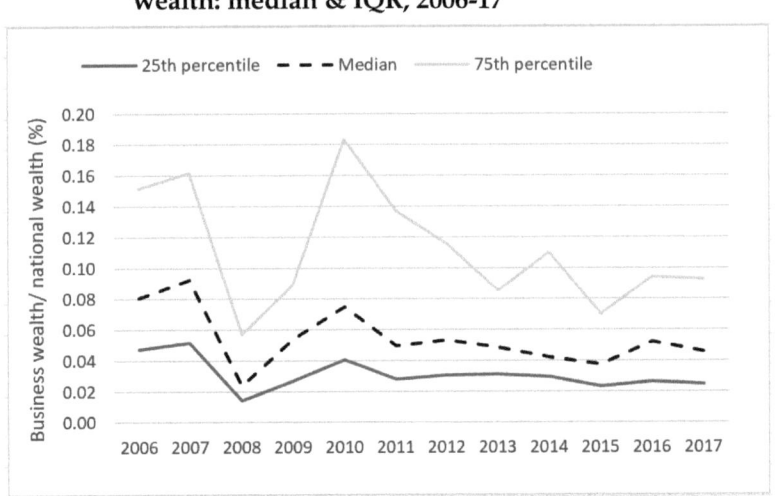

Source: Focus.ua. Focus Ratings archive for 2006-17 data is available at: https://focus.ua/rating/archive. SSSU (2019a), experimental balance of non-financial assets in 2017 and archive. Available: https://bit.ly/3ltmrz0. SSSU (2019b), experimental balance sheets of financial assets and liabilities in 2017 and archive. Available: https://bit.ly/3rQGrN6. Shorrocks et al (2018b), Table 2.4, pp. 66-102. Own calculations.

The median business wealth of the Focus-100 group (the black dashed central line on the chart) averaged 0.057% of national wealth in 2010-13, but fell in 2014-17 to 0.045%. Moreover, in 2014-17 the spread of the central 50% of the distribution was a little lower and narrower than in the previous four years, as the "floor" (the 25th percentile) fell modestly and the "ceiling" (the 75th percentile) more markedly, although it had already come down significantly under Yanukovych. Although in the Yanukovych era the middle portion of the Focus list members held individual wealth equal to 0.033-0.130% of national wealth (an IQR of 0.098 percentage points), this has fallen to 0.026-0.092% in the first four years after the Euromaidan, an IQR of just 0.066 percentage points, more tightly clustered about the median. That is, between the Yanukovych and the Poroshenko eras, the potential material power of the representative distribution of individuals on the rich list became more equal at a lower level. As with the wealth totals for the Focus-100 group as a whole, therefore, this suggests a weakening of the potential domestic material power of the typical rich-list member. Whether this is likely to have translated into a loss of political influence will be answered in the conclusion to this chapter.

Why does the domestic "material resource power" of the Focus-100 fall?

What explains the broad fall, or "dilution", in the observable domestic business wealth of the very rich in relation to Ukrainian national wealth in 2010-17, both at the level of the rich list as a whole and of the typical list member? And why did it fall more markedly under Yanukovych than in the general crisis that followed his political demise?

In the introductions to the wealth rankings, as well as the more detailed accounts of individual wealth trajectories that they sometimes provide, the (unnamed) Focus editors offer a sufficient account across a range of specific, plausible factors — taking in the global, regional, domestic and sectoral levels — to explain this downward trend. In short, under Yanukovych, the main factors were adverse global economic trends alongside intensified state economic predation at home. Following the collapse of his administration, a more generalised societal crisis ensued. In each case, the effects of political and economic development on the material power of the Ukrainian economic elite were mediated through the impact on the local stockmarkets, and so on the company valuations on which the Focus-100 rich list is based.

The fall in the domestic business wealth of the very rich thus corresponds mainly to stockmarket performance. This is shown in Figure 4.6 below by the broad similarity in the movement over time of the domestic material resource power of the 100 richest Ukrainians (the black line in the chart, read against the right-hand scale), viewed against the movement of the PFTS index, which tracks share valuations on the largest of Ukraine's two stockmarkets (the lower grey line, read against the left-hand scale). By tracking the movement of an externally verified data series — ie the PFTS index — this similarity of movement offers some "quality assurance" regarding the Focus-100 data, potential concerns about which were raised earlier in the chapter.

135

Figure 4.6: Domestic material power of the Ukrainian economic elite vs PFTS stock index, 2006-17

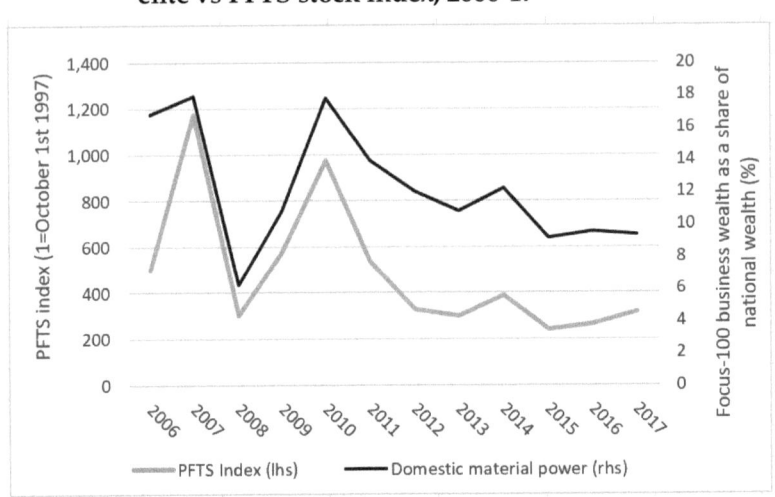

Sources: National Bank of Ukraine (NBU), Financial Sector Statistics, Data: PFTS Index. Available: https://bank.gov.ua/ua/statistic/sector-financial/data-sector-financial#2fs. Focus.ua. The Focus Ratings archive for 2006-17 data (published the following year) is available at: https://focus.ua/rating/archive.

The fall in domestic material power under Yanukovych

The introductions to the Focus wealth rankings for 2011 (published in March 2012) and for 2012 (published in April 2013) place us in the middle of the action, so to speak—that is, with the Yanukovych presidency already under way and its authoritarian trajectory understood. At the level of the Focus rich list as a whole, the Focus editors suggest two broad sets of factors driving the steep fall in business wealth in this period, and one affecting the relative fortunes of specific individuals within it.

The first broad economic factor is a sharp decline in company valuations on the Ukrainian stockmarket in 2010-13, linked primarily to a fall in global stockmarkets. This was an effect of the then ongoing European sovereign debt crisis, undermining the public finances of several EU states, while generating serious intra-EU conflict over the best means of tackling high levels of public debt. In Ukraine, this had a depressing knock-on effect on the fortunes of businesses—and so also their valuations and the net worth of their owners — in agriculture and metals, linked to Ukraine's main commodity exports, wheat and steel.

The second broad factor, originating from domestic political developments, was an intensification of state predation of businesses. This created strong incentives for the wealthy to invest abroad, and to obscure asset ownership or to create the appearance of poor performance to render the business an unattractive target for coercive takeover[14]. Thus, write the Focus editors, "businessmen whose relations with the current government are not so close prefer to diversify their businesses and acquire assets abroad" (Focus, 2011). The businessmen they name include high-profile figures such as Andriy Verevskyi, the chair of Kernal Holding, a large agribusiness concern; Vyacheslav Bohuslayev, the head of Motor Sich, a large aircraft engine manufacturing business in Zaporizhzhya; and Kostyantyn Zhevaho, who runs the Finances and Credit conglomerate. All of these are leading oligarchs in their own right, and all appear on the list of the wealthiest, longest-lasting members of Ukraine's contemporary economic elite (see Table 4.12).

The Focus texts paint a picture of an extremely tough business operating environment in Ukraine in this period — even as the country began to make forward strides in international indexes, such as the Ease of Doing Business rankings (World Bank, 2013) — when the struggles between business-political networks of the "Orange" era gave way to a phase in which Yanukovych had consolidated his position in the state sufficiently both to reward favoured oligarch backers (primarily Akhmetov and Firtash) with under-priced sales of state assets, and to begin to develop his own proto-business network, known as "the family", and centred on Yanukovych's elder son, Oleksandr, and his associates (Tkach and Dalton, 2013, pp. 10-11). Along with the operation of poor macroeconomic policy, symbolised by the maintenance of a fixed exchange-rate regime, even amid rapid deterioration in the current account, this is likely also to have undermined business confidence, further eroding Ukrainian company valuations.

---

[14] As Kolomoyskyi did, the Focus editors suggest, to protect his ownership of Ukrainian Airlines.

A third factor, this time helping to explain the changing relative fortunes of specific individuals among the very rich, and implied by the second factor, is proximity to official political power. Although it is a theme that runs through the political economy of Ukraine since independence, during the Yanukovych presidency, maintaining good ties with the politically dominant network as a strategy for sustaining wealth took on a special importance. In the succinct phrase of the Focus editors, "the best results are shown by those close to Viktor Yanukovych" (Focus, 2011).

The fall in domestic material power after Yanukovych
In the period after the flight of Yanukovych and his associates in late February 2014, signalling the onset of a protracted general crisis, wealth-holders were in preservation mode, according to Focus (Focus Ratings, 2015). In this period, the three main factors behind the fall in domestic business wealth are as follows:

- the depressing effect on the confidence of economic actors because of domestic political turmoil and uncertainty;
- the economic impact of military conflict with Russia, not only in terms of loss and destruction of assets following the annexation of Crimea and the instigation of armed conflict in the Donbas, but also of the loss and destruction of sales potential, both through the suspension of production facilities and the closure of shopping outlets; and
- the onset of a protracted phase of recession and macro-financial instability, linked to the first two points, but an outcome also of the unwinding of the macroeconomic imbalances built up under Yanukovych.

4.2.4 Do the richest Ukrainians stay rich longer? Who are they?

Turnover and stability among Ukraine's economic elite
As well as showing the dynamics of the domestic wealth of Ukraine's super-rich, personnel changes on the Focus-100 list shine a light on the patterns of turnover, cohesion and even inequality within the Ukrainian economic elite over more than a decade. Had the entire list been replaced each year with a new set of individuals,

for example, total membership across all 12 years would have produced 1,200 separate cases. That there are only 239 such cases indicates a degree of institutional stability across time.

For these 239 cases, divergent patterns of longevity of membership on the list can be discerned. These patterns suggest that there has been considerably more positional stability at the very top end of the wealth spectrum than lower down. The results are set out in Table 4.10 below. This shows that in almost half of all cases (116), membership on the list lasted for three years or fewer (the first three rows of the table). Just over 70% were on the list for six or fewer years (168 cases). This means that only 30% of those appearing on the list, or 71 cases, maintained their presence for seven or more years. Of these, just 32 cases (31 individuals plus the Surkis brothers) qualified for inclusion for the whole 12-year period, or 13% of the total.

Table 4.10: Individual longevity on Focus-100 rich list, 2006-17

Years present	Frequency (no.)	Share (%)	Cumulative share (%)
1	47	19.7	19.7
2	33	13.8	33.5
3	36	15.1	48.5
4	17	7.1	55.7
5	22	9.2	64.9
6	13	5.4	70.3
7	6	2.5	72.8
8	16	6.7	79.5
9	6	2.5	82.0
10	7	2.9	84.9
11	4	1.7	86.6
12	32	13.4	100.0
Total	239	100.0	100.0

Sources: Focus.ua. The Focus Ratings archive for 2006-17 data (published the following year) is available at: https://focus.ua/rating/archive. Own calculations. Note: For each year of the ratings, the relevant web page on wealth is usually titled "100 samykh bogatykh lyudey Ukrainy", "Ukraine's 100 richest people".

Although membership of the Focus-100 rich list represents a very small group within Ukrainian society, this analysis suggests that an even smaller group is persistently present within it. That is, although the rich list itself tends to undergo a high rate of replacement of personnel at the bottom end of the distribution, a much smaller number of individuals were able to maintain their position on the list for a decade or more.

A quarter of the Focus-100 had domestic assets of above US$300m
Prompted by the theory of oligarchy set out in chapter 2, this raises the question of whether the ability to last on the rich list is linked to the level of wealth held. To investigate this, I first generated a variable for the average annual US dollar domestic business assets of each wealthy individual (or family couple), then grouped this data into categories to make it easier to see an overall pattern. The frequency distribution of this new variable is set out in Table 4.11.

Table 4.11: Average annual business wealth of individuals on the Focus-100 rich list, 2006-17

Wealth (US$ m)	Frequency (no.)	Share (%)	Cumulative share (%)
0-100	44	18.4	18.4
101-200	79	33.1	51.5
201-300	52	21.8	73.2
301-500	27	11.3	84.5
501-1,000	24	10.0	94.6
1,001-10,000	13	5.4	100.0
Total	239	100.0	100.0

Sources: Focus.ua. The Focus Ratings archive for 2006-17 data (published the following year) is available at: https://focus.ua/rating/archive. Own calculations. Note: For each year of the ratings, the relevant web page on wealth is usually titled "100 samykh bogatykh lyudey Ukrainy", "Ukraine's 100 richest people".

Table 4.11 shows that, for just over 50% of cases, average annual domestic business wealth was at or below US$200m (the first two rows of the table), and for almost three-quarters (73%), at or below US$300m (the first three rows). Although roughly the top quarter of wealth-holders therefore had annual average assets of more than US$300m, only around 5% of Ukraine's richest people (13 individuals) had average annual business wealth of US$1bn-10bn. This suggests that wealth distribution is highly skewed even among leading wealth-holders, with a significant gap between the top 5% and the rest.

Material power and longevity on the rich list: wealth sustains wealth

Turning now to the relationship between wealth and longevity on the rich list, the pair of charts below show the (uncategorised) distribution of average business wealth as a share of national wealth for each individual on the Focus-100 rich list in 2006-17 by the number of years they appeared on it. The switch from US dollar data is again because the central concern of this chapter is elite wealth relative to Ukrainian society, as a potential social and especially political power.

Figure 4.7, the higher of the pair of charts directly below, shows the full picture, including conspicuous outliers, signified by the two grey dots hanging well above the body of the distribution. The first dot, on the left-hand side of this chart, represents Lakshmi Mittal, an Indian steel tycoon whose investments in Ukraine led to his (temporary) inclusion on the Focus list. The second outlier, towards the top right of the chart, represents the relative wealth of Rinat Akhmetov. It shows that, on average in 2006-17, his domestic business assets equal to just over 2% of Ukraine's national wealth.

By greatly reducing the scale, the lower chart zooms in on the data distribution, excluding the outliers from view and so making clearer a mild but definite positive slope in the relationship—ie, that higher individual wealth appears associated with more time on the rich list, but with a spike for those who have "gone the distance", remaining on the list for the maximum 12 years.

A correlation coefficient can be used to assess the strength and direction of linear association of this relationship, on a graded scale of -1 (perfectly negatively associated) to +1 (perfectly positively associated), with zero indicating the absence of a linear relationship. For the data in the top chart, the coefficient (produced using a simple command in Stata) is 0.324—that is, positive in direction, but relatively weak. (Without the outliers, this would rise to 0.514, interpreted as an association of moderate strength.) According to this analysis, then, there is some evidence that level of business wealth is associated with longevity on the Focus-100 rich list.

Figures 4.7 & 4.8: Business wealth of the rich as a share of national wealth vs years on the rich list, 2006-17 (top chart); zoomed-in version of the same (bottom chart)

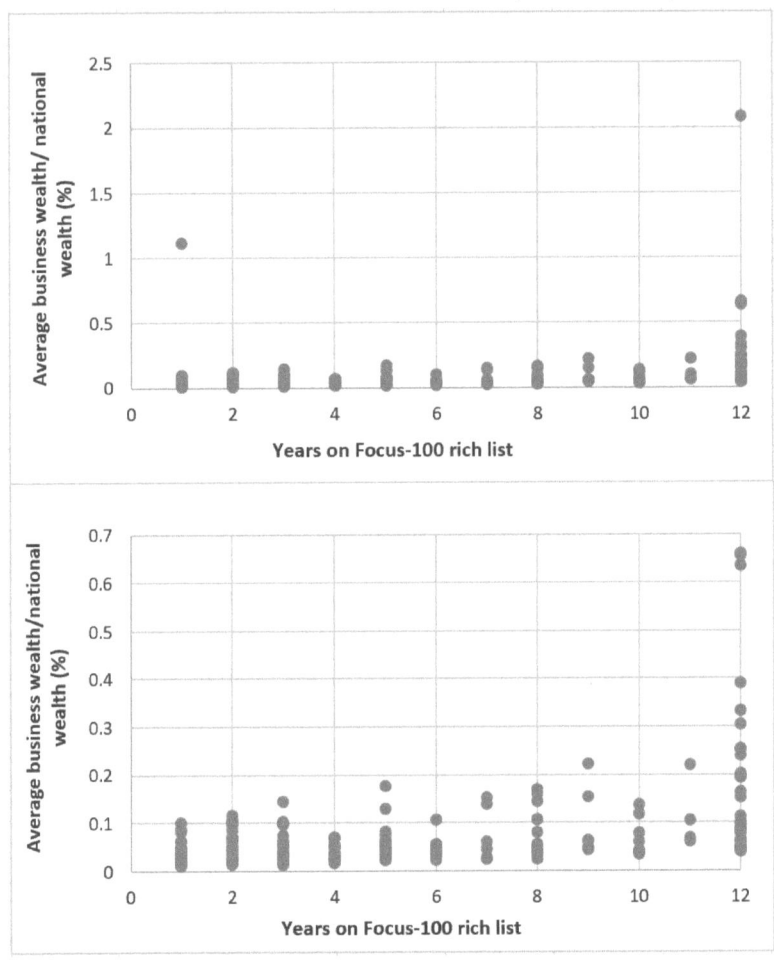

Sources: Focus.ua. The Focus Ratings archive for 2006-17 data is available at: https://focus.ua/rating/archive. SSSU (2019a), experimental balance of non-financial assets in 2017 and archive. Available: https://bit.ly/3ltmrz0. SSSU (2019b), experimental balance sheets of financial assets and liabilities in 2017 and archive. Available: https://bit.ly/3rQGrN6. Shorrocks et al (2018b), Table 2.4, pp. 66-102. Own calculations.

To get an idea of the size of effect of levels of wealth on longevity on the rich list in a more meaningful way—that is, in terms of the scale in real world units of measurement—we can perform a linear regression on the same data. This is a statistical technique that "fits" a line to the data points by minimising the distance between them, producing also a value (the beta coefficient) that indicates both the direction of the relationship (positive or negative) and the steepness of the gradient of the slope. With years present on the rich list as the dependent variable (the one to be predicted or explained) and individual business wealth as the single independent or explanatory variable (here, as a share of national wealth averaged over the number of years present on the list), Stata tells us that the relationship is a positive one (as wealth rises, time present on the list tends to rise).

More precisely, it suggests that for an increase in business wealth equal to 1% of national wealth, you could expect to last an additional 7.17 years on the rich list. Dividing both sides by 7.17, we can say that, on this data, an increase in business wealth equal to 0.14% of national wealth is associated with an additional year on the rich list. The software confirms that, with a probability value (p-value) of below 0.05, a common benchmark used in social research, this relation is statistically significant, meaning that it is unlikely to have occurred by chance. However, the Stata readout indicates that average relative wealth predicts only around 10% of the variation in the "years present" variable (the R-squared value), which means, of course, that other explanatory factors are also in play.

How might wealth explain longevity on the rich list?
How might this relationship be explained? The theory of wealth defence (Winters, 2011, pp. 20-26) outlined in chapter 3 offers one strategy. To recap, wealth as a power resource is distinguished by its capacity to be deployed flexibly in its own defence. Holders of concentrated wealth are able to buy the services they need—whether coercive or professional—to allow them to see off the threats that wealth-holders face, thereby defending their property claims. How this is done depends on the specific threats and the political institutions in place. But with greater wealth comes a greater, and perhaps more effective, range of protective options, so that there is a better chance of staying rich for longer.

However, institutional economics supplies a broad explanatory principle, of circular and cumulative causation, which would also explain the correlation observed in the strip charts. This is an approach that stresses the self-perpetuating quality of processes driving socio-economic inequality, so that "divergence rather than convergence is the norm" (Stilwell, 2019, p. 115). A contrast is with the conception of economic dynamics governed by equilibrium processes, which is at the heart of neo-classical thinking. In the case of concentrated riches, circular and cumulative causation translates into the idea that "wealth breeds wealth", first because it permits the generation of wealth-enhancing income — through profits, rents or interest — without having to resort to paid work and, second, over generations, because of the educational, social networking and material benefits (such as inheritance) that birth into a rich family brings (Stilwell, 2012, pp. 223-225; 2019, pp. 115-117).

It may be possible, however, for wealth defence to be viewed as a subset of the mechanisms by which circular and cumulative causation operates in the case of wealth inequality, as a special set of mechanisms of a more general process — although any attempt to reconcile the two may be complicated by the very different social ontologies, or views of what the social world is, underlying them.

For modern Ukraine, in addition to the above "virtuous circle" of wealth-holding as an explanation for enduring wealth, should be added a Ukraine-specific one, already referred to in the section on privatisation above, which is the institutionalisation of a range of adaptable, extractive economic practices or schemes — illustrated with examples from the energy sector in chapter 6 — as a normal part of political life centred on transactional relationships between business-political networks. In other words, the oligarchy itself is an institutionalised set of adaptable economic and political practices for perpetuating wealth inequality.

The "core" rich

Finally in this section, Table 4.12 below presents a shortlist of the "core" rich, who are the most enduringly successful business leaders on the Focus-100 rich list for 2006-17. This group is made up of those who managed both to remain in the top quarter of cases in terms of domestic material power[15], while also appearing on the rich list for ten years or more. With most of the well-known "old" oligarchs clustered towards the top of the list, I have added to the table information on individuals' main companies and business sectors, where available. As well as owning high-value domestic business assets, many of the "core" rich have also held seats in parliament, or positions in government or public office (several have headed the board of the central bank, for example), so meeting the criteria of "oligarch" used in this study. From the table and the information on this group of the Ukrainian rich in the data set, several points can be drawn. These are that the "core" rich:

- are a tiny minority within a tiny minority, comprising just 28 individuals, or 11.7% of all cases, on the Focus-100 rich list in 2006-17;
- tend between them to own the bulk (60-70%) of domestic business wealth held by the top 100 in any one year; and
- held between them average business wealth equal to 8.2% of national wealth for 2006-17 as a whole.

While not all of the individuals on the Focus-100 rich list are likely to be oligarchs, the top-tier of oligarchs, defined in this research after Heiko Pleines (2016a) as wealthy business leaders involved in national politics, are likely to be concentrated among the "core" rich. This, then, is a starting point for identifying individual oligarchs by name outside the handful of those regularly referred to in the Ukrainian press. A final point from the table is that it suggests a degree of sectoral specialisation within the group, so that metallurgy, energy, media and banks could be identified as characteristically "oligarch" or rent-seeking economic sectors in Ukraine.

---

[15] US dollar wealth measured as a share of national wealth, averaged over the number of years on the rich list: the fourth column in Table 4.12.

Table 4.12: Ukraine's "core" rich, 2006-17

No	Name	Wealth (US$ m; av)	Av % of national wealth	Years on Focus	Main business	Main sectors
1	Rinat Akhmetov	9,989	2.08	12	SCM	Metals, engineering, electricity, media, banks
2	Ihor Kolomoyskyi	3,005	0.66	12	Privat Group	Metals, oil, media, banks
3	Viktor Pinchuk	2,999	0.66	12	Interpipe	Metals/steel, media
4	Hennadiy Boholyubov	2,898	0.63	12	Privat Group	Banking
5	Vadym Novynskyi	1,899	0.39	12	Smart Holding	Metals, ships, machinery, agriculture
6	Kostyantyn Zhevaho	1,558	0.33	12	Finance & Credit	Banks, mines machinery, chemicals
7	Dmytro Firtash	1,461	0.30	12	Group DF	Gas, media chemicals, banks
8	Kostyantyn Hryhoryshyn	1,171	0.25	12	Energy Standard	
9	Vitaliy Hayduk	1,164	0.25	12	IUD 2009	Heavy industry
10	Serhiy Taruta	1,097	0.22	11	IUD	Metals, media
11	Yuriy Kosyuk	1,029	0.24	12	MPKh	Food
12	Oleksandr Yaroslavskyi	860	0.20	12	Ukr-Sibbank; DCH	Finance, construction, agriculture, insurance
13	Petro Poroshenko	846	0.20	12	Ukrprominvest (to 2012); Roshen	Sweets, vehicles, boats, media, banking,
14	Andriy Verevskyi	821	0.20	12	Kernel	Food
15	Leonid Yurushev	852	0.19	12	Forum Group	
16	Serhiy Tihipko	703	0.16	12	Privat Group; TAScombank	Finance, machinery, insurance

Table continued overleaf...

Table 4.12: Ukraine's "core" rich, 2006-17

No	Name	Wealth (US$ m; av)	Av % of national wealth	Years on Focus	Main business	Main sectors
17	Leonid Chernovetskyi	640	0.15	12	Pravex	
18	Viktor Nusenkis	704	0.14	10	Energo	
19	Valeriy Khoroshkovskyi	558	0.12	10	Ukrsotsbank	Metals, media, banking
20	Vasyl Khmelnytskyi	531	0.11	12	Kyiv Investment Group	Steel, property, utilities
21	Oleksiy Martynov	510	0.11	11		
22	Vyacheslav Bohuslayev	429	0.10	12	Motor Sich	Machines
23	Vitaliy Antonov	426	0.10	12	Universal Investment Group	
24	Andriy Ivanov	420	0.09	12		
25	Hryhoriy & Ihor Surkis	411	0.09	12	Dynamo?	Food, energy, hotels
26	Oleksandr & Serhiy Buryak	370	0.08	10		Banking, machines, chemicals, mining, vehicles
27	Mykola Yankovskyi	335	0.08	12	Stirol	Chemicals
28	Volodymyr Kostelman	331	0.08	12		
	Total	38,015	8.21			

Sources: Focus.ua. The Focus Ratings archive for 2006-17 data (published the following year) is available at: https://focus.ua/rating/archive. Verkhovna Rada. Available: https://iportal.rada.gov.ua/. Pleines (2016b). Chernenko (2018). Matuszak (2012). Own calculations.

4.3 Chapter summary and conclusions

4.3.1 Recap of key empirical findings and economic effects

On estimates derived from national accounts, Ukraine's national wealth is considerably larger than indicated by some high-profile sources (namely, Credit Suisse). Moreover, despite the disparity in the size and structure of their economies, before the onset of war in 2014, the broad picture of productivity of the Ukrainian economy, as shown by wealth-income ratios of 400-450%, was similar to that of Russia, probably rooted in a common Soviet institutional-technical inheritance. On wealth distribution, several indicators in combination strongly suggest that modern Ukraine and Russia are among the most unequal countries in Europe, and perhaps the world. This reflects similarities of the post-communist wealth accumulation processes, and especially of the modes of privatisation. Similarities in the original and ongoing elite wealth extraction and accumulation schemes, by way of personal network connections to the state, are again rooted in the two countries' shared late Soviet institutional-political culture, or practical understanding among elites of the fusion of the political and the economic.

Personnel changes over time in the composition of the Focus-100 ranking point to greater positional stability at the top end of the wealth spectrum, associated with the higher levels of wealth. This offers some support to theory of wealth defence, but also to the concept of circular and cumulative causation. By identifying those in the top quarter of wealth-holders who have remained on the Focus-100 ranking for ten years or more, it is possible to identify a small group of individuals (28) who constitute the "core" rich. These are among the most enduringly successful members of the contemporary Ukrainian economic elite, a minority within a minority, among whom oligarchs (the politically active rich) are well represented.

"Offshoreisation" may be seen as an important outcome of the process of wealth concentration in a situation in which property rights are weak, and so as a practice both to protect wealth from business rivals and to evade taxes. This is both a key "external" mechanism in the reproduction of the Ukrainian oligarchy as an institution (allowing oligarchs to survive with wealth, the source of their material power, intact through periods of political marginalisation) and may be the process that weighs most heavily on Ukraine's long-term economic prospects. However, the economic effects of offshoreisation include not just the removal of funds from the economy, but also reduction in the financial capacity of the state, while a strong central state is one of the crucial ingredients, according to the institutional theory of prosperity, for creating a reasonably level legal "playing field" for capital accumulation. By reducing the capacity of the state to implement legal rules relatively even-handedly, this feeds back into the recreation of the incentives that had helped to drive offshoreisation originally — namely, unstable property rights — as well as preventing the development of the conditions needed to attract modernising investment, on which a sustained rise in productivity and living standards depends.

4.3.2 Does the fall of domestic business wealth mean that the oligarchs' political influence also fell after the Euromaidan?

The key finding of this chapter, however, is of a marked fall in the domestic business wealth of the very rich relative to the wealth of Ukrainian society, from around 18% in 2010 to about 9% in 2017. But does this decline, interpreted as a drop in material resource power of the economic elite, correspond to a fall in their political influence, and of oligarchs' political influence, following the flight of Yanukovych? Some commentators have argued so. Aslund, for example, in an interview in late 2016, argues that "the power of the oligarchs has declined" in Ukraine, because "in the last 2 years the oligarchs as a group have lost 2/3 of their wealth, and several of them...are completely out. The oligarchs are not a problem anymore, because they suffered heavy losses" (Filipiak, 2016).

There are a number of reasons for believing that this may not be the case, however.

First, on the definition adopted in this study, oligarchs are only a subset of all those who appear on the Focus-100 rich list — that is, they are owners of great wealth who use their riches politically in order to further their business aims.

Second, although the share in national wealth held by the "core" rich also declined, from just over 7% in 2013, at the end of the Yanukovych era, to 6% in 2017, almost four years into the Poroshenko presidency, and although the mean relative wealth of the group fell too (the downward-sloping dashed black line in Figure 4.9 below), this mainly reflected a steep fall in share at the very top of the wealth-holding distribution.

Figure 4.9: Changing share of domestic business wealth of the "core" rich in national wealth, 2013 vs 2017

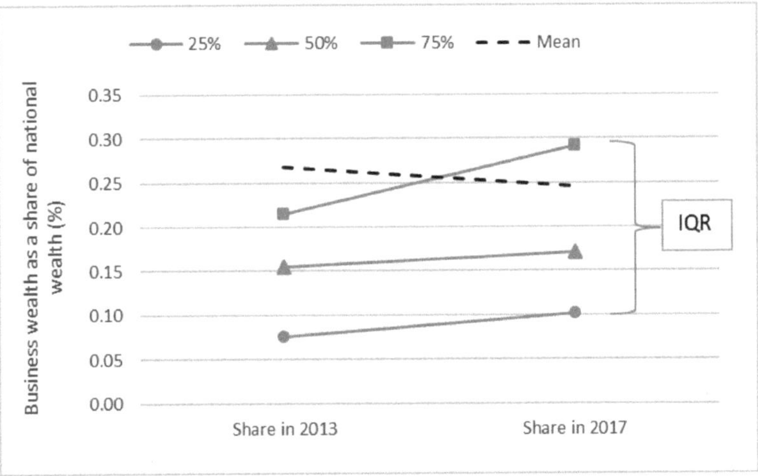

Source: Focus.ua. The Focus Ratings archive for 2006-17 data is available at: https://focus.ua/rating/archive. SSSU (2019a), experimental balance of non-financial assets in 2017 and archive. Available: https://bit.ly/3ltmrz0. SSSU (2019b), experimental balance sheets of financial assets and liabilities in 2017 and archive. Available: https://bit.ly/3rQGrN6. Shorrocks et al (2018b), Table 2.4, pp. 66-102. Own calculations.

In contrast, the median value, as well as the 25th percentile and the 75th percentile — the floor and ceiling of the interquartile range (IQR) as the representative central body of the distribution — all climbed a little. This is represented in the chart above by the upward-sloping grey lines joining geometric markers, indicating a widening of the IQR between 2013 and 2017. In other words, while the main hit to material resource power in this oligarch-dominated group was at the top end, for the central representative body, it tended to rise.

Third, in times of uncertainty, such as a change in the faction of the elite that comes to the fore politically, we might expect not only a rise in capital flight and outward investment, as wealth-holders try to protect their financial assets from predation of currently politically successful network rivals, but also, on immovable business properties, the proliferation of business defence measures, including greater efforts to obscure business ownership and performance, so reducing the level of business wealth that the compositors of the rich list can record. This is likely to have been one reason why observable domestic business wealth fell more steeply under Yanukovych than after his departure.

A fourth reason to doubt that the material political influence of the Ukrainian oligarchs declined in the wake of the Euromaidan Revolution is that domestic business wealth of the Ukrainian super-rich is likely to be only a portion of the total wealth owned by them, with some volume held overseas. A way of tracking this is to examine the country's illicit capital outflows. Going by the estimates from Global Financial Integrity, a US think-tank, which are based on trade invoices and balance-of-payments data, illicit outflows from Ukraine were equal to about 10% of Ukraine's GDP annually in the Yanukovych era in 2010-13 (Kar and Spanjers, 2015, p. 33).

On research into the measurement of accumulated illicit capital flows globally, Gabriel Zucman is a leading authority. To investigate the scale of financial assets held in contemporary tax havens, he takes as a starting point a marked discrepancy in the international investment position at the global level—that is, recorded foreign liabilities of all countries combined tend to be larger than total foreign assets. From this, he estimates global illicit offshore financial wealth in early 2014 at US$7.6trn, or around 8% of all household financial wealth (Zucman, 2015, pp. 35-37), implying a tax loss for governments around the world of US$190bn (pp. 47-50). A later study estimates the hidden wealth of private individuals in 2015 at the equivalent of more than 10% of global GDP, rising to 50% of GDP in the case of Russia (Alvaredo et al, 2018, pp. 263-264).

From these calculations, it is possible to make a rough estimate of the stock of illicit offshore wealth held by the Ukrainian rich in 2013, on the eve of the Euromaidan Revolution. At the lower end, based on the global average of 10% of GDP, this comes to US$18bn. A higher-end estimate, based on the 50%-of-GDP estimate for Russia, yields a figure of US$90bn. That year, Focus-100 domestic business wealth (of US$69bn) was equal to 11% of Ukraine's national wealth. To this, the lower-end estimate of offshore wealth adds 3 percentage points of "material resource power", taking the total to 14% of Ukrainian national wealth. The upper estimate raises the figure by 14 percentage points, to 25% of national wealth.

Which of these estimates is more plausible? I would opt for the higher one, for two reasons. The first is the GFI's estimate of accumulated illicit outflows from Ukraine in 2004-13, of US$117bn. This is above my high-end estimate, but it can probably be assumed that a significant portion of the total sent abroad will have been recycled back into Ukraine periodically—for example, around election times. A second factor supporting the upper estimate is a comparison of the illicit outflow data for Ukraine and Russia to GDP data. For Russia, annual outflows average 7% of annual output, whereas for Ukraine it is 8.3%. Outflows from Ukraine over the same period are therefore likely to have been at least as high as those for Russia, relative to its economic output. Cumulatively, then, for Ukraine these outflows are likely to sum to a similar size of its GDP as for Russia—hence, closer to 50% of GDP than to 10%.

Whatever the size of this stock of illicit financial wealth held by Ukrainians abroad in 2013, it will have been expanded by a step-up in capital outflows in response to the overlapping political, geopolitical, financial and economic crises of 2014-15. Moreover, the local-currency material power of any foreign wealth held abroad in foreign currency will have been greatly magnified by the drastic depreciation of the hryvnya to the US dollar from February 2014, boosting its scale relative to shrinking Ukrainian national wealth, measured in US dollars. This implies that Ukrainian oligarchs' total available material resource power in relation to Ukrainian society may not have fallen much or at all after Euromaidan. Although between 2010 and 2017 domestic business wealth halved as a share of national wealth, therefore, the local-currency material power of illicit foreign-currency assets abroad will have been amplified by exchange-rate effects. This is shown in Figure 4.10 below.

Figure 4.10: Dynamics of domestic & external material resource power of the Ukrainian economic elite, 2006-17

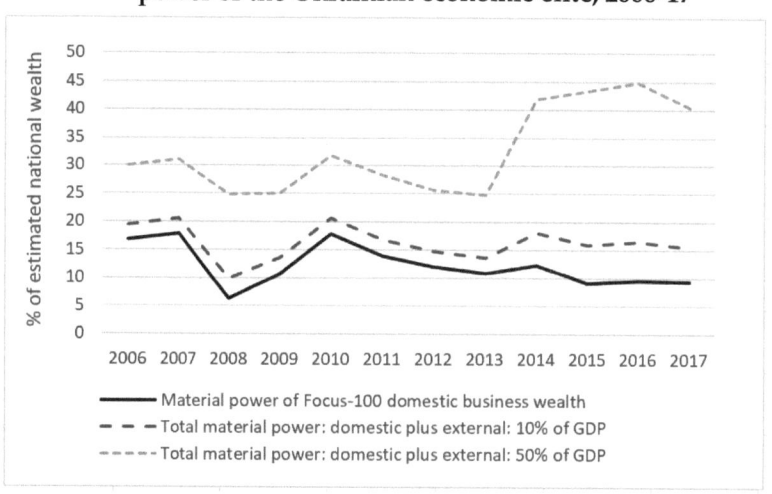

Source: Focus.ua. The Focus Ratings archive for 2006-17 data (published the following year) is available at: https://focus.ua/rating/archive. Own calculations.

At the lower estimate of foreign-held financial wealth in 2013, of 10% of GDP, total material resource power rises above 15% of Ukrainian national wealth from 2014; at the higher estimate, it rises to 40-45% of Ukrainian national wealth. This again underscores the vital role of the international wealth-management industry in the process of reproduction of the Ukrainian oligarchy.

A final reason for believing that the material basis for the political influence of oligarchs probably did not decline following the Euromaidan events, despite the fall in the value of their assets in Ukraine, is more theoretical and sociological. This is that wealth itself is a potential social and political power, realised, as Winters suggests, only in a specific institutional setting. What, then, is material resource power, or the power of highly concentrated wealth, considered in this light? It is the capacity to tilt the structure of incentives, of punishment and reward, that others face so that their interests align with yours, placing their skills and capacities in the service of your interests.

Moreover, although wealth is a potential resource power with a strong quantitative dimension—that is, the more you have of it, the more, and perhaps better-quality, professional and coercive services you are able to hire—the relation of wealth to political power is not a straightforwardly quantitative one, since its realisation must be mediated through the practices of institutional actors, sometimes in co-operation, sometimes in competition, so that strategy, tactics and contingency must come in to play, making intended political outcomes less than fully certain.

In modern Ukraine, this means that the power of wealth is realised (and replenished) primarily through business-political networks. These networks developed originally out of the late Soviet regional nomenklatura networks, which had formed somewhat distinct identities through the process of competition for party and government posts at republic level (Minakov, 2019, pp. 226-227). On this basis, the post-communist regional business-political networks were recast in the course of the struggles with rival forms of elite organisation in the 1990s, winning out over them to form a lasting, but evolving institutional relation to presidential power particular (Minakov, 2019, pp. 229-230). It is this set up, as recounted in chapter 3, that, through its flexibility and adaptability, has remained the dominant political economy structure in post-communist Ukraine ever since. Despite initial setbacks for some of the previously "ruling" business-political networks right after the Euromaidan Revolution, most of the main ones remained intact, so that their relationship with one another and with the holders of formal positional state authority continued to inform, and to be shaped by, subsequent political and economic events. Following this investigation of the dynamics of concentrated wealth and its broad relation to political power, it is time to look at the role of wealth as a means of political influence by way of an examination of patterns of voting in the Verkhovna Rada, the Ukrainian parliament, and what this reveals about its role in the reproduction of the country's political economy regime more widely.

5 Voting on institutional prosperity bills in the Verkhovna Rada, 2014-17

5.1 Preliminaries

5.1.1 Introduction and aims

The material mode of political influence of the Yanukovych era...

In 2016 a series of articles appeared in the Ukrainian press offering a glimpse into the operation of a wide-ranging and expensive system of political payments run by the Party of Regions (PoR), the political organisation of Viktor Yanukovych, in the years leading up to and during his presidency in 2010-14. Originating in the "black ledger" (off-book accounts) of Yanukovych and his circle, the documents that these articles are based on had been handed to the National Anti-Corruption Bureau of Ukraine (NABU) by Viktor Trepak, a former deputy head of the Ukrainian Security Service (SBU), allegedly in response to the blocking of his investigation into the financial crimes of the Yanukovych era (Kuznetsov, 2017; Sukhov, 2016; Tucker, 2016).

Supporting these accounts, in an interview from 2017, Taras Chornovil, who ran Yanukovych's presidential campaign in 2004, says that the PoR practice of "paying for deputies from other parliamentary factions to vote in legislative projects the party needed" was formalised and centralised from 2006. This was on the initiative of Borys Kolesnikov, a parliamentary deputy for the Opposition Bloc who is close to Rinat Akhmetov, arguably Ukraine's leading oligarch. This accounting function, says Chornovil, was taken over more narrowly by Yanukovych and his group following his victory in the 2010 presidential election (Kuznetsov, 2017).

According to the ledger, for the four years of the Yanukovych presidency, the PoR's illicit payments came to US$2bn, equal to US$500m per year (Tucker, 2016). This is a remarkably high figure for a country with an average annual GDP in this period of around US$164bn (IMF, 2019b).

Reports concur on the central role of PoR political fixers in delivering large cash sums to journalists, judges, and electoral and local authority officials, in return for favourable coverage or decisions, as well as to a well-connected US political consultant, Paul Manafort. The documents also record the details of payments to a number of political parties — both allies and opponents of the PoR — as well as to individual people's deputies (MPs) in the Verkhovna Rada, the Ukrainian parliament. The "chief curators" in the process are identified by Sevgil Musayeva, the editor of *Ukrayinska Pravda*, a Ukrainian-language online news outlet, as Yevhen Genner, one-time head of the parliamentary budget committee, and Vitaliy Kalyuzhnyi, a PoR MP (Ukrainian Crisis Media Centre, 2016). As examples of the kinds of transactions involved, the ledgers record a PoR intermediary, one V.N. Slaba, receiving US$250,000 in December 2009 to pay to Yuriy Kostenko of Our Ukraine, the party of the then president, Viktor Yushchenko (the report does not say what the payment was for). A second entry records the allocation in April 2010 of US$500,000 to Kalyuzhnyi for payment to Inna Bohoslovska (Sukhov, 2016). The suggestion is that this was in return for Bohoslovska's resignation from the PoR to stand as a candidate in the 2010 presidential election, with the aim of drawing votes away from Yuliya Tymoshenko, Yanukovych's main rival in the contest.

... carried over into the post-Euromaidan period
One of the principal demands to emerge from the Euromaidan protests of 2013/14 was for a break with just these kinds of corrupt procedures in public life (Umland, 2017). However, the revelation in 2018 of the WhatsApp texts of Oleksandr Onyshchenko, through an investigation by Hromadske TV's Slidstvo.info programme, demonstrates the continuation into the post-Euromaidan era of material means of political influence in Ukrainian public life.

The texts show Onyshchenko — at the time of the communications in 2015 a Rada deputy for People's Will — discussing the practicalities of buying votes in the Rada with deputies linked to Petro Poroshenko, who succeeded Yanukovych as Ukraine's head of state. Onyshchenko's mobile phone dialogues, in Russian, are peppered with short-hand code or slang words. One exchange from May 2015 is with Serhiy Berezenko, a faction leader in Poroshenko's eponymous party, the Petro Poroshenko Bloc (PPB). It relates to attempts to secure the appointment of Oleksiy Malovatskyi, who had worked as a lawyer for Poroshenko during his presidential campaign, to the High Council of Justice, which deals with staffing the judiciary. In the text, Onyshchenko seems to be arranging a deal to buy the voting support of Fatherland deputies on the issue, in exchange for cash. He reports that he has spoken with "Y.V." (Yuliya Vladimirovna Tymoshenko, the leader of the Fatherland party, then still part of the governing coalition), and relays that she awaits the "documents" (said to be code for an illicit monetary fee) the following day. In another exchange on an unspecified vote, Ihor Kononenko, a close business associate of Poroshenko, appears to signal his readiness to pay "the girl" (again, Tymoshenko) US$1m (Sukhov, 2018; Slidstvo, 2018).

The text dialogues implicate key Poroshenko lieutenants and cast Tymoshenko in a poor light. They also point to a continuity in informal political practices between the pre- and post-Euromaidan parliaments. This picture of continuity in the informal, material means of political influence between Rada convocations provides a backdrop for interpretation of the results of the analysis of voting patterns on institutional "prosperity" laws in the Rada later in the chapter, as well as informing its overall conclusion on the way the Rada operates within the Ukrainian political system.

At the same time, leaks to the press concerning illicit political practices cannot be taken at face value. For instance, it is alleged that the selective leak of information from Yanukovych's "black ledgers" shows one oligarchic group (that of Dmytro Firtash and Serhiy Lyovochkin) attempting to undermine another (that of Rinat Akhmetov), since the leakers were careful not to expose the names of their own associates (Kuznetsov, 2017). Using Winters' terminology, this could be read as a concrete, routine example of "lateral" competition between oligarchs (Winters, 2011, p. 66).

Focus of the chapter

As recounted in chapters 2 and 3, the political means of influence of the Ukrainian oligarchs are numerous and include election funding, network payments within the state apparatus, domination of the media, as well as the hiring of private armed force. Of these, I examine the second (payments within the state apparatus), in part because it is an under-researched channel of influence.

The focus of this chapter is therefore on tracing patterns of voting in the Rada, especially of deputies identified as associated with the "old" oligarch sub- and cross-factional groups. The aim is to investigate a key means by which oligarchs have maintained influence after the Euromaidan, in order to answer the question of whether voting patterns in the Rada in 2014-17 support the idea that the politically active heads of leading business-political networks continue to use their wealth to influence economic policy outcomes.

A key conclusion to the chapter is that, although evidence of a direct relationship of oligarchs' financial influence and the blocking of economic legislation was not as systematic as envisaged, this result may align with other findings on the way the operation of the oligarchy is expressed in the Rada—that is, as a certain fuzziness, or blurring of lines, in its internal organisational forms. The loose organisational structures of (usually not very ideological) parties and formal parliamentary factions, shot through with sub- and cross-factional formations, it is argued, are not accidental features of the Rada's workings, but characteristic ones, expressive of its role in the operation of politics within the oligarchy as a whole. In this context, oligarchs' control of votes through material means may be seen as a way of securing a seat at the negotiating table with leaders of other business-political networks, and with the holders of other kinds of power resources, in the broader contest for position and rents. The flexible mode of operation of the Rada is shown by the break of factional voting patterns between the second government of Arseniy Yatsenyuk and that of Volodymyr Hroysman. This indicates, I argue, the full recreation of the oligarchy as a transactional relation between successful politicians, state officials and most of the main big business groups.

Why the Rada?

The three governments in place between late February 2014 and December 2017 between them instituted probably the most extensive range of economic, administrative and institutional reforms undertaken so far in post-Soviet Ukraine. However, I argue, experienced political practitioners managed to pursue reform without doing fundamental damage to the institutional "essentials" of the old oligarchic system. A reason for choosing the Rada for examination, therefore, is because it is one such "essential" state institution. Specifically, the Rada performs the function of a venue for elite alliance- and deal-making, a place in which formal and informal politics intertwine, making it one of the institutional sites of the state on which the oligarchy — both as an institutional relation between the business, political and state elites, and as a forum for transactional deal-making — is realised. This is why Serhiy Leshchenko, a journalist who became a Rada deputy following the parliamentary election of October 2014, describes the Rada as "Europe's biggest business club" (Leshchenko, 2016). In this sense, it can be considered as performing some of the co-ordination and transactional functions of Lucky Luciano's "Mafia commissions" in Winters' account of oligarchy (Winters, 2011, p. 69). Moreover, my choice of the Rada voting as a topic for investigation, and its positioning in my study, is informed both by the notion of the primacy of political institutions set out in the "conjoined theory" of chapter 2, and by the cyclical "currency flow" scheme of institutional reproduction with which this study begins and ends.

The judiciary might also be considered one such "essential" state institution, since, conceived to include the "gatekeeping" role of the prosecutor general, it protects the positional and material power of the elite — especially of the part of the elite currently holding the main positions of public office — from the spectre of the even-handed application of the law. At the same time, it is one of the terrains on which the struggle of elite networks against one another takes place. Although examples of this appear in chapter 6, which examines elite economic enrichment schemes in the energy sector, in this chapter I restrict my investigation to the Rada.

5.1.2 The Rada in Ukraine's political system

Introduction

To understand the value of attempting to influence voting outcomes in the Rada, it will be helpful to know something about Ukraine's modern political system, the role of the Rada within it, as well as the functions of the Rada's main bodies. The aim is to establish the position and role of the Rada within the Ukrainian state at the onset of the post-Euromaidan era, and to address the relation of formal and informal political practices within it.

The distinction between formal and informal politics is crucial for understanding the political economy of contemporary Ukraine because, in its first post-Soviet decade, the delayed and incomplete process of state-building led to "a low degree of differentiation between the political and economic domains" and "the dominance of personal networks over legal rules" (Zimmer, 2006, p. 276). Neglect of these phenomena has left some kinds of Western scholarship unable to describe the societies of post-communist eastern Europe in their own terms, according to a framework of analysis proposed by Bálint Magyar and Bálint Madlovics (2020, pp. 8-9). Whereas formal politics deals with the officially articulated basic principles and procedures of public life—often written down as a constitution, for example—informality refers to patterns of unwritten, customary behavioural norms or rules, known implicitly to insiders, and of the personal, interest-based political actions informed by these rules that, happening behind the scenes, describe "how things really work" (Meyer, 2006, p. 14). On the relation between the two, Kerstin Zimmer argues that, rather than conceiving of them proceeding alongside or in conflict with one another, in practice the line between formal and informal political rules is blurred, as they "are not neatly separated and do not refer to different spheres of influence" (Zimmer, 2006, p. 274).

Formal politics: a changing institutional framework

The Ukrainian constitution specifies the single chamber, 450-seat Verkhovna Rada (Supreme Council) as the sole legislative body of the Ukrainian state. However, periodic change in the form of the government and of electoral rules has been a feature of Ukraine's political life since independence.

Ukraine's constitutions

Ukraine's first post-Soviet constitution was agreed only in mid-1995, and approved by the Rada a year later. Despite some amendments, linked primarily to the country's separation from the Soviet Union, this means that before 1996, the 1978 constitution of Soviet Ukraine, with its formal (but not factual) emphasis on the supremacy of the Rada, remained in place (Whitmore, 2004, p. 22, 32). In the independence era, the 1996 constitution has twice switched places with a later document, the 2004 constitution, introduced after the Orange Revolution. In the absence of a clear delineation of roles between executive and legislative branches, and exacerbated by this pattern of constitutional alternation, "the two institutional bodies engaged in turf wars over exclusive prerogatives, appointment powers, and policy priorities, which resulted in frequent political crisis" (Kudelia and Kazianov, 2021, p. 14).

The 1996 constitution introduced a semi-presidential system of governance. This is a "dual executive" mode of rule, in which "a popularly elected fixed-term president exists alongside a prime minister and cabinet which are also responsible to parliament" (Whitmore, 2004, p. 6). The two kinds of semi-presidentialism, president-parliamentary and premier-presidential, offer more or less power to the head of state within the system of joint rule. Leonid Kuchma, independent Ukraine's second president, managed during his first term in 1994-99 to secure the first version, with stronger presidential powers.

Two parliamentary elections (in 1998 and 2002) and two presidential elections (in 1999 and 2004) took place under the 1996 constitution. A significant overhaul was only agreed in December 2004 as a central element in talks between the two sides in the Orange Revolution. Preparations for constitutional change were already under way, however. Confronted with the prospect of a win for Viktor Yushchenko, the opposition leader, "Kuchma initiated another round of constitutional revisions, now meant to transfer most of the president's powers over cabinet formation to parliament" (Kudelia and Kazianov, 2021, p. 16). Kuchma's motivation, these authors suggest, was not just to retain for his own group key positions in the executive through their slight majority in the legislature, but also to protect himself from investigations over past serious wrongdoings, including his alleged instigation of the murder of a journalist, Georgiy Gongadze. For the Orange camp, agreement on a new constitution may have been a way of avoiding violence and containing threats of "separatism" (Wilson, 2015, p. 321).

Implemented only at the start of 2006, the 2004 constitution reduced the powers of the president and enhanced those of parliament. Most importantly, under the 2004 constitution, the prime minister is selected and dismissed by parliament, rather than by the president (Zimmer, 2006, p. 280; Europa, 2018, pp. 542-543).

After his election as president in early 2010, Yanukovych was able by October to pressure the Constitutional Court into reinstating the 1996 constitution (Wilson, 2015, p. 344). By the end of February 2014, however, political fortunes had turned again and the Rada voted to restore the 2004 constitution (Wilson, 2014, p. 92), so that the formal capacities of the president and prime minister were again more evenly distributed.

Rules for elections to the Rada
Likewise, the system used to elect deputies to the Rada has been altered several times since independence. Starting in the immediate post-Soviet period with a territorial "single mandate" system, ahead of the 1998 general election Kuchma initiated a switch to a "mixed" system, whereby half the seats in the legislature (225) continued to be chosen by single mandates, but the other half were allocated by a proportional system, according to placement on each party's list of ranked candidates. In the single-mandate system, parliamentary deputies are elected by simple majority in single-seat constituencies. Under Ukraine's proportional system, the country represents a single constituency, with seats distributed to parties according to the size of their vote, so long as they pass a 5% threshold. For the Rada elections of 2006 and 2007, a pure proportional system was in operation. In 2012, the mixed system was restored. This allowed the PoR

to maintain its parliamentary dominance in the election of that October via the single-mandate system, amid falling support in the polls (Fedorenko et al, 2016, p. 611).

The formal political framework in 2014 vs 2012
Moving from the more presidential system in place for most of the Yanukovych era, this means that a more balanced version of the "dual executive" system of government was in operation from late February 2014, limiting the range of formal presidential powers available to Petro Poroshenko after his election victory in May. Attempts post-Euromaidan to switch back to a proportional electoral system were unsuccessful until 2015, so that the October 2014 parliamentary elections took place under the "mixed" system reintroduced in 2012. A common criticism of the single-mandate scheme is that it is more susceptible to manipulation at the local level, acting as a link between local and national elites (Andrusiv et al, 2018, p. 64), and weakening the party system by making single-mandate candidates dependent on financiers rather than parties (Dabrowski, 2017b). An argument in favour of the proportional party list is that it helps to institutionalise party politics (Fedorenko et al, 2016, p. 611).

This alignment in 2014 of a more "open" premier-presidential constitution with the "mixed" system for electing deputies to the Rada has been unique in the independence period, signalling relatively weak presidential powers (as under Yushchenko after 2006), but with retention of the single mandate perhaps favouring a return to the legislature of experienced representatives of informal networks, even amid high rate of turnover in people's deputies.

Informal politics in action
The role of the constitution has been central to recent theorisations of the dynamics of power in political systems such as Ukraine's. While key informal actors, often at the head of powerful networks, are seen to dominate the political process, their political actions are structured by expectations about who ultimately will control formal rules and powers. This is a central theme of the general political sociology of post-Soviet space of Henry Hale (2015), whose

approach has been taken up by other authors. In particular, interest has focused on the way in which constitutional change affects the behaviour of these informal actors, including the overlapping networks of business leaders, politicians and officials which I am referring to as "the oligarchy".

In countries with political cultures similar to that of Ukraine — variously described as either "neo-patrimonial" (Zimmer and Matsiyevsky) or "patronal" (Hale) — the kind of constitution in place is characterised as encouraging the development of either unified or competing informal network "pyramids". These are hierarchical organisations of personal links that reach up to the "chief patron", who sits atop the formal structures of power. The chief patron is often the president, but could be the holder of another high public office. Neo-patrimonialism is a concept developed from two of the categories of political authority originally proposed by Max Weber, a German social theorist. Whereas patrimonialism can be described as traditional authority based on personal kinship ties, "rational-legal" authority is associated with the rise of administrative bureaucracy within the modern nation state (Giddens, 1971, pp. 156-160). The "neo" signifies a fusion or equilibrium of the two, "where the patrimonial logic in encrypted into the formal institutions" (Zimmer, 2006, p. 284). In contrast, patronalism, according to Hale, is a broader concept, indicating the way in which neo-patrimonial polity is itself embedded in a society, the interlinks with which help to sustain it (Hale, 2015, pp. 24-25).

For the enquiry of this chapter, the specific constitutional and electoral arrangements in place post-Euromaidan are important, therefore, because the form of the constitution affects the distribution of formal governmental powers. Not only does this set the position and powers of the Rada within the Ukrainian political system more broadly, but it also shapes the expectations of leading political actors, thereby influencing the dynamics of alignment of formal and informal Rada factions, and so also voting outcomes. Meanwhile, the electoral rules in place in October 2014 conditioned how the members of the Rada for the eighth convocation were chosen — and therefore who was chosen.

5.1.3 Rada factions and committees

A basic distinction made in this chapter is between formal Rada factions on the one hand, and sub- or cross-factional formations on the other, the compositions of which can be fluid in the course of a parliamentary term. The dynamics of factional change in the seventh and eighth parliamentary convocations will be shown in due course. Addressed here is the role of the internal bodies of the Rada most relevant to this study, especially the factions system.

What are parliamentary factions?

Blocs, parties, factions and deputy groups are all terms used to refer to formal political groupings in the Verkhovna Rada, ranging from the most to the least encompassing. Precisely how they differ, however, is harder to pin down. For instance, the Rada's official regulations (*rehlament*) mention parliamentary factions and groups, rather than political parties, as the main organising units for the activity of people's deputies (Verkhovna Rada, 2010). Factions and groups are treated slightly differently in the document, but deputy groups have the same rights as factions, and there seems to be no attempt to distinguish between them in terms of functions.

Tentatively, factions could be assumed to be based more on shared political criteria, and deputy groups on MPs' shared policy interests (such as security or budget issues). The first assumption is in line with the definition of factions, offered by Sarah Whitmore, as politically based associations of deputies, which are supposed to be organised around a party, but need not be (Whitmore, 2004, pp. 49-50). On the second, in an investigation of Poroshenko's party in parliament after the 2014 general election, *Ukrayinska Pravda* notes that deputy groups may be formed around MPs' common policy or lobbying interests, or used as a means of party management (Romanyuk and Kravets, 2016a). The dividing line between the categories can appear indistinct, however. So, for example, according to the website of the Rada, the leading parliamentary parties of the seventh and eighth convocations (the PoR and the PPB) are listed as factions, whereas others, smaller and of more recent creation, are listed as groups (eg Economic Development).

Factions remain weakly institutionalised

Sarah Whitmore outlines the constitutive role of the Rada in the formation of the post-Soviet Ukrainian state—that is, by laying its legal foundation—and the slow process of its institutionalisation in a wider political context in the 1990s and early 2000s (Whitmore, 2004, p. 31). By institutionalisation, she means the creation and observation of procedural norms that enhance organisational coherence and autonomy (Whitmore, 2004, pp. 10-11, p. 179).

Whitmore details the emergence of parliamentary standing committees and factions as the main organisational subdivisions for the allocation of parliamentary work. By 2003, parliamentary factions had "assumed prime position in structuring and organising the Verkhovna Rada...and were the dominant force inside parliament influencing deputies' voting decisions and articulated alternative policy proposals" (Whitmore, 2004, p. 185). Despite their position in the Rada after 1998, however, Whitmore concludes that the institutionalisation of the faction system had occurred patchily and in spurts, so that factions "remained fluid and mutable units, unable to co-operate beyond ad hoc agreements" (Whitmore, 2004, p. 185). Continuing institutional weakness was shown by the routine violation of the legislature's rules, alongside the survival of "customs" of operational behaviour outside of this formal framework. This has hindered the ability of the Rada as a whole to act independently, she argues, and to hold the executive to account (Whitmore, 2004, p. 92, 185).

The weakness of the Ukrainian party system

One way of understanding the predominance of the factional system in the Rada is through a grasp of the persistent weakness of Ukraine's party system. Fedorenko et al argue that, while stronger political competition was achieved after the fall of Yanukovych, Ukraine's party system remains weakly institutionalised (2016, p. 628). Over the long term, this is seen in the large number and high turnover of parties. The factors behind the underinstitutionalisation of the Ukrainian party system include frequent changes in electoral law; the tendency for parties to be vehicles for leading politicians; and long-term inconsistency in voter preferences.

The Ukrainian Institute for the Future (UIF), a local think-tank, goes further. It suggests that three kinds of relations between Rada deputies and the heads of large financial industrial groups (FIGs) help to explain the formation of the cross-factional groupings that run through the Rada. The first is of deputies on the payroll of oligarchs whose place on a party list has been paid for by them. The second is of deputies who made it into the legislature independently, but who have entered into mutually beneficial relations with an oligarch. The third is of deputies who run their own businesses, but need protection (Andrusiv et al, 2018, p. 8). Alongside the personality-based political vehicles, the authors suggest, a kind of organisation flourishes which they call "leader-type" parties (*partiyi vozhdystskoho typu*; Andrusiv et al, 2018, p. 64). The raison d'être of these organisations is to operate as a service provider to the very rich — in this case, providing legislative votes. This reading ties in well with the theory that oligarchs' politics tends to focus on the acquisition of wealth-defence services, which vary by political-institutional context. Named among this group are Oleh Lyashko's Radicals, Fatherland under Yuliya Tymoshenko and Svoboda (Freedom). The report concludes that the crosscutting of informal political groupings through and within formal ones is a key impediment to the development of a functioning party system. "If the backbone of any faction consists of lobbyists for the interests of individual financial and industrial groups," they add, "there is no chance of any ideology" (Andrusiv et al, 2018, p. 64). The tendency for Ukrainian parties to lack a clear or consistent ideological platform is noted by all of the above authors, while the stress on political organisation based on networks of personal links rather than a shared political world view is a feature of Hale's account of a patronal political culture. It further helps to explain the parties' institutional infirmity, but has broader implications. This is because it is said to hinder the establishment of an exchange process vital for the development and maintenance of socio-political cohesion and stability in a democratic polity, whereby competitive parties act as a medium for representing divergent social interests in the political sphere, so inculcating trust in political institutions and strengthening their legitimacy (Fedorenko et al, 2016, p. 615).

5.1.4 Data sources, data sets and methods

Data sources
The main data set analysed in this chapter is of voting results across formal and cross-factional parliamentary formations on 23 laws associated with the conditions required for economic prosperity. The sources are the website of the Verkhovna Rada, along with the Ukrainian business and political press. The methods are descriptive and inferential statistics, combined with document analysis.

Legislative roll-call results
The Rada maintains an online archive, in Ukrainian, of its plenary meetings (*plenarni zasidannya*), stretching back to 1990. Here, it is possible to search through the laws of each plenary meeting by convocation and session. "Convocation" (*sklykannya*) is the name for the whole parliamentary term following a general election. The focus of this chapter is on the last two sessions of the seventh convocation (February-November 2014) after the Euromaidan, and the first seven (out of ten) sessions of the eighth convocation (December 2014-December 2017). The reason for concentrating on voting patterns after the Euromaidan is that the central interest of this book is to trace the reconstitutive process of the institutional cycle.

Deputies' formal factions
For each bill, the Rada archive reports voting roll-calls by deputy (in alphabetical order) and by formal parliamentary faction. From these tables, it is possible to work out the factional voting patterns as recorded at the time of each vote, and from this, the dynamics of the formal parliamentary factions over time. For this study, I transcribed into two data sets the composition of these factions at three points during the final stages of the seventh convocation (from the end of February 2014), and at four points over a span of the eighth convocation (from December 2014 to December 2017).

Sources for sub- and cross-factional Rada groupings
Informal Rada associations of MPs operate within, as well as across, the formal ones. These formations are recognised among specialist local journalists to be headed either by a prominent politician within

a formal faction or to fall in the "orbit" a high-profile "old" oligarch. In the eighth convocation, there were at least six such "old" oligarch formations identifiable—three larger and three smaller. These are shown in Table 5.1. All of the figures mentioned have appeared on the Focus Ratings rich list. Vitaliy Khomutynnik, the Renaissance faction leader, is perhaps the least recognisable of them, but is included because, according to media reports, in 2014 he was the richest Ukrainian MP, and became an independent player during Hroysman's premiership (Chernyshev et al, 2017).

To take account of the fluidity of cross-factional Rada groupings, I make use of earlier and later versions of the "old" oligarch groups. The "early" snapshot is taken from an account by Kristina Berdinskikh in *Novoye Vremya* from May 2015 (Berdinskikh, 2015; the fourth column of Table 5.1). For a later period, I compiled a picture of the composition of cross-factional Rada formations mainly from a series of articles in *Ukrayinska Pravda* (Romanyuk and Kravets, 2016a, 2016b, 2016c, 2017a, 2017b, 2017c, 2018). In these, the authors detail the genesis, composition and changing political alliances between many of the formal political factions and their cross-factional subcomponents. This information was checked and augmented using a long article (Chernyshev et al, 2017) on Liga.net, an online news outlet. Finally, the purported informal factional divisions for the later period were checked against the factional subgroups in the eighth convocation that were quantified in a report by the UIF (Andrusiv et al, 2018). The results are recorded in the fifth column of Table 5.1.

The table shows a considerable, but not perfect, overlap of the deputies included in the earlier and later accounts of the cross-factional formations. There are 66 named Rada deputies identified as belonging to an "old" oligarch faction in the earlier cohort, and 53 in the later one, with the number on at least one list coming to 74. This is a small portion of all of the MPs in the eighth convocation, and may well be smaller than the actual figure of those who were working in co-operation with the leaders of big business. However, the table includes a reasonable number of cases with which to conduct a meaningful analysis of the interweaving voting patterns of formal and cross-factional Rada political groups.

Table 5.1: Deputies in the 8th convocation of the Rada by "old" oligarch group & formal faction

	Deputy		Informal faction			Formal faction	
No.	Surname	Initials	1	2	3	4	5
1	Batenko	T.I.	K	K	K	PPB	NF
2	Bereza	YU.M.	K	-	K	PF	PF
3	Bondar	V.V.	-	K	K	Ren	Ren
4	Herashchenko	A.YU.	K	-	K	PF	PF
5	Hyeller	YE.B.	K	K	K	Ren	Ren
6	Denysenko	A.S.	K	K	K	NF	NF
7	Didych	V.V.	K	K	K	NF	NF
8	Dubinin	O.I.	K	K	K	NF	NF
9	Kupriy	V.M.	K	K	K	NF	NF
10	Parasyuk	V.Z.	K	-	K	NF	NF
11	Savchenko	N.V.	-	K	K	Father	Father
12	Savchuk	YU.P.	-	K	K	PF	PPB
13	Semenchenko	S.I.	K	-	K	SP	SP
14	Filatov	B.A.	K	-	K	NF	-
15	Shevchenko	O.L.	K	K	K	PPB	NF
16	Shypko	A.F.	K	K	K	Ren	Ren
17	Yarosh	D.A.	K	-	K	NF	NF
18	Bakhteyeva	T.D.	A	A	A	OB	OB
19	Bilyi	O.P.	A	A	A	OB	OB
20	Vilkul	O.YU.	A	A	A	OB	OB
21	Voropayev	YU.M.	A	A	A	OB	OB
22	Halchenko	A.V.	A	A	A	OB	OB
23	Husak	V.H.	A	A	A	OB	OB
24	Dobkin	D.M.	A	A	A	OB	OB
25	Dobkin	M.M.	A	A	A	OB	OB
26	Dolzhenkov	O.V.	A	A	A	OB	OB
27	Zvyahilskyi	YU.L.	A	A	A	OB	OB
28	Kolyesnikov	D.V.	A	A	A	OB	OB
29	Korolevska	N.YU.	A	A	A	OB	OB
30	Martovytskyi	A.V.	A	A	A	OB	OB
31	Moroko	YU.M.	A	A	A	OB	OB
32	Novynskyi	V.V.	A	A	A	OB	OB
33	Omelyanovych	D.S.	A	A	A	OB	OB
34	Pavlov	K.YU.	A	-	A	OB	OB
35	Sazhko	S.M.	A	A	A	OB	OB
36	Solod	YU.V.	A	A	A	OB	OB
37	Shpenov	D.YU.	A	A	A	OB	OB
38	Kozak	T.R.	M	M	M	OB	OB
39	Nimchenko	V.I.	M	M	M	OB	OB
40	Shurma	I.M.	M	-	M	OB	OB
41	Shufrych	N.I.	M	M	M	OB	OB
42	Bezbakh	YA.YA.	P	-	P	NF	NF

Table continued overleaf...

Table 5.1: Deputies in the 8th convocation of the Verkhovna Rada by "old" oligarch group & formal faction

No.	Deputy Surname	Initials	Informal faction 1	2	3	Formal faction 4	5
43	Byelkova	O.V.	P	-	P	PPB	PPB
44	Katser-Buchkovska	N.V.	-	P	P	PF	PF
45	Klympush-Tsyntsadze	I.O.	P	-	P	PPB	-
46	Ostapchuk	V.M.	-	Kh	Kh	Ren	Ren
47	Pysarenko	V.V.	-	Kh	Kh	Ren	Ren
48	Svyatash	D.V.	-	Kh	Kh	Ren	Ren
49	Khomutynnik	V.YU.	K	Kh	Kh	Ren	Ren
50	Ahafonova	N.V.	L	-	FLB	PPB	PPB
51	Bakulin	YE.M.	B	FLB	FLB	OB	OB
52	Bereza	B.YU.	L	-	FLB	NF	NF
53	Boyko	YU.A.	B	FLB	FLB	OB	OB
54	Dunayev	S.V.	B	FLB	FLB	OB	OB
55	Ioffe	YU.YA.	B	FLB	FLB	OB	OB
56	Kaplin	S.M.	L	-	FLB	PPB	PPB
57	Kunitsyn	S.V.	F	-	FLB	PPB	PPB
58	Larin	S.M.	L	FLB	FLB	OB	OB
59	Lytvyn	V.M.	L	FLB	FLB	PW	PW
60	Lyovochkin	S.V.	L	FLB	FLB	OB	OB
61	Lyovochkina	YU.V.	L	FLB	FLB	OB	OB
62	Melnychuk	S.P.	L	FLB	FLB	PW	PW
63	Myrnyi	I.M.	F	FLB	FLB	OB	OB
64	Miroshnychenko	YU.R.	L	FLB	FLB	OB	OB
65	Moskalenko	YA.M.	B	-	FLB	PW	PW
66	Nechayev	O.I.	F	-	FLB	OB	OB
67	Pavlenko	YU.O.	L	FLB	FLB	OB	OB
68	Papiyev	M.M.	-	FLB	FLB	OB	OB
69	Prodan	O.P.	F	-	FLB	PPB	PPB
70	Skoryk	M.L.	L	FLB	FLB	OB	OB
71	Tryhubenko	S.M.	F	-	FLB	PPB	PPB
72	Fursin	I.H.	F	FLB	FLB	PW	PW
73	Chepynoha	V.M.	L	-	FLB	PPB	PPB
74	Chervakova	O.V.	L	-	FLB	PPB	PPB

Sources: Berdinskikh (2015), *Novoye Vremya*. Romanyuk & Kravets (2016a), (2016b), (2016c), (2017a), (2017b), (2017c), (2018), *Ukrayinska Pravda*. Chernyshev et al (2017), LIGA.net. Key: a) K = Kolomoyskyi; A = Akhmetov; M = Medvedchuk; P = Pinchuk; F = Firtash; L= Lyovochkin; B = Boyko; Kh = Khomutynnik. b) PPB = Petro Poroshenko Bloc; PF = People's Front; Ren = Renaissance; NF = no faction; Father = Fatherland; SP = Samopomich; OB = Opposition Bloc; PW = People's Will. c) A dash means no information was given for network association. d) Informal factions: 1: Apr-May 2015; 2: 2016-17; 3: 2015-17. e) Formal factions: 4: Apr 9th 2015; 5: Jun 2nd 2016.

Timeline and periodisation

Since a large number of laws were submitted and processed by the Rada over the period of study, the criteria for choosing which ones to examine is one important consideration. Another is the periodisation of the timeline in which the voting took place.

With the aid of two sources in particular – a US political science paper by Magelinski et al (2019) that identifies marked shifts in the pattern of voting in the Ukrainian parliament by means of computer modelling, and the *Europa Regional Survey* (2018), which provides political timelines for east European countries – I derived three broad political divisions for my study. The first analytical period starts with the "critical juncture" of the Euromaidan, paving the way for the first, interim administration of Arseniy Yatsenyuk, from late February 2014 until November 2014. The second is marked by the span of the subsequent Yatsenyuk government, from December 2014 until April 2016. It follows the pre-term general election of late 2014 and ends with the appointment of the new administration of Volodymyr Hroysman, which lasted past the end of my study period, of December 2017. This scheme allows me to propose explanations for the disruption in Rada voting patterns, and the factional realignments underlying them, in terms of key political and economic events of the preceding period.

Choice of laws

On the choice of laws, I restrict my analysis to those that correspond to the "inclusive" political economy rules associated with the generation of broad-based economic affluence, according to modern institutional economics. In the first instance, this means selecting laws that align with the criteria taken from the theory of Acemoglu and Robinson, as outlined in chapter 2. Private property rights, and an impartial judiciary with the capacity to enforce them, are among the main inclusive economic rules. Others are low barriers to market entry and active state support for entrepreneurial activity.

What I am calling the institutional theory of prosperity is similar to, but not identical with, some alternative approaches to assessing an economy's legal and institutional preparedness to encourage investment and productivity growth as a means of expanding the capacity to generate output and accumulate wealth. One such alternative approach assesses the factors affecting the conditions in which a country's firms function. An example of this is the Doing Business index (World Bank, 2020), which ranks countries according to how easily their regulations allow companies to operate. A second hones in on innovation. Drawing on the ideas of Joseph Schumpeter, an Austrian economist, Janos Kornai, for example, outlines the "general" systemic characteristics required for dynamic entrepreneurial innovation. This includes decentralisation of initiative, the prospect of a "gigantic" reward, competition, space for experimentation and access to financing (Kornai, 2010, pp. 640-641). These alternative approaches offer more room for manoeuvre in the choice of "prosperity" laws than just using the criteria from *Why Nations Fail* alone.

Data set preparation

With the analytical timelines and criteria for law selection in place, and using the Rada's legislative archive and information gathered from local journalistic sources, I prepared two data sets of voting by individual people's deputies on selected "prosperity" laws by faction—one for the fourth and fifth sessions of the seventh convocation, after February 2014, and one for the eighth convocation, up until December 2017. To identify bills, I combed through the lists of legislation presented in the Rada's plenary meetings across the three analytical periods. The first data set consists of six "business environment" laws, although I was unable to find specific information on the informal groups aligned to "old" oligarchs in this period. For the second data set, for which information on such cross-factional associations was outlined above, I selected 17 laws across three categories, relating to aspects of reform of the business environment ("BE" on Table 5.5), to institutional political or judicial changes ("PP", for "political pluralism"), or to sectoral laws ("S") linked to the business interests of leading "old" oligarchs. For the three analytical periods, Table 5.5 below, placed just ahead of the second analysis of this chapter, presents a summary of the 23 selected bills and the voting results in chronological order.

5.2 Voting patterns in the Rada on "prosperity" legislation: three analyses

5.2.1 Outline of the Rada analyses

With an analytical timeline in place and the legislation selected for examination, the second half of the chapter presents the results of three interlinked analyses.

The first analysis addresses the political situation in the run up to the pre-term parliamentary election of October 2014, along with its results. It focuses on the patterns of change and continuity within and between legislative convocations, as well as overlaps of Rada deputies with the Focus-100 rich list from chapter 4. These offer a glimpse into the means of reproduction of Ukraine's elite after the Euromaidan victory, and of the fusion of economic power and political office in the persons of key actors.

A second analysis examines the intertwining voting patterns of the formal factional with sub- and cross-factional Rada formations on the selected "institutional prosperity" bills across the three analytical periods. The investigation is structured around a distinction between the *propensity* of Rada groups to support reform laws (the changing shares of each group backing the bills) and their *capacity* to do so (their voting weight in parliament). The results are put into their political and economic context by way of explanation. A key finding is that, after the disintegration of the five-party coalition, additional backing for the legislation came from the successor parties of Yanukovych's PoR, as well as the sub- and cross-factional groups of the "old" oligarchs linked with them.

A third analysis uses cross tables and inferential statistics to check for a systematic relationship between membership of the purported "old" oligarch Rada factions and the pattern of support for political-economic reform legislation in the eighth convocation. An apparent statistically significant relationship showing "old" oligarch MPs failing to support "prosperity" legislation more consistently than other MPs breaks down, however, when controlled for the distinction between "coalition" and "opposition".

5.2.2 Continuity and change in and between Radas

In late July 2014 a pre-term election was initiated by the withdrawal of two parties from the first post-Euromaidan governing coalition. The new president, Petro Poroshenko, dissolved parliament a month later, in accordance with the restored 2004 constitution (Shevel, 2015, p. 159).

Aspects of change

Factional dynamics in the seventh convocation
In the Rada, the period of the interim government is characterised by two main developments. The first was the rise to dominance of an unofficial coalition of parliamentary parties, formerly in opposition, led by politicians who had backed the Euromaidan protests. This coalition included Fatherland, with Arseniy Yatsenyuk and Oleksandr Turchynov taking the main leadership roles; UDAR, of Vitaliy Klychko, a successful boxer; and the nationalist Svoboda (Freedom) party, headed by Oleh Tyahnybok.

The second was the rapid but incomplete disintegration of the formerly ruling Party of Regions (PoR). Its breakaway MPs tended to re-form into two new deputy groups, Economic Development and Sovereign European Ukraine. The period saw the formal disappearance of the Communist faction, the junior party in the outgoing Yanukovych administration, many of whose members formed the core of the For Peace and Stability group following the passage of de-communisation laws in July 2014. In Figure 5.1 below I have gathered together these three breakaway groups under the "post-Euromaidan" label. The chart conveys the scale of the factional change. It shows the number of deputies registered as members of the PoR (the leftmost cluster of bars) dropping from 183 MPs towards the start of the parliamentary term (the tallest, darkest grey of the leftmost bars) to just 76 by August 2014, a loss of 107 MPs, or almost 60% of the total. The rise of the "post-Euromaidan" groupings, represented by the two bars second-farthest to the right, is almost a mirror image of this, rising from just one MP at the start to 112 MPs by August. The absence of third, light grey column for the Communists indicates their disappearance as a formal political formation after July. These seismic shifts in parliamentary organisation were driven mainly by the institutional rupture triggered by political violence and the toppling of the Yanukovych presidency as a culmination of the Euromaidan mass protests.

Of the pro-Euromaidan parties, only Fatherland suffered noticeable losses in this period. In contrast, the parliamentary factions of UDAR and Svoboda maintained broad organisational integrity throughout, so that their bar clusters are almost flat.

Figure 5.1: Formal factional dynamics in the 7th convocation of the Rada, 2012-14

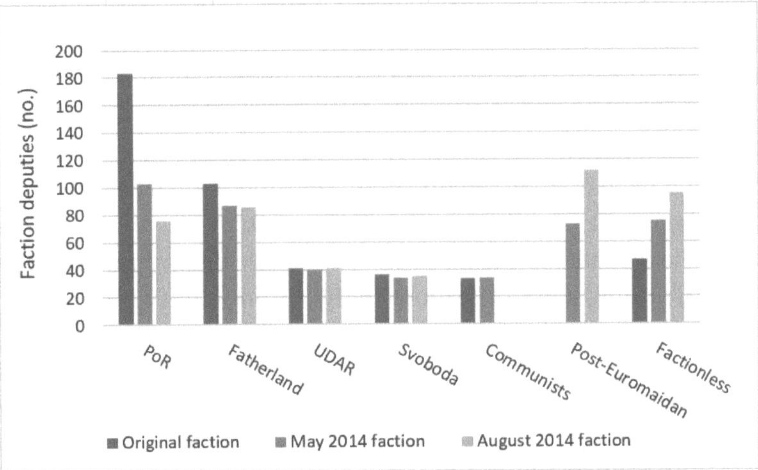

Sources: Verkhovna Rada, online archive. Available: https://iportal.rada.gov.ua/. Own calculations. Note: PoR: Party of Regions.

Party-political changes between elections

The Rada that emerged from the pre-term parliamentary election of October 2014 was quite different from those that came before — featuring, for example, a high turnover in personnel, so that about two-thirds of deputies in the new parliament had not been present in the seventh convocation[16].

---

[16] This was estimated by comparing the Rada lists of MPs for each parliamentary term using the conditional formatting function in Excel.

With a "mixed" electoral system in place in both cases, Table 5.2 below sets out the results for the 2012 and the 2014 legislative elections. It is based on the parties' performance in the (proportional) national vote, but shows also the single-mandate seats for the parties that passed the 5% national threshold. It gives an indication of the parties' legislative voting weight at the start of the seventh and eighth convocations. The table shows the PoR as the dominant party at the start of the seventh convocation in late 2012, with a total of 185 seats in the 450-seat chamber. Similarly, in 2014 the new president's party, the Petro Poroshenko Bloc (PB), led the field at the start of the eighth convocation, with 132 seats. In combination with 82 seats of the other main coalition party, People's Front (PF), this took their total to 214. A commonality between the two parliamentary terms is that, in both, "presidential" parties relied on single-mandate districts for most of their seats.

The 2014 contest marked the emergence, for the first time since independence, of a (nominally) pro-Western, pro-market parliamentary majority in the Rada. With the formation of a five-party governing coalition in its wake, this developed into a constitutional majority, including through co-option of independents to the president's PPB (Shevel, 2015, p. 160). Centring on the PPB and PF of Arseniy Yatsenyuk, returning as prime minister, the coalition included other parties that had supported the mass protests against the Yanukovych government. These were Samopomich (Self-Reliance), with its roots in western Ukraine; the Radical Party, headed by a former journalist, Oleh Lyashko; and a much-reduced Fatherland, again led by Yuliya Tymoshenko.

The converse of the success of these "Westernising" political forces was a poor electoral showing of the parties that evolved from the PoR, alongside the disappearance from the Rada — for the first time in the contemporary era — of an organised Communist faction. The main body of the PoR's surviving MPs reconstituted themselves as the Opposition Bloc, but with only 29 seats, greatly diminished in size and shorn of some of the most prominent PoR leaders.

Table 5.2: Results of Rada elections in Ukraine for parties taking seats in the national vote, 2012 & 2014

Party	National vote (%)	Seats (no.) Party list	Single mandate	Total	Share (%)
October 2012 election					
Governing					
Party of Regions (PoR)	30.0	72	113	185	41.1
Communist Party (CPU)	13.2	32	0	32	7.1
Opposition					
Fatherland	25.6	62	39	101	22.4
Ukrainian Democratic Alliance for Reform (UDAR)	14.0	34	6	40	8.9
Svoboda (Freedom)	10.5	25	12	37	8.2
October 2014 election					
Governing					
People's Front	22.1	64	18	82	18.2
Petro Poroshenko Bloc (PPB)	21.8	63	69	132	29.3
Samopomich (Self-Reliance)	11.0	32	1	33	7.3
Radical Party	7.4	22	0	22	4.9
Fatherland	5.7	17	2	19	4.2
Opposition					
Opposition Bloc	9.4	27	2	29	6.4
Other					
Independents	-	-	96	96	21.3

Sources: The Central Election Commission of Ukraine, (2012, 2014), Election of people's deputies of Ukraine. Available: https://bit.ly/391gkuj. Shevel (2015).

Between them, these two developments left the "pro-Russian" camp in the Rada greatly weakened. This reflected not just the discrediting of Yanukovych's associates, or revelations following his fall of the exorbitant corruption that had flourished under his rule, or the process of "de-communisation", but also Russia's drastic response to his flight, reducing the traditional voting base of the PoR/Opposition Bloc through its military takeover of Crimea and destabilisation of east Ukrainian regions. In due course, however, the parliamentary numbers of the opposition were bolstered by the emergence, from MPs returned to the legislature as independents, of other successor factions to the Yanukovych-era ruling party — namely, People's Will and Renaissance.

As a consequence of these developments, expectations on the prospects of rapid and thoroughgoing reform were raised to their highest pitch since the immediate aftermath of the Orange Revolution, almost a decade before. Moreover, contrary to the thrust of Russia's large-scale propaganda campaign, portraying the downfall of Yanukovych as the result, not of domestically generated popular protest, but of a foreign-inspired fascist coup, the Ukrainian far right—in the form of Svoboda and Pravyi Sector—performed poorly in the 2014 election, receiving between them only a handful of single-mandate seats.

Although it is possible, therefore, to depict the results of the 2014 election in ideological terms—as greatly diminishing or excluding the parties of the far left and far right, for example—the application of such labels can be misleading, since Ukrainian parties do not tend to perform the same role as in liberal democratic political systems, precisely because of enduring strong overlaps of the public and private worlds, of political and economic institutions and personnel. A recent account underscores this point, contrasting the role of parties in a liberal democratic setting with those in similar settings to Ukraine. Rather than a means of articulating popular policies through established political channels, so helping to legitimise them, in a post-communist setting, with its specific institutional and political culture, parties are viewed as a vehicle for the integration and operation of hierarchical informal networks within the formal political framework (Magyar and Madlovics, 2020, pp. 150-151). This understanding resonates with the account earlier in the chapter of the purported role of certain parties of the eighth convocation—the Radicals and Fatherland, according to some sources (Andrusiv et al, 2018, p. 63)—which appeared to act as a "buffer" between the population and the elite, showing a populist, anti-establishment face to the electorate to win seats, but then marketing to the elite the parliamentary voting rights so gained.

Factional dynamics in the eighth convocation
Compared with the seventh convocation, the scale of factional change is much less dramatic in the eighth convocation, despite the increased fragmentation of the parliamentary scene. Key developments include not only the disappearance of Economic Development, a "post-PoR" grouping, and the corresponding rise

of Renaissance, a nominally "pro-Russian" grouping linked to Kolomoyskyi (Romanyuk and Kravets, 2017a), but also the reduction in membership of the president's party in the course of the parliamentary term, which may have been due both to the loss of some MPs following a fallout with Kolomoyskyi in March 2015, as well as by the "loan" of some MPs to People's Will later that year to allow it to form an independent parliamentary faction (Romanyuk and Kravets, 2017b).

Aspects of continuity

Factional origin and destination of re-elected deputies
The re-election of people's deputies from the seventh convocation represents a notable line of continuity between the two parliaments. For the period under study, up until December 2017, 156 out of 454 individuals who sat as deputies in the eighth convocation had also been deputies in the seventh[17]. This means that roughly one-third of the legislators in the new parliament were "old hands", while around two-thirds were first-time deputies — a high ratio in comparison with previous parliaments, reflecting the disruptive impact of revolutionary political events. Table 5.3 below shows the factional change for 148 of these "old hands" between the end of the seventh convocation, in August 2014, and early on in the eighth convocation, in April 2015. The figures emboldened in the body of the table show the main destination faction, set out in the row headings, of each origin faction in the column headings.

- The largest contingent of these MPs — one-quarter of the total, or 37 deputies — ended up in the new president's party, the PPB.
- Around one-quarter of the re-elected parliamentarians came from the Fatherland faction, the biggest single supplier of returning MPs (38). Of these, only about one-fifth remained in the party under Tymoshenko, while 55% joined People's Front (PF), the new organisation of

---

[17] The figure of 454 is higher than the number of MPs elected in October 2014, of 423, as some MPs left the institution and were replaced.

Yatsenyuk and Turchynov, the Fatherland leaders at the time of the Euromaidan. Another fifth joined the PPB.
- Just over one-third of the politicians re-elected to the eighth convocation came from the one of the formerly ruling parties under Yanukovych, or one of the factions formed from them. Of those from the PoR proper, just over 60% (13 out of 21 returning MPs) ended up in the Opposition Bloc, while the bulk of the "post-Euromaidan" deputies from the seventh convocation, or about 80% of them (26 out of 32), split evenly between the People's Will and Renaissance successor groups in the eighth.
- Unaligned MPs accounted for roughly one-fifth of the parliamentary veterans who managed to enter the new parliament, and UDAR a little less than that. While almost the entire UDAR contingent joined the president's PPB (reflecting a pre-election deal between the two leaders), only 17% of factionless deputies did likewise.
- Although returning MPs formed only one-third of the complement of the new parliament, they made up around 46% of the "old" oligarch informal factions identified by *Novoye Vremya* and *Ukrayinska Pravda* (Table 5.1).

Table 5.3: The changing formal factional allegiances between Radas of re-elected deputies, 2014-15

Destination Apr 2015 (v)	Origin Aug 2014 (>) PoR	Post-PoR	No faction	Fatherland	UDAR	Svoboda
PPB	-	3.1	17.2	21.1	95.8	-
PF	-	3.1	3.5	55.3	-	-
OB	61.9	-	20.7	-	-	-
No faction	14.3	12.5	31.0		-	100.0
Self-Reliance	-	-	-	2.6	-	-
Radicals	-	-	6.9	-	4.2	-
PW	4.8	40.6	13.8	-	-	-
Fatherland	-	-	-	21.1	-	-
Renaissance	19.1	40.6	6.9	-	-	-

Source: Verkhovna Rada, ARKHIV ZA SKLYKANNYAMY (online archive of legislative votes). Available: https://iportal.rada.gov.ua/. Own calculations.

Focus-100 and "core" rich MPs
We turn now to the overlap in personnel between the deputies of both parliamentary convocations and the Focus-100 rich list from the previous chapter. Correspondences between the names on these lists were again checked using the conditional formatting function in Excel. The results are summarised in Table 5.4 below. Some points to draw from the table are as follows.

- Of the MPs who sat in the earlier term of the Rada, 40 (or about 9% of the total) also appeared on the Focus-100 rich list in 2006-17. Seven of these are listed among the "core" rich, identified in the last chapter as among the most enduringly successful business owners of the period. In the column two of Table 5.4, their surnames are emboldened.
- In the eighth convocation (up to December 2017), the number of "Focus MPs" fell almost by half, to 23 (or 5% of the total), while the number of "core rich MPs" declined to four. Of these 23, 16 had retained their seats from the earlier parliamentary term (out of the total of 156 such deputies identified above). In the first of the "8th convocation" columns, their names are underlined.
- Those whose names for the eighth convocation are both emboldened and underlined in Table 5.4 are therefore among the wealthiest and most enduring of Ukraine's lawmakers in the period examined, each wielding two or three "power resources" (material, positional and mobilisational power) over an extended period.
- This underscores the important point that, while definitional distinctions are indispensable analytically (here, between wealth-holders and office-holders), in practice, among the top tier of the Ukrainian elite, such distinctions blur. In looking to identify the membership of Ukraine's "oligarch class" — extremely rich business figures with political influence at the national level — the names emboldened and underlined here augment those of the "core" rich list from the last chapter (Table 4.12).

Table 5.4: People's deputies of the 7th & 8th convocations who appear on Focus-100 rich list, 2006-17

No.	7th convocation Last name	Initials	8th convocation Last name	Initials
1	Baysarov	L.V.	Berezkin	S.S.
2	Berezkin	S.S.	Bobov	H.B.
3	Bobov	H.B.	**Bohuslayev**	V.O.
4	**Bohuslayev**	V.O.	Vadaturskyi	A.O.
5	Boyko	V.S.	Hereha	O.V.
6	**Buryak**	S.V.	Hirshfeld	A.M.
7	Vasadze	T.SH.	Hranovskyi	O.M.
8	Vasylyev	H.A.	Derkach	A.L.
9	Hereha	O.V.	Yeremeyev	I.M.
10	Hirshfeld	A.M.	**Zhevaho**	K.V.
11	Derkach	A.L.	Zahoriy	H.V.
12	Yedin	O.Y.	Zvyahilskyi	YU.L.
13	Yeremeyev	I.M.	Ivakhiv	S.P.
14	Zhvaniya	D.V.	Klimov	L.M.
15	**Zhevaho**	K.V.	Klyuyev	S.P.
16	Zvyahilskyi	YU.L.	Kostenko	P.P.
17	Ivanyushchenko	YU.V.	Lyovochkin	S.V.
18	Ivakhiv	S.P.	Mykytas	M.V.
19	Kyi	S.V.	**Novynskyi**	V.V.
20	Klychko	V.V.	Svyatash	D.V.
21	Klimov	L.M.	**Taruta**	S.O.
22	Klyuyev	S.P.	Feldman	O.B.
23	Kolesnikov	B.V.	Shufrych	N.I.
24	Kurovskyi	I.I.		
25	Landyk	V.I.		
26	Moshenskyi	V.Z.		
27	Mkhitaryan	N.M.		
28	**Novynskyi**	V.V.		
29	Polyakov	V.L.		
30	**Poroshenko**	P.O.		
31	Pryhodskyi	A.V.		
32	Prodyvus	V.S.		
33	Rudkovskyi	M.M.		
34	Svyatash	D.V.		
35	Sihal	YE.YA.		
36	Tabalov	O.M.		
37	**Tihipko**	S.L.		
38	Feldman	O.B.		
39	**Khmelnytskyi**	V.I.		
40	Shufrych	N.I.		

Sources: Focus.ua, the Focus Ratings archive for 2006-17 data; Verkhovna Rada. Note: Those MPs who also appear on the list of the "core" rich are emboldened; those who survived as MPs between the two convocations are underlined.

What significance for the reproduction of the Ukrainian oligarchy?

The two dimensions of the intersection of personnel examined here—between parliaments, and between legislative and economic institutions—provide evidence of continuity in Ukraine's political-economic elite, even in the wake of the political disjuncture of the Euromaidan events. The first opens a window onto the process of reconstitution, renewal and transformation of formal factions in the Rada across terms. Going by the wholesale movement of "old hands" between formal factions from one parliament to the next, it also supports the view that factional associations are more fluid and pragmatic, and based more on the attractions of currently powerful political network leaders, than ideological groupings. The second dimension offers some support for the notion that wealth, and wealth-holders, remained central in Ukrainian politics.

Lastly, the continuity of even relatively small numbers of political-economic network leaders and sub-leaders means that they bring with them, and can therefore transmit to newcomers, know-how of "customary" elite political and economic practices, so perpetuating the "regime".

These results are suggestive of a direct fusion of the institutions of Ukraine's political and economic elites, in the persons of key individual wielders of position and wealth, reminiscent of the "power elite" approach to understanding the operation and reproduction of elite rule, associated with the US sociologist C Wright Mills. He offers a sweeping, stylised account of the shifting relative positions of US elites heading the main institutions of economic, political and military power up to the 1950s, of a small ruling group "laced together" by personal relationships, shared social activities, but chiefly by overlapping interests and personnel, who between them "make decisions with terrible consequences for the underlying populations" (Mills, 1956, p. 278). As with Winters' "political materialism", it offers a useable approach to empirical analysis, an example of how the narration of the power relations between distinctive groups within elites might be handled, while drawing attention to overlaps of personnel as a means for achieving elite cohesion between component institutions.

5.2.3 Interaction of formal factional with sub- and cross-factional voting patterns on institutional prosperity bills after the Euromaidan Revolution

Introduction and summary of voting results

Having identified the "stables" of people's deputies that "old" oligarchs are reported to have maintained, or whose votes they procured for specific bills, how do the formal and informal (sub- and cross-) factional voting patterns in the Rada interweave to produce legislative outcomes? This is a key question that the detailed descriptive and contextual analysis that follows aims to answer, identifying the patterns of parliamentary factional support for, and obstruction of, political-economic reform legislation.

Table 5.5 below presents a summary of the roll-call results across three periods for the 23 political economy bills selected for analysis. In the Ukrainian parliament, deputies can respond to a legislative voting opportunity in one of five ways. The online archive records these as "for", "against", "abstained", "did not vote" and "absent". For ease of analysis, I simplified the voting results into three categories, of "for", "not for" (covering explicit opposition, abstention and the failure to vote), and "absent".

The size of the last two categories ("not for" and "absent") account between them for the instances in which a bill was not adopted. To pass, cumulative backing for a bill must rise above the 50% threshold, equal to 226 or more seats in the single, 450-seat Rada chamber. For each bill, the columns of results on the right-hand side of the table show the shares of Rada deputies voting "for" or "not for" (incorporating votes against and the failure to vote), as well as those MPs absent from the voting chamber. Of these bills, 12 were adopted and 11 were not.

Table 5.5: Voting results on 23 "institutional prosperity" bills, Feb 2014-Dec 2017

Voting result (% of seats)

Bill no.	Official no.	Topic	PE category	For	Not for	Absent
1	4586	Investment protection	BE	54.9	20.2	24.2
2	3614-1	SME state support	BE	21.6	49.8	27.8
3	2037	Joint-stock firms	BE	34.0	35.6	29.3
4	4101a	Tax on capital income	BE	59.3	8.9	30.7
5	0937	Economic intervention	BE	52.0	2.4	44.4
6	4930	Corporate taxes	BE	28.0	39.6	31.3
7	1580	Deregulation	BE	58.9	16.4	18.2
8	1839	Shareholder rights	BE	38.9	40.0	14.7
9	2250	Gas market	S	64.4	13.6	15.6
10	2382	Doing Business	BE	41.6	19.6	32.4
11	2138a	Party finances	PP	51.6	18.4	23.8
12	2431	Competition policy	BE	38.7	34.7	20.2
13	3755	Anti-corruption	PP	52.9	22.0	18.4
14	3755-P1	Blocking anti-corruption	PP	24.2	23.6	45.6
15	2286a	Financial system	S	46.9	28.4	18.0
16	4734	Judiciary	PP	62.4	22.2	7.8
17	2413a	Financial system	S	40.0	37.6	14.9
18	5368	Investment climate	BE	52.2	27.8	13.8
19	2302a-d	Corporate governance	BE	56.9	21.3	15.8

Table continued overleaf...

Table 5.5: Voting results on 23 "institutional prosperity" bills, Feb 2014-Dec 2017

Bill no.	Official no.	Topic	PE category	Voting result (% of seats)		
				For	Not for	Absent
20	4840	Mining	S	49.6	14.2	30.0
21	6232	Judicial procedures	PP	56.2	26.0	11.6
22	7276	Anti-corruption	PP	32.4	41.1	20.2
23	3096d	Oil & gas	S	51.3	25.3	17.3

Source: Verkhovna Rada, ARKHIV ZA SKLYKANNYAMY (online archive of legislative members & votes). Available: https://iportal.rada.gov.ua/. Note: Political economy (PE) category key: BE: business environment; PP: political pluralism or rule of law; S: sectoral.

Period 1: The interim government and the dominance of the "pro-Euromaidan" factions

The first period is delimited at one end by the flight from Kyiv of Yanukovych and his lieutenants, and at the other by the formation of a new government in the wake of the early parliamentary election of October 2014. Within this, the election of Petro Poroshenko in late May marks a shift in political leadership from the "duumvirate" of Oleksandr Turchynov (as interim president and parliamentary speaker) and Arseniy Yatsenyuk (as interim prime minister) to the more uneasy one between Yatsenyuk as the head of government and Poroshenko as head of state that followed, conditioned by the more even distribution of powers between the president and parliament after the restoration of the 2004 constitution.

Period 1: Propensity of formal factions to back reforms

Under the first Yatsenyuk government, in late February-November 2014, it was the political formations backing the new, hastily formed administration in parliament that tended to be the most well-disposed towards economic reforms. These were the parties (Fatherland, UDAR and Svoboda) that had formed the opposition to Yanukovych's PoR following the October 2012 Rada election, and whose leaders had supported the Euromaidan protests. During the fourth and fifth sessions of the seventh convocation, the share of MPs from these factions backing the six proposed business environment (BE) laws was high, averaging above 60%.

Figure 5.2 below presents three kinds of information on these voting results. First, the horizontal dashed black line indicates the average level of voting "for" the six proposed bills across the Rada (42%). Second, the grey bars represent the average level of voting "for" the bills by formal parliamentary faction. These show that the share of MPs from each of the "pro-Euromaidan" factions backing the six laws tended to well above the average. In contrast, the shares of the Yanukovych-era ruling factions (the remains of the PoR and the Communists) voting for the bills were well below the average. Meanwhile, the "post-PoR" factions (Economic Development and Sovereign European Ukraine, here merged into one bar) were modestly above the chamber average, in keeping with the notion that some of these deputies were willing to co-operate with the new authorities (Romanyuk and Kravets, 2017a, 2017b).

Figure 5.2: Share of formal Rada factions voting "for" business environment laws, Feb-Nov 2014

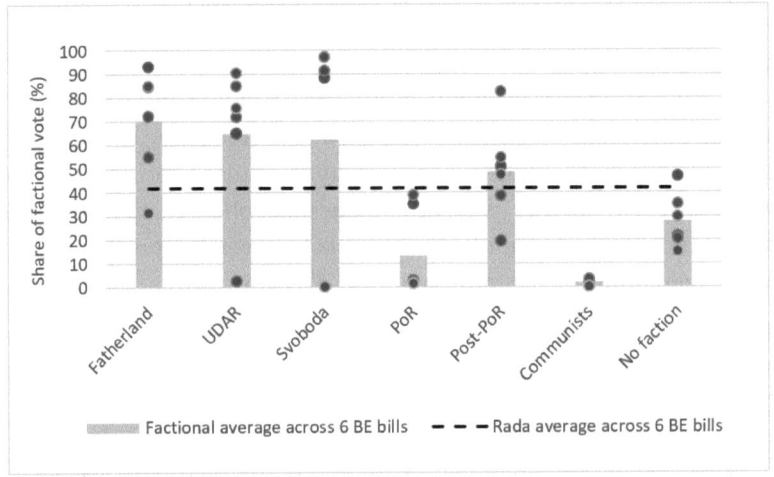

Sources: Verkhovna Rada, online archive. Available: https://iportal.rada.gov.ua/. Own calculations.

Third, the dark dots, aligned vertically with the factional bars to which they correspond, show the "for" shares of each faction on each bill individually. A key point to draw from these patterns is that although the main clusters of course tally with the average pattern for the groups, they also show considerable variation in backing for the bills within each. So, for example, although the share of support from Svoboda MPs is exceptionally high for four of the six laws, clustering around 90%, it is zero for the other two. Whereas the relative closeness of the dots could be interpreted as an indication of the broad factional disposition towards economic policy reform overall, factional voting towards the very top of the chart (100% in favour) and the very bottom (0% in favour) could be read as an indicator of factional discipline. If so, this seems to show the Communists, and especially Svoboda, as the most disciplined formal Rada factions in this period, perhaps reflecting their origins as more ideologically based organisations.

Period 1: Capacity of formal factions to back reforms

Overall. The analysis so far tells us about the broad orientation of the Rada factions to the selected economic reforms in this period. However, we must also assess which of the formal factions made the strongest voting contributions to passing or blocking reforms, which depends on their relative voting weight in parliament.

In the final sessions of the Rada's seventh convocation, the pro-Euromaidan parties continued to command a maximum of just 35-36% of the chamber vote. Backing from at least some deputies associated with the Yanukovych administration was therefore necessary to pass legislation. Three of the six business environment reforms examined were adopted — numbers one, four and five. This is shown in Figure 5.3 below by the stacked bars, representing the cumulative "yes" votes of deputies across all formal Rada factions, with successful votes pushing above the dashed black line, representing the 50%-of-seats threshold for a law to be adopted.

Successful bills. The "for" votes of the three pro-Euromaidan factions — Fatherland, UDAR and Svoboda — between them made a contribution to the passage of the laws equal to more than 30 percentage points of the required 50%. In the chart below, these are the three plain grey cells, differently shaded but unpatterned, at the base of each stacked bar. However, the sizeable positive voting contributions of the post-PoR factions, of between eight and 14 percentage points (vertically striped cells), were crucial in pushing the "yes" votes above the threshold in these cases. So too was support from some PoR deputies (horizontally striped cells), worth 8-9 percentage points. "For" votes from factionally unaligned legislators made a difference on bills one and five (diagonally patterned cells).

Figure 5.3: Contribution of "for" votes of formal Rada factions on business environment laws, Feb-Nov 2014

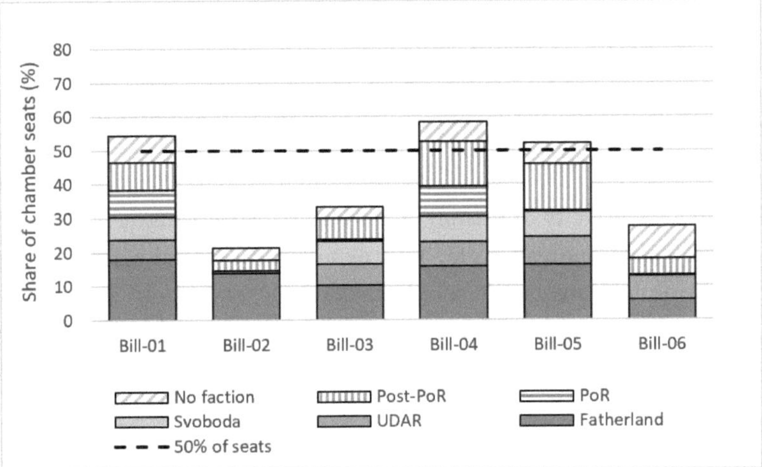

Sources: Verkhovna Rada, online archive. Available: https://iportal.rada.gov.ua/. Own calculations. Note: PoR: Party of Regions.

Rejected bills. Conversely, there were two main factors behind the rejection of the reforms put forward in bills two, three and six. The first was a large "not for" cumulative vote by the factions linked to the former ruling group. Moreover, the total "not for" votes subsumed within them a very high level of absences, accounting for 25-45% of all seats on the bills examined (see Table 5.5 above). In this period, absence from parliament seems to have been a tactic by which legislators associated with the Yanukovych-era authorities were able to contribute to the defeat of some legislation, without explicitly voting against it. This recalls a point made by Sarah Whitmore, when she identifies "non-voting" as one of the "subroutines" of MPs' political performance in the Rada (2019, p. 1,492).

However, at least early on after the Euromaidan, this phenomenon may have been more linked to the highly charged political atmosphere generated by the upsurge in deadly violence preceding the collapse of the Yanukovych administration, as well as a rise in patriotism following the onset of the Russia-Ukraine conflict.

A second factor behind the rejection of these reforms, more unexpected than the first, is the low level of support from one or more of the pro-Euromaidan factions themselves. For example, on bill two, dealing with state support for small business, the total "not for/absent" votes of the successors to the former ruling parties diverted 43% of all chamber mandates away from a positive result. At the same time, the combined "non-positive" contributions of UDAR and Svoboda deputies were around 16 percentage points. That is, the pro-Euromaidan factions themselves were not always united in their approach to reforms of the business environment.

What explains differences in voting between periods 1 and 2?
One way of making sense of the voting patterns in each of the three periods of analysis is to read them broadly as the outcome of the main political and economic developments in the lead up to them.

Looking at the interim government, this means centrally the three-month anti-government protests of the Euromaidan, leading in early 2014, in the wake of political violence that left scores dead in Kyiv, to the downfall of the Yanukovych administration, at once discrediting and fragmenting the political forces associated with it, while lifting into power those parliamentary forces most supportive of the demonstrators. This explains both the switch in institutional power positions of the pro- and anti-Euromaidan factions, and the broad split in their voting patterns.

Although destabilisation of the financial system and increasingly open military conflict with Russia developed during this period, their domestic political effects did not show fully on the composition of the Rada until after the 2014 elections, which is the period of the second Yatsenyuk government. In this sense, key developments that took place in the first period of analysis help to explain the transition to the Rada of the second period, with its changed political composition and character. Among the most relevant such developments should be included:

- the re-introduction of the 2004 constitution, bolstering the powers of parliament and the prime minister relative to those of the president;
- the failure to roll back the "mixed" election laws, and especially the single mandate, considered a route into parliament for "network" or oligarchic-linked deputies;
- the rise to the presidency of a second-tier oligarch, Petro Poroshenko, along with his Vinnytsya-based business-political network;
- the plummeting popularity of politicians and parties associated with Yanukovych or seen as "pro-Russian", alongside a reduction in the size of the "pro-Russian" electorate as a consequence of territorial annexation or *de facto* occupation; and
- the gradual re-integration of leading oligarchs and their business networks.

These developments, along with the rise of patriotic and pro-Western sentiment in reaction, left pro-Euromaidan factions in a strong position in parliament, with enhanced powers, not requiring too much co-operation from the diminished PoR opposition successor factions for as long as they remained relatively united — which, as after the Orange Revolution, was not for long.

Period 2: The second Yatsenyuk government; the formation and disintegration of the five-party coalition

The second analytical period, from December 2014 until mid-April 2016, is that of the five-party Rada coalition formed to support the second Yatsenyuk government. At the start, the political forces that came out on top following the Euromaidan protests were at the height of their political power, holding both the presidency and premiership, and dominating the legislature. However, it was also the period of the onset of the progressive disintegration of the five-party coalition, as the ramifications of a second serious military defeat by Russian-led forces in the Donbas in early 2015 played out in domestic politics, even as a struggle for political pre-eminence within the government (between the president and the prime minister) and between the president and leading oligarchs (in particular, Kolomoyskyi) also fed into splits within the governing camp and to an eventual factional realignment in the Rada.

Period 2: Propensity of formal factions to back reforms
In the new parliament, the nine proposed bills covered not only reforms of the business environment, but also bills on countering corruption and financing political parties, as well as the energy and financial sectors. Four of the nine were adopted.

With the greater parliamentary weight of "pro-Euromaidan" forces aligned, at least nominally, to a reformist agenda, support for the laws examined rose across the Rada under the second Yatsenyuk government compared with the first, to 49%, from 42%.

The patterns of formal factional propensity of support show some similarities with those in the previous Rada, albeit complicated by the proliferation and evolution of parties, factions and deputy groups. Specifically, the average shares of factional "for" votes among the five-party coalition were higher than for the successor factions of the PoR. However, factional legislative support was not equally solid among coalition members, but appeared to depend on relative closeness to the dominant political leaders, Poroshenko and Yatsenyuk. Across all nine bills, support from the president's PPB, and especially Yatsenyuk's PF, was high, averaging above 60% and 70%, respectively. On a tier below this, support from both Fatherland and Self-Reliance averaged just under 60% across the nine bills, with the more erratic stance of the Radicals bringing the average level of support offered down towards 40%. Meanwhile, backing from factions with their origins in the PoR were almost uniformly low, with an average of just 9% of deputies of the Opposition Bloc voting for these reforms.

These points are shown in Figure 5.4 below, with the grey bars again representing average factional "for" votes. For the PPB and the PF, these are well above the dashed black line, representing the average "for" vote across the chamber, and for Self-Reliance and Fatherland, a little less so. But the average factional "for" shares are below the line for the Radicals. The "opposition" formations—the Opposition Bloc, People's Will and Economic Development/Renaissance—tend to offer the least support, all below 20%.

Figure 5.4: Factional shares of 5-party coalition voting "for" prosperity bills, Dec 2014-Apr 2016

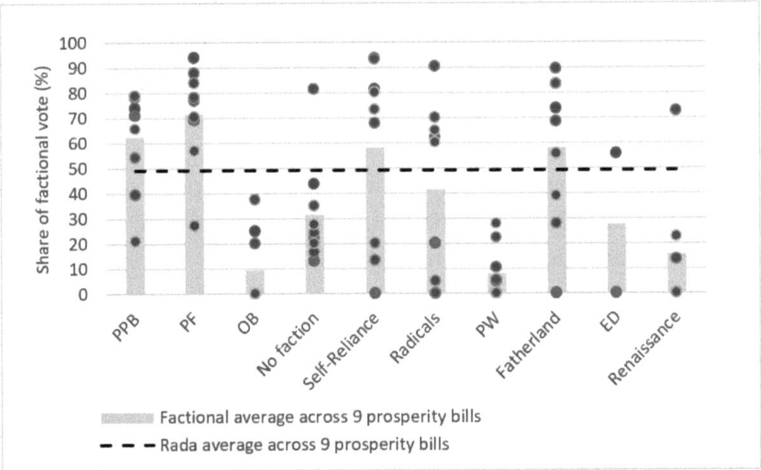

[Chart showing share of factional vote (%) for factions: PPB, PF, OB, No faction, Self-Reliance, Radicals, PW, Fatherland, ED, Renaissance, with factional average across 9 prosperity bills (bars) and Rada average across 9 prosperity bills (dashed line at ~50%).]

Sources: Verkhovna Rada, online archive. Available: https://iportal.rada.gov.ua/. Own calculations. Note: PPB: Petro Poroshenko Bloc; PF: People's Front; OB: Opposition Bloc; PW: People's Will; ED: Economic Development.

On this chart, moreover, a more varied pattern of factional voting, compared with the first period, is shown by the wider spread of the dark grey dots associated with each faction's bar, indicating greater variation in attitude to political economy reforms within formal factions across bills. So, for example, although clusters of dots above the bars for Self-Reliance, Fatherland and the Radicals show high levels of support for several pieces of reform legislation individually, they each also display quite low levels of support for at least another three bills. In hindsight, this may be indicative of the five-party coalition's inherent limitations as a vehicle for the pursuit of broad and sustained reform policy.

Period 2: Alignment of formal and "old" oligarch voting
Under the second Yatsenyuk government, the willingness of the "old" oligarch sub- and cross- factional groups (comprised of 66

MPs in this period; see Table 5.1) to back the selected prosperity laws was much lower than for the formal factions, with just 19% of such MPs doing so, against 49% across the chamber. The small number of deputies reported as linked to Viktor Pinchuk were more inclined to support the legislation, and those of Kolomoyskyi's larger group (15 MPs), somewhat less so. Of the others, Akhmetov's group (with 20 MPs) were the least well-disposed on average.

However, the shares of these sub- or cross-factional MP groups associated with the "old" oligarchs not only peak on different laws, but appear to align with the voting patterns of different formal factions, perhaps reflecting specific business interest and/or their current political alliances in the Rada. These patterns of "associated voting" remain intact even when the MPs identified with the "old" oligarchs are removed from their formal factions to avoid "double counting", as in the pair of charts below. So, in the topmost of the two of graphics (Figure 5.5), the jagged upper and lower lines, with different geometric markers, rise and fall in accord across the proposed bills, suggesting that a portion of MPs associated with the FLB (Firtash-Lyovochkin-Boyko) oligarchic network may have been working in informal alliance with the dominant formal Rada factions (the PPB and the PF), with more backing from People's Will on later bills. The lower chart (Figure 5.6) shows a simultaneous rise in the shares of MPs from the Akhmetov and Medvedchuk groups, as well as of the Opposition Bloc, voting for bills seven and 12, but withholding support in unison on almost all the others, suggesting a degree of voting co-ordination.

This second pattern of alignment may be less surprising than the first. However, the first makes sense, too, considering the reports of an informal agreement between Poroshenko and Firtash made in Vienna, the Austrian capital, ahead of the presidential election of May 2014 (Matsiyevsky, 2018, p. 351). Moreover, after the departure of the Radicals from the coalition in late 2015, People's Will are reported to have reached a mutually beneficial arrangement with the PPB (Romanyuk and Kravets, 2017b).

Figures 5.5 & 5.6: Associated "for" votes of core coalition with PW & the FLB group (top chart); & of the Opposition Bloc with Akhmetov & Medvedchuk groups (bottom chart), period 2

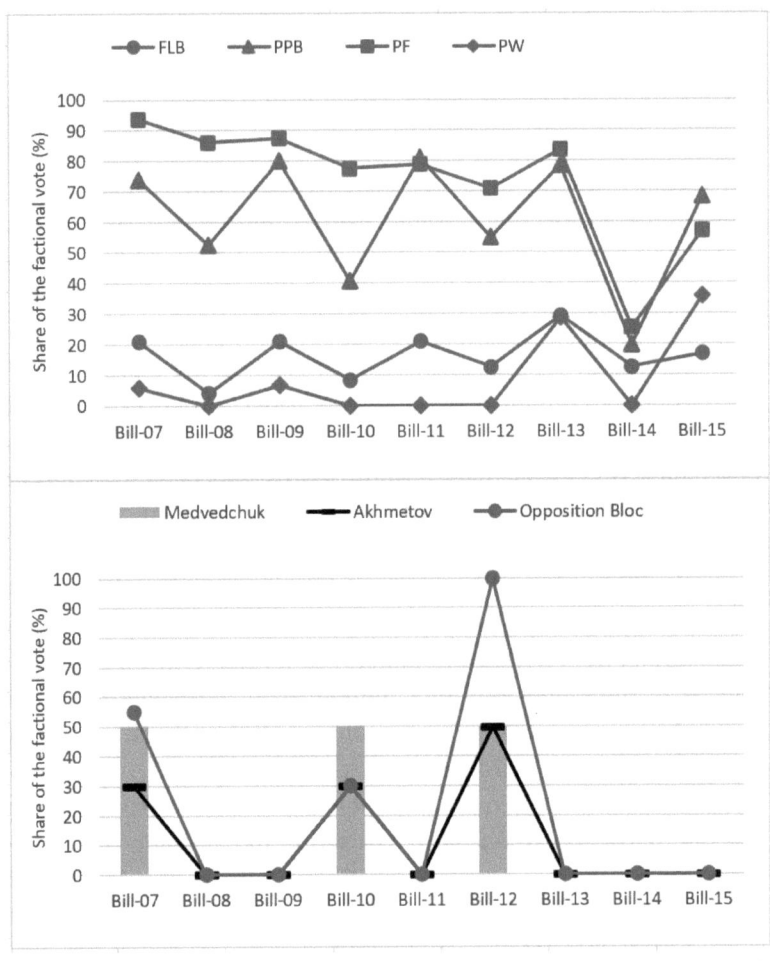

Sources: Verkhovna Rada, online archive. Available: https://iportal.rada.gov.ua/. Berdinskikh (2015), *Novoye Vremya*. Romanyuk & Kravets (2016a), (2016b), (2016c), (2017a), (2017b), (2017c), (2018), *Ukrayinska Pravda*. Chernyshev et al (2017), LIGA.net. Own calculations. Note: FLB: Firtash-Lyovochkin-Boyko; PPB: Petro Poroshenko Bloc; PF: People's Front; PW: People's Will; OB: Opposition Bloc.

Period 2: Contributions of formal factions to backing reforms

Overall. In the second period, the voting contribution of the leading government parties, the PPB and the PF, remained high, averaging 32 percentage points over the nine votes examined. This reflected not only high factional commitment to the legislation, but also the numerical weight of these parties in the new parliament. However, the contributions of the smaller coalition parties were also vital, with Self-Reliance, the most ideologically liberal of them, offering the most solid support. Positive contributions from the parties to emerge from the PoR were low to zero. This contrasts with the opposition's factional forebears under the interim government. This was so not just for the Opposition Bloc, but also for the factions that arose from those that broke from the PoR. This change in relations between parliaments ties in with the accounts of the leaders of these factions that they were side-lined by the second Yatsenyuk government for as long as their votes were unnecessary to complete parliamentary business (Romanyuk and Kravets, 2017a, 2017b).

Because of the rise in the number of formal factions in the eighth convocation, in Figure 5.7 below I merged factional voting contributions into broader groups. The lower, plain cells of the stacked bars represent the voting contributions of the main coalition groups (the PPB and the PF; dark grey), while the minor coalition groups are in light grey above them, and the smaller contributions of the combined opposition are marked with vertically striped cells atop the bars. This was the period of maximum polarisation in the Rada, or mutual alienation between the political forces on opposite sides of the Euromaidan protests.

Successful bills. In the period up to mid-April 2016, the PPB and the PF were the major backers of those prosperity bills adopted by the Rada, contributing 39-42 percentage points of the required 50%. The starting position of the parties was much more advantageous than for the interim government. The combined voting capacity of the two peaked at around 51% of the maximum possible votes early in eighth convocation, but dropped below 50% by October 2015, amid departures from the president's faction, possibly linked to his earlier clash with Kolomoyskyi. Crucial to the passing of the successful bills in this phase was the support of at least two of the three smaller coalition parties (light grey cells) and/or a portion of factionless MPs (diagonally striped cells). So, for example, on a law on gas market reform (bill nine), the combined backing of the Radicals and Fatherland, of 11 percentage points, was enough to push support for the legislation above 50%, when added to the votes of the PPB and the PF.

Figure 5.7: "For" votes of formal Rada factions on prosperity laws, Dec 2014-Mar 2016

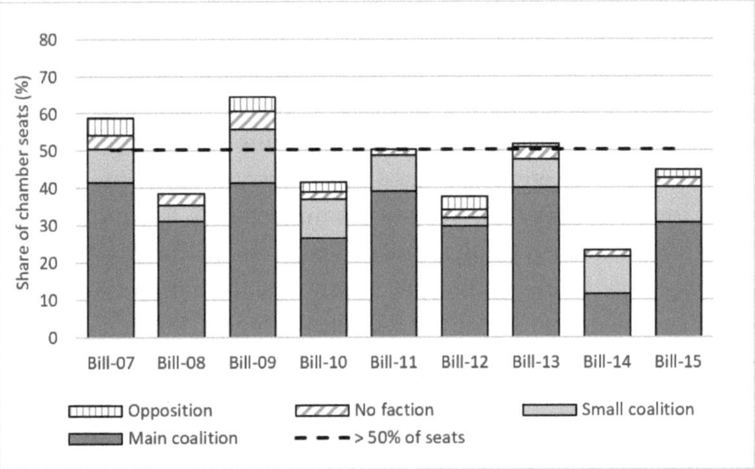

[Chart: Share of chamber seats (%) for Bill-07 through Bill-15, with categories: Opposition, No faction, Small coalition, Main coalition, and dashed line > 50% of seats]

Sources: Verkhovna Rada, online archive. Available: https://iportal.rada.gov.ua/. Own calculations.

Rejected bills. Although the Opposition Bloc was often a significant detractor from the passage of bills that failed in the Rada, diverting 7-9% of the total chamber vote, on its own, this was usually insufficient to block a law, even in combination with the non-positive votes of other post-PoR formations. The most striking feature of the data for this period, however, is that, under the second Yatsenyuk administration, a large part of President Poroshenko's own party consistently failed to back the government's political economy reforms. Typically, this was the main reason for a bill's failure. On the bills that were not adopted (bills eight, ten, 12, 14 and 15), the combined mandates of PPB deputies failing to support the legislation made up 11-20 percentage points of all votes. This may reflect the origins of the PPB as a hastily assembled political vehicle for Poroshenko after his presidential victory; the weakness of the party system; and the related phenomenon of informal political formations in the Rada operating in and across formal ones.

Changing political economy context of period 2 as explanation for the shift in Rada alliances and voting patterns in period 3

As before, the key political and economic developments of the second analytical period help to provide the context for understanding the broad change in political alignments, and so voting patterns, in the third. The resignation of Yatsenyuk as prime minister and his replacement by Hroysman corresponds, therefore, to a switch in parliamentary alliances, as the loss of three of the five coalition parties left the authorities more reliant on the opposition factions that emerged from the PoR, and on deputies linked to a handful of "old" oligarchs, often with an overlap between the two.

This switch in factional Rada alliances, moreover, corresponds to a shift in the relations of the main business-political networks underlying them. In particular, 2016 is the year of the political "rehabilitation" of Rinat Akhmetov. After spending 2014-15 in the (relative) political wilderness, reportedly as part of the developing network pyramid around Yatsenyuk, he switched his support to Poroshenko (Chernyshev et al, 2017). Although Poroshenko's clash in 2015 with Kolomoyskyi may have reduced the latter's inclination to co-operate, Yatsenyuk, on departure from the premiership, may have been able to negotiate favourable conditions for his party and business base (Konończuk, 2016, p. 37). This development seems to mark a crucial stage in backtracking on "de-oligarchisation".

One subdivision within the second period runs from the formation of the administration in December 2014 until March 2015, with the second stretching from April 2015 to mid-April 2016. There are several candidates for the events that could have altered broad political-economic alliances between the two.

The most obvious of these, perhaps, is the domestic political fall-out from the second Minsk peace deal in the war with Russian and Russian-backed forces in eastern Ukraine, following the defeat of the Ukrainian army at Debaltseve in early 2015 (Kudelia and Kazianov, 2021, pp. 47-48). More precisely, the provision for embedding autonomous status for the Donbas into the Ukrainian constitution had serious repercussions in Ukrainian politics, culminating in late August 2015 in a deadly grenade attack by Ukrainian nationalists outside parliament (Europa, 2018, p. 520), followed by the withdrawal of the Radicals from the coalition (Romanyuk and Kravets, 2017c). This initiated the coalition's drawn-out disintegration, which moved into a second phase in February 2016 with the withdrawal of Fatherland and Self-Reliance. In turn, this followed the resignation of the reforming economy minister, Aivaras Abromavičius, in protest at the meddling in ministry appointments of Ihor Kononenko, one of President Poroshenko's key political overseers, and left the government's Rada majority in jeopardy (Kalymon and Havrylyshyn, 2016).

Another important development was a serious clash between Poroshenko and Kolomoyskyi, a prominent "old" oligarch, in early 2015, around the same time as Minsk II. The story behind this clash, investigated in more depth in the next chapter, helps to understand the increased reliance of the Poroshenko-Hroysman government on political forces linked to the Yanukovych-era ruling groups to counter the influence of Kolomoyskyi and his Privat group, with whom Yatsenyuk and the PF were informally aligned.

Period 3: A realignment of government and former Yanukovych factions under the Hroysman administration
The third phase of analysis begins with the appointment of the Hroysman government in mid-April 2016, bringing to an end a period of open conflict within the government. It ends in December 2017, marked internationally with the grant of military aid to Ukraine by the Trump administration in the US (Europa, 2018, p. 521). Half of the eight laws examined here were accepted. They covered judicial reform, improvements in the investment climate and corporate governance, as well as mining and banking reforms.

Period 3: Propensity of formal factions to back the bills
On patterns of formal factional shares of support for "prosperity" legislation from mid-April 2016, there are again points of similarity and difference with earlier periods.

The voting coherence displayed by the remaining parliamentary factions of the governing coalition, the PF and the PPB, stayed intact, with each recording rates of support of around 70% across the eight bills (the two leftmost pairs of bars in Figure 5.8 below). An explanation for the PF sticking with the coalition, even after the replacement of Yatsenyuk as prime minister, is that, with its ratings very low (Razumkov Centre, 2017), owing in part to its open pursuit since the early post-Euromaidan period of "kamikaze" policies, including steep increases in household energy tariffs, the party's MPs feared not only losing their connection with executive power but also, should the fall of the coalition have led to early elections, their seats (Romanyuk and Kravets, 2016b).

The most pronounced feature of the period, however, is a turnabout in the relative willingness of the smaller formal parliamentary factions to support these bills. The level of support among its former members dropped markedly—for Fatherland, from close to 60% in the second period (the dark grey factional bar, fourth from the left, in Figure 5.8) to below 25% in the third (the corresponding lighter grey bar). Conversely, the incidence of support for this legislation rose sharply for the Opposition Bloc, People's Will and especially Economic Development/Renaissance, among whose MPs the average level of backing rose from around 18% in the second period to close to 50% in the third. These developments point to increased co-operation between the remaining "core" government factions and the opposition, marking a sea-change in political alliances in the legislature.

In Figure 5.8 below the horizontal dashed lines, rising from the dark grey of the second period to the lighter grey of the third, show parliament as a whole becoming better-disposed to the proposed bills. This may suggest that, under the Hroysman administration, the arrangements with opposition and former coalition groups were a more effective means of generating support for reform legislation than the five-party coalition. Chaisty and Chernykh (2015) identify control of a legislative majority as an important feature of Ukrainian politics in the Rada that has sometimes helped to stabilise Ukraine's presidential political system – albeit, at times, at the expense of democratic accountability. A second change in the Rada in this period is a fall in the level of parliamentary absences, as the immediate post-Euromaidan stigma attached to the former ruling factions began to fade.

Figure 5.8: Change in formal Rada faction shares voting "for" prosperity laws, periods 2 & 3

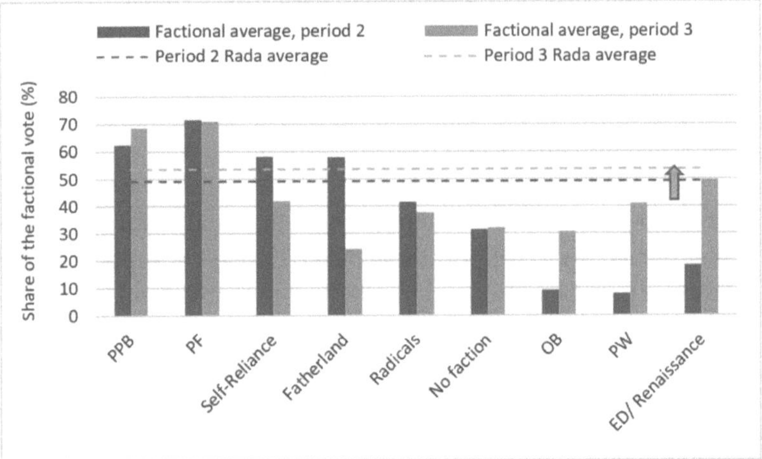

Sources: Verkhovna Rada, online archive. Available: https://iportal.rada.gov.ua/. Own calculations. Note: PPB: Petro Poroshenko Bloc; PF: People's Front; OB: Opposition Bloc; PW: People's Will.

Period 3: Re-alignment of "old" oligarch deputy groups
Similarly, in the first year and a half of the Hroysman administration, the willingness of the "old" oligarch formations to back the eight bills rose on average to 32%, from 19% in the second period, suggesting an increased propensity of some MPs associated with these groups to co-operate with the government. Although still quite low, this rise, of 13 percentage points, was more marked than for the formal factions. The change in the average "for" vote among such MPs is shown in Figure 5.9 below by the upward movement,

denoted by arrows, from the lower, darker grey dashed line under the second Yatsenyuk administration (period 2) to the higher, lighter grey dashed line of period 3. An increase in the factional incidence of support was seen across all the "old" oligarch groups, except Pinchuk's small one, but was strongest for the Akhmetov and Medvedchuk groups. The increased willingness of these formal and informal factions to back government legislation distinguishes the third period of analysis from the second, seeming to mark their institutional re-integration into the work of the Rada.

Figure 5.9: Changing shares of "old" oligarch groups voting "for" prosperity bills, period 2 & 3

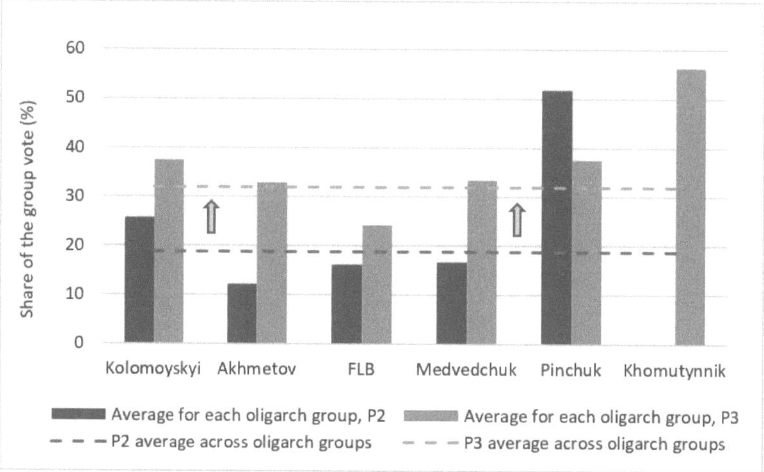

Sources: Verkhovna Rada, archive. Available: https://iportal.rada.gov.ua/. Berdinskikh (2015), *Novoye Vremya*. Romanyuk & Kravets (2016a), (2016b), (2016c), (2017a), (2017b), (2017c), (2018), *Ukrayinska Pravda*. Chernyshev et al (2017), LIGA.net. Own calculations. Note: FLB: Firtash-Lyovochkin-Boyko.

Period 3: Alignment formal with "old" oligarch groups

Again adapting the formal factional voting data to subtract the MPs (53 in this period) identified with one of the "old" oligarch groups so as to avoid double counting, the alternation in voting proportions, illustrated in the twinned charts below, seems to show a high degree of voting co-ordination on the prosperity bills.

Voting patterns in the Rada

Figures 5.10 & 5.11: Associated "for" votes of core coalition parties & FLB group (top chart); & of post-PoR parties & informal factions (bottom chart), period 3

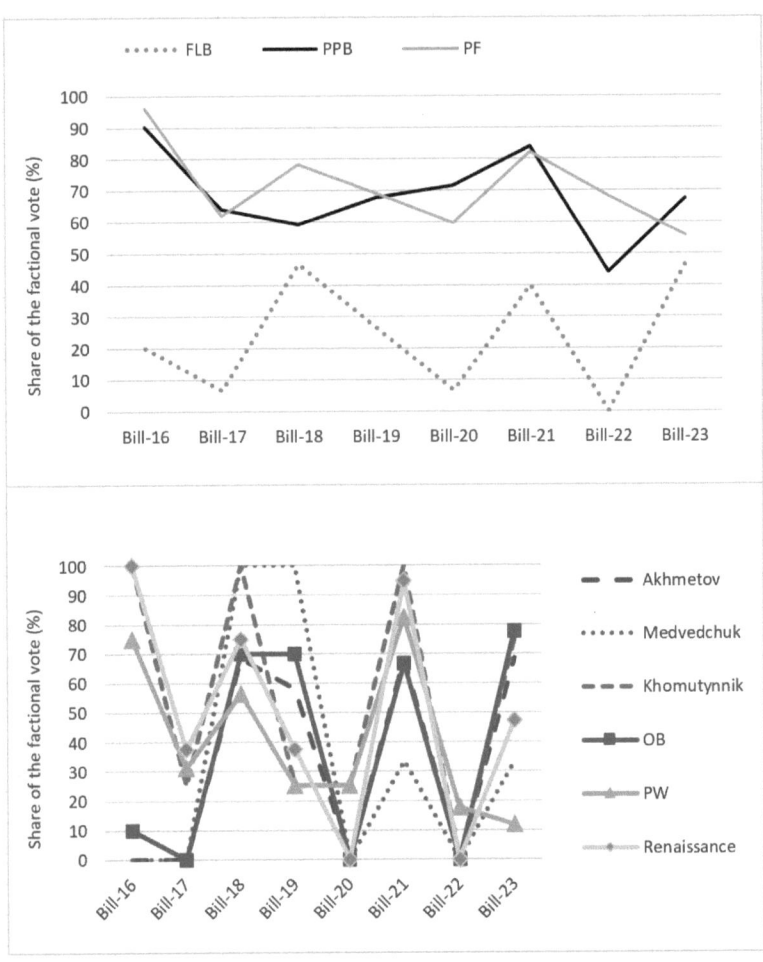

Sources: Verkhovna Rada, online archive. Available: https://iportal.rada.gov.ua/. Berdinskikh (2015), *Novoye Vremya*. Romanyuk & Kravets (2016a), (2016b), (2016c), (2017a), (2017b), (2017c), (2018), *Ukrayinska Pravda*. Chernyshev et al (2017), LIGA.net. Own calculations. Note: FLB: Firtash-Lyovochkin-Boyko; PPB: Petro Poroshenko Bloc; PF: People's Front; OB: Opposition Bloc; PW: People's Will.

On the lower of the pair of charts above (Figure 5.11), this co-ordination is between three "old" oligarch groups (Akhmetov,

Medvedchuk and Khomutynnik) and three formal "opposition" factions (the Opposition Bloc, People's Will and Renaissance). Because the information conveyed is quite intricate, I have indicated old oligarch factions with different kinds of broken line, but formal factional shares with solid lines, each with a different marker. The central point to take from this is that the shares of MPs from these groups voting for reforms alternate broadly in unison. The upper chart, Figure 5.10, meanwhile, appears to show a level of continued co-ordination of some MPs from the Firtash-Lyovochkin-Boyko (FLB) group with the government parties.

Period 3: Contributions of the formal factions to backing bills

Overall. In this period, marking a shift in parliamentary alliances, the voting contribution of the PPB and the PF in support of the eight political economy bills under consideration rose from an average of 32% of the Rada votes in the second period to 34% in the third, mainly reflecting the improved factional coherence of the PPB. However, the share of the vote at the command of the core government factions on paper, already below 50% at the beginning of the Hroysman administration, fell further over the next 18 months.

For the smaller formal factions, the change in pattern of average legislative contributions to prosperity reforms between periods is shown in the bar chart below (Figure 5.12). Among the former coalition factions — Self-Reliance, Fatherland and the Radicals — the average positive voting contribution for prosperity laws dropped, from a combined 8.6 percentage points in the second phase to 5.3 percentage points in the third.

Conversely, the legislative support from the post-PoR "opposition" factions rose abruptly, from a contribution of 2 percentage points to more than 7 percentage points between periods. Although the Opposition Bloc had the largest voting weight of the three post-PoR factions, the change in behaviour between periods was most marked for Renaissance and People's Will.

Figure 5.12: Change in average contribution of small Rada parties to "for" votes, periods 2 & 3

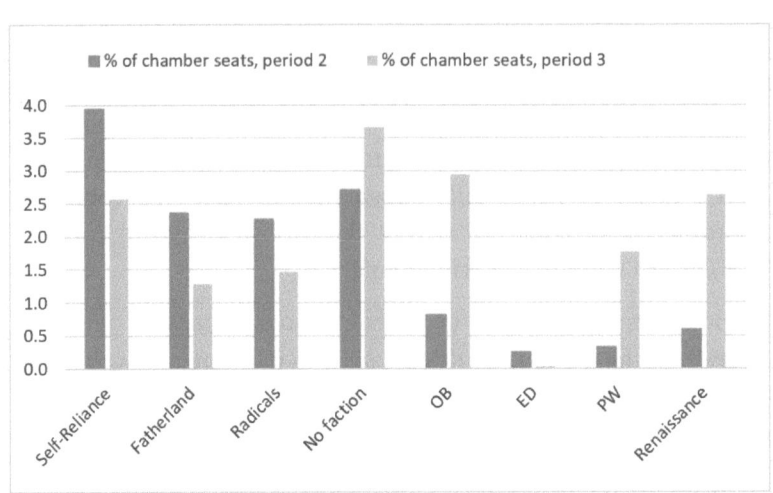

Sources: Verkhovna Rada, online archive. Available: https://iportal.rada.gov.ua/. Own calculations. Note: OB: Opposition Bloc; ED: Economic Development; PW: People's Will.

Successful bills. Because the supporting contributions for the first of the five adopted bills (number 16, on judicial reform) from the remaining "core" coalition parties (the PPB and the PF) was so high, at 45.8% combined (the lower, darker, plain grey cell at the base of the first stacked bar in Figure 5.13 below), it required only a little additional support to pass, with the combined "opposition" making the largest contribution, of 8.7 percentage points (the vertically striped cell on top of the stack, mostly from Renaissance).

For bill 18, however, on the investment climate, and bill 23, on energy-sector reform, a lower level of backing from the governing coalition necessitated the support of a broader range of factions, most substantially from the Opposition Bloc, but with relatively strong support from Self-Reliance and the Radicals pushing it over the 50% threshold. In this period, Ukrainian sources report, the Radicals switched allegiance from the Firtash-Lyovochkin-Boyko (FLB) network to that of Akhmetov (Romanyuk and Kravets, 2017a; Andrusiv, 2018, p. 64; Chernyshev et al, 2017).

On top of PPB and PF backing, the support that allowed bill 21, on judicial reform, to pass again came from the post-PoR groupings (the Opposition Bloc and Renaissance). A conspicuous feature in the data in this period is the very low contribution of Fatherland, which had earlier been a stalwart of the pro-Euromaidan coalition. This perhaps reflects the relative side-lining of the Yatsenyuk-Kolomoyskyi political-business axis.

Figure 5.13: "For" votes of formal Rada factions on prosperity laws, Apr 2016-Dec 2017

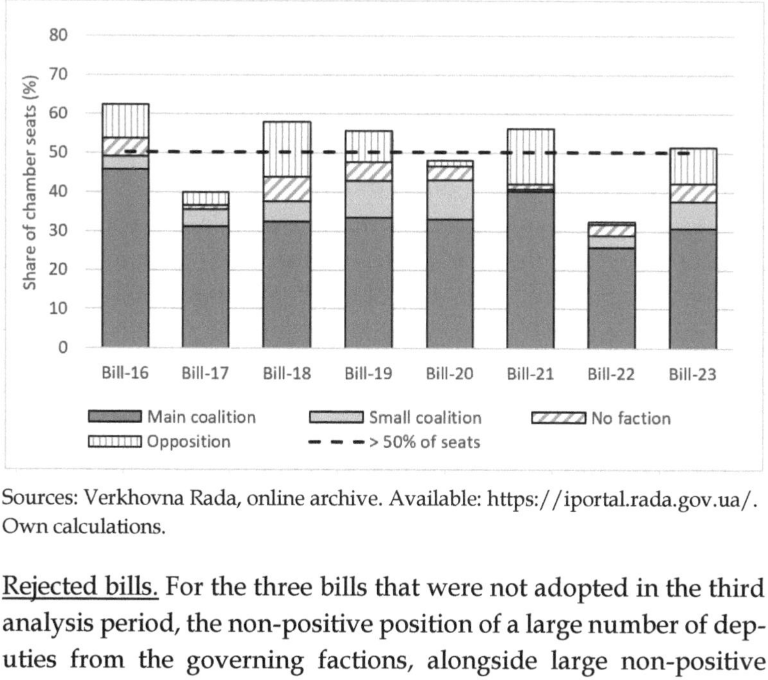

[Stacked bar chart showing share of chamber seats (%) for Bill-16 through Bill-23, with categories: Main coalition, Small coalition, No faction, Opposition, and a dashed line at >50% of seats.]

Sources: Verkhovna Rada, online archive. Available: https://iportal.rada.gov.ua/. Own calculations.

Rejected bills. For the three bills that were not adopted in the third analysis period, the non-positive position of a large number of deputies from the governing factions, alongside large non-positive votes from the Opposition Bloc and "no faction" MPs, were the main factors causing the bills to fail.

Period 3: Change in "for" contributions of "old" oligarch groups
The overall voting weight of the "old" oligarch factions in the eighth convocation is quite low—perhaps somewhat above the 12-17% of Rada deputies indicated by the lists of aligned MPs compiled from local investigative sources (Table 5.1). Moreover, the

degree of coherence of some oligarchic factions appears weaker than others. In combination, this is likely to mean that although these formations have the capacity to steer or nudge voting on particular bills, they lack the capacity individually, and perhaps even in combination, to determine legislative outcomes. This is in line with Heiko Pleine's view that oligarchs might best be seen as rule-takers (Pleines, 2016a, p. 105, 110).

Under the second Yatsenyuk government, the average positive contributions, or "yes" votes, of the "old" oligarch factions taken together was equal to just 2.7 percentage points of total possible chamber votes, rising to 3.9 percentage points under the Hroysman administration, in line with the broader trend of increased official legislative co-operation with opposition forces.

The voting impact in the Rada of the oligarch groups appears relatively small, then. This does not mean, however, that they cannot between them make a direct difference to a bill's course. Under the second Yatsenyuk government, for example, there are two instances in which the "for" votes of the "old" oligarch factions "tipped the balance" in favour of a bill, albeit on votes that were anyway close to the acceptance threshold. These are bills 11 and 13. On three other bills (eight, 10 and 15), the "not for/absent" vote of the old oligarchic factions would have been sufficient to push the bills over the line had they gone the other way, and in this sense could be said to have "blocked" the bills' adoption. In the third period, the vote of oligarch-linked MPs tipped the balance for bills 18 and 23, but held back bills 17 and 20. However, the ability to tip or block particular votes, based on voting weight alone, is contingent on factors that such groups may be unable to influence.

5.2.4 Chi-square test on the relation of "old" oligarch groups to voting on prosperity bills

Outline

The final analysis of this chapter is a statistical examination of the relationship between membership of the "old" oligarch Rada sub- and cross-factional groups and the patterns of voting on the selected "prosperity" bills in the eighth convocation. To examine this, two sets of dichotomous variables (that is, with only two possible values) were created by re-categorising the observations of the collected roll-call data. The independent variable (the one assumed to be doing the causing) distinguishes deputies identified as belonging to an "old" oligarch group (Table 5.1) from other MPs, while the dependent variable, of voting results, distinguishes "not for/absent" from "for" votes.

There are four elements to this analysis: a cross-table analysis; the chi-square test; the Cramér's V measure of association; and a controlled comparison of the results. A cross table allows examination of the distribution of the dependent variable in terms of the categories of the independent variable. To check whether a relationship shown by the cross tables could have happened by chance, their statistical significance is checked using the chi-square test. The strength of any relationship is assessed using Cramér's V. The last stage involves the use of a control variable to check for the presence of shared unseen factors underlying an observed relationship.

Although evidence from the cross-table analysis appeared to support the research hypothesis, showing a pattern of "old" oligarch groups failing to vote for prosperity laws more than other deputies, and although the chi-square tests and Cramér's V measures appeared to confirm for many votes a statistically significant relationship of at least moderate strength, this pattern was in many cases confounded when controlled for the broad distinction between coalition and opposition factions.

Despite this, I have kept the chi-square analysis in this book for two reasons. First, it illustrates the importance in statistics of the control stage for avoiding spurious causal inference. Second, alongside other findings from the chapter, its results affected my conclusions. In particular, it raised the question of whether the method used was appropriate for the subject matter — of a public institution in which the formal and informal dimensions of political life are fused — or did violence to it. In other words, the results of this analysis aided my arrival at the conclusion that it was a mistake to treat the Rada as if it were a liberal democratic legislative body. Rather than a liberal democracy, Ukraine's political system may best be described as a patronal democracy (Magyar and Madlovics, 2020, pp. 221-223), or a popular democracy structured around political-economic networks.

Cross-tables analysis, chi-square tests and measure of association

Cross-table analysis

The first stage of the analysis was to produce cross tables for the new dichotomous variables. From this, if the research hypothesis is right, we would expect to see a systematic pattern of "old" oligarch MPs failing to vote for prosperity legislation. Table 5.6 below shows the results of a cross-table investigation for the second analytical period of the eighth Rada convocation.

The way to interpret these results is to compare the share of each MP group voting "for" and "not for" on each bill—ie, horizontally, across rows. For example, turning to the top left-hand corner of the results for bill 7, which addressed deregulation of the business environment and was accepted, this shows that, of the 66 deputies in this period identified as linked to the "old" oligarchs (see Table 5.1), 62% failed to vote in the bill's favour, whereas only 32% of other MPs did so—a gap, or "effect", of almost 30 percentage points. This broad pattern is replicated across all of the selected prosperity bills under the second Yatsenyuk government, albeit with a varying effect size. In other words, a much larger share of the "old" oligarch vote is to be found in the "not for" cells. So, although the gap in the voting shares of the two MP groups is close to or above 30 percentage points for seven of the nine bills, it is smaller for two others (bills 12 and 14).

In the third period of analysis, the pattern (not shown here in table form owing to limitations of space) becomes more erratic. The voting patterns of the (53) deputies associated with the "old" oligarchs are similar to those of the second period for four of the eight laws (bills 16, 17, 20 and 22). That is, the size of the effect of membership of the different MP groups shows the same polarisation in the shares of voting "not for/absent" on each piece of legislation.

Table 5.6: Do "old" oligarch groups tend to vote against prosperity bills in period 2? (%)

	"Old" oligarch deputies	Other deputies	% of all deputies
Bill-07			
Not for/absent	62.1	32.4	37.1
For	37.9	67.6	63.0
Bill-08			
Not for absent	95.5	51.6	58.4
For	4.5	48.4	41.6
Bill-09			
Not for/absent	74.2	23.1	31.1
For	25.8	76.9	68.9
Bill-10			
Not for/absent	81.8	50.7	55.6
For	18.2	49.3	44.4
Bill-11			
Not for/absent	87.9	37.1	45.0
For	12.1	62.9	55.0
Bill-12			
Not for/absent	70.8	56.5	58.7
For	29.2	43.5	41.3
Bill-13			
Not for/absent	80.0	36.6	43.3
For	20.0	63.4	56.7
Bill-14			
Not for/absent	90.8	71.0	74.0
For	9.2	29.0	26.0
Bill-15			
Not for/absent	87.7	42.8	49.8
For	12.3	57.2	50.2

Source: Verkhovna Rada. ARKHIV ZA SKLYKANNYAMY (online archive of legislative members & votes). Available: https://iportal.rada.gov.ua/. Own calculations.

For three others bills, however — 19 and 21 and 23 — the degree of polarisation shrinks, and for a fourth (bill 18), is reversed. This change between periods of analysis matches the earlier finding of a break in voting patterns under the Hroysman cabinet. Nonetheless, the cross-table results may be interpreted as providing initial evidence of a relationship that supports the research hypothesis.

Chi-square test and Cramér's V measure

Alongside this initial evidence for a broad, systematic relationship between categories of MPs and their voting patterns, it would be useful to know something of its strength and likelihood of having happened by chance. So, whereas the Cramér's V formula measures the strength of the relationship between nominal variables, the chi-square test provides a check for statistical significance, or how likely it is to be explained by the systematic influence of the independent on the dependant variable, as hypothesised, rather than by chance.

A chi-square test has two components. The first generates the chi-square statistic, which measures the discrepancy between the actual frequencies of each cell of the cross table and their expected frequencies. Expected frequencies are the distributions that would be seen if the independent variable had no effect on the dependent variable. In our case, this would happen if membership of one of the "old" oligarch groups had no impact on voting outcomes. The contributions of each cell are calculated from their individual discrepancies, which are summed to arrive at the chi-square statistic. If the observed frequencies conformed to the expected frequencies—that is, if the null hypothesis of an absence of a relationship had been true—the chi-square statistic would be zero. Broadly speaking, however, the chi-square statistics for period 2 are quite high (the second column in Table 5.7 below), suggesting the presence of a causal effect between the two variables across votes. While this remains the case for half of the laws in period 3, overall, the chi-square statistics for this group of bills tend to be lower.

The second part of the chi-square test is to establish a level of significance as a benchmark against which to compare the probability value (p-value) that accompanies each chi-square statistic (the third column in the table). The level of significance marks the degree of risk that the researcher is willing to accept that they might reject a null hypothesis that is true (a "Type I" error). If the p-value is below this, then the null hypothesis can be rejected, leading to the conclusion that the relationship is statistically significant. If the p-value is above this threshold, we cannot conclude, at the chosen benchmark, that the relationship did not happen by random variation. The bigger the chi-square statistic, the less plausible it is that the observed relationship could be a freak occurrence. In the social sciences, it is common to set this threshold value at the $p < 0.05$ level, which is the one I adopt. In turn, a value of zero on the

Cramér's V measure indicates no association between variables, while a value of 1 indicates perfect association. Table 5.7 below summarises the results for the chi-square tests and the Cramér's V association measure (the fifth column) on the sets of dichotomous variables for the two analytical periods.

Table 5.7: Chi-square test & Cramér's V measure for voting of "old" oligarch groups on prosperity laws, 2014-17

	Chi-square statistic	p-value		Cramer's V value
Period 2, Dec 2014-Mar 2016: 66 old oligarch MPs				
Bill-07	21.085	0.000	***	0.2238
Bill-08	44.169	0.000	***	0.3239
Bill-09	67.916	0.000	***	0.4016
Bill-10	21.823	0.000	***	0.2277
Bill-11	58.049	0.000	***	0.3709
Bill-12	4.641	0.031	**	0.1050
Bill-13	42.104	0.000	***	0.3166
Bill-14	11.189	0.001	***	0.1632
Bill-15	44.257	0.000	***	0.3246
Period 3, April 2016-Dec 2017: 53 old oligarch MPs				
Bill-16	34.866	0.000	***	0.2895
Bill-17	31.575	0.000	***	0.2755
Bill-18	1.760	0.185	ns	-0.0646
Bill-19	6.695	0.015	**	0.1180
Bill-20	41.936	0.000	***	0.3152
Bill-21	2.997	0.083	ns	0.0843
Bill-22	25.450	0.000	***	0.2456
Bill23	0.077	0.781	ns	0.0135

Sources: Verkhovna Rada. ARKHIV ZA SKLYKANNYAMY (online archive of legislative members & votes). Available: https://iportal.rada.gov.ua/. Own calculations. Key: * $p < 0.1$; ** $p < 0.05$; *** $p < 0.01$.

Conclusions from the chi-square test

Extending the findings of the cross-table analysis, from Table 5.7 it can be seen that, for all nine bills in the second period and for five of eight in the third, the chi-square tests show these relationships to be statistically significant at the 0.05 level. For these, the Cramer's V measure assesses the impact of the independent variable—of membership or not of an "old" oligarch group—as between medium small and medium large in the majority of cases. In these cases, we can reject the null hypothesis and conclude that the negative relationship between "old" oligarch faction membership and voting behaviour identified in the cross-table analysis is statistically significant at the 95% confidence level.

Control stage

Which control variable?

So far, then, there appears to be good evidence in support of the hypothesised relationship. However, the control stage of the analysis permits a check for the presence of possible confounding factors — that is, of a common third influence, as yet unconsidered, that explains the observed relationship.

As possible alternative causal factors underlying the observed relationship, I decided to use membership of the original government coalition, or the parliamentary "opposition" to it, as my control variable. To this end, I created a new variable assigning Rada deputies to one of three categories — the five-party coalition; the opposition, made up mostly of factions that emerged from the PoR; or those not participating in any of the formal Rada factions.

Table 5.8: Distribution of "old" oligarch Rada MPs by simplified formal faction, Dec 2014-Dec 2017; (no.)

Factions	"Old" oligarch deputies	Other deputies	Total
5-party coalition	14	295	309
Opposition	44	35	79
No faction	16	50	66
Total	**74**	**380**	**454**

Sources: Verkhovna Rada, ARKHIV ZA SKLYKANNYAMY (online archive of legislative members & votes). Available: https://iportal.rada.gov.ua/. Own calculations. Berdinskikh (2015), *Novoye Vremya*. Romanyuk & Kravets (2016a), (2016b), (2016c), (2017a), (2017b), (2017c), (2018), *Ukrayinska Pravda*. Chernyshev et al (2017), LIGA.net.

A frequency distribution of Rada deputies between "old" oligarch and other MPs on this re-classification is shown in the Table 5.8

above. A prominent feature of the table is the uneven distribution of "old" oligarch deputies across factions — and, in particular, that the bulk of them appeared in opposition ranks (44 of the 74 such deputies identified); and that the majority of opposition MPs were also "old" oligarch MPs (44 out of 79), supporting the intuition that the government vs opposition distinction may be important.

Control results
Controlling the relationship of old oligarch MPs to voting behaviour for the division of Rada deputies into broad coalition or opposition groups, a quite different pattern of voting on the prosperity legislation emerges. In many cases, following control, the chi-square statistic was greatly reduced or disappeared, compared with the uncontrolled test, and many of the variable relationships were rendered no longer statistically significant at the 5% level. Such a fall in the chi-square statistic is what we would expect when controlling for a common third factor. This change in pattern points to "old" oligarch MPs as chiefly an opposition phenomenon, rather than one underlying the operation of the Rada as a whole.

5.3 Chapter findings and conclusions

The focus of this chapter has been an investigation of voting patterns in the Rada, following the Euromaidan revolt, on laws associated with the conditions favourable to economic prosperity.

Some evidence was found for "associated voting" between formal Rada factions and "old" oligarch formations on the selected political economy reforms. However, I did not find statistically robust evidence for the greater preponderance of direct blocking of prosperity legislation among "old" oligarch deputies, compared with other MPs, once this was controlled for the post-Euromaidan government vs opposition divide, as most "old" oligarch deputies identified were associated with political forces close to the Yanukovych administration, driven into opposition by its demise.

With hindsight, when composing my research question, I probably brought to bear too liberal democratic a conception of the Ukrainian legislature. By the end of this strand of research, however,

I had come to a different view of the Rada and how it works within Ukraine's modern political economy system. Specifically, the relationship of "old" oligarch factions to political economy laws is probably less direct than originally envisaged, and should be viewed rather as mediated by the current "balance of power" within the evolving political economy structures of the oligarchy as a whole (ie the current state of relations of the main business-political networks to one another and to the currently dominant political network leaders). An account of some features of this revised view of the Rada forms the substance of my conclusions for this chapter, to which I will return after a brief recap of the chapter's main findings, on which these broader conclusions are based.

5.3.1 Key findings: Continuity of personnel and informal political influence practices

In this chapter, I set out some changes in the character and composition of the Ukrainian legislature — in terms of a marked reduction in representation of the left and right wings of the ideological spectrum, for example — between the convocations elected either side of the Euromaidan. However, it is the continuities between convocations, of personnel, rules and practices, that must be stressed to understand how the Ukrainian oligarchy as an institution of informal political and economic rule managed to survive.

Continuity of personnel was shown by the roughly one-third of MPs who retained a seat in parliament, with these "old hands" identified as a possible channel through which customary informal political practices were transmitted to new cohorts of MPs, so helping to recreate the "regime" across Rada convocations, despite the high turnover of deputies. Relatedly, parliamentary opposition to a proposed change in the electoral rules ahead of the October 2014 general election kept in place the "mixed" electoral system, and so the single-mandate element of it through which many of the "old hands", as well as many of the "old" oligarch MPs, were able to retain a seat in parliament. Moreover, many of the new "revolutionary" leaders were themselves products of the old system and will have become accustomed to informal practices as the regular way of proceeding, bringing to post-Euromaidan governments this understanding of how politics is done. In the persons of Rada legislators who also appeared on the Focus-100 rich list was noted an overlap of key institutions of Ukrainian political and business elite reminiscent of a "power elite", which helps to understand the means by which institutional coherence is achieved. A second intersection, contained within the first, of the "old hands" and the "core" rich represents a smaller-still contingent of the most enduringly successful of Ukraine's political economy actors, among whom oligarchs, as nationally politically active business leaders, were well represented.

Continuity in the operation of material resource power at the highest levels in Ukrainian political life between the pre- and post-Euromaidan periods was illustrated by revelations from the secret accounts kept under Yanukovych, and of text exchanges under Poroshenko, concerning the informal political practice of vote-buying in the Rada. This, it was suggested, should be seen as a backdrop against which to interpret the sub- and cross-factional voting patterns observed in this chapter's second analysis as materially informed. The mode of vote-buying can be refined into "sub-routines" or styles, including the maintenance of a roster of MPs as "retainers" (as with Akhmetov); the continual negotiation of one-off payments for votes on specific pieces of legislation (associated with Kolomoyskyi); or the purchase of a block of votes from one of the parties that market themselves to the competing business-political networks as reliable providers of voting services.

Although vote-buying was the "carry over" political practice focused on in this chapter, it is, of course, just one in a wider repertoire. Other central examples include media backing and electoral funding. Matsiyevsky notes, moreover, the routine conclusion of behind-the-scenes political deals within the Ukrainian elite, as well as an unofficial quota system for the distribution of government posts (2018, p. 349). Along with the "extractive" political and economic schemes outlined in chapter 3, it is these practices, in sum and joined up, that constitute the "regime". Moreover, the continuity and adaptation of the whole interconnected ensemble of political and economic practices across the "critical juncture" of the

Euromaidan revolt is what is meant by the institutional reproduction of the oligarchy. It is the continuity of the ensemble of practices in the round that largely explains the resilience of the oligarchy as an institution, even across bouts of severe political-economic crisis.

5.3.2 Some observational conclusions

The systemically appropriate looseness and flexibility of the Rada's internal organisational arrangements

From the analyses of this chapter, I come to some observational conclusions. The first is that a certain looseness or flexibility in the internal organisational structures of the Rada — of parties, factions, MP groups, as well as the sub- and cross-factional formations — and of the alignments between them is not an incidental institutional feature, but an integral one, expressive of the role of the Rada within Ukraine's political economy regime more broadly.

As in other areas of Ukraine's oligarchic system, where formal political or economic rules undergo regular contestation and alteration, or may be lightly observed, this means that the lines between parties, factions, and business-political networks are often blurred or porous, and associations within and between them fluid. This fluidity is shown not just by the transformation of formal factions in survival mode in a crisis, as with the disintegration of the PoR in 2014, or by their reinvention between convocations, but also by marked realignments of parliamentary forces, as after the collapse of the five-party coalition in 2016.

This is because, as I have argued previously, the Rada operates as a venue for the deal- and alliance-making between the leaders of the strongest business-political networks, through which the transactional relationships of leading wealth-holders to the current holders of state office are continually made, broken and re-forged. Flexibility is therefore an organisational quality that facilitates and corresponds to a mode of elite politics conducted by way of flexible informal networks. That is, a loose factional system emerged as the dominant internal organisational unit of the Rada in the course of the 1990s (Whitmore, 2004, p. 9, 92), and remains so because it suits and is explained by the broader "personalist" context of Ukrainian politics, in which the role of parties is subordinated to the workings of the informal network system (Andrusiv et al, pp. 63-64).

In this light, rather than a basically liberal democratic institution, tainted by the persistent transgressions at the margins, the Rada appears as an institution shot through with informal practices, the operation of which may have to reckon with, or work around and neutralise, the encroachment of formal democratic and ideological party norms. What appears as a transgression from the perspective of the norms of "market society" (Polanyi, 2001, p. 32, 74), where it is assumed that business should be kept at arm's length from the formal political process, is in fact the Ukrainian system, where the practices of high politics and big business are more fused, working correctly according to its own internal logic.

It is possible that this is too harsh an assessment of the Rada as an institution, conditioned by my examination of it through the lens of wealth as political power. The account that comes closest to this, however, is that of the UIF (Andrusiv et al, 2018), a Ukrainian think-tank reported to be close to Volodymyr Zelenskyi, the comic actor-manager who became president of Ukraine in April 2019.

Deals and alliances amplify oligarchs' material resource power, while reducing risks to it

On the data examined here, the absolute voting weight in the Rada of each of the oligarch groups appears insufficient to do anything but tip the balance for or against individual bills, as the situation permits. Of course, as suggested by the observation of "associated voting" between formal and cross-factional Rada groups, the total number of deputies under each oligarch's influence is not the only factor affecting voting outcomes, which are affected also by alliances with other faction leaders. This suggests a second conclusion. This is that, for leading oligarchs, the main purpose of material control of Rada votes may be to buy them a "seat at the table" with the other power resource holders, and their networks, allowing the negotiation of deals and of broader alliances that not only amplify individual oligarch's political influence, but through this offer a more reliable means of achieving legislative goals and of reducing the risk of wealth confiscation. That is, they need to buy MPs' votes to take part in the transactional deal- and alliance-making between networks that is at the heart of the politics of the Ukrainian elite, and it is through this process that they are best able to protect and augment their material interests.

Factional realignment in the Rada signals full reconstitution of the oligarchic system

Probably the most striking finding of the analysis of this chapter is that, with the institution of the Hroysman government, there was a marked break in the pattern of parliamentary support for political economy reforms, distinguishing the third period of analysis from the previous two. This corresponds to a significant realignment of parliamentary and network forces linked to the disintegration of the five-party coalition, and to the struggle between competing political-economic "pyramids" for pre-eminence, encouraged in part by the reversion to the 2004 premier-presidential constitution.

The significance of this is that it indicates a third or final stage of "reintegration" into formal politics of both the "old" oligarch networks and the remains of the Yanukovych era elite—and with it, the full recreation of the oligarchy in the Rada as a transactional relation between successful politicians, state officials and the main business-political networks—following a brief phase of the rhetoric of "de-oligarchisation" in the aftermath of the Euromaidan victory. Earlier stages in the process of institutional reintegration include the appointment in early 2014 of leading oligarchs as regional governors as a defensive measure against Russian military incursion, followed by the reliance on oligarch's financial and media backing in the electoral campaigns later that year.

As a consequence of this shift in alliances, the level of support for prosperity laws rose across the Rada as a whole. This suggests that the new arrangement proved more effective as a vehicle of support for the government's legislative programme than the five-party coalition under Yatsenyuk. The question is, in return for what? This is a key subject of the investigation of the next chapter.

6 Post-Euromaidan energy rent-extraction schemes, amid energy-sector reforms

6.1 Introduction and approach

6.1.1 Why energy-sector case studies?

The political economy framework outlined earlier in this book points to oligarchy, centrally, as the politics of wealth defence, a form of extractive or exclusionary politics, while suggesting that extractive political institutions tend to foster extractive economic ones (chapter 2). The previous chapter examined voting patterns in the Verkhovna Rada (parliament) as a key institutional setting for certain political practices — namely, of the conversion of material resource power into political influence by means of control of parliamentary votes and, through this, the ability to forge parliamentary deals and alliances with the leaders of other business-political networks — crucial to the reproduction of Ukraine's extractive political economy regime. But what do extractive economic practices look like in contemporary Ukraine? And how do they connect with the extractive mode of elite politics that prevails?

To answer these questions, this chapter focuses on oligarchic rent-extraction schemes in the Ukrainian energy sector, against a backdrop of sectoral reform and political change. One reason for choosing the energy sector for this part of my research is its importance to an economy that has historically been highly energy intensive. The reason for narrowing the focus still further to the gas industry is that it, in turn, has been central to the formation of the Ukrainian oligarchy since the 1990s, largely owing to the size of economic rents available (Balmaceda and Rutland, 2014).

To recap, in orthodox economics, an economic rent implies a level of income above what is needed to induce the delivery of factor supplies (land, labour and capital) to the market (Stilwell, 2019, pp. 101-102). On the one hand, temporary or "dynamic" rents are seen as a vital mechanism for the proper operation of a market economy, facilitating both innovation and adjustment to economic shocks, as price changes signal to investors and suppliers the location of profitable business opportunities, so encouraging the reallocation of resources between sectors and re-equilibrating market supply and demand. When rents are persistent, however, they may be considered a sign of market failure (Sethi et al, 2017). Less formally, such rents can be thought of as increasing one's share in current wealth, without contributing to the creation of new wealth (Matsiyevsky, 2018, p. 349).

The kind of politically constructed money-making opportunities that have tended to replenish the material basis of elite rule in post-communist Ukraine can frequently be considered as persistent forms of economic rents. According to a well-informed source, energy schemes in modern Ukraine have generated annual flows of rents of "up to 5% of the country's GDP (approximately £3.5bn) in peak years" (Balmaceda and Rutland, 2014). Lastly, the gas-sector rent-seeking schemes provide examples for comparison across time of extractive economic practices with a family resemblance which, in combination, have had a lasting impact on, and been significantly affected by, Ukraine's political economy institutions.

6.1.2 Contribution, "contextualising" tools, findings and key argument

The main original contribution of this chapter is an analysis of rent-extraction schemes in the Ukrainian gas industry across the general crisis of 2014-15, helping to concretise an understanding of what the overlap of the political and economic spheres of social life looks like in practice. This is done by comparing these with earlier "benchmark" schemes in terms of the kinds of actors, institutions and mechanisms involved, and the relations between them, in an evolving political context. In the first half of the chapter, I develop two contextualising "tools" to aid analysis of the operation of these post-Euromaidan schemes in the second half. By emphasising context, concrete detail and specificity as a mode of analysis, this chapter draws on the approach of "old" institutional economics, a brief account of which was given at the end of chapter 2.

The first contextualising tool is an account of the long-term problems of reform of the energy sector, its dysfunctional condition at the end of the Yanukovych presidency and the main lines of sectoral reform from 2014, which altered the structure of opportunities available for rent extractors. The second tool is an account of the operation of two large intermediary rent-extraction schemes that dominated the Ukrainian gas sector earlier in the post-communist era[18]. The purpose of these is to provide a benchmark against which to compare the case studies of gas-sector rent-extraction schemes in the post-Euromaidan era, thereby bringing out elements of continuity and change in their operational features in an evolving political-institutional environment. A key output of this analysis is a "taxonomy" of rent-extraction schemes in the Ukrainian energy sector over the past three decades (Table 6.4), followed by a brief account of what this suggests about the nature and mode of regeneration of the contemporary Ukrainian oligarchy as a whole.

A stylised account of Ukraine's evolving national political economy governance structures is a third contextualising device. Focusing chiefly on the contrast between the Yanukovych and Poroshenko eras, it shows how the dominant operational relations between key formal political actors in the government and state apparatus on the one hand, and the politically involved leaders of large business organisations (oligarchs) on the other, shifted across presidencies, post-independence. This was positioned to follow my account of the generative phase of the Ukrainian oligarchy, and forms the final section of chapter 3.

Among the main findings of this chapter are that, although Russia's military interventions in Ukraine following the collapse of the Yanukovych administration helped the Ukrainian oligarchy to survive the Euromaidan revolt, the halt to direct gas imports from Russia that it induced proved one of the main "anti-corruption"

---

[18] In business, an intermediary is a firm that stands between the producer and the buyer, specialising in value-adding services such as distribution, branding or sales. In the case of the energy intermediaries established in post-independence Ukraine, however, they are often charged with merely inserting themselves into the supply chain without performing any economically useful function, existing merely to extract economic rents for business-political elites.

measures of the period. This and other developments, such as the stepped rise in household gas tariffs, helped to restrict the scope for rent-seeking opportunities, especially at the height of the crisis in 2014-15. A key argument, however, is that rent-seeking opportunities began to open up again in the gas sector thereafter, and to shift to other parts of the energy sector, following the passing of the worst of the economic crisis and a re-balancing of political-economic forces domestically from 2016.

The analysis of the politically enabled context for elite rent-extraction schemes is placed last of the empirical investigations of this book. This positioning reflects the notion of political institutions as conditioning economic ones. By detailing a series of cases in the energy sector showing how the main networks are able to convert their political influence back into wealth, the chapter completes the circuit of the "currency flow" model of institutional reproduction set out in the opening and closing chapters.

6.2 Contextualising tools

6.2.1 Reform of the Ukrainian energy sector

Energy-sector reform before 2014

On independence in 1991, Ukraine inherited from the Soviet Union an economy, centred on heavy industry, that was "hooked on cheap hydrocarbons" (Balmaceda and Rutland, 2014). Within a decade, the share of industry in Ukraine's economic structure had fallen from one-half to around one-third, owing to a long and deep "transition" slump (Turley and Luke, 2011, p. 77). However, the energy intensity of the Ukrainian economy — the ratio of energy used to output produced — stayed high in international comparison, while overreliance on Russian natural gas imports continued into the Yanukovych presidency. The first acted as a drag on economic efficiency, while the second proved a chronic threat to the country's energy security.

In his assessment of Ukraine's energy sector before the onset of post-Euromaidan reforms, Karel Hirman argues that, by early 2014, there had been "no changes in the structure of the energy sector in Ukraine over the past 20 years" (2019, p. 78). It is not that there were no attempts at reform, however, but rather that each time they were stopped in their tracks by "vested interests", a common euphemism for the association of economic interest groups and political power holders that I am calling "the oligarchy".

The problem of large-scale corruption in Ukraine's gas-supply business was not addressed until 2000, when Viktor Yushchenko, as head of a reforming government, appointed Yuliya Tymoshenko as energy minister. She eliminated ITERA as "intermediary" in the post-Soviet gas trade, reverting to direct trade between Naftogaz, Ukraine's state energy holding, and Gazprom, its Russian counterpart. In early 2001, however, under pressure from the domestic gas-trading lobby, Tymoshenko was sacked by the president, Leonid Kuchma, and the Yushchenko government fell a few months later, while the intermediaries were soon re-established (Havrylyshyn, 2017, pp. 230-231).

Two further concerted attempts at energy reform were made, in 2005 and in 2008/09 — on each occasion led by Tymoshenko, this time as prime minister. In 2005, following the Orange Revolution, Tymoshenko tried to remove RosUkrEnergo (RUE) as the main intermediary in the gas trade with Russia, but was sacked that September by Yushchenko, now president, and RUE was reinserted into the gas business in a still more lucrative role (Havrylyshyn, 2017, p. 231). In a dispute with Russia over a new gas contract in 2008/09, Tymoshenko, back leading the government, went over Yushchenko's head to strike a deal with Vladimir Putin, her Russian counterpart, again restoring direct trading links between the two countries' state energy firms, but paying a higher price for imported gas. This may have been aimed, in part, at cutting financial flows to Dmytro Firtash, a key backer of Yanukovych, her main political rival in the then upcoming 2010 presidential contest (Hale, 2015, p. 336). From this, Balmaceda suggests that a large part of the infighting in the Orange camp from 2005 was driven by contestation over gas rents (Balmaceda, 2013, pp. 122-123).

The events leading up to the 2009 deal — in particular, another halt in Russian gas supplies that winter — seem finally to have prompted the Ukrainian leadership, during the presidency of

Viktor Yanukovych, to start to diversify the country's gas imports (see Figure 6.3 below). However, Yanukovych's victory against Tymoshenko in the presidential contest of 2010 paved the way for Firtash, as one of his main backers, to reinvent his intermediary scheme under a new name, OstChem, and in late 2011 Yanukovych used Tymoshenko's 2009 energy deal with Putin as a premise to imprison her on charges of abuse of office (Wilson, 2015, p. 347).

From this brief account, it is possible to summarise the story of reforms in the Ukrainian energy sector before 2014 as follows: starting late, and usually triggered only by a serious economic or political crisis, energy reforms were often truncated once the danger had passed and usually quickly reversed.

The dysfunctional condition of the energy sector in 2014

In late February 2014, therefore, at the point where the Yanukovych period gave way to the post-Euromaidan era, the energy sector was rundown and dysfunctional. Perhaps the clearest expression of this was the very low household tariffs for gas and heating. For example, according to IMF data, reproduced in the pair of charts below, in 2013 some of Ukraine's east European neighbours were paying between three and six times as much as Ukraine for domestic gas, and between two and three times as much for home heating (IMF, 2014b, pp. 17-18). Figure 6.1 shows that, while the price of gas was close to US$500 per 1,000 cu metres for Moldova and US$600 for Poland, in Ukraine it was just US$100 (the light grey bars on the chart, read against the left-hand scale); and while heating cost US$30 per gigacalorie in Ukraine, it was around US$80 in Moldova and Romania (the darker grey dots, read on the right-hand scale).

At the same time, in Ukraine groups of users were subject to different gas tariffs (Figure 6.2), with private- and most public-sector firms paying full cost-recovery price of around UAH4,750 (US$594) per 1,000 cu metres, but households and heating utilities paying less than one-quarter of this. Low household energy prices have often been identified as a key source of corruption in Ukraine, offering members of the elite significant rent-seeking opportunities. Hirman suggests that, in addition, prices for this segment of the gas market were kept low in part to compensate consumers for poor service and unreliable infrastructure (Hirman, 2019, p. 75). Low energy prices also gave households a stake in the dysfunctional situation, which helps to explain why it endured.

Figures 6.1 & 6.2: Ukraine's gas & heat tariffs in east European comparison, 2013 (top chart); retail gas tariffs for different users in Ukraine, 2013 (bottom chart)

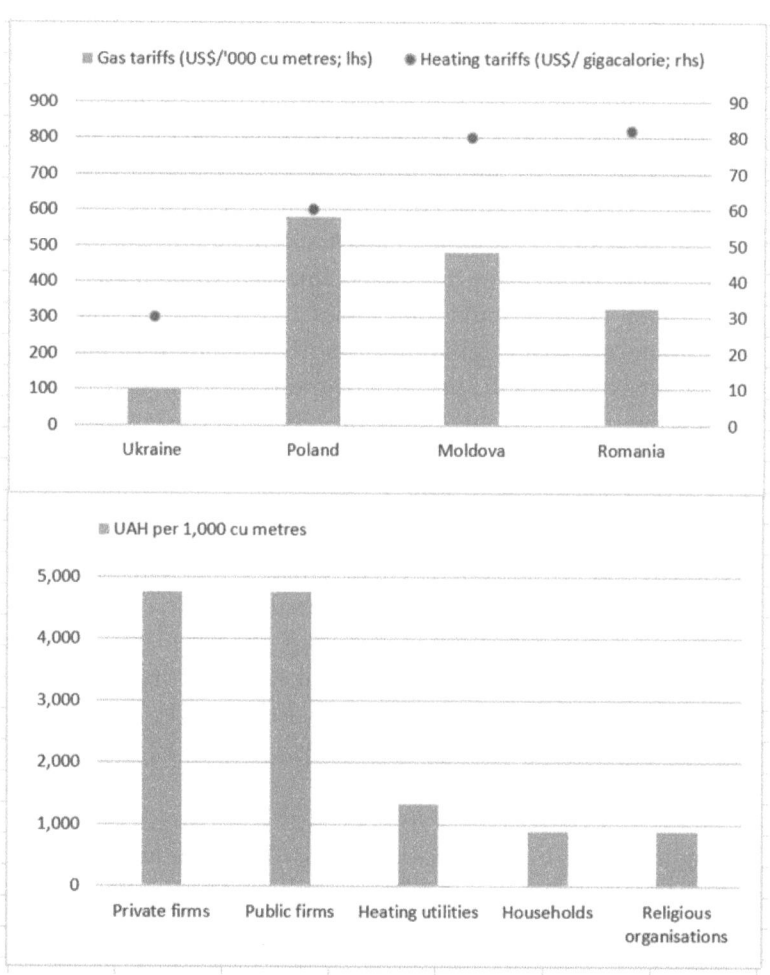

Source: Adapted from IMF (2014b, p. 18).

Creating weak incentives to economise on energy use, while undermining the incentives and ability of energy firms to invest in exploration, production, and distribution, selectively low energy prices were both a cause and symptom of sectoral dysfunction, manifesting as a range of negative economic effects, including low energy efficiency, high levels of pollution, and chronic damage to public finances. On energy efficiency, while in 2013 Ukraine produced output worth US$5 per kilogramme of oil equivalent—measured in constant US dollars at purchasing power parity (PPP) to aid international comparison—in the UK, it was US$15 per kilogramme, according to the *World Development Indicators*.[19] On public finances, low domestic energy tariffs produced large persistent losses at Naftogaz, which were covered by the state (Table 6.1 below shows these for 2010-15). A Ukrainian think-tank cites a range of estimates on the scale of damage to public finances from under-priced energy. One estimate puts total losses to Naftogaz in 2005-15 at UAH620bn (not easily convertible into US dollars because of the marked weakening of the hryvnya over this period), while another assesses the cost to the government at US$53bn. The IMF calculates gas subsidies at 5% of GDP in 2012, and all energy subsidies at 8% of GDP (Burakovsky et al, 2018, p. 25).

From the perspective of this study, however, the main deleterious effect of low household energy prices is that they acted as an incentive for the reproduction of Ukraine's political economy regime, the oligarchy. As a result, "in the long run, ordinary Ukrainians are paying the price of being trapped in an economic model that depends on rent extraction rather than investment in competitive industries" (Balmaceda and Rutland, 2014).

The main energy-sector reforms from 2014

During the Yanukovych presidency, populist economic policies at home, alongside an overvalued exchange rate, produced very large fiscal and current-account deficits (IMF, 2014a, pp. 5-6). In

---

[19] It may be that the degree of energy inefficiency in Ukraine is exaggerated somewhat by the failure of its GDP statistics to capture the activity of the shadow economy, which remains sizeable (Balmaceda and Prokip, 2021, p. 140).

early February 2014 the soon-to-be-outgoing authorities were forced by the low level of reserves to switch to a floating currency regime. With the domestic political crisis reaching its violent denouement at the end of the month, triggering Russia's military takeover of Crimea, by early 2014 the conditions were in place for these macroeconomic imbalances to begin to unwind, destabilising the Ukrainian economy. In 2014, therefore, the return to energy-sector reform was again driven by crisis, becoming central to the macroeconomic stabilisation plans of Arseniy Yatsenyuk's interim government, owing to its impact on public finances.

Because of the circumstances of their prompting, the momentum behind energy reforms took them further than before. This was not just a reflection of the scale of the crisis, but also of the time it took for "vested interests" to regain a foothold in politics, which only happened in stages. Once these were complete, the authorities' backing for energy reforms seemed to lose steam. With opportunities stymied in the gas trade, owing to reorientation of imports away from Russia, the attention of prominent oligarchs switched to rent-seeking schemes in other parts of the energy sector.

The energy reforms undertaken in Ukraine from 2014 were set out in the interim government's Letter of Intent to the IMF and an accompanying Memorandum of Economic and Fiscal Policies of April 2014 (IMF, 2014a, pp. 59-60; 63; 72-74), covering household energy tariffs, energy diversification, market regulation and institutional restructuring. These reforms were important, separately and in combination, because they changed the structure of opportunities facing rent-seeking actors. By following the progress, delays or setbacks on these reforms, it is possible to chart the impact of developments in both popular democratic and elite politics — in this instance, the re-alignment from 2016 of business-political networks, their reintegration into formal institutional politics and the corresponding strengthening of the network "pyramid" around Poroshenko, at the expense of the one around Yatsenyuk. This corresponds to an increasing resistance from the authorities to implementing energy reforms, and so to a re-opening of energy-sector rent-seeking opportunities, albeit on a smaller scale than before.

Reform of energy tariffs

A central aim of the reforms was to raise residential gas and heating tariffs to cost-recovery level, so eliminating the gap with industry prices (IMF, 2014a, pp. 20-22). Although designed to address some of the serious, chronic economic side-effects of low household energy prices noted above, amid a deep recession, this policy was "the most politically and socially sensitive topic of the entire four-year period" (Hirman, 2019, p. 79). Nonetheless, under successive Yatsenyuk governments, household tariffs were raised in three steps between May 2014 and April 2016 (see Figure 6.5 below).

The main result of this, making it a "flagship" economic policy success story of the period, was the elimination of the "quasi-fiscal" deficit at Naftogaz by 2016, two years ahead of schedule, marking the first year of its contribution to the budget since 2011, and the first of doing without a subsidy since 2006 (Burakovsky et al, 2018, p. 26). This is shown in the Table 6.1 below, with the "quasi-fiscal" deficit at Naftogaz, already significant before the crisis, shooting up to 5.5% of GDP in 2014, boosting the overall budget shortfall to 10% of GDP, which is very high. This contributed to a dramatic rise in the public debt burden, from 40% of GDP in 2013 to 70% in 2014 (another key factor was the collapse of the exchange rate).

Table 6.1: Ukraine's public finances, 2010-17; % of GDP

	2010	2011	2012	2013	2014	2015	2016	2017
Government balance	-5.8	-2.8	-4.3	-4.8	-4.5	-1.2	-2.2	-2.2
Naftogaz deficit	-1.6	-1.5	-1.2	-1.9	-5.5	-0.9	0.0	0.0
Overall budget balance, incl Naftogaz deficit	**-7.4**	**-4.3**	**-5.5**	**-6.7**	**-10.0**	**-2.1**	**-2.2**	**-2.2**
General government debt	40.6	36.9	37.5	40.5	70.3	79.5	81.2	71.6

Sources: IMF, 2014a, 2014b, 2016a, 2016b, 2019a; World Economic Outlook (WEO) Database, October 2019.

Owing mainly to the tariff increases, the deficit at Naftogaz shrank rapidly to less than 1% of GDP the following year, before disappearing in 2016-17. By contributing to a slide in political support in the polls (Razumkov Centre, 2017), however, the impact of these measures on Ukrainians' already low living standards seems to have motivated the government of Arseniy Yatsenyuk to backtrack thereafter, in late 2015 reaffirming the operation of price controls in the household segment (Burakovsky et al, 2018, p. 29, footnote 41).

Diversification of gas imports

Diversification of energy supplies, long delayed or ignored, was aimed at reducing Ukraine's dependence on energy imports directly from Russia, to deprive it of a means of geo-economic coercion. Ukraine's elimination by 2016 of all direct imports of natural gas from Russia, and their import instead by "reverse" supply from Central Europe, became another high-profile post-Euromaidan policy success, therefore. The combination of recession, the loss of some energy intensive industries to the war in eastern regions and the hikes in household tariffs led to a steep drop in gas consumption in Ukraine, from about 50bn cu metres in 2013 to 32bn cu metres in 2016-17 (Naftogaz, 2021). This is shown below by the shortening of the darkest grey bars from left to right in Figure 6.3.

Figure 6.3: Volumes of production, import & use of natural gas in Ukraine, 2010-17

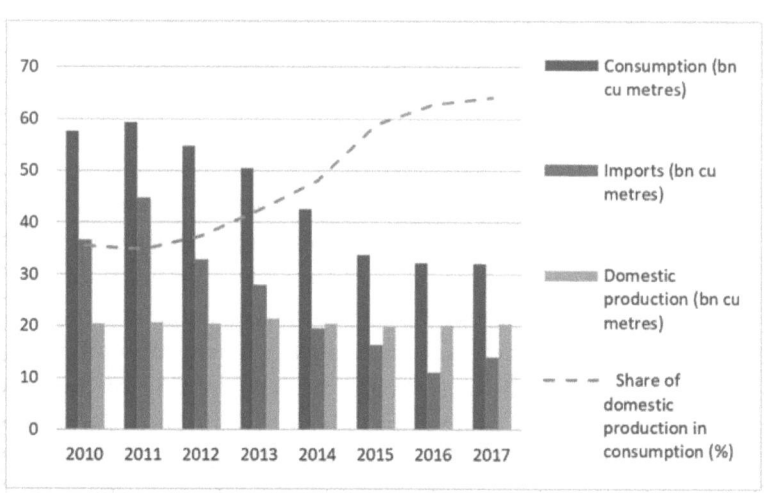

Sources: Naftogaz (2020). *VYDOBUVANNYA HAZU*. Available: https://bit.ly/3tWO1ag. Naftogaz (2021), *Vykorystannya pryrodnoho hazu*. Available: https://bit.ly/3nOf869. Own calculations.

Within these totals, the share supplied by domestic gas production rose from around 40% of all consumption in 2013 to more than 60% by 2016-17 (shown on the chart above by the rising dashed grey line). However, this was because of a halving of all gas imports between 2013 and 2017, rather than an expansion of domestic gas production, the volume of which remained broadly stable at just above 20bn cu metres (Naftogaz, 2020), suggesting no quick turnaround in investment and productivity in the sector.

Reform of energy market regulations
The goal of the final two post-Euromaidan gas-sector reforms — of the regulatory framework and of Naftogaz — was to develop a more transparent and competitive gas market compatible with Ukraine's membership of the EU's Energy Community (EC), which it had joined in 2011, and with the EU's so-called Third Energy Package in particular (Bayramov and Marusyk, 2019, p. 77). The basic "roadmap" for energy reform was already contained, therefore, in the framework of the country's EU association agreement (AA) and deep and comprehensive free-trade agreement (DCFTA), covering the political, economic policy and trade dimensions of Ukraine's planned EU integration. Although thwarted temporarily by Yanukovych's failure to sign the AA in November 2013 — thereby triggering the mass protests that eventually brought him down — the agreement was signed by Petro Poroshenko in June 2014, following his election to the Ukrainian presidency, but did not come into force until the start of 2016.

On the regulatory dimension of gas-sector reforms, therefore, the most important goal was the development of a legal framework, in line with EU energy laws, to be overseen by an independent regulator. Central measures of the legislative alignment included allowing third-party access to the national gas transmission system, hitherto monopolised by Naftogaz, and the raising of domestic household gas prices, as described above. By late 2016, the authorities had also "committed to introducing a quarterly adjustment mechanism to ensure prices stay on a par with import prices" (IMF, 2016a, p. 14), in part to "depoliticise" the issue.

In September 2016 a law was passed on the establishment of a new energy market regulator with enhanced powers. Thereafter, the government is reported to have delayed the appointment of a management team at the new regulator (Konończuk and Matuszak, 2017). Moreover, although household gas prices were supposed to rise by a further 17% in October 2017, "Fearing a political backlash, the authorities suspended the adjustment mechanisms" (IMF, 2019, p. 16). Hirman notes the slow pace of alignment with EU energy laws, so that by the time of a 2018 report on overall progress, although legislative alignment on 24% of the *acquis communautaire* (the body of EU law) had taken place, the figure was only 6% for energy sector laws, mostly on the gas market (Hirman, 2019, p. 80). Moreover, Bayramov and Marusyk underscore the crucial distinction in post-Euromaidan Ukraine between the passing of energy reform legislation and its practical implementation (2019, p. 75).

Naftogaz restructuring

Naftogaz and its subsidiaries dominate the Ukrainian oil and gas sectors. As an institution central to the political economy of Ukraine since its establishment in the late 1990s, purportedly as a means of centralising energy rents (Balmaceda, 2013, p. 113), the issue of its governance and restructuring were high on the list of energy reforms proposed by the post-Euromaidan authorities and their international backers. The interim government suggested that reform of Naftogaz was necessary in the short term to reduce the strain on public finances, and over the longer term to attract investment to the sector (IMF, 2014a, p. 63). It was not until 2016, however, that any of the plans for reform of Naftogaz began to take shape. This included:

- the appointment in May of a more independent supervisory board, for which the powers of control of Naftogaz subsidiaries were expanded in December (Burakovsky et al, 2018, p. 27);
- the delivery to the EU by July of an official plan to "unbundle" Naftogaz — that is, to separate the gas transmission and gas storage elements of the business; and

- the development of a "corporate governance action plan" for Naftogaz, to reduce costs and increase transparency.

Soon after this, however, according to a later IMF report, "Despite some initial success in advancing energy [and banking sector] reforms...reforms increasingly faced resistance" (IMF, 2019, p. 14). As a result, in September 2017, the independent members of the new supervisory board resigned (Antonenko et al, 2018), accusing the government of disrupting "unbundling" preparations, and of interfering in the activities of Ukrgazvydobuvannya (UGV), the state-owned gas producer, and Ukrtransgaz (UTG), the gas pipelines operator. Figure 6.4 below depicts in simplified form the relation of Naftogaz to its main subsidiaries, along with the main functions of each. The purpose is to make it easier for the reader to follow the subsequent analyses of the chapter, in which these portmanteau names of Ukrainian energy enterprises will often be used.

Figure 6.4: Naftogaz & main subsidiaries: structure & functions

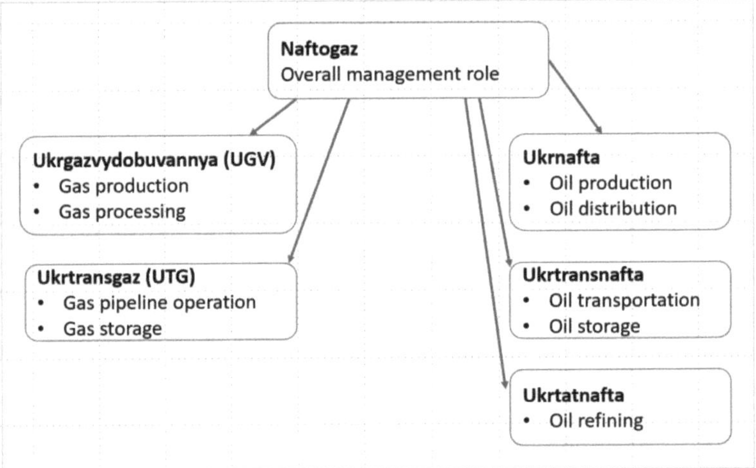

```
                    ┌─────────────────────────┐
                    │ Naftogaz                │
                    │ Overall management role │
                    └─────────────────────────┘

┌───────────────────────────────┐     ┌───────────────────────────────┐
│ Ukrgazvydobuvannya (UGV)      │     │ Ukrnafta                      │
│  • Gas production             │     │  • Oil production             │
│  • Gas processing             │     │  • Oil distribution           │
└───────────────────────────────┘     └───────────────────────────────┘

┌───────────────────────────────┐     ┌───────────────────────────────┐
│ Ukrtransgaz (UTG)             │     │ Ukrtransnafta                 │
│  • Gas pipeline operation     │     │  • Oil transportation         │
│  • Gas storage                │     │  • Oil storage                │
└───────────────────────────────┘     └───────────────────────────────┘

                                      ┌───────────────────────────────┐
                                      │ Ukrtatnafta                   │
                                      │  • Oil refining               │
                                      └───────────────────────────────┘
```

Source: Naftogaz Europe (2014). Available: https://bit.ly/3AM8q45.

Interim observations

To conclude this section, two observations can be made. The first is that Naftogaz appears as one of the "essential" institutional settings in which the leading business-political networks struggle with one another for resource control, often by trying to place associates into key management positions. In this sense, it may be seen, alongside the Rada, the courts and the presidential administration, as one of "essential" sub-institutional sites on which the Ukrainian oligarchy as a whole is recreated, regulated and evolves. A second observation is that the energy reforms discussed above were undertaken during a severe crisis in order to meet IMF loan conditions. That such reforms have tended to be externally imposed, rather than internally driven, and so better adapted to Ukraine's political and economic circumstances (Bayramov and Marusyk, 2019, p. 13), probably helps to explain their relative lack of purchase.

6.2.2 Two "historical" gas intermediary case studies

Lazarenko's United Energy Systems of Ukraine (UESU), 1995-98
The essence of the rent-extraction scheme of Pavlo Lazarenko in the Ukrainian gas sector in 1995-98, with Yuliya Tymoshenko as his chief adjunct, was the use of his formal political position as a high-level government official to award energy contracts to a business, the earnings of which he and his business-political network were the "ultimate beneficiaries" — a fact that they went to some lengths to obscure. His operation can perhaps be seen as a prototype for later large-scale rent-extraction schemes, not just in the energy sector, but across the Ukrainian economy. It must have shown what was possible when political connections, organisational knowledge and an imaginative leap in scale come together, paving the way for a succession of similar later schemes, several linked to Dmytro Firtash, the main Ukrainian "gas" oligarch, who has had a more lasting impact on modern Ukrainian politics than Lazarenko.

So how did the Lazarenko scheme work within the political set up of the day? What were its mechanisms? Which political and business actors, and institutions, were involved, and what were the relations between them?

Central here is the development of regional business-political networks in the early 1990s out of the social, organisational and political material of late Soviet society. In Ukraine, the roots of these structures, Mikhail Minakov suggests, go back as far as the bans on ideological factions in the Soviet Communist Party under Stalin (Minakov, 2019, pp. 221-222). Developing in-group patterns of hierarchical personal loyalty, in part in competition with rival regional party-administrative structures for the leading official posts in Soviet Ukraine, these left the regional elite networks with a degree of cohesion, administrative and management skills, as well as political experience, that proved a competitive advantage — and for network members, a source of security — in the chaotic and sometimes dangerous period of the 1990s. In the course of that decade, these advantages saw them win out over rival kinds of elite organisation (Minakov, 2019, pp. 229-230). From these formations, leading regional political actors were able to launch careers in national politics as a way of claiming for themselves and their group a share of the resources available only at national level.

The biographies of both Lazarenko and Tymoshenko, straddling independence in 1991, fit into this picture, which recalls also the discussion in chapter 3 on the generative phase of the Ukrainian oligarchy. That is, both Lazarenko and Tymoshenko seem to have been trained in late Soviet institutions to prepare them for lives as functionaries in the Dnipropetrovsk regional administrative-economic apparatus, him as an agronomist, her in mining technology, then economics (*Ukrayinskyi doshch*, 2020). With Gorbachev's reforms in the late 1980s, they were among the relatively privileged stratum of Soviet society with the knowledge, connections, training and skills, and perhaps self-confidence, to make the most of the business opportunities then starting to appear.

Over time, and by way of sometimes violent struggles over resources and position, the late Soviet networks of personal economic and administrative connection developed into the post-communist regional networks, the two most important centring on the industrial regions of Dnipropetrovsk and Donetsk, but with less powerful networks based in other regions or cities — as in the case of the Kyiv network — and with much internal differentiation. For example, after Kuchma was elected, the Dnipropetrovsk network "split into several competing and hostile groups seeking to control resources through the privatisation process and the control of trade flows (oil, gas)" (Avioutskii, 2010, p. 122).

Amid Kuchma's attempt to combine informal political know-how with enhanced presidential powers to stabilise the relations of post-Soviet political and economic power by "balancing" the interests of the leading business-political networks (Balmaceda, 2013, p. 98), Lazarenko, as another key political representative of the Dnipropetrovsk group, rose to the position of deputy prime minister with responsibility for restructuring the energy sector (Hirman, 2018, p. 77). This gave him the formal political authority to set the rules on energy imports and distribution.

In this role, in the mid-1990s Lazarenko awarded to United Energy Systems of Ukraine (UESU) the exclusive contract to import and distribute natural gas supplies for the Dnipropetrovsk region, so that in 1995-97 UESU became Ukraine's largest energy importer, generating annual turnover of US$10bn (Hirman, 2019, p. 77). UESU was founded by Tymoshenko in 1995, but 85%-owned by United Energy International (UEI), another of her business creations. At some point, the title of UESU's gas contracts were transferred to UEI, while the payments of Ukrainian gas consumers went into UEI's bank accounts. In 1996 UEI transferred US$140m to Cyprus-registered Somolli Enterprises, controlled by Tymoshenko. In 1996-97 Somolli paid Lazarenko US$162m (Hirman, 2019, p. 77).

Two crucial international dimensions of Lazarenko's scheme can be identified. The first is the energy supply link with Gazprom and the Russian officials assumed to have authorised and benefited from it. This was necessary for the generation of what Balmaceda terms "external" rents (2013, p. 6). The second was use of the legal and financial services of the international wealth-management industry, such as registration of firms in tax havens. This was necessary both to complete and to obscure the circuit of conversion of political authority into private material gain, as well as to keep the wealth accumulated out of the reach of the national government and business rivals, underlining a point already made in chapter 4.

These steps could not have happened outside of a conducive political environment — that is, not just the specific political institutions that aid rent-extraction, but also the particular way that the interpenetrating worlds of politics and economics are articulated and align.

In the end, Lazarenko's personal political ambitions seem to have been his undoing, as Kuchma only brought charges of embezzlement of state funds against him when he suggested he might run against Kuchma for the presidency in 1999 (Kudelia and Kasianov, 2021, p. 22). That year, Lazarenko fled Ukraine to the US, where he was arrested by the authorities and eventually convicted of money-laundering (Wayne, 2016). Up to half a billion US dollars were confiscated from Lazarenko's US accounts following his arrest (Hirman, 2019, pp. 77), testifying to the scale of his personal financial benefit from the scheme, while a decade and a half later, according to the US authorities, he still had up to US$250m hidden abroad (Wayne, 2016).

Dmytro Firtash's RosUkrEnergo (RUE), July 2004 to January 2009

The story of RosUkrEnergo (RUE), the intermediary that dominated the Ukraine-Russia gas trade for a significant chunk of the 2000s, takes place in two parts. The first runs from its founding in July 2004 until the agreement that followed a serious gas dispute with Russia in January 2006. The second runs from then until late January 2009, when a new deal struck between Yuliya Tymoshenko and Vladimir Putin, as the prime ministers of Ukraine and Russia, respectively, cut RUE out of the gas trade.

The mechanism of rent extraction of the RUE scheme was simple: with political backing at the highest levels in both Russia and Ukraine, RUE was able to buy gas from Gazprom at low prices and sell it at higher prices both in Ukraine — including to Naftogaz after 2006 — and to central eastern and western Europe (Burakovsky et al, 2018, p. 24; Grey et al, 2014).

RUE was established as a joint venture between Ukrainian and Russian partners, 50%-owned by Rosgas Holding and 50% by Centragas Holding, all three registered in Switzerland. Rosgas held the share of the business belonging to Russia's Gazprom, whereas that of Centragas was held for Group DF, with Dmytro Firtash as its majority owner (giving him 45% ownership of RUE) and Ivan Fursin, a sometime MP for the Party of Regions (PoR), holding a minority share that gave him a 5% stake in RUE (Grey et al, 2014).

The RUE scheme was similar to Lazarenko's UESU, involving the two countries' state-owned energy conglomerates and licensed by powerful formal political connections at home and abroad, for whom it generated private incomes at the expense of Ukrainian and Russian public finances, but with the proceeds stowed away in business structures registered in countries specialising in "wealth protection" services (such as Cyprus and Switzerland).

At the same time, the RUE scheme, especially in its final form between 2006 and 2009, was both more comprehensive and larger in scale in terms of its financial and political impact. While RUE started life in a deal between Leonid Kuchma and Vladimir Putin in July 2004 to replace the earlier Eural Trans Gas intermediary, Balmaceda stresses the qualitative change in its position in the gas trade as a result of the agreement put in place from late January 2006, which contractually embedded RUE's control over the whole Ukraine-Russia gas import business. Alongside the takeover of gas imports, moreover, the establishment of a connected company, UkrHazEnergo (UHE), was an aspect of the 2006 deal that had significant long-term macroeconomic ramifications for Ukraine. This was because, by awarding to UHE the right to market gas to industrial consumers in Ukraine, it took from Naftogaz the most profitable segment of the domestic gas market. In combination with its statutory obligation to sell gas to households and household heating enterprises below cost (Balmaceda, 2013, p. 128), this helps to explain the development of a chronic "quasi-fiscal" deficit at Naftogaz, by which financial shortfalls at the company were for many years covered from the state budget (see Table 6.1 above).

RUE's profits are recorded at US$755m in 2005, US$785m in 2006 (RosUkrEnergo, 2007) and US$795m in 2007, the last on turnover from gas sales of US$10bn (Grey et al, 2014). On reported annual average gas volumes of 50bn cu metres in 2005-08, and using average German border prices for gas (Balmaceda, 2013, p. 124), the total potential turnover of the gas handled by RUE at market prices comes to an annual average of around US$16bn.

Firtash was involved in other gas-sector rent-extraction schemes, but RUE is the one that launched him into the premier league of very wealthy and politically influential Ukrainians whom

I am calling oligarchs. The value of Firtash's domestic business assets peaked in 2012 under Yanukovych, at US$3.4bn (0.5% of national wealth), taking him to 4th place on the Focus rich list. Although this value fell sharply post-Euromaidan, he remained among the ten wealthiest Ukrainians. Compared to Lazarenko and Tymoshenko, however, Firtash is of a different "social type", also familiar from the generation story of the Ukrainian oligarchy — an entrepreneurial outsider whose chief asset is his political, and reportedly underworld, connections. Since 2014, he has been held in Austria on bail after accusations by the US authorities of bribery in a titanium deal with Indian businesses (Brown, 2019), although this has not prevented him from playing an active role in Ukrainian politics at a distance, by way of his network representatives. Another contrast with the Lazarenko case is that Firtash seems to have risen to prominence primarily through Russian political-administrative links rather than through association with one of the Ukrainian regional networks.

The RUE scheme was, then, the most comprehensive and largest in scale of the gas intermediary rent-extraction schemes. Perhaps because of this, however, it did not durably fit with the "multiple pyramid" political context of the "Orange" years. At the same time, the weakening of the constitutional powers of the president relative to parliament and the prime minister encouraged increased competition for rents among networks. In time, this showed itself politically as a campaign by Tymoshenko as prime minister to re-centralise the gas trade between the two countries' state gas enterprises. Public hostility was linked to the view that the RUE intermediary performed no useful economic function (Miklos, 2019, pp. 20-21) that Gazprom and Naftogaz could not have done themselves. Rather, as a business structure, it was interposed between the producer and the consumer as a way of extracting wealth for well-placed special interests. An earlier rationale for the intermediaries had been that they were able, through barter, to supply gas at low prices to Ukraine in conditions of low liquidity (Balmaceda, 2013, p. 110). Once this situation passed, the justifications for such schemes became more spurious still.

Observations on the UESU and RUE schemes

In retrospect, if Lazarenko's operation appears as that of the informal innovator, Firtash's RUE intermediary is more that of the copyist who scales up and "perfects" the original. The most direct economic costs of both schemes were felt as losses to Ukrainian and Russian public finances. The RUE scheme appears not just on a larger scale, however, but also a deeper or more thoroughgoing mode of rent extraction, not just damaging public finances, but contributing to large-scale, chronic macroeconomic imbalance that increased the Ukrainian economy's vulnerability to economic shocks. The most serious long-term impact of these schemes may be at the political-institutional level, however — UESU through prompting the establishment of Naftogaz as an institution within the Ukrainian polity for control of energy rents, which has been a focus for network rivalry ever since; and RUE not only by helping to perpetuate macroeconomic imbalance, but also by inserting into Ukrainian politics a wealthy political actor (Firtash), primarily dependent on the Russian elite for his material power and position, who helped to pave the way for Yanukovych's disastrous presidency.

6.3 Rent-extraction schemes in the Ukrainian energy sector, post-Euromaidan: three case studies

6.3.1 Energy sector analyses and main sources

The second half of the chapter explores three case studies of post-Euromaidan rent-extraction schemes in the gas sector, based on an analysis of the reports of Ukrainian investigative journalists, think-tanks and anti-corruption bodies. The case studies were chosen on a number of criteria, including the level of detail provided and the reputation of the provider. Also, the three cases illustrate both continuity of extraction practices and something of their range.

As with the older, large-scale intermediary gas schemes, the aim is not just to show the mechanisms by which rent extraction was achieved, but also the alignments of political-economic actors and institutions that made them possible. From these accounts, similarities and contrasts can be drawn with the older schemes, in order to arrive at a "taxonomy" of some characteristic features of Ukraine's gas-sector rent-extraction schemes. Locating each post-Euromaidan gas scheme in my accounts of energy policy and the evolution of Ukraine's political economy governance regime (chapter 3) will help to make sense of these continuities and adaptations.

While the previous chapter examined the means by which holders of concentrated wealth have been able to transform this into a political negotiating position through their material control of votes in the Rada, the energy case studies illustrate concretely some channels through which economic rents continued to be extracted and defended in the post-Euromaidan era by way of networks of political influence running through and acting upon the component institutions of the state — so completing a simple "national" circuit of material and political power.

One of the post-Euromaidan gas schemes analysed arises from an investigation of the National Anti-corruption Bureau of Ukraine (NABU), a law-enforcement agency set up in the wake of the Euromaidan revolt to tackle corruption in public life. It centres on the construction of an arbitrage opportunity as part of a production-sharing agreement (PSA) of a number of private energy firms with Ukrgazvydobuvannya (UGV), the wholly state-owned gas-production company. The information is taken mainly from the website notices on the investigation issued by the NABU (2016a, 2016b, 2017a, 2017b, 2017c, 2017d, 2018a, 2018b, 2019).

A second scheme involved the creation by a gas-supply company in Kirovohrad region of gas accounts for non-existent households to benefit from the divergence in gas tariffs charged to households and industrial consumers, following a period of convergence from 2014. The main details are taken from a report by a Naftogaz research team (Naftogaz, 2017).

The case examined first and in greatest depth, however, is the award of a valuable gas-extraction permit for an already developed gas-field to a firm with no track-record in the energy business, which, the journalists at the aptly named Schemes (*Skhemy*) TV programme demonstrate, was linked to figures close to President Poroshenko (Chornovalov, 2018). There are three parts to this analysis, looking at: i) the mechanics of the scheme and the evidence of its connection to Poroshenko's circle; ii) the scheme viewed as an episode in a wider power struggle between oligarchic networks; and iii) the multi-pronged strategy for the scheme's defence via state institutions. These produce a picture of how the scheme was generated, how it worked and how it was protected.

Schemes is a Ukrainian weekly investigative TV programme, run by First (*Pershyy*), the main TV channel of Ukraine's national broadcaster, and Radio Svoboda, the Ukrainian service of the US-funded Radio Free Europe/Radio Liberty (RFE/RL). The show, which came on air after the Euromaidan Revolution, specialises in uncovering official corruption, using a mix of public and company records, communiqués and websites, as well as legal documents and interviews with institutional actors and politicians, sometimes by "door stepping" them (that is, confronting them with questions in a public space without prior arrangement). Each episode is then written up for the websites of the show and of Radio Svoboda, reproducing facsimiles of the evidence and infographics used. The main Schemes articles detailing the gas-permit case are from 2018-19, but the events they cover occur in 2014-17.

6.3.2 The Poltava gas-permit scheme

Arkona Gas-Energy "wins" the gas permit

Operation of the scheme and its value

In May 2017 the State Service of Geology and Subsoil of Ukraine (Gosgeonadr) awarded to Arkona Gas-Energy, a small, recently created company, a 20-year permit to extract gas and gas condensate from the Svistunkivsko-Chervonolutsk deposit in the Poltava region in central Ukraine (Chornovalov, 2018). At the time of the award, Arkona was owned by two relatively low-level "business-administrative" officials from Donetsk region, Ihor Mychko and Oleksandr Neshchotny. With authorised capital of just UAH4,000 (US$150 at the exchange rate then current) and Mychko initially its sole owner, Arkona had first expressed an interest in the licence in March 2016. Later in that year, the share capital of the company was raised to UAH5.6m (US$214,400), in return for which Neshchotny obtained a 50% stake.

According to Schemes, the mechanism of rent extraction in this case was through securing formal, legal access to a valuable resource cheaply using administrative connections within the state apparatus. The Geology Service was the crucial administrative link, as it accepted a low estimate for the Poltava field's reserves and issued the permit without a competitive tender. These factors suggest that the price Arkona paid for the licence, of UAH3.8m (US$143,400 at the May 2017 average exchange rate), was below the sales value it could have achieved. This view is supported by alternative estimates for the energy reserves at the deposit. According to Arkona, exploitable gas reserves at the field totalled 320m cu metres, with gas condensate of 46,000 tonnes. Ukrnafta, the majority state-owned oil production company that had been developing the Svistunkivsko-Chervonolutsk deposit since the 1990s, estimated gas reserves at around four times higher, or 1.6bn cu metres, with gas condensate estimated more than twice as high, at 130,000 tonnes. In light of this, Ukrnafta claimed that it had been prepared to offer UAH45m (US$1.7m) for the right to exploit the deposit, more than ten times above what was paid by Arkona, but suggested that the licence might have fetched up to UAH110m (US$4.5m) in a competitive tender. As part of its pre-trial investigation, the NABU estimates a permit value about double this figure, of UAH200.6m (US$9.1m; NABU, 2021), implying larger losses still to state coffers. Based on Ukrnafta's reserve estimates, and using the market prices then current, Schemes estimates the total resource value of the deposit at UAH12bn, or US$450m.

Ukrnafta says that it applied for the Poltava extraction licence in 2014, following the expiration of its exploration and development permit, but was refused. When it applied again in 2016, it was again turned down, for two reasons. The first was that the documents the company had submitted were inconsistent. The second was that Ukrnafta lacked the funds to pay for the licence, since it had a backlog of unpaid taxes (Chornovalov, 2018).

It is possible to calculate the value of the resource independently. The results are shown in Table 6.2 below. On estimated international gas prices of between US$192 and US$203 per 1,000 cu metres in 2017, the year the permit was awarded, the market value of the gas from the Poltava deposit would have been US$61m-65m on Arkona's reserves estimate, but US$307m-325m on Ukrnafta's higher one, a difference of around US$250m. To arrive at these estimates, which exclude the value of gas condensate, I used the data on annual "German border" gas import prices from bp's *Statistical Review of World Energy 2020* (bp, 2020, p. 39). As these are listed in US dollars per million Btus (British thermal units), and I wanted to extend the series of Ukraine's gas import prices collected by Balmaceda for 1991-2010, which are in US dollars per thousand cu metres (Balmaceda, 2013, p. 104), I used a "low" and a "high" conversion rate to arrive at the gas price estimates in the table. The lower rate was taken from the methodology section of bp's report (bp, 2020, p. 64). The higher one is the average conversion rate implied by comparison of bp's Btu prices and Balmaceda's prices per thousand cu metres for 1991-2010.

Table 6.2: Value of the Svistunkivsko-Chervonolutsk gas deposit, by contrasting reserve estimates

	Arkona	Ukrnafta
Estimated gas volume ('000 cu metres)	320,000	1,600,000
German border price (US$/'000 cu metres)		
Low estimate	191.8	191.8
High estimate	202.9	202.9
Gas deposit value (US$ m)		
Low estimate	61.4	306.9
High estimate	64.9	324.6

Sources: Chornovalov, (2018), Schemes/Radio Svoboda. Available: https://bit.ly/3izyOYf. BP (2020). *bp Statistical Review of World Energy 2020*, p. 39. Available: https://on.bp.com/3ol8l3Z. Own calculations.

Without factoring in expected production costs, these estimates do not indicate the scale of the profits available to the permit holders, of course. What they show, however, is the scale of the losses to public finances implied by the divergent estimates of gas volumes, both in terms of permit fees and future income foregone, since the Ukrainian state holds a 50%-plus-one share in Ukrnafta, which is a subsidiary of Naftogaz (see Figure 6.4 above).

How was the Arkona scheme linked to Poroshenko's circle?

In mid-2017 two new partners came on board at Arkona. The first, with a 5% stake, was Oleksiy Hrebenchenko, who had previously worked at Ukroptkulttovary (Chornovalov, 2018), a food wholesaler owned by Poroshenko (*Ekonomichna Pravda*, 2018). The second was Ashburi Universal, registered in Belize to a Panamanian citizen. It took a 49.5% stake in Arkona, so reducing the stakes of the two original shareholders to 22.5% each. It is mainly through Ashburi, an offshore legal structure that invested in Arkona only after the gas permit had been obtained at a knock-down price, that Schemes is able to trace the control of the licence to a sub-network of legal officials close to President Poroshenko. In particular, Schemes links the acquisition of Ashburi's stake with the transfer of UAH1.39m (US$52,000) each to Mychko and Neshchotny in the second quarter of 2017 by a Kyiv notary, Natalya Malovatska.[20] She is the wife of Oleksiy Malovatskyi, a member of Ukraine's High Council of Justice, the state body responsible for the appointment and dismissal of judges. Malovatskyi has already been mentioned in the previous chapter, when Rada approval for his appointment to the High Council appeared as the subject of a vote-buying negotiation, via mobile text, between Oleksandr Onyshchenko and Serhiy Berezenko, one of Poroshenko's Rada fixers (Sukhov, 2018).

During Poroshenko's run for the presidency in 2014, Malovatskyi had been on his legal team, but is described as a protégé of Berezenko (Chornovalov, 2018), himself a central figure in Poroshenko's Vinnytsya business-political network and the leader of a deputy group in the Rada within the Petro Poroshenko Bloc/ PPB (Andrusiv et al, 2018, p. 66). Many of the other players in the Arkona gas-permit scheme are linked to Malovatskyi through the legal profession. Both Hrebenchenko and Oleksiy Bondar, registered as the legal agent of Ashburi for a company general meeting, were connected to Malovatskyi through a law firm, Ekovis, Bondar and Bondar, where all three had previously worked. Meanwhile, Liliya Kobzar, the lawyer with power of attorney for Arkona,

---

[20] In the Ukrainian legal system, the main role of a notary is to authenticate legal documents.

managed another legal firm, Yus Novitas, which was owned by Malovatskyi.[21] By 2019, perhaps in response to the original story, possession of Ashburi's 49.5% share in Arkona had been transferred to one Oleh Olkhovyi, the director of a fitness centre in Kyiv owned by Poroshenko and another of his long-time associates, Ihor Kononenko (Chornovalov et al, 2019; *Ekonomichna Pravda*, 2018).

The permit scheme in the context of a power struggle over the oil sector
The Schemes journalists portray the Arkona case somewhat neutrally, almost apolitically. That is, in their treatment of the story, Ukrnafta is presented more or less unproblematically as a public enterprise that has been swindled out of an asset (the gas deposit), in which it had already invested, by the sharp practices of well-connected political insiders, at the expense of the national budget.

Standing back, however, the Arkona scheme appears as an episode in a broader power struggle between rival business-political networks, each conducting their moves through the influence they are able to exert on and within key administrative, judicial and economic institutions of the state. Specifically, this was the struggle between the networks around Poroshenko as the new president, and the Privat network of Ihor Kolomoyskyi, arguably the most successful of the "oligarch governors" following the fall of Yanukovych. This conflict is one of the threads that runs through many of the defining developments of the Poroshenko presidency, and may be detected also, perhaps, in the snap nationalisation of PrivatBank at the end of 2016 (Buckley, 2016), as well as events around the Donbas blockade the following year (Olearchyk, 2017). In the post-Euromaidan era, however, it originated in a high-profile clash over control of the domestic oil sector.

Kolomoyskyi and the Privat network
With the value of his recorded domestic business assets averaging around US$3bn (equal to 0.66% of national wealth) in 2006-17, according to the Focus rich lists, Kolomoyskyi, like Poroshenko,

---

[21] The significance of this network connection with legal specialists will become clear in the outline of the means of defence of the Arkona permit scheme below.

appears among the "core" rich—that is, high on the list of the richest and most enduring members of Ukraine's economic elite. It is clear, however, from legal cases in Britain and the US in which Kolomoyskyi has been involved—as well as from his own accounts in interviews, if these are taken at face value (Berdinskikh, 2019a, 2019b)—that he also holds significant wealth abroad, on top of his business assets in Ukraine, some of which may also have been deliberately obscured using complex legal structures (Focus Ratings, 2008). Both Poroshenko and Kolomoyskyi were among the high-profile wielders of either formal factional, or cross-factional, political influence in the Rada formed after the October 2014 parliamentary election (chapter 5). Both can be described, therefore, as leading oligarchs[22], with each consolidating their rise in the ranks of influential network leaders as a result of the Euromaidan victory and its aftermath, albeit by different routes. Moreover, their educational backgrounds are somewhat similar, suggesting that before the demise of the Soviet Union, they, as with Lazarenko and Tymoshenko, were on a path to becoming state functionaries, Kolomoyskyi in metallurgy, Poroshenko in trade (Havrylyshyn, 2017, pp. 204-205). Kolomoyskyi's Privat network, with holdings in banking, metallurgy and the media, originated in the Dnipropetrovsk region, which was dominated in the 1990s by Kuchma and Lazarenko (Avioutskii, 2010, p. 122, footnote 3).

During the Orange Revolution of 2004/05, Poroshenko and Kolomoyskyi found themselves backing the same side politically, and did so again in the early post-Euromaidan period, when the interim government under Yatsenyuk is reported to have struck up a "tactical alliance" with Kolomoyskyi (Konończuk, 2017, p. 23), so that conflict with Privat manifested itself at governmental level as an uneasy relationship between Poroshenko and Yatsenyuk, rooted in the divergent interests of their network alliances. The conditions for the development of their rivalry, post-Euromaidan, are not to be found only in the elevation of Poroshenko to the presidency and his

---

[22] That is, persistently successful national political actors at the head of extensive business-political networks, who are backed by substantial individual material power, relative to Ukrainian society.

attempts to consolidate his political position, however, but also in the elevation of Kolomoyskyi to the position of regional governor.

The appointment of a number of leading oligarchs with roots in eastern Ukraine as regional governors by the interim government in March 2014 took place amid the onset of military conflict with Russia. In light of the weakness of the Ukrainian army at the start of the conflict, the authorities looked to these oligarchs to shore up the country's defences. This was a first, very early step in the political reintegration of the "old" oligarchs following the flight of Yanukovych, underscoring the weakness of the central state relative to oligarchs' business groups. The testimony of Oleksandr Turchynov during the trial *in absentia* of Yanukovych in 2018 suggests that the appointment of these oligarchs was an emergency measure. In particular, Turchynov, who was acting Ukrainian president and head of the National Security and Defence Council after the fall of Yanukovych, said that, at the onset of the hostilities, the Ukrainian state had just 5,000 battle-ready soldiers. Fearing a full-blown Russian invasion from the north and east, none of these were available to counter Russia's military takeover of the Crimean parliament at the end of February 2014 (Wilson, 2014, p. 110), ahead of its annexation of the peninsula in March (Unian, 2018).

As a result, Kolomoyskyi was appointed governor of his home region of Dnipropetrovsk in south-east Ukraine. Over the next year, he ran a broadly successful campaign to counter the spread of the Russia's neo-imperial "Novorossiya" project, including by offering bounties for the capture of enemy combatants and their weapons, and by funding new military formations (Chazan and Weaver, 2014). Following the collapse of Yanukovych's "power vertical" in early 2014, and amid the official post-Euromaidan rhetoric of "de-oligarchisation", the political position of the leading oligarch networks under Yanukovych (primarily, those of Akhmetov, Firtash and of Yanukovych himself) had been greatly undermined. In contrast, Kolomoyskyi's resolute actions in the south-east helped to improve his standing within this small group of "old" oligarchs, just as their "stars" were in decline. Moreover, his official post inserted him and his organisation at an early stage and at a high level into the post-Euromaidan "revolutionary" political order.

Control of Ukrnafta allowed Privat to dominate the oil sector

Although the clash of the Poroshenko and Kolomoyskyi networks was triggered by an attempt by the authorities to wrest control from the Privat Group of key public-sector oil enterprises, Privat's domination of the domestic oil business can be traced back to the late Kuchma era, when management control of Ukrnafta, which accounts for the bulk of Ukraine's domestic oil production, was ceded to Privat. Presumably, this was as part of the system for balancing the interests of the strongest business-political groups as a principle of institutional stability. By negotiating deals with each subsequent government, Kolomoyskyi was able to maintain this arrangement over the following decade (Konończuk, 2017, p. 23).

One factor that is said to have aided Privat's maintenance of management control of Ukrnafta, despite holding just 42% of the enterprise (Konończuk, 2016, p. 18), is a joint-stock law that required the backing of 60% of shareholders to convene a general assembly — in effect, preventing any change in the leadership at the company without Privat's consent (Konończuk, 2017, p. 23). Another factor was an informal alignment with state-institutional insiders. On this, Schemes offers some detail in the case of Ihor Didenko, an official with long experience of high office overseeing public energy assets and policy. He reports having an extended, co-operative relationship with Kolomoyskyi (Chornovalov, 2015). As an example of the use of his positional influence in Privat's favour, between rounds of the 2010 presidential election, Didenko, then deputy head of Naftogaz, is reported to have helped to prepare an agreement formalising the Kuchma-era understanding of Privat's management role at Ukrnafta (Chornovalov, 2015).

Starting with Ukrnafta, Privat was eventually able to extend its reach to a "complete cycle" of the oil business, gathering together operational control of key firms in oil production, processing, transport and retail sales, allowing the network to dominate the domestic oil sector and so the rents generated from it. Of Didenko's part in this, the Schemes team writes, "it was due to his direct...participation that certain financial and industrial groups gained control over a number of strategic state-owned enterprises"

(Chornovalov, 2015). They report that, in his role at Naftogaz, Didenko supported the appointment of Oleksandr Lazorko, who had previously worked for Kolomoyskyi, as head of Ukrtransnafta, the state oil pipeline operator; and facilitated Privat's acquisition of a majority (56%) stake in Ukrtatnafta, which operates a large oil refinery at Kremenchuk in Poltava region (see Figure 6.4).

Konończuk notes two consequences of Privat's long-standing control of Ukrnafta. The first is that "structures controlled by Kolomoyskyi have been siphoning off money from the company for more than ten years" (2017, p. 23). Second, this mode of management, with its emphasis on fund extraction rather than investment in business modernisation, has contributed, he thinks, to a 45% decline in oil production, to 2.25m tonnes, between 2009 and 2016 (2017, p. 22). This ties in with the account presented earlier on the dysfunction and deterioration in the Ukrainian energy sector before the 2014 reforms. Lastly, illustrating the transactional nature of Ukraine's political economy governance regime, "the informal price that Privat has paid for maintaining control of Ukrnafta is the need to pay bribes to members of the government and support them in Kolomoyskyi's media" (2017, p. 23).

Naftogaz restructuring sets off a network conflict

In early 2015 the new leadership at Naftogaz tried to replace the heads of Ukrnafta and Ukrtransnafta, as two of its subsidiaries, with its own candidates, so threatening Privat's control, not just of these firms, but also its "full cycle" dominance of the oil sector, even as the importance of oil in the Ukrainian energy sector had been enhanced by the need to diversify supplies away from Russia.

Perhaps emboldened by his "ascendancy" in the early period following the Euromaidan, Kolomoyskyi seemed to overplay his hand, bringing his private militia to the headquarters of Ukrnafta in the Ukrainian capital, Kyiv, apparently to try to enforce the position of his preferred candidate for CEO. By "crossing the Rubicon", however, Kolomoyskyi issued a direct challenge not only to the state's monopoly on the legitimate use of force, but also to the leading position of Poroshenko's developing network pyramid, so that Poroshenko removed him as Dnipropetrovsk governor

(Olearchyk, 2015). Although Kolomoyskyi's actions were considered unorthodox, even by the fairly ruthless standards of the Ukrainian elite, they were not too dissimilar either from the methods for which he had been praised in the Donbas conflict, or from those with which his business practice was already associated.

The sacking of Kolomoyskyi as governor marks not just the completion of the first phase in the contest of network strength, in which the groups around Poroshenko came out on top, but also a way-point of consolidation in Poroshenko's attempt to construct a pre-eminent "network pyramid" around his presidency, in spite of the weaker constitutional powers at his disposal.

Despite this setback, Privat was able to retain effective control of both Ukrtransnafta and Ukrnafta. How did it do so? Alongside the failed attempt to use physical force, the organisation seems to have pursued legal and administrative-political means of defence. It is also possible that the situation was defused by way of a behind-the-scenes deal within the Ukrainian elite. The legal defensive factor, aiding continued management control of Ukrnafta at least, was the joint-stock law, mentioned above, requiring the backing of 60% of Ukrnafta shareholders to convene a general assembly. The government's attempt to dismantle this line of defence seems to have been protracted. So, in April 2015, although the authorities pressed ahead with amendments to reduce to 50% the proportion of shareholders required to call a general meeting at joint-stock companies, so allowing it to change Ukrnafta's leadership with its 50%-plus-one share, People's Front (PF) Rada deputies, aligned with Kolomoyskyi through Yatsenyuk, the party's leader, managed to delay its passage until later in the year (Konończuk, 2016, p. 18).

Privat's administrative-political tactics to retain control of Ukrtransnafta also were twofold. First, Lazorko, faced with the prospect of his replacement by Naftogaz's candidate, seems to have taken sick leave to avoid this, at the same time appointing his own choice of successor, Natalia Parakonyak, who had also worked previously for Privat. Second, Didenko, now deputy minister of energy and coal in the second Yatsenyuk government, ensured that Parakonyak was hired to head Ukrtransnafta, so ensuring Privat's continuing *de facto* management control (Chornovalov, 2015).

At Ukrnafta, meanwhile, in the wake of the clash with Poroshenko, the Privat group not only retained management control but, perhaps fearing the potential loss of a lucrative income stream, intensified the pace of extraction of funds from the business, while running up a backlog of unpaid taxes. "As a result, in 2016, Ukrnafta sustained a loss of US$250m and the debt owed to the state reached US$470m" (Konończuk, 2017, p. 24).

Seen in this light, the Arkona gas-permit story seems to show one network (Poroshenko's) side-stepping the institutional control of another (Kolomoyskyi's) to win control of valuable resource, with both offensive and defensive manoeuvres conducted on the terrain of state institutions. Moreover, this account supports one of the rationales offered by the Geology Service for its rejection of the Ukrnafta's application for the Poltava gas-extraction permit in 2016: that, under Privat's *de facto* management control, Ukrnafta had built up significant tax debt. The story offers a detailed illustration of the contention that the Ukrainian hydrocarbons market is a "classic example of political corruption where government authorities representing political forces competed for the right to appoint Naftogaz management" (Burakovsky et al, 2018, p. 24). Finally, Naftogaz was at the epicentre of this network struggle precisely because it was set up in the late 1990s as a centralised institution for the collection and distribution of energy rents among the Ukrainian elite (Balmaceda, 2013, p. 113).

Lutsenko's rear-guard action

A third instalment of the Arkona permit story offers another glimpse into how elite rent-extraction schemes can be defended institutionally, with actors' formal actions belied by their inferred informal purpose. The quite elaborate defence strategy of the Poltava gas permit, following its award, has three components: a "friendly" or intentionally ineffective prosecution; the commissioning of an expert report, allegedly to minimise the estimated financial losses to the state; and the use of judicial oversight procedures to pressurise the appeals judge into producing the desired ruling.

The first element of this part of the story is a legal case launched by the Office of the Prosecutor General over the issue of the award of the gas-permit to Arkona, following the broadcast of Schemes' original story. Initially, it seems as though the prosecutor's office was just doing its job. Reflecting an inheritance of judicial traditions of both the Tsarist and Soviet state systems, in modern Ukraine its functions are to oversee pre-trial investigations and to prosecute court cases for the state. A follow-up Schemes investigation strongly suggests, however, that the legal case was launched as part of a larger co-ordinated plan to protect the permit transaction, both from legal contestation by a rival political network and from examination by the NABU (Chornovalov et al, 2019).

A telling event in this account is the appointment in May 2016, in the wake of the formation of the Hroysman cabinet, of Yuriy Lutsenko as prosecutor general, after the position of his predecessor, Viktor Shokin, became politically untenable (Subramanian, 2019). The appointment of Lutsenko was widely criticised because of his lack of formal legal qualifications. Lutsenko came to prominence in the early 2000s as a campaigner against the increasingly authoritarian rule of Leonid Kuchma. He was interior minister in the governments of Yuliya Tymoshenko after the Orange Revolution. Like her, he was jailed on spurious charges during the Yanukovych presidency (Minakov and Rojansky, 2021, p. 329). More pertinent to the current story is his association with Poroshenko, within whose remit as president the appointment of the prosecutor general fell.

Following the initial Schemes investigation, outlined above, the prosecutor's office took to court a case against the award of the Poltava gas permit to Arkona, but the Kyiv Administrative Court ruled the award legal. The follow-up Schemes investigation begins therefore with the prosecutor's office taking its case to appeal (Chornovalov et al, 2019). However, as Schemes points out, the case that the prosecutor's office took to court and lost was made on purely procedural grounds — that is, in awarding the licence without conducting a competitive tender, official procedures had not been followed. In contrast, the issue of accepting a low estimate of reserves at the deposit, so permitting a low payment for the licence, was not raised, leaving an important dimension of the case untried. This part of the case was followed up by "rival" legal bodies — the

NABU and the Specialised Anti-Corruption Prosecutor's Office (SAPO) — which only finished their pre-trial investigations into the low price paid for the gas permit some years later (NABU, 2021).

The procuracy did appoint an expert, Oleksandr Ruvin of the Kyiv Forensic Research Institute, to assess the scale of these losses to the public purse. Schemes suggests, however, that the aim was to whitewash the untried dimension of the case. In particular, they suggest, "a draft expert opinion is being prepared which confirms that the special permit was sold at an adequate price" (Chornovalov et al, 2019), reproducing a photograph of Ruvin at a Kyiv restaurant with Pavlo Vovk, the head of the Kyiv Administrative Court, and Oleksandr Hranovsky, and influential MP in the Petro Poroshenko Bloc (PPB). Although this is suggestive of collusion, which may even be very likely based on a broad understanding of the ubiquity of the informal dimension of elite Ukrainian politics, this is the weakest part of the journalists' investigation, relying more on guilt by association than on detailed, convincing documentation, as in the original Arkona story.

A third line of defence of the permit transaction involves the High Council of Justice, to which the appointment of Malovatskyi, the key legal link with Poroshenko in the Arkona gas-permit award, appears to have been secured by way of a cash payment for votes in the Rada (chapter 5). Specifically, Schemes reports, at the time of the appeals case, the High Council happened to select from its files for review a complaint against Halina Zemlyana, the judge at Kyiv's 6th Administrative Appeals Court chosen to hear the appeal. The implication is that the actions of the High Council were aimed at pressurising the judge into producing a ruling on the permit case favourable to the Poroshenko network by raising the threat of the judge's dismissal from her job.

Once all the elements of the "defence" phase of the story are assembled — the lost but only partial prosecution, the possibly diversionary assessment of the scale of public financial losses, and the attempt to coerce the appeals judge — the actions of the prosecutor's office appears to have been quite helpful to the defendants. That is, they seem designed to look like a serious prosecutorial intervention, while preventing a real investigation from taking place, as part of a broader strategy to defend the permit award by well-placed associates of the Poroshenko network — not only against the contestation of the Kolomoyskyi and his Privat network, but also against the takeover of the case by a rival investigative authority, the NABU, from which the prosecutor's office are reported to have withheld documents (Chornovalov et al, 2019). Supporting this overall picture of an "orchestrated" network defence from within and from outside of a range of state institutions, another source suggests that the Arkona permit case was allocated to a department of the prosecutor's office controlled informally by Ihor Kononenko, a stalwart of Poroshenko's Vinnytsya business network and of his presidency (*Ekonomichna Pravda*, 2018). In sum, the prosecution appears as part of a multi-pronged network campaign both to thwart a rival network and the effective operation of the rule of law, while seeming to do the opposite.

What does the permit scheme tell us about the Ukrainian oligarchy?
On its own, the Arkona scheme shows associates of Ukraine's head of state using administrative connections to gain access to a valuable energy asset at a low price, at the expense of public finances. Understanding something of the clash of personalities and organisations over the control of public enterprises in the oil sector (Ukrnafta and Ukrtransnafta) helps to make sense of the gas-permit scheme by adding its informal political economy context. This seems to show one business-political network attempting to sidestep the institutional reach of a public enterprise (Ukrnafta) controlled by a rival network, using its connections to another state body (the Geology Service) amid a long-running network feud. Both Privat's attempts to maintain *de facto* management control of a majority state-owned energy asset, as well as the actions of the prosecutor's office and other judicial bodies to do similarly for Poroshenko's "pyramid", illustrate the multiple means by which the most powerful Ukrainian networks are able to mount a defence of their rent-extraction schemes.

The Arkona scheme offers insights into the mode of operation of the Ukrainian oligarchy as an informal institution of political-economic rule across several organically connected dimensions, and allows us see how these dimensions can be joined or articulated into a single line of action. It allows us, for example, to connect the application of material resource power for political influence in one institution (vote-buying in the Rada to place an associate on the High Judicial Council) to the orchestration and protection of the process of conversion of political influence back into wealth elsewhere, making clear the purpose of a practice in one area through its furthering of network goals elsewhere.

Lastly, two broader observational conclusions may be drawn linked to the appointment of oligarchs in a defensive capacity following Russia's military takeover of Crimea from late February 2014. The first is that weakness of the Ukrainian state and the relative strength of the oligarchic networks could be understood as two sides of the same coin — the state weakened financially by networks' rent-extraction schemes, and organisationally by way of the placement of network personnel into key positions throughout the state apparatus, in combination undermining state capacity and coherence. The second is that, because it led to the "rehabilitation" of leading oligarchs, and so the reintegration of their informal networks into "post-revolutionary" politics, Russia's military interventions helped to save the Ukrainian oligarchy as an institution of informal rule, just at its point of maximum vulnerability to popular mobilisational power at home.

6.3.3 The Onyshchenko-Nasirov gas scheme

In mid-2016 the head of a small private gas-production company, Nadra Geocentre, was arrested, following an investigation by the NABU into a wider scheme of suspected embezzlement of public funds (NABU, 2016a). Linked to production-sharing agreements (PSAs) in Ukraine's gas sector, whereby participants divide the income from joint gas-extraction projects, and involving up to 30 people (*Ekonomichna Pravda*, 2019), this second post-Euromaidan rent-extraction scheme became known as the "Onyshchenko case" after its main organiser, described by the NABU as the "creator and head of a criminal organisation" (NABU, 2018b).

Oleksandr Onyshchenko has already appeared in the previous chapter of this book, where he is depicted organising vote-buying in the Rada via mobile phone texts with Poroshenko's parliamentary fixers. With business interests in the energy sector, Onyshchenko was a people's deputy in the seventh and eighth Rada convocations, first for Yanukovych's Party of Regions (PoR) and then for one of its offshoots, People's Will. Ahead of the lifting of his parliamentary immunity and planned arrest in July 2016, he fled abroad (NABU, 2016b), apparently forewarned.

Following the victory of the Euromaidan, the NABU was set up as a new law-enforcement agency to tackle corruption in public life. The case against Onyshchenko and his associates, initiated in late 2015 (NABU, 2017a), was one of the agency's first high-profile investigations to come to fruition that involved politically well-connected figures holding positions of authority in the state.

The Onyshchenko scheme was made up of two separate extraction mechanisms, whose operation overlapped between January 2013 and January 2016 (NABU, 2018a, 2018b; *Ekonomichna Pravda*, 2016b), so straddling the Yanukovych and Poroshenko presidencies, and illustrating continuity of rent-seeking practices between them. One mechanism, an artificially constructed arbitrage scheme, was run with the knowledge of the management of Ukrgazvydobuvannya (UGV), the state-owned gas-production firm. The second, a tax and rent evasion scheme, was conducted in collusion with leading officials from the State Fiscal Service (SFS).

Scheme A. Construction of an arbitrage opportunity, 2014-15

The first extractive mechanism focused on the embezzlement of the earnings from gas produced as part of a PSA between UGV and its private production partners.

In the post-communist era, the volume of Ukraine's domestic gas production has been relatively stable at 18bn-20bn cu metres annually (Balmaceda and Prokip, 2020, p. 141), with UGV accounting for around 80% of this output (Balmaceda and Prokip, 2021, p. 144). Despite possessing the second-largest natural gas reserves in Europe (Balmaceda and Prokip, 2021, p. 141), however, Ukraine has continued to import around one-third of its gas requirement, even following the marked reduction in gas consumption and reorientation of supply away from Russia from 2014 (see Figure 6.3). In large part, the inability to expand gas production reflects the long-term dysfunction of the energy market, described earlier in this chapter, in which low household tariffs, implying thin or non-existent profit margins, have tended to deter investment. Ostensibly, PSAs, a form of public-private partnership, were introduced, therefore, as a means of addressing the problem of underinvestment in the sector.

The main rent-extraction sequence in this first component of the scheme involved control of the commodity exchanges on which the gas produced under the PSAs was sold (NABU, 2018a; *Ekonomichna Pravda*, 2019). This allowed the scheme's operators to set a gas purchase price close to cost (UAH2,600 per 1,000 cu metres, according to the NABU) to predetermined intermediaries, which then sold the gas on at the much higher market price (UAH6,900 per 1,000 cu metres) to real industrial consumers (NABU, 2018a; *Ekonomichna Pravda*, 2016a), with the difference, of UAH4,300 per 1,000 cu metres — implying a profit of 160%, the NABU notes in its case outline — assigned to the accounts of firms linked to the scheme's organisers (NABU, 2018a). According to these case notes, "officials at UGV…were informed about this scheme, and…contributed to the implementation of criminal activities" (NABU, 2018a). Andriy Kobalev, then head of the Naftogaz board, claimed that Onyshchenko did not create the PSA-UGV rent-extraction scheme, but took it over from earlier practitioners — including, under Yanukovych, Serhiy Kurchenko (*Ekonomichna Pravda*, 2017a), a prominent figure in the network that Yanukovych attempted to build to support his presidency by way of the associates of his elder son, Oleksandr (Wilson, 2015, p. 345).

Scheme B. Evasion of subsoil rents, 2015-16
According to the NABU, the trigger for the establishment of a second extractive element of the Onyshchenko scheme, running in parallel with the first, was a change in policy, as part of the government's wider post-Euromaidan energy reforms. This involved a sharp increase in the subsoil rents charged to private mining firms

participating in the PSAs at the UVG sites they were exploiting. In response, the NABU writes of the schemes' participants, "they also decided to save on paying taxes" (NABU, 2018a).

Roman Nasirov, the head of Ukraine's fiscal service, was the leading public official implicated in the operation of this second mechanism. In particular, without informing the Ministry of Finance, he is reported to have allowed private gas-production firms participating in the PSAs and controlled by Onyshchenko — Nadra Geocentre, Khas and Karpatnadinvest (NABU, 2017b) — to defer payment on the subsoil rents owed for exploitation of UGV gas sites (*Ekonomichna Pravda*, 2019), and to pay instead in instalments over 2015-16, although it was outside the remit of his position to do so (NABU, 2017a, 2017d). Moreover, the firms in question did not pay the rent instalments. Instead, Nasirov, along with officials from the debt redemption department of the fiscal service, it is claimed, falsified data to indicate that the firms in question did not owe any tax debt (NABU, 2017c), so reducing income flows to the state budget, but boosting the retained rents of the two-part extraction scheme.

Once news of his involvement in the scheme broke in early 2017, Nasirov seems to have feigned illness to try to avoid arrest (NABU 2017a, 2017d). Although bail was set at the considerable sum of UAH100m (US$4m), family and high-profile friends from his network — including Mykola Martynenko, a political ally of Yatsenyuk who was himself earlier embroiled in an energy scandal linked to the nuclear industry (Andrusiv, 2018, p. 16) — were quickly able to raise the sum to secure his release (NABU, 2017d; Umland, 2017). By way of Martynenko, this seems to link Nasirov with the network "pyramid" around the recently replaced prime minister. On the one hand, some reports suggest that Nasirov was chosen to head the tax service as a compromise candidate between the key parliamentary parties and their allied business factions. On the other hand, while Nasirov is reported as being associated with the Poroshenko's BBP, *Ekonomichna Pravda* suggests that, under Nasirov's leadership, the fiscal service was under the control of Ihor Kolomoyskyi (*Ekonomichna Pravda*, 2017b), then informally aligned with Yatsenyuk's People's Front (PF), and involved at the same time in a running battle with President Poroshenko and his networks for political pre-eminence.

Over the full three years of the combined scheme, financial losses to the state came to about UAH3bn (US$120m at average 2016 exchange rates), according to the NABU — with UAH1.6bn-worth of gas "seized" through the production and selling scheme, translating into UAH740m in lost UGV income, but with a further UAH2bn lost to the state through unpaid subsoil rent (NABU, 2019a). Less than a year after the termination of the PSAs, the NABU reports, UGVs profits had risen considerably, to UAH1.3bn, from just UAH25m in the three years of the PSA scheme with private gas-production firms (NABU 2017b).

Why did the scheme come to an end when it did?
The question that comes to mind regarding the Onyshchenko-Nasirov scheme is why it ended when and how it did, in prosecution by the NABU — especially as we have seen Onyshchenko performing a useful organisational role for the authorities in parliament. Considering the political associations of the individuals involved, as well as the timing to the scheme's demise, it may have been a case of the authorities strategically permitting the law to take its course, unhindered, for reasons beneficial to them. The first reason is that key personnel affected by the prosecution of the scheme seem to have been associated with the competing network "pyramid" around Yatsenyuk, corresponding to the period of a marked network realignment in the Rada observed in chapter 5. That is, the authorities may have been happy to see its main competitor group weakened. A second reason is that allowing the NABU to proceed with such a high-profile case would have acted as a useful demonstration to Ukraine's external partners that the country's anti-corruption campaign was making progress, but without hampering the activities of the dominant network alliance around Poroshenko. If this reasoning is along the right lines, then the sacrifice of Onyshchenko as a mid-level operative in the political economy system could have been considered acceptable "collateral damage" (Hromadske International, 2016).

6.3.4 Gas-market "manipulations" of RGCs

Kirovohradgaz gas tariff arbitrage scheme

My final post-Euromaidan rent-extraction case study examines two gas-sector schemes linked to the Group DF conglomerate of Dmytro Firtash. The details are taken mainly from a report by Naftogaz (Naftogaz Research, 2017), which is analysed also by the Institute for Economic Research and Policy Consulting (IERPC), a Ukrainian think-tank, in its own report on post-Euromaidan economic reforms (Burakovsky et al, 2018, pp. 28-31). Key elements of the story are corroborated using local investigative articles.

The Naftogaz authors describe their evidence and reasons for believing that "manipulations" in the regional gas market, which continued on a reduced scale even in the immediate post-Euromaidan reform period, had expanded from 2017 amid a revival of arbitrage opportunities, which involves making money from a disparity in the buying and selling prices of commodities in different markets or market segments. The data sources that the report draws on include some privileged information that reflects Naftogaz's position as Ukraine's national oil and gas company. So, while its analysis uses macroeconomic data, it also draws on Naftogaz's own monthly gas data (volumes and sales), as well as its audit of a regional gas company (RGC).

From this "internal audit" of late 2017, Naftogaz reports its discovery of a long-running "manipulation" of a regional gas market by Kirovohradgaz, one of the companies responsible for delivering gas to end-users in Ukrainian regions through their control of the local gas-pipeline infrastructure.[23]

According to Naftogaz, the general mechanism of rent extraction was that volumes of gas recorded as destined for households, and so qualifying for lower, subsidised prices, were in fact supplied to industry, either at the market price (arbitrage), so yielding rents

---

[23] It was only in July 2017, after the change in the joint-stock law requiring 60% of shareholders to approve management changes (Kupfer and Kovensky, 2019), that Naftogaz was able to retake operational control of Kirovohradgaz, on the basis of its 51% stake in the business. Before that, the firm was run for a decade by Group DF, which dominates Ukraine's regional gas-distribution business.

to the RGCs, or to a connected industry at the household price, so reducing its input costs (transfer pricing). The impact on public finances was either on the state budget directly by boosting the cost of the household energy subsidy, or indirectly by adding to Naftogaz debt.

In particular, Naftogaz found that in 2009-16, Kirovohradgaz had created accounts for 384 non-existent households across the Kirovohrad region to this end (Naftogaz Research, 2017, p. 6) — although more cases were later uncovered, taking the total to almost 500 (Kupfer and Kovensky, 2019). From its original audit of the firm, Naftogaz reports that the incidence of this practice at Kirovohradgaz, while small in scale, picked up during the post-Euromaidan period. While in 2015, therefore, gas sales to such "dead souls" (*mertvi dushi*) accounted for 1.5% of all the gas the enterprise had recorded as being delivered to regional households, and for 2.6% of the total in 2016, this rose to 6% of the total in January-August 2017 — that is, before Naftogaz regained management control (Naftogaz Research, 2017, p. 6).

The significance of the Kirovohradgaz scheme is that, from this relatively small-scale development, the story of a re-opening of rent-extraction opportunities based on changing incentive structures in the domestic gas market can be traced, with the re-appearance of such opportunities shaped by developments on world energy markets, in domestic politics and by the broad re-balancing of business-political networks within the post-Euromaidan political order from 2016. As with the Onyshchenko scheme, the one operated at Kirovohradgaz in 2009-17 is reported to have emerged earlier (Borosovsky, 2018), and was simply reused by the firm's management from the existing stock of rent-extraction routines.

The return to tariff divergence

The Naftogaz researchers ascribe this pick-up in the attribution of gas supplies to fictitious accounts to a re-divergence of household and industry gas prices from late 2016, following their earlier brief convergence. The first factor in this overall development was the series of increases in household gas tariffs, outlined above, which led in 2014-16 to the gradual elimination of a plethora of price distinctions offered to households. A second factor was the passage in April 2015 of a new law on the gas market, which switched the industrial sector to payment for gas at market prices (Burakovsky, 2018, p. 29, footnote 40). Although prices to industrial users spiked initially, as a consequence of these developments the marked disparity between household and industrial tariffs narrowed considerably over time. The results are show in Figure 6.5 below.

Figure 6.5: Convergence & re-divergence of gas tariffs for household & industrial users, 2013-17

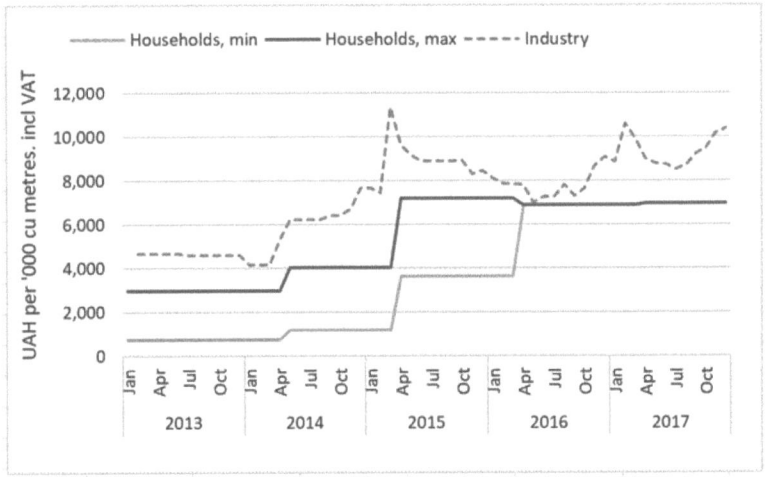

Sources: Naftogaz (2018). Available: https://bit.ly/2VRwkvU. Based on Burakovsky et al (2018, p. 29). IERPC. Available: https://bit.ly/3jY3aEw.

In the chart, gas prices charged to industrial consumers are represented by the dashed, light grey line, and prices to households, rising in steps, by the solid dark and lighter grey lines. To simplify the complex and shifting array of household tariffs ahead of their unification in April 2016, only the minimum and maximum household tariffs are shown (these are prices to the end-user, including VAT and transport, rather than cost price). In the course of 2015 and early 2016, it can be seen, the household and industrial tariffs began to converge. This is indicated by the approach of the lighter grey dashed line and the solid dark line to one another in early 2016. The tariffs for the two market segments quickly returned to divergent paths thereafter, however, so that, by 2017, industry was paying 35% more for its gas on average than households (Burakovsky et al, 2018, p. 29), so incentivising a return to gas-market "manipulations", such as that of Kirovohradgaz above.

Alongside price movements on global energy markets, the recreation of conditions conducive to the re-divergence in gas prices corresponds to domestic political developments. The first was the passage in October 2015 of legislation by the second Yatsenyuk government reasserting the public service obligation (PSO) of Naftogaz (Burakovsky et al, 2018, p. 29, footnote 41) — in effect, reaffirming price regulation for the household segment, albeit with household prices now at a higher level. This was probably conditioned by plummeting support in the polls, not only for the government, but especially for Yatsenyuk's own party, People's Front (PF). So, having won just above 22% of the popular vote in the general election of October 2014, already by 2015 opinion polls showed PF support below 5% (Razumkov Centre, 2017). A second political development came in 2017 when, faced with a proposal from Naftogaz for another rise in household gas prices from October 2017, in line with a previously agreed adjustment mechanism, the Hroysman cabinet balked, and voted against (Dabrowski, 2017, pp. 5-6). Although this decision, too, may have been influenced by declining popular support, it also appears to have been part of a broader campaign by the authorities to undermine the reformist leadership at Naftogaz, with a view to reasserting control over the company, and so too the income streams of its most profitable subsidiaries (Ukrnafta and Ukrtransnafta), possibly with an eye on funding the next round of elections, then scheduled for 2019 (Konończuk and Matuszak, 2017). In turn, the scene for the authorities' campaign had been set, first by the onset of economic recovery, reducing the pressure to pursue reforms in order to qualify for external loans, and second by the network rebalancing of 2016, one result of which was the easing aside of the main rival network pyramid of around Yatsenyuk.

"Top down" evidence for re-emergence of a transfer pricing scheme

Over the period of operation of the Kirovohradgaz scheme, the gas volumes diverted to non-existent households by the firm's management is reported at 9.8m cu metres, then valued at UAH80m, or US$3m (Kupfer and Kovensky, 2019). However, the "bottom-up" evidence from the audit of Kirovohradgaz's accounts, Naftogaz believes, supports a suspicion, based on an analysis of sectoral trends, that such practices are likely to have been more widespread among Ukrainian RGCs, between them accounting for the misallocation of an estimated 0.6 bn cu metres of natural gas per year in 2015-16 (Naftogaz, 2017, p. 6), out of a total of around 32bn cu metres consumed annually (see Figure 6.3). Although this sounds quite small in scale, the market price of this volume of natural gas, using the average "German border" import prices calculated earlier, would have been around US$100m-150m per year. The calculations are set out in Table 6.3 below.

Table 6.3: Estimated value of volumes of gas involved in regional "manipulations"

	2015	2016
Estimated gas volume ('000 cu metres)	600,000	600,000
German border price (US$/'000 cu metres)		
Low estimate	229	168
High estimate	243	178
Value of "manipulated" gas volume (US$ m)		
Low estimate	137.4	100.8
High estimate	145.8	106.8

Sources: Naftogaz Research (2017). Available: https://bit.ly/3rC9wvC. Prices estimated from *bp Statistical Review of World Energy 2020*. Available: https://on.bp.com/3ol813Z. Own calculations.

The Naftogaz authors present a second, tightly argued example of exploitation of the opportunity for rent-extraction from the redivergence of domestic gas tariffs from mid-2016, but this time based on evidence from divergent trends in macroeconomic data for gas consumption and the production of fertiliser inputs

(Naftogaz Research, 2017, pp. 4-5). They show that, in 2009-12, according to this data:

- household consumption of natural gas in Ukraine climbed from 16.6bn cu metres to 17.3bn cu metres;
- fertiliser output rose from 3m tonnes to 5m tonnes; and
- there was a fall in the average volume of natural gas used per unit of ammonia produced.

These divergent trends, the authors suspect, correspond to the diversion of cheaper, subsidised gas, earmarked for households, to fertiliser production by Firtash's Group DF, facilitated by its dominance of the both regional gas-supply network and the chemicals sector (Burakovsky et al, 2018, pp. 29-30). This is reminiscent of the practice of transfer pricing, as outlined in chapter 3, with the state covering the cost of cheap production inputs supplied to a related business. With the onset of energy reforms from 2014, the trends suggestive of transfer pricing come to a halt, the data show — so that the intensity of gas used in production of ammonia, a key input for fertiliser production, reverts back to its 2009 level — but then resumes in 2017 as the divergence in household and industrial gas tariffs again offered savings in input costs for the manufacture of ammonia. The evidence on which the Naftogaz researchers base this conclusion includes:

- a year-on-year rise in household gas consumption in January-August 2017;
- a decline in gas use by Group DF companies supplying thermal power (heating) to the population; and
- the resumption of ammonia production at Group DF plants from February 2017.

It is unreasonable, but indicative, the authors think, that trends in household gas consumption and heating supply — assumed both to be driven by changes in temperature — should move in opposite directions, deducing from this a return to the profitable misallocation of gas supplies from connected RGCs to Group DF fertiliser producers (Naftogaz Research, 2017, p. 5).

Section conclusions

The "twin" case study on the purported rent-extraction schemes of Group DF RGCs sheds light on the political and economic dynamics of implementation of energy-sector regulations in this period. Specifically, the revival of rent-seeking opportunities, following the general crisis of 2014-15, can be seen as a response, not only to economic developments (fluctuations in global energy prices abroad and the onset of economic recovery at home), but also to falling government popularity linked to energy policy, as well as to the state of relations between elite networks. On this last point, the realignment of networks in the Rada in the course of 2016, involving the political reintegration of those groups side-lined by the Euromaidan events, sets the basis for the consolidation of the leading position of the "government camp" around Poroshenko as president and Hroysman and prime minister.

With the worst of the crisis past, and the requirement for external financial assistance no longer so urgent, it was from this more secure position that the dominant "pyramid" was able to launch its campaign to reassert control over Naftogaz by attempting to undermine the company's reformist management, including by refusing to raise household gas prices in line with the agreed mechanism, failing thereby to curb the re-divergence of gas tariffs. One of the authorities' steps in the clash with Naftogaz management was to raise from five to seven the membership of Naftogaz's supervisory board, so "diluting" its reformist element (Konończuk and Matuszak, 2017). This is the background to the resignation in September 2017 of the more independent members of the supervisory board — appointed only the year before — which, in effect, marks the end of the phase of energy reform that began in 2014 (Antonenko et al, 2018).

If, then, the relation of the two gas-market "manipulations" by the RGCs alleged by Naftogaz appear more reflexive than the result of another intra-elite agreement — that is, of an explicit exchange of political support in parliament in return for greater room for manoeuvre in the pursuit of rent-extraction opportunities — then a more direct line of connection can be seen in the construction in relatively large-scale rent-extraction schemes outside of the gas sector. Namely, the political reintegration of Akhmetov and his SCM network corresponds chronologically with his initiation of the so-called Rotterdam plus scheme, by which the price of Ukrainian-mined coal supplied to local power plants was set according to coal prices on Rotterdam commodity markets, plus transport costs from the Netherlands. Serhiy Leshchenko ties the political go-ahead for this scheme to Akhmetov's purported control of half of the MPs of the Opposition Bloc (Leshchenko, 2016) in the Rada.

For the Naftogaz researchers, because the re-affirmation of price regulation implied by the passage of the PSO law in October 2015 was a key factor behind the re-divergence in domestic gas tariffs, the reunification of gas tariffs is the appropriate measure with which to tackle this. If my account above is right, however, this mistakes an effect for a cause. That is, the policy proposal skirts a more fundamental problem underlying the one the researchers identify. This is that, in a crisis, while the flexible political economy regime submits to the pursuit of reform, and so the restriction of rent-seeking opportunities, as a measure of systemic preservation, it also permits a return to the status quo ante, and so to the reopening of rent-extraction opportunities, once the crisis passes.

Two other small points drawn from the twin case study are relevant to my investigation. First, the Naftogaz researchers argue that Ukraine's RGCs are energy intermediaries of the same kind as the "historical" UESU and RUE intermediaries, but in miniature — that is, run to extract value, rather than to provide value-added services. Second, the alleged Group DF transfer-pricing scheme was facilitated by its dominance of related economic sectors (gas-supply infrastructure and chemicals production), which itself has a history bound up with the evolution of the dominant political economy regime. In particular, Firtash was able to acquire the bulk of the RGCs (70%) in phases, starting in 2007-08 (Burakovsky, 2018, p. 30, footnote 43) on the back of his accumulated RUE wealth, then again through "crony" privatisation under Yanukovych, as well as four out of six of the biggest chemical producers (Burakovsky, 2018, p. 30), as "payback", it is usually assumed, for his financial and media backing of Yanukovych's presidential campaign.

6.4 Chapter findings and conclusions

6.4.1 A comparative taxonomy of the rent-extraction schemes

From the five energy-sector rent-extraction case studies examined in this chapter—two historical and three post-Euromaidan—it is possible to draw up a shortlist of the kinds of actors and institutional structures, and the relations between them, involved in each scheme's rent-extraction mechanism. To bring out the similarities and differences, Table 6.4 below summarises each across a range of recurring institutional and operational features. The presence of a feature—whether the scheme made use of shell companies, for instance—is marked by a tick. A cross indicates either the absence of that feature from the scheme, or that no specific information on it was given in the source material.

The first point to note from the table is the high number of features listed, indicating the relatively complex alignment of business and political elements required to execute such schemes. A second point, indicated by the prevalence of ticks in the body of the table, across features 4 to 12, is that there is considerable overlap in the means used to run the schemes and the kinds of institutions involved, across political, economic and bureaucratic spheres. That is, the schemes often include similar operational components—in terms of the kinds of business vehicles deployed, for example—conducted by networks' positional institutional contacts. This recalls the "structural-relational" definition of the Ukrainian oligarchy from the opening chapter of this book, as a ruling political economy institution made up not just of the very rich, but also of their business networks in alignment with position-holders in the state and the bureaucracy.

What, then, does an "archetype" Ukrainian gas-sector rent-extraction scheme entail? From the table, we can suggest that its operation centrally involves public-private collaboration, of oligarchs' business-political networks in alignment with and reaching into the state apparatus, often using a non-value-adding intermediary inserted in the supply chain between producer and consumer as the business structure of extraction, possibly in co-operation with like-minded political economy actors from the external supplier, but usually licensed by high level political authority, and usually making use of the international financial and legal infrastructure of the wealth-management industry to protect the material gains of the extraction scheme.

On the historical "benchmark" rent schemes, it was noted that where Lazarenko and his associates had innovated, the RUE intermediary seemed to scale-up and deepen the rent-extraction process. A second distinction between these older schemes — indicated in Table 6.4 as a cross under the RUE scheme against feature 9 — is that Firtash does not seem to have risen to his position in the front rank of Ukrainian oligarchs primarily by way of one of the Ukrainian regional business-political networks, but rather through political-administrative links to Russia. In this sense, his business network appears to an extent to have been inserted into Ukrainian politics from the outside as a kind of "political intermediary", just as RUE itself was as an economic one.

Between these benchmark schemes and the more recent post-Euromaidan ones, the main contrast is one of scale. This is shown on the Table 6.4 by the line of crosses marked under these later schemes against feature 4. That is, all of the post-Euromaidan gas schemes examined here appear much smaller in scope — whether in terms of the size of the rents accruing to the schemes' operators, the gas volumes involved, or their economic and political-institutional impact — as well as more geographically delimited than the earlier ones, particularly the RUE scheme. The crucial explanatory factor here is the re-orientation of gas imports away from Russia, which is shown in Table 6.4 by the series of crosses under the post-Euromaidan schemes on feature 5, mirroring those on scale directly above. This leads to a striking conclusion, which is that the break in direct imports of gas from Russia in 2014-16 was itself one of the most effective "anti-corruption" measures of the post-Euromaidan period, because it cut access to "external" rents. By changing the opportunity structure, this may also have stoked rivalry among rent-seeking actors over the remaining domestic energy rent opportunities, encouraging a shift to energy sectors other than gas.

Table 6.4: Key features of elite rent-extraction schemes in the Ukrainian gas sector, 1995-2017

	UESU	RUE	Gas permit	Onyshchenko	RGC schemes
A. Scheme Identification					
1. Main energy companies	UESU; UEI; Somolli	RUE; UkrHazEnergo	Arkona; Ashburi	UGV; Nadra Geocentre, Khas, Karpatnadinvest	Kirovohradgaz; Group DF
2. Dates	1995-18	2005-08	2016-17	2013-16	2016-17
3. Mechanism	State position allows award of gas import contracts	Cheap gas from Gazprom sold at a higher price	Permit bought on low reserves estimate, without tender	Constructed arbitrage via PSA; evasion of subsoil rents	Allocation of gas to non-existent households
B. Scale					
4. Was it large?	✓	✓	✗	✗	✗
C. Positional-institutional authority/ links					
5. Russia the main gas supplier?	✓	✓	✗	✗	✗
6. High-level domestic political backing?	✓	✓	✓	✓	✗
7. State personnel involved?	✗	✓	✓	✓	✗
8. Collaboration of public & private?	✓	✓	✓	✓	✗
9. Associated with a regional business-political networks?	✓	✗	✓	✓	✓
D. Operational elements					
10. Non-value-adding intermediary?	✓	✓	✗	✓	✓
11. Fictional firm/ shell company?	✓	✓	✓	✓	✗
12. Use of international "wealth management"?	✓	✓	✓	✗	✗
Other contextualising tools					
13. Political economy regime					
How does scheme reflect balance of relations of political authority with main networks?	Upsets network balance: energy rents centralised in Naftogaz	Source of network rivalry in the Orange period; aids victory of Yanukovych	Poroshenko network alliance clashes with Kolomoyskyi/Privat, aligned with Yatsenyuk	The authorities around Poroshenko/Hroysman permit the law to take its course against rival network	Reflects opportunities from 2016 network realignment, & authorities' reassertion of Naftogaz control
14. Shaped by post-Euromaidan energy policy?					
Tariff hike					✓
Energy diversification			✓	✓	✓
Reform of energy sector regulation				✓	✓
Restructuring of Naftogaz			✓		

Source: Own compilation from the analysis of the chapter. Note: tick = feature present; cross = feature not present or not specifically noted in source.

I have argued that evolution in Ukraine's overarching political economy regime in the post-communist period has both shaped, and been shaped by, the operation of large-scale energy rent-extraction schemes. So, if the Lazarenko intermediary impinged on the interests of rival regional networks, upsetting the balance of relationships to the Kuchma presidency and triggering the establishment of Naftogaz, the RUE scheme was a source of network contestation in the "multi-pyramid" Orange era. Similarly, the smaller post-Euromaidan gas schemes were shaped by developments in institutional relationships within Ukraine's political economy regime, and so the pursuit of energy reforms, and then partial retreat from them. The workings of the Poltava gas-permit scheme were shown in the context of a struggle between elite networks, while the ending of the Onyshchenko-Nasirov scheme seems to have fallen foul of the realignment of such networks during 2016. The gas-market "manipulations" by Group DF RGCs, by contrast, may not have been pre-agreed in the same way as the Rotterdam plus project, but rather as a more opportunistic and reflexive response to a return of rent-seeking opportunities as these appeared, linked to the wider network reset. On energy policies, although in their scale all three post-Euromaidan schemes seem to show the impact of the diversification of gas imports away from Russia, the gas-permit scheme was pictured on a backdrop of government attempts to restructure Naftogaz; the Onyshchenko-Nasirov scheme, in part in response to a change in gas-sector regulations on PSA subsoil payments; while the RGC manipulations were first constrained by the impact of the rise in household gas tariffs, then opened up again by the government's failure to keep household and commercial gas tariffs in line.

6.4.2 Some wider systemic observations

The low degree of separation of public political from private economic activity, characteristic of the political economy setting of modern Ukraine, has already been touched upon. In the five rent-extraction schemes examined, however, it is possible to observe this phenomenon in operation. Specifically, in the management of

Kirovohradgaz by Firtash's Group DF, until the reassertion of control by Naftogaz in late 2017, we see a parallel with the relation of Kolomoyskyi's Privat Group to Ukrnafta, recounted in the gas-permit study. In each case, we see a majority state-owned business being managed over the long-term by a minority private shareholder, highlighting ambiguities in the nominal distinction between public and private property. To take the point further, it could be argued that it is a property form that expresses well the character of the Ukrainian oligarchic system more broadly — that is, a fusing public and private, of formal and informal, of political and economic, the institution existing as all of these simultaneously. This highlights a more general point, often glossed over in mainstream economics, which is that forms of ownership are themselves culturally variable and institutionally determined.

Alongside the many similarities in organisational components systematised in Table 6.4, a notable feature of the gas schemes, also telling of the institutional whole and of the mode of its recreation, is the repetition, recycling, re-combination and recreation of "stock" scheme elements, or extraction mechanisms, drawing on rent-seeking models stretching back to the generative phase of the oligarchy in the 1990s. That is, there is a fairly limited repertoire of rent-extraction routines, which for informal actors can be reused in different combinations, depending on the political circumstances and opportunities. So, for example, rather than a response to the misalignment of prices between markets, as with the original arbitrage schemes of the 1990s, the first part of the Onyshchenko scheme appears as the artificial construction of an arbitrage opportunity. As with the Onyshchenko case, the two RGC schemes show the routine redeployment of traditional rent-extraction practices (arbitrage and transfer pricing), as political and economic conditions allow. Even if, as in 2014-15, therefore, customary rent-extraction schemes are forced to continue in a more limited manner amid reforms prompted by crisis, both the transmitted network knowledge and personnel remain in place and ready to resume such schemes when opportunities open up politically once more.

7 Conclusion

7.1 What kind of institution is the Ukrainian oligarchy? How did it survive the Euromaidan?

The central concern of this book has been to investigate the generation and reproduction of Ukraine's dominant post-communist political economy regime, "the oligarchy". The aim has been to trace the role of wealth as a material resource power in this process, looking for connections between its economic and political practices to understand how the Ukrainian oligarchy as an institution managed to survive the shock of the Euromaidan revolt and its aftermath more or less intact, despite an official "de-oligarchisation" drive, the onset of war with Russia, and the country's perennially sub-par economic performance. The main findings and arguments of the empirical chapters were as follows.

- Although the domestic business wealth of the Focus-100 fell by half as a share of national wealth between 2010 and 2017, from 18% to 9%, this need not imply a fall in the potential material power available to oligarchs to influence politics, not least because of the scale of wealth they are likely to hold abroad.
- There was a break in the pattern of voting on political economy reform bills in the Verkhovna Rada (parliament) following the formation of the government of Volodymyr Hroysman in April 2016, linked to a realignment of parliamentary factions and business-political network forces. This was interpreted as indicating a final stage in the reconstitution of the Ukrainian oligarchy as a transactional relation between elites following the systemic disruption of the Euromaidan Revolution.
- Amid energy-sector reform brought on by the general crisis of 2014-15, rent-extraction schemes in the Ukrainian gas sector became smaller, compared with earlier, high-profile intermediary schemes. This was probably linked to the reorientation of gas imports away from Russia, which

reduced the scale of "external" rents available to local actors. With the political consolidation of the network "pyramid" around Poroshenko and an abatement of the financial and economic crisis, however, from 2016 rent-seeking opportunities in the energy sector appear to have opened up again.

To aid the development of a more rounded, but still concrete picture of the Ukrainian oligarchy as a resilient political economy institution, some of the main conclusions of the empirical chapters are brought together below.

So, while an analysis of the Focus-100 series shows the top echelon of Ukraine's economic elite as a small group controlling a high share of society's wealth, a range of indicators suggest that wealth inequality in Ukraine is high in international comparison. Within this group, it was shown that a relatively higher level of wealth was one explanation for longevity at the top end of the rankings, in line with the broad prediction of the theory of wealth defence. Key factors behind the concentration of wealth in Ukraine in the post-communist era include the original generative and ongoing institutionally licensed rent-extraction schemes of the Ukrainian oligarchy; the skewing of privatisation in their own favour by the same emergent political economy elites; and the large scale of the "external rents" available by way of intermediary schemes run with Russian counterparts, at least up until 2014.

Evidence of institutional continuities across the Euromaidan events was shown between parliaments, as well as between parliament and the economic elite, in the form of personnel overlap of MPs with the Focus-100 rich list. Those lawmakers who held seats in both the seventh and eighth Rada convocations ("old hands"), and who were also among the wealthiest and longest-lasting members of the Focus-100 (the "core" rich), were identified as among the most enduringly successful of Ukraine's political economy actors — a tiny group dominated by oligarchs, defined as the nationally politically active rich. Moreover, revelations in the Ukrainian press regarding "black ledger" payments of Yanukovych's inner circle, and of WhatsApp text exchanges in parliament under Poroshenko, point to continuity in the informal practice of vote-buying, which helps to explain the mechanics behind sub- and cross-factional Rada voting patterns. Despite a degree of systemic rupture in 2014, signalled by collapse of Yanukovych's "power vertical", the carry-over of institutional personnel, and especially of the whole repertoire of adaptable, informally understood and interlinked political and economic practices, it was argued, go a long way towards explaining the resilience of the Ukrainian oligarchy across crises. This is what is meant by the institutional continuity of the political economy regime. It is this institutional context that helps to explain why the decline in domestic material resource power of Ukraine's economic elite, and especially of the subset of oligarchs among them, need not imply a decline of potential political influence. This argument is backed also by the likely scale of wealth that Ukraine's leading political economy actors are assumed to hold abroad, underscoring the institutionally supportive role of the international financial system in sustaining them as oligarchs in the face of political setbacks at home.

The Rada can be viewed as one in an ensemble of "essential" sub-sites within the state apparatus on which the oligarchy as an informal institutional relation between the leaders of the main business-political networks and current state positional elites is continually renegotiated and reachieved. In this light, the goal of the leading oligarchs in exerting material control over Rada votes may not be to influence the voting outcome of any specific legislation, as the votes they control are often too few in number to make a decisive difference to the voting outcome. Rather, it may be to give them a seat at the bargaining table with other leading wielders of resource powers, as the least risky strategy for the protection and development of their business interests. Another way of putting this is that the effective application of the material resource power of individual oligarchs is mediated by the current state of relations of the main business-political networks to each other and to the state.

Detailed descriptions of the operation and modes of protection of elite rent-extraction schemes in the Ukrainian energy sector, viewed as affected by the policy and political economy environments that they also helped to shape, allowed for the connection of network actions in one location with network material goals in another, across the oligarchy's constituent sub-institutions, illustrating what a low degree of separation between politics and economics looks like in contemporary Ukraine, as well as the means by which the institutional whole is continually "laced" together.

"Flexibility" is a quality integral to the operation of Ukraine's political economy regime, manifesting itself in several ways. That is, not only in the porous organisational forms in the Rada, but also in the room for manoeuvre this allows for network and political realignment, through which the Ukrainian oligarchy as an institution evolves in response to political and economic developments. Not only in a relaxed approach to the observance of laws and other formal regulations, but also the submission to external conditions of reform to qualify for foreign loans as a means of systemic preservation in a crisis, but without relinquishing the means by which such reforms can be bypassed, subverted or reversed once the crisis has passed. In short, flexibility, porousness and looseness are qualities required for the normal operation of a political economy model in which networks of personal connection are central.

The picture that emerges of the Ukrainian oligarchy from the assembly of these findings and conclusions is of an adjustable institution which, founded upon extreme economic inequality that it helps to perpetuate, has been able to survive and adapt in the wake of disruptive crises by way of a stock of customary, reusable, informal political and economic schemes conducted by sometimes rivalrous, sometimes co-operative hierarchical networks.

7.2 A "currency flow" model

7.2.1 The national circuit

It is possible, however, to abstract from the main research findings and conclusions of this book to develop a broader, more general account of how the Ukrainian oligarchy operates and keeps going. In this account, set out schematically in the diagram below (Figure 7.1), each of the capacities or practices examined in this study — of extreme wealth concentration, of the deployment of wealth as material power for political influence, and of wealth extraction by way of political links to the state—can be seen as parts of an interconnected, iterative process. The circular depiction is supposed to suggest the idea that the stock of wealth, as elite material power over society, once generated, operates as both a practical facilitator and motivational end-goal—as both the motor and the prize—of the political and economic routines that constitute the Ukrainian oligarchy as a self-reproducing institution. The notion of a "currency flow" aims to convey a sense of wealth in motion as both money and power, the first recalling the "circular flow of income" model from mainstream macroeconomics, and the second the flow of electric current on a circuit, with the diagram's inner loop perhaps evoking the image of a benzene ring, in which the sharing of electrons binds the structure.

The parts of this process investigated in depth in this study correspond to points 1, 3, 4, and 5 of Figure 7.1, forming the "national"-level circuit of institutional reproduction. These are:

- the original rent accumulation schemes described in chapter 3, including, for example, commodity arbitrage and subsidised credits (point 1);
- the changing patterns of wealth of the richest Ukrainians as a material resource power, or stock of wealth relative to Ukrainian society, analysed in chapter 4 (point 3);
- the control of votes in the Rada by material means, the subject of chapter 5, as an example of an "extractive" domestic political practice (point 4); and
- the adaptation to the changing politics and policy of post-Euromaidan gas-sector rent-extraction schemes (chapter 6) as an example of the operation of extractive economic rules conditioned by extractive political ones (point 5).

Moreover, the role of privatisation (point 2 on the diagram) in the formation of the Ukrainian oligarchy in the 1990s—aided by wealth generated from the original rent accumulation schemes, but in turn boosting the stock of elite material resource power—was discussed in chapter 4 as one of the explanations for the very high degree of wealth concentration in Ukraine.

7.2.2 Regional and international supportive links

Of course, the buying of legislative votes and the extraction of energy rents do not constitute a complete account of the range of political and economic practices, and systems of support, through which Ukraine's post-communist political economy regime is continually replicated, even at the national level, since there are many other schemes — some set out in chapter 3, and others encountered elsewhere in the book — that could be placed in slots 4 and 5 of the "national circuit".

At the same time, the national-level processes are conditioned by feed-ins and outflows at the regional or international levels. To acknowledge this — as well as to forestall the possible charge of "methodological nationalism", by which social processes are investigated as if they took place wholly within the bounds of the nation state — the "currency flow" model indicates several points of connection to the national circuit, both from "below" and from "above", representing links with regional- and international-level practices that, at different times, have helped to generate or to stabilise the national-level system, holding it together or aiding its recovery following a crisis.

At the regional level (point 6 on the diagram), relatively resource poor provincial elites may be able to use their network influence in local politics to deliver votes or seats to larger, better-resourced networks able to exert an influence nationally, in exchange for access to national-level rent opportunities or positions (Andrusiv et al, 2018, p. 12). This is the level of Henry Hale's "bosses" and their "territorially circumscribed" political machines, whom he describes as one of the three broad kinds of actors, along with oligarchs and state officials, around which political economy networks coalesce in patronal societies (Hale, 2015, p. 10, 29).

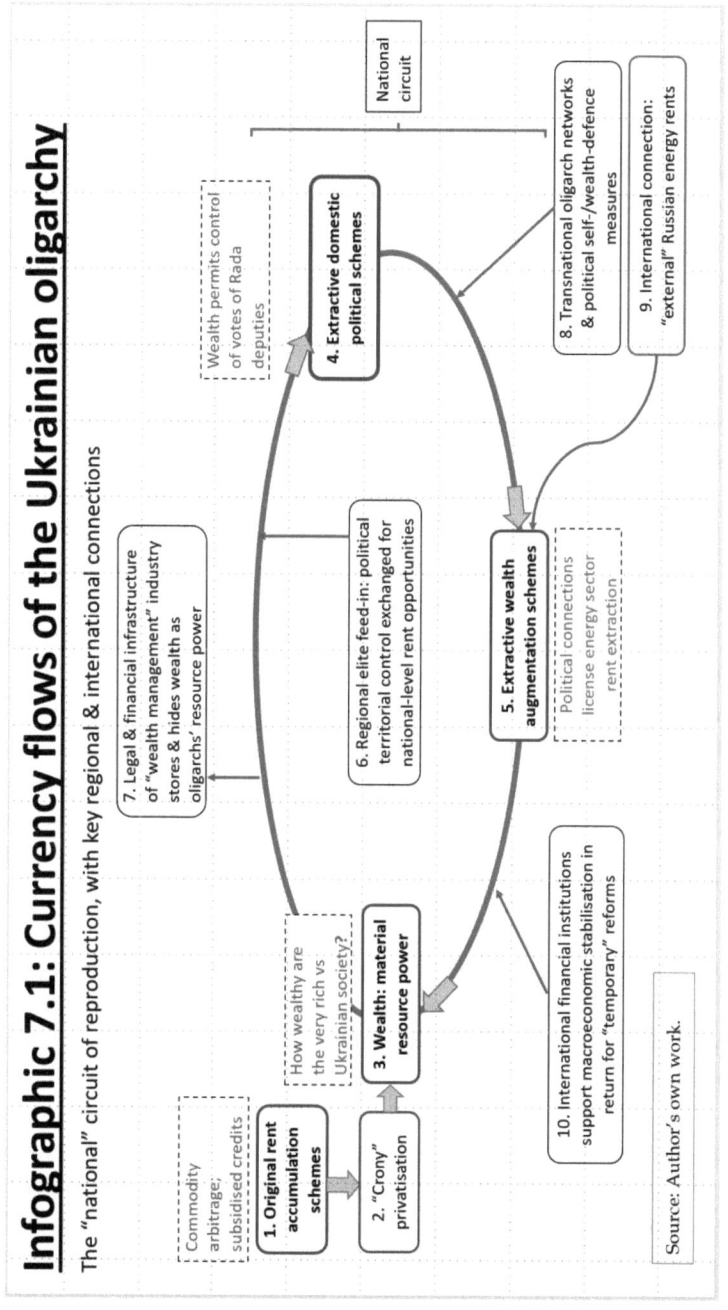

In the case of leading individual oligarchs, the ability to make use of the international legal and financial systems—each, like the Ukrainian oligarchy, composed of formal and informal dimensions—to register firms, and to channel profits and economic rents abroad to store as hidden wealth (point 7), permits their survival in case of political defeat or side-lining at home, but with their material resource power (and oligarchic network know-how) intact, facilitating a return to politics when events allow. The side-lining of Ihor Kolomoyskyi during the Poroshenko period, and his return at the start of the presidency of Volodymyr Zelenskyi in 2019, whom Kolomoyskyi had backed for the post, could be viewed in these terms.

Examining the post-communist period in Ukraine as a whole it is possible to argue that both the services of the international wealth-management industry and the interventions of the international financial institutions (IFIs), such as the IMF (point 10 on the chart), have acted as vital supporting mechanisms for Ukraine's political economy regime. That is, I have argued, successive IFI interventions to stabilise the Ukrainian economy in a crisis have tended to be used by the Ukrainian elite for their own ends, just as with privatisation. Specifically, Ukrainian elites tend to allow reforms to proceed for as long as external aid is required to prevent an economic crash that could threaten the survival of the political economy system, but to halt or row back on these reforms once the crisis has passed, carrying on much as before. (This may not be a wholly planned occurrence, but rather a settling back into everyday routine.) In different ways, therefore, the roles of both kinds of external actor help to explain the longevity of oligarchic system across crises.

The "external" rents (Balmaceda, 2013, p. 95) generated via energy supplies from Russia (point 9) were identified in chapter 6 as one of the key factors, alongside early rent-accumulation schemes and skewed privatisations, that provided the means and incentives for the formation and perpetuation of Ukraine's oligarchic system. The disappearance of these rents following the onset of war with Russia from 2014, I suggest, was perhaps the major "anti-corruption" policy success of the early post-Euromaidan era, as it greatly reduced the size of external rents available.

Point 8 of the "currency flows" graphic, "transnational oligarchy", refers to co-operative interpersonal links between wielders of material resource power or their representatives across national boundaries. A clear and recent high-profile example of this may have been the attempt by Ukrainian oligarchs and network operatives to take advantage of a complicated conspiracy theory propagated by the administration and support networks around Donald Trump, then US president, both to deflect charges that Russia had interfered on Trump's behalf in the 2016 presidential campaign, and to discredit his rival, Joe Biden, in the then approaching 2020 presidential election.

In sum, the joined-up series of political-economic practices are the moving parts of the oligarchy, the oligarchy in motion, with the external feeds from "above" and "below" acting as critical support systems for it—that is, for the constitution and reconstitution of the same or very similar political and economic practices, the political economy regime—across disruptive junctures.

7.3 The Ukrainian oligarchy as a process

From this schematic outline, it is possible to arrive at a revised definition of the Ukrainian oligarchy as **an institution habitually reproduced by its extractive political and economic practices, interconnecting at regional, national and international levels, motivated and facilitated by wealth**. In combination, the process conception, the reproduction schema and the revised definition of the modern Ukrainian political economy regime that follow from them is one of the key results and contributions of this study.

Compared with the definition given earlier—of the Ukrainian oligarchy as the relation between the business-political networks of oligarchs and successful politicians—the revised one offers an understanding of Ukraine's political economy regime as an institution made up of its moving parts, which shape and adapt within an evolving whole, which they also help to shape. Both definitions can be useful, as the right tools for addressing different kinds of question. The structural conception was helpful, for example, as a starting point of the investigation, and remains so for the diagrammatic "snapshot" approach to representing presumed network "orbits" of key political and economic actors, such as the one by Kononczuk (Figure 3.1). However, it presents a more static image, and the second a more flexible and fluid one. That is, I would say, the second concept is a more informative generalisation because it approaches more closely the way that the oligarchy as an institution actually works. Another advantage of this second, process formulation is that it helps to separate out analytically key capacities, practices and roles in institutional reproduction that, in reality, are fused. It offers a flexible framework for locating an examination of other oligarchic practices, not covered in this book, in the context of their connections with the wider, developing whole. Other advantages of the second formulation stem from its cyclical perspective and its explicit recognition of the international dimension in the recreation of Ukraine's political economy model. These are worth dwelling on for a moment, not least because of their potential practical implications for a more effective development policy.

7.3.1 Elite cycles

The cyclical conception of reproduction of elites presented in Figure 7.1 is broadly in line with a burgeoning scholarly consensus concerning patterns of elite political dynamics in the post-communist world, linked to inherited political-economic values and culture. From the cyclical perspective, the periodic political disjunctures in post-communist politics can best be understood, not as instances of democratic breakthrough or backsliding, as they were often portrayed by an earlier, rival school of political analysis, but rather as cycles of elite adaptation and reordering, as informal business-political networks interact with, and adjust to, changes in official politics.

In this light, the outcome of the Euromaidan events can be described as a revolution, but only a political one, since, despite the change in political leadership personnel—drawn mostly from the ranks of the pre-existing elite—there was also considerable carry over of elite political and economic practices, as I have detailed. That is, if the leading business-political networks survive, and the network personnel and network practices that constitute them survive, then the "regime" of the Ukrainian oligarchy survives. The cyclical conception of elite reproduction thus produces, I think, an account of post-Euromaidan developments in Ukraine that better fits the available data than the alternative reading of democracy as periodically advancing or in retreat. It brings with it a fresh perspective on the problems of democratisation and the construction of market economies compared with the earlier, more linear approach, helping to explain past policy failures and to inform policies for the future that, recognising local institutional specificities, may have a better chance of success.

Within this emerging academic consensus, Henry Hale's book on patronalism in Eurasia (Hale, 2015) could be considered a landmark contribution, which other authors—such as Heiko Pleines (2016), Andreas Umland (2017), Yuriy Matsiyevsky (2018) and Sarah Whitmore (2019)—have taken up and applied to post-Euromaidan developments in Ukraine. A more recent publication by two Hungarian scholars, Bálint Magyar and Bálint Madlovics (2020), offers a similar, but still more ambitious approach, proposing a general "ideal type" framework of analysis, not just for the former Soviet region, as with Hale's book, but for post-communist eastern Europe as a whole. My research does not contradict either of these. Although it examines similar processes and issues, of the overlap of formal and informal practices that, in combination, provide individual and group actors with distinctive incentive structures, it does so: i) through the relatively restrictive lens of wealth, or of practices pertaining to the use and replenishment of wealth as a material resource power; ii) for Ukraine only, albeit with some externally comparative elements impinging on the narrative; and iii) for the political and economic dimensions of the social world (whereas Hale and Matsiyevsky concentrate mainly on the political dimension of regime continuity, the ideal-type framework of Magyar and Madlovics encompasses the political, communal and market "spheres of social action").

7.3.2 The international dimension

Finally, the cyclical model of institutional production outlined here, suggests that, if the conditions for perpetuation of Ukraine's sub-optimal political economy model are conceived to be rooted solely in Ukraine's domestic conditions, and not also as supported from the outside by a range of external actors and institutions, then proposals on how to bring about positive institutional and developmental change within Ukraine — as with President Zelenskyi's "de-oligarchisation" campaign — are likely to go awry.

7.4 Economic side-effects of institutional reproduction

The main focus of this study has been on the ways in which the oligarchy, as Ukraine's dominant political economy regime, has been able to recreate itself across disruptive crises by way of a limited set of adaptable, customary, informal political and economic practices. The cyclical framework elaborated above aims to show how my detailed, national-level empirical investigations could be conceived as fitting into a broader process of institutional reproduction, with supportive feed-ins at the regional and international levels. This framework could be useful for envisaging how existing research on this topic might be viewed as part of a wider, developing institutional whole, while perhaps also stimulating ideas for further research (on which I make some suggestions below).

However, as the "other side of the coin", drawing on the two-part thesis set out in the introduction to this study, a secondary aim has been to draw attention to some economic side-effects of the process of institutional reproduction, so helping to explain Ukraine's poor post-communist economic performance, as described in the first chapter. As with the gathering of findings and conclusions on institutional reproduction above, the aim here is to bring together the economic side-effects from the empirical analyses into a more unified, coherent picture. It is possible to group together into three or four main channels the negative economic effects of this process of institutional reproduction. In combination, these might be conceived as weighing on Ukraine's economic development as depicted in Figure 7.2 below.

First, "offshoreisation", identified in chapter 4 as an outcome of the process of rapid wealth concentration amid insecure property rights, was portrayed as a way of protecting accumulated wealth against confiscation by business or political rivals—not least, in the 1990s, amid sometimes violent network competition—as well as of evading taxes, thereby simultaneously removing capital as a ready source of investment in the domestic economy and weakening inflows of public revenue. This can be considered the initial or "set-up" phase of a negative economic feedback loop between weak state capacity and low investment. This gets to the nub of the question of the mechanisms by which Ukraine's post-communist political economy regime has tended to act as a fetter on the country's economic growth.

Second, alongside offshorerisation, oligarchic rent-extraction schemes conducted by way of political connections to the state — such as those detailed in chapter 6—recurrently undercut the state's financial capacity. This was seen most readily in the chronic "quasi-fiscal deficits" run at Naftogaz until 2016, linked to the joint operation by Ukrainian and Russian political and economic elites of large-scale gas intermediary rent-extraction schemes. Another, equally important effect of the operation of such schemes on state capacity, I have argued, is through their undermining the state's organisational coherence and public administrative purpose. This occurs, in particular, through the penetration across the component institutions of the state by business network personnel, whose main allegiance may not be defined by the formal administrative positions they hold, but whose formal positional authority can be used to further the private interests of the informal business-political networks with which they are aligned.

In combination, the persistent undermining of public finances and use of formal state authority for private advancement and material gain hampers the ability of the state to offset the impact of economic shocks—contributing, for example, to the scale of the fall in Ukraine's output in 2009 as a result of the global financial crisis — as well as of its judicial and law-enforcement bodies to apply laws relatively even-handedly. In other words, the ability to perform the standard function of a rule-of-law state, of constituting the legal framework needed for a market economy to run, is significantly constrained. Under such conditions, an absence of fully secure property rights continually recreates incentives for further wealth offshorisation, while maintaining business risks for both domestic and foreign investors at a high level.

In economic theory, capital accumulation through sustained investment is an essential means by which prosperity may be achieved. On the one hand, this is because it allows an increase in capital intensity, or rising provision of productive equipment to workers, that produces the boost to labour productivity on which lasting improvements in living standards depend. It is technological progress, however — or the application of new knowledge to the design of still-more productive machinery and work processes, itself in part the product of investment in research — that counters the effect of the tendency of returns to capital to fall as capital accumulation proceeds, thereby maintaining incentives for investing in domestic production rather than the alternatives (Algan et al, 2017, p. 3,022, 3,042). At the same time, while productivity boosts the economic surplus, whether and to what degree this is translated into higher average living standards across the population depends on how the additional surplus is distributed, which in turn depends on the relative bargaining power of the parties involved, of employers relative to employees (Algan et al, 2017, p. 3,158).

Lastly, by contributing to the economic conditions that keep wages and living standards in Ukraine low in European comparison (chapter 1), the institutional recreation of the Ukrainian oligarchy, and the negative economic feedback loop it sets up, has a knock-on demographic effect that also damages the economy's long-term growth prospects. That is, through encouraging labour migration, including a "brain drain" effect (the loss to the domestic economy of the "human capital" that has been developed within it), it is a key factor behind population decline. Although this has affected a number of post-Soviet societies, it has been especially severe in Ukraine. So, according to the World Bank, Ukraine's population peaked at 52.2m in 1993. Between then and 2017, however, it contracted by just over 14%, to an estimated 44.8m, a proportionately larger fall even than for Estonia, the east Europe country with the next-steepest pace of population decline (World Bank DataBank, *World Development Indicators*). This stylised account of the main economic impacts of institutional reproduction of the Ukrainian oligarchy is represented visually in Figure 7.2, below, with the "set-up" and "knock-on" effects placed either side of the negative feedback loop as the central element, moving left to right.

Figure 7.2: Institutional recreation of the Ukrainian oligarchy sets up a negative economic feedback loop

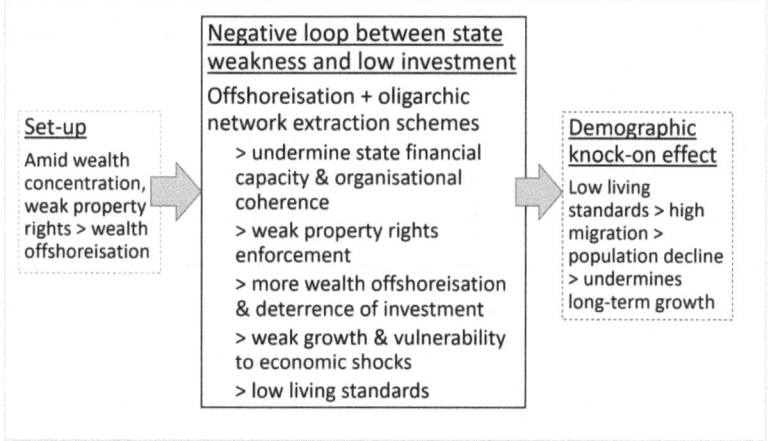

Source: Author's own work.

My account here ties in with the argument of Balmaceda and Rutland (2014), referred to in an earlier chapter, that one of the main negative outcomes of the political economy model of modern Ukraine, dominated by a small number of oligarchs and their organisations, is that it incentivises the pursuit of economic rents over investment, with long-term costs in terms of living standards to the Ukrainian population. Another way of expressing this is that, in this model, it pays leading economic actors to focus more on the struggle over the division of the existing economic surplus than on its expansion. Although this conclusion will not surprise many close observers of Ukraine's post-Soviet economic development, what is new in this study is that it shows concretely how poor overall economic outcomes can be connected to specific political-material processes of institutional reproduction.

7.5 Suggestions for further research

Drawing on the discussion of this chapter, it is possible to derive some suggestions for further research related to the political economy of contemporary Ukraine. This could include:

- Investigations of key sites and sectors of operation of oligarchic material political influence and economic extraction at the national level, other than the Rada and the energy sector (points 4 and 5 on Figure 7.1). Research opportunities might include an examination of the systemic role of the presidential administration, of law-enforcement agencies and the courts, or of PrivatBank in Kolomoyskyi's network before the bank was nationalised in late 2016.
- A study of the operation of institutional support mechanisms at the regional or international level, and how they interact with national-level processes, including perhaps a more detailed empirical assessment of the scale of wealth held by Ukrainians abroad.
- Concrete, detailed micro-level descriptions of how business-political networks operate, and how they interact with one another and with public officials and institutions, as these are processes at the heart of Ukraine's contemporary political economy regime, but are understudied.
- A working out of the implications for Ukraine's development policy of the recast conception of the Ukrainian oligarchy proposed in this study. More specifically, what is implied for political and economic governance reforms — whether those recommended by the international financial institutions (IFIs), or developed as "de-oligarchisation" drives in Ukraine — by an understanding of the oligarchy as motivated not only by the material incentives, but by these mediated by the shared habits of institutional actors? This "thickens" somewhat the broadly "rational actors" approach of the conjoined political economy theory assembled in

chapter 2 by making it more sensitive to local cultural-institutional factors. It helps to explain why standard reform prescriptions, conceded in an emergency, often fail to take hold, since they do not take into account the socially pervasive "logic" of operation of political economy regimes characterised by patronal relations.

- My recast conception of the oligarchy as a stock of linked, adaptable, institutionalised informal practices may also help to explain a key development conundrum of the post-communist era. This is that Ukraine has been unable to build a fully rule-of-law state, even though oligarchs, as the leading wealth holders, would seem to have a strong material interest in ensuring such a development, as it would reduce the cost to them of defending their property claims personally. My somewhat "thickened" explanatory approach suggests that this is because of the shared institutional conventions affecting actors' perceptions of the proper or customary ways of securing and maintaining wealth and power, as well as perhaps what these are, and what they are for.
- In light of Russia's most recent invasion of Ukraine, starting in late February 2022, and the large-scale human and material destruction it has brought, the topic of Ukraine's governance reforms, and of why standard Western reform prescriptions have often failed to take hold over the past three decades, seems likely to be of central importance for the success of Ukraine's post-war domestic reform and reconstruction policy, should it come through the fighting essentially intact. Even more clearly than before, this is because institutional reform holds implications not only for national prosperity and security, but also for whether Ukraine is able to survive as a sovereign nation state over the longer term.

References

Acemoglu, D. & Robinson, J. A. (2012). *Why Nations Fail: The Origins of Power, Prosperity and Poverty.* London: Profile Books.

Algan, T., Carlin, W., Bowles, S. & Segal, P. (2017). "Technological progress, employment and living standards in the long run". Unit 16 in *The CORE Team, The Economy.* Available: https://www.core-econ.org/.

Alvaredo, F., Chancel, L., Piketty, T., Saez, E. & Zucman, G. (2018). *World Inequality Report 2018.* World Inequality Lab. Available: https://wir2018.wid.world/files/download/wir2018-summary-english.pdf [Accessed September 18th 2019].

Andrusiv, V., Ustenko, O., Romanenko, Y. & Tyshkevich, I. (2018). *The Future of the Ukrainian Oligarchs.* Ukrainian Institute for the Future, Kyiv. Available: https://www.wilsoncenter.org/sites/default/files/media/documents/event/the_future_of_ukrainian_oligarchs.pdf [Accessed June 24th 2020].

Antonenko, A., Nitsovych, R., Pavlenko, O. & Takac, K. (2018). *Reforming Ukraine's Energy Sector: Critical Unfinished Business.* Carnegie Europe. Available: https://carnegieeurope.eu/2018/02/06/reforming-ukraine-s-energy-sector-critical-unfinished-business-pub-75449 [Accessed July 2nd 2021].

Aristotle (1996). *The Politics and The Constitution of Athens.* Cambridge Texts in the History of Political Thought. Revised student edition. Everson, S. (ed.) Cambridge: Cambridge University Press.

Aslund, A. (2001). The Myth of Output Collapse after Communism. *Carnegie Endowment for International Peace* [Online], Working Paper 18. Available: https://carnegieendowment.org/2001/03/13/myth-of-output-collapse-after-communism-pub-644 [Accessed July 27th 2021].

Aslund, A. (2009). *How Ukraine Became a Market Economy and Democracy.* Washington, DC: Peterson Institute for International Economics.

Aslund, A. (2014). Why Ukraine is so poor, and what could be done to make it richer. *Eurasian Geography and Economics*, 55, 3, pp. 236-246.

Aslund, A. (2015). *Ukraine: What Went Wrong and How to Fix It.* Washington, DC: Peterson Institute for International Economics.

Avioutskii, V. (2010). The Consolidation of Ukrainian Business Clans. *Revue international d'intelligence économique* [Online], Volume 2. Available: https://r2ie.revuesonline.com/gratuit/R2IE2_1_12_AvioutskiHD.pdf [Accessed July 1st 2021].

References

Backhouse, R. (2002). *The Penguin History of Economics*. London: Penguin Books.

Balcerowicz, L. (2019). "Report on Reforms in 2016-17." In: Miklos, I. & Kukhta, P. (eds.) Annex 1 in: *Reforms in Ukraine after Revolution of Dignity: What was done, why not more and what to do next*. Strategic Advisory Group for Support of Ukrainian Reforms/SAGSUR. pp. 162-165. Available: https://ces.org.ua/wp-content/uploads/2019/07/SAGSUR-book_WEB_ed.pdf [Accessed July 1st 2021].

Balmaceda, M. M. (2013). *The Politics of Energy Dependency: Ukraine, Belarus, and Lithuania between Domestic Oligarchs and Russian Pressure, 1992-2012*. Toronto: University of Toronto Press.

Balmaceda, M. & Rutland, P. (2014). Ukraine's gas politics. [Online] openDemocracy. Available: https://www.opendemocracy.net/en/odr/ukraines-gas-politics/ [Accessed July 1st 2021].

Balmaceda, M. & Prokip, A. (2021). "The Development of Ukraine's Energy Sector." Chapter 4 in: Minakov, M., Kasianov, G. & Rojansky, M. (eds.) *From 'the Ukraine' to 'Ukraine': A Contemporary History, 1991-2021*. Stuttgart: ibidem-Verlag.

Bayramov, A. & Marusyk, Y. (2019). Ukraine's unfinished natural gas and electricity reforms: one step forward, two steps back. *Eurasian Geography and Economics*, 60, 1, pp. 73-96.

Berdinskikh, K. (2015). Deputatskiy rasklad. Kakim oligarkham i politikam podkontrolny narodnyye izbranniki v Rade. *Novoye Vremya*. Available: https://nv.ua/publications/kakie-politiki-i-biznesmeny-vliyayut-na-resheniya-narodnyh-izbrannikov-v-rade-49044.html [Accessed June 24th 2020].

Berdinskikh, K. (2019a). Milliarder, kotoryy smeyetsya. Intervyu Igorya Kolomoyskogo NV — pervaya chast. *Novoye Vremya*. Available: https://nv.ua/ukraine/politics/igor-kolomoyskiy-intervyu-nv-novosti-ukraina-50030191.html [Accessed September 27th 2019].

Berdinskikh, K. (2019b). Ne boyus ya nikogo, krome Boga odnogo. Intervyu Igorya Kolomoyskogo NV — vtoraya chast. *Novoye Vremya*. Available: https://nv.ua/ukraine/politics/igor-kolomoyskiy-intervyu-nv-chast-2-novosti-ukraina-50030322.html [Accessed September 27th 2019].

Bojcun, M. (2020). *Towards a Political Economy of Ukraine, Selected Essays 1990-2015*. Ukrainian Voices. Umland, A. (ed.) Stuttgart: ibidem-Verlag.

Bondarenko, A., Kelm, N., Bodnar, P. & Drozdova, Y. (2019). *Try etapy Rady. Yak fraktsiyi i deputaty parlamentu vosmoho sklykannya holosuvaly za reformy*. TEXTY.ORG.UA. Available: https://texty.org.ua/d/2019/verhovna-rada/ [Accessed June 24th 2020].

Borosovskyi, T. (2018), Skhemy obkradannya derzhavy ta prykhovuvannya prybutkiv Zhytomyrhazu. *Ukrayinska Enerhetyka*. Available: https://ua-energy.org/uk/posts/skhemy-obkradannia-derzhavy-ta-prykhovuvannia-prybutkiv-zhytomyrhazu [Accessed March 20th 2022].

Boytsun, A. (2019). "Privatisation and SOE reform." Chapter 7 in: Miklos, I. & Kukhta, P. (eds.) *Reforms in Ukraine After Revolution of Dignity. What was done, why not more and what to do next*. Strategic Advisory Group for Support of Ukrainian Reforms/SAGSUR. pp. 112-130. Available: https://ces.org.ua/wp-content/uploads/2019/07/SAGSUR-book_WEB_ed.pdf [Accessed July 10th 2021].

BP. (2020). *bp Statistical Review of World Energy 2020*. Available: https://www.bp.com/content/dam/bp/business-sites/en/global/corporate/pdfs/energy-economics/statistical-review/bp-stats-review-2020-full-report.pdf [Accessed July 1st 2021].

Brown, D. (2019). Billionaire Putin supporter Dmitry Firtash faces extradition to US for bribery. *The Times*. Available: https://www.thetimes.co.uk/article/billionaire-putin-supporter-dmitry-firtash-faces-extradition-to-us-for-bribery-zt2p32p5n [Accessed September 30th 2021].

Buckley, N. (2016). Ukraine takes needed steps to clean up its banks: Nationalisation of PrivatBank could face legal challenges from bondholders. *The Financial Times*. Available: https://www.ft.com/content/162c55a6-cc26-11e6-864f-20dcb35cede2 [Accessed March 13th 2022].

Burakovsky, I., Anhel, Y., Betliy, O., Butin, A., Havronyuk, M., Koliushko, I., Kravchuk, V., Kuziakiv, O., Movchan, V. & Volokh, K. (2018). *Ukraine's Fight Against Corruption: The Economic Front. Economic Assessment of Anticorruption Measures Implemented 2014-2018*. Research Report. The Institute for Economic Research and Policy Consulting. Kyiv. Available: http://www.ier.com.ua/en/publications/reports?pid=5993 [Accessed December 12th 2022].

Caporaso, J. A. & Levine, D. P. (1992). *Theories of Political Economy*. Cambridge: Cambridge University Press.

Casais, E. Jr & Casais, E. Sr. *The Complete World Billionaire Lists*. areppim website. Available: https://stats.areppim.com/stats/links_billionairexlists.htm [Accessed September 27th 2019].

Chaisty, P. & Chernykh, S. (2015.) Coalition presidentialism and legislative control in post-Soviet Ukraine. *Post-Soviet Affairs*, 31:3, pp. 177-200.

Chazan, G. & Olearchyk, R. (2015). Ukraine: An oligarch brought to heel. *The Financial Times*. Available: https://www.ft.com/content/b0b04474-d232-11e4-a225-00144feab7de [Accessed July 1st 2021].

References

Chazan, G. & Weaver, C. (2014). Ukraine partisans battling separatists raise concerns. *The Financial Times*. Available: https://www.ft.com/content/b525af9a-e191-11e3-9999-00144feabdc0 [Accessed July 1st 2021].

Chernenko, D. (2019). Capital Structure and Oligarch Ownership. *Economic Change and Restructuring*, 52, 4, pp. 383-411.

Chernyshev, R., Golovatyuk, E., Samofalov, A., Sorochan, O., Katsilo, D. & Brovinskaya, M. (2017). Strategicheskaya vosmerka: Chto izmenilos za tri goda pravleniya Poroshenko - kto iz oligarkhov stal pervym, kto okazalsya nepotoplyayemym i komu ne povezlo bolshe vsekh. LIGA.net. Available: https://project.liga.net/projects/3_goda_poroshenko/ [Accessed August 18th 2021].

Chornovalov, O. (2015). Zastupnyk ministra enerhetyky Didenko vyyavyvsya biznes-partnerom Kolomoyskoho — rozsliduvannya. Radio Svoboda. Available: https://www.radiosvoboda.org/a/26953743.html [Accessed July 7th 2021].

Chornovalov, O. (2018). Novyi hazovyi biznes otochennya Petra Poroshenka (rozsliduvannya). Radio Svoboda. Available: https://www.radiosvoboda.org/a/29049145.html [Accessed July 7th 2021].

Chornovalov, O., Tolstyakova, K. & Sedletska, N. (2019). «Hra v piddavky»: chy vidsudyt henprokuror Lutsenko hazovyi biznes otochennya Poroshenka? Radio Svoboda. Available: https://www.radiosvoboda.org/a/schemes/29770600.html [Accessed July 8th 2021].

Dabrowski, M. (2017a). Ukraine's unfinished reform agenda. Bruegel Policy Contributions. 24. [Online] Brussels: Bruegel. Available: https://www.bruegel.org/policy-brief/ukraines-unfinished-reform-agenda [Accessed August 10th 2021].

Dabrowski, M. (2017b). Ukraine's oligarchs are bad for democracy and economic reform. [Online] Brussels: Bruegel. Available: https://www.bruegel.org/blog-post/ukraines-oligarchs-are-bad-democracy-and-economic-reform [Accessed June 25th 2020].

Dadkhah, K. (2009). *The Evolution of Macroeconomic Theory and Policy*. Berlin Heidelberg, Springer-Verlag.

Dalton, D. (2016). Belarusian Economic Recovery May Downgrade Intended Reforms for Competitiveness. Emerging Europe. Available: https://emerging-europe.com/voices/belarusian-economic-recovery-may-downgrade-intended-reforms-for-competitiveness/ [Accessed September 9th 2021].

Dalton, D. (2021). How did the Ukrainian oligarchy keep going after the Euromaidan? *Vox Ukraine*. Available: https://voxukraine.org/en/how-did-the-ukrainian-oligarchy-keep-going-after-euromaidan/ [Accessed May 14th 2021].

D'Anieri, P. (2019). *Ukraine and Russia: From Civilised Divorce to Uncivil War*. Cambridge: Cambridge University Press.

Douarin, E. & Mickiewicz, T. (2017). *Economics of Institutional Change: Central and Eastern Europe revisited*. Studies in Economic Transition. Cham, Switzerland: Palgrave Macmillan.

Drake, M. S. (2010). *Political Sociology for a Globalizing World*. Cambridge, UK; Malden, MA: Polity.

Ekonomichna Pravda. (2016a). Leshchenko pokazav perepysku Onyshchenka z Kononenkom na 7 milyoniv hryven. Available: https://www.epravda.com.ua/news/2016/12/11/614063/ [Accessed March 12th 2022].

Ekonomichna Pravda. (2016b). Hroysman obyasnyl, kak rabotala tak nazyvaemaya skhema Onyshchenko. Available: https://www.epravda.com.ua/rus/news/2016/12/14/614390/ [Accessed March 12th 2022].

Ekonomichna Pravda. (2017a). Kobolyev pro "skhemu Onyshchenka": U skhemi bahato politykiv. Available: https://www.epravda.com.ua/news/2017/01/5/616784/ [Accessed March 12th 2022].

Ekonomichna Pravda. (2017b). 100 milyoniv za Nasirova. Malo chy bahato? Available: https://www.epravda.com.ua/publications/2017/03/10/622542/ [Accessed March 12th 2022].

Ekonomichna Pravda. (2018). Eks-dyrektor "5 elementu" Poroshenka stav osnovnym vlasnykom skandalnoyi hazovoyi kompaniyi. Available: https://www.epravda.com.ua/news/2018/11/15/642662/ [Accessed March 13th 2022].

Ekonomichna Pravda. (2019). Obvynuvalnyy akt shchodo Onyshchenka skeruvaly do sudu. Available: https://www.epravda.com.ua/news/2019/02/18/645370/ [Accessed March 12th 2022].

Estrin, S., Hanousek, J., Kocenda, E. & Svejnar, J. (2009). The Effects of Privatization and Ownership in Transition Economies. *Journal of Economic Literature*, 47, 3, pp. 699-728.

Europa Publications (2018). "Ukraine." In: Europa Publications (ed.) *Eastern Europe, Russia and Central Asia 2019*. 19th ed.: Routledge. pp. 515-559.

European Bank for Reconstruction and Development. (2018). *Transition Report 2017-18: Sustaining Growth.* London: EBRD. Available: https://www.ebrd.com/transition-report-2017-18 [Accessed December 6th 2022].

European Commission, IMF, OECD, UN & World Bank. (2009). *System of National Accounts 2008.* United Nations/UN. New York. Available: https://unstats.un.org/unsd/nationalaccount/docs/sna2008.pdf [Accessed August 5th 2021].

Fedorenko, K., Rybiy, O. & Umland, A. (2016). The Ukrainian Party System before and after the 2013-2014 Euromaidan. *Europe-Asia Studies*, 68, 4, pp. 609-630.

Filipiak, T. (2016). "The oligarchs are not a problem in Ukraine anymore". Interview with Anders Åslund — Senior Fellow at the Atlantic Council. eastbook. Available: http://www.eastbook.eu/en/2016/12/02/the-oligarchs-are-not-a-problem-in-ukraine-anymore-interview-with-anders-aslund-senior-fellow-at-the-atlantic-council/ [Accessed September 18th 2019].

Forbes' List. (2008). *Billionaires, 2008.* Available: https://www.forbes.com/forbes/2008/0324/080.html?sh=256f220410f2 [Accessed December 14th 2018].

Foucault, M. (2002). "The Subject and Power." In: Faubion, J. D. E. & (Trans.), R. H. a. O. (eds.) *Power. Essential Works of Foucault 1954-1984.* London: Penguin Books.

Francis, D. (2016). Stolen Future. Atlantic Council. Washington, DC. Available: https://www.atlanticcouncil.org/in-depth-research-reports/issue-brief/stolen-future/ [Accessed February 10th 2021].

Freedom House. (2021). Freedom in the World: All Data, FIW 2013-2021. Available from: https://freedomhouse.org/report/freedom-world [Accessed July 3rd 2021].

Galbraith, J. K. (1973). Power and the Useful Economist. *The American Economic Review*, 63, 1, 1-11.

Garside, J., Harding, L., Watt, H., Pegg, D., Bengtsson, H., Bowers, S., Gibson, O. & Hopkins, N. (2016). Ukraine's leader set up secret offshore firm as battle raged with Russia. *The Guardian.* Available: https://www.theguardian.com/news/2016/apr/04/panama-papers-ukraine-petro-poroshenko-secret-offshore-firm-russia [Accessed July 3rd 2021].

Giddens, A. (1971). *Capitalism and modern social theory: An analysis of the writings of Marx, Durkheim and Max Weber.* Cambridge: Cambridge University Press.

Goldstone, J. A. (2014a). *Revolutions: A Very Short Introduction.* Very Short Introductions. Oxford; New York: Oxford University Press.

Goldstone, J. A. (2014b). The Revolution in the Ukraine. *NewPopulationBomb* [Online]. Available: https://newpopulationbomb.com/2014/03/02/the-revolution-in-the-ukraine/ [Accessed September 17th 2021].

Grey, S., Bergin, T., Musaieva, S. & Anin, R. (2014). Putin's allies channelled billions to oligarch who backed pro-Russian president of Ukraine. Reuters. Available: https://www.reuters.com/investigates/special-report/comrade-capitalism-the-kiev-connection/ [Accessed July 3rd 2021].

Hale, H. E. (2015). *Patronal Politics: Eurasian Regime Dynamics in Comparative Perspective*. Cambridge, UK: Cambridge University Press.

Halling, S. & Stewart, S. (2016). "Deoligarchisation" in Ukraine: Promising Visions, Murky Realities. *SWP Comment 2016/C 51*. German Institute for International and Security Affairs. Available: https://www.swp-berlin.org/en/publication/deoligarchisation-in-ukraine [Accessed March 19 2022].

Hartwell, C. (2016). *Two Roads Diverge: The Transition Experience of Poland and Ukraine*. Cambridge: Cambridge University Press.

Hass, J.K. (2020). *Economic Sociology: An Introduction*. 2nd ed. London and New York: Routledge.

Havrylyshyn, O. (2017). *The Political Economy of Independent Ukraine: Slow Starts, False Starts, and a Last Chance?* Studies in Economic Transition. London: Palgrave Macmillan UK.

Havrylyshyn, O., Meng, X. & Tupy, M. L. (2016). 25 Years of Reforms in Ex-Communist Countries: Fast and Extensive Reforms Led to Higher Growth and More Political Freedom. *Policy Analysis no. 795*. Washington, DC: Cato Institute. Available: https://www.cato.org/policy-analysis/25-years-reforms-ex-communist-countries-fast-extensive-reforms-led-higher-growth [Accessed June 16th 2021].

Hayek, F. A. (1948). The Meaning of Competition. Excerpt from *Individualism and Economic Order*. Mises Institute. Available: https://mises.org/library/meaning-competition [Accessed December 9th 2022].

Heinrich, M. (2012). *An Introduction to the Three Volumes of Karl Marx's Capital*. Locascio, A. (trans.). New York: Monthly Review Press.

Henn, M., Weinstein, M., Foard, N. (2009.) *A Critical Introduction to Social Research*. 2nd ed. London, California, New Delhi, Singapore: Sage Publications.

Hellman, J. S. (1998). Winners Take All: The Politics of Partial Reform in Postcommunist Transitions. *World Politics*, 50, 2, pp. 203-234.

References

Hirman, K. (2019). "Energy policy." Chapter 4 in: Miklos, I. & Kukhta, P. (eds.) *Reforms in Ukraine After Revolution of Dignity. What was done, why not more and what to do next*. Strategic Advisory Group for Support of Ukrainian Reforms/SAGSUR. pp. 75-85. Available: https://ces.org.ua/wp-content/uploads/2019/07/SAGSUR-book_WEB_ed.pdf [Accessed July 1st 2021].

Hodgson, G. M. (1998). The Approach of Institutional Economics. *Journal of Economic Literature*, 36, 1, pp. 166-192.

Hodgson, G. M. (2019). *Is Socialism Feasible? Towards an Alternative Future*. Northampton: Edward Elgar Publishing.

Hromadske International. (2016). The Onyshchenko Case: A Step Toward The Anti-Corruption Struggle? Available: https://en.hromadske.ua/posts/Onyshchenko_Case_Step_Toward_Anticorruption_Struggle [Accessed September 25th 2021].

IMF. (2014a). Ukraine: Request for a Stand-by Arrangement—Staff Report; Supplement; Staff Statement; Press Release; and Statement by The Executive Director for Ukraine. *Country Report No. 14/106*, IMF. Available: https://www.imf.org/external/pubs/ft/scr/2014/cr14106.pdf [Accessed February 16th 2019].

IMF. (2014b). Ukraine: Staff Report for the 2013 Article IV Consultation and First Post-Program Monitoring. *Country Report No. 14/145*, IMF. Available: https://www.imf.org/en/Publications/CR/Issues/2016/12/31/Ukraine-Staff-Report-for-the-2013-Article-IV-Consultation-and-First-Post-Program-Monitoring-41599 [Accessed February 16th 2019].

IMF. (2016a). Ukraine: Second Review under the Extended Fund Facility and requests for waivers of non-observance of performance criteria, rephrasing of access and financing assurances review. *Country Report No. 16/319*, IMF. Available: https://www.imf.org/en/Publications/CR/Issues/2016/12/31/Ukraine-Second-Review-Under-the-Extended-Fund-Facility-and-Requests-for-Waivers-of-Non-44318 [Accessed September 20th 2021].

IMF. (2016b). Republic of Belarus: Staff Report for the 2013 Article IV Consultation. *Country Report No. 16/298*, IMF. Available: https://www.imf.org/en/Publications/CR/Issues/2016/12/31/Republic-of-Belarus-Staff-Report-for-the-2016-Article-IV-Consultation-Press-Release-Staff-44279 [Accessed September 9th 2021].

IMF. (2019a). Ukraine: Request for Stand-By Arrangement and Cancellation of Arrangement Under the Extended Fund Facility-Press Release; Staff Report; and Statement by the Executive Director for Ukraine. *Country Report No. 19/3*, IMF. Available: https://www.imf.org/en/Publications/CR/Issues/2019/01/08/Ukraine-Request-for-Stand-By-Arrangement-and-Cancellation-of-Arrangement-Under-the-Extended-46499 [Accessed September 20th 2021].

IMF. (2019b). World Economic Outlook (WEO) Database. International Monetary Fund (IMF). Available: https://www.imf.org/en/Publications/WEO/weo-database/2019/October [Accessed July 10th 2021].

Inglis, D. & Thorpe, C. (2019). *An Invitation to Social Theory*. 2nd ed. Medford MA: Polity Press.

Kalymon, B. A. & Havrylyshyn, O. (2016). What's Behind the Resignation of Minister Abromavicius? Atlantic Council. Available: https://www.atlanticcouncil.org/blogs/ukrainealert/what-s-behind-the-resignation-of-minister-abromavicius/ [Accessed September 30th 2021].

Kar, D. & Spanjers, J. (2015). *Illicit Financial Flows from Developing Countries: 2004-2013*. Global Financial Integrity. Available: https://gfintegrity.org/report/illicit-financial-flows-from-developing-countries-2004-2013/ [Accessed August 8th 2021].

Kenny, A. (2010). *A New History of Western Philosophy*. Oxford: Clarendon Press.

Kinder, T., Plimmer, G., & Pickard, J. (2020). Watchdog criticises government over awarding of £17bn Covid contracts: National Audit Office raises concerns over lack of transparency and potential conflicts of interest. *The Financial Times*. Available: https://www.ft.com/content/ee4f2220-9b22-4a4d-87c2-85e8034f8e8c [Accessed September 30th 2019].

Konończuk, W. (2016). *Keystone of the system. Old and new oligarchs in Ukraine*. Ośrodek Studiów Wschodnich (OSW) im. Marka Karpia. Warsaw. Available: https://www.osw.waw.pl/en/publikacje/point-view/2016-08-18/keystone-system-old-and-new-oligarchs-ukraine [Accessed February 16th 2019].

Konończuk, W. (2017a). *The never-ending collapse. The state of the Ukrainian oil sector*. Ośrodek Studiów Wschodnich (OSW) im. Marka Karpia. Warsaw. Available: https://www.osw.waw.pl/en/publikacje/osw-report/2017-05-04/never-ending-collapse-state-ukrainian-oil-sector [Accessed July 1st 2021].

References

Konończuk, W. & Matuszak, S. (2017b). Dark clouds over the Ukrainian gas market reform. *OWS Commentary*. Available: https://www.osw.waw.pl/en/publikacje/osw-commentary/2017-10-04/dark-clouds-over-ukrainian-gas-market-reform [Accessed September 11th 2021].

Kornai, J. (2010). Innovation and dynamism: Interaction between systems and technical progress. *Economics of Transition and Institutional Change*, 18, 4, pp. 629-670.

Korpi, W. (1998). "Power Resources Approach vs Action and Conflict: On Causal and Intentional Explanations in the Study of Power." In: O'Connor, J. S. & Olsen, G. (eds.) *Power Resource Theory and the Welfare State: A Critical Approach*. University of Toronto Press. pp. 37-69.

Kravtsov, H. & Hrabarska, A. (2015). Partiya "Vidrodzhennya": kolyshni rehionaly na orbiti Kolomoyskoho. *Ukrayinska Pravda*. Available: https://www.pravda.com.ua/articles/2015/10/23/7085959/ [Accessed June 24th 2020].

Kudelia, S. & Kasianov, G. (2021). "Ukraine's Political Development after Independence." Chapter 2 in: Minakov, M., Kasianov, G. & Rojansky, M. (eds.) *From 'the Ukraine' to 'Ukraine': A Contemporary History, 1991-2021*. Stuttgart: ibidem-Verlag.

Kupfer, M., & Kovensky, J. (2019). In Ukraine, gas is even sold to people who don't exist. *Kyiv Post*. Available: https://www.kyivpost.com/business/in-ukraine-gas-is-sold-even-to-people-who-dont-exist.html [Accessed March 20th 2022].

Kuzio, T. (2016). Analysis of Current Events: Structural Impediments to Reforms in Ukraine. *Demokratizatsiya: The Journal of Post-Soviet Democratization*, 24, 2, pp. 131-138.

Kuznetsov, S. (2017). Yanukovych-era corruption schemes implicate Ukraine's current elites. Transparency International Ukraine. Available: https://ti-ukraine.org/en/news/yanukovych-era-corruption-schemes-implicate-ukraine-s-current-elites/ [Accessed February 8th 2020].

Lange, G.M., Wodon, Q. & Carey, K. (2018). *The Changing Wealth of Nations 2018: Building a Sustainable Future*. Washington, DC: World Bank. Available: https://openknowledge.worldbank.org/bitstream/handle/10986/29001/9781464810466.pdf [Accessed September 18th 2019].

Ledeneva, A. (2013.) *Can Russia Modernise? Sistema, Power Networks and Informal Governance*. Cambridge, UK: Cambridge University Press.

Leshchenko, S. (2016). Ukraine's Verkhovna Rada: an oligarchs' club or a real parliament? openDemocracy. Available: https://www.opendemocracy.net/en/odr/ukraine-s-verkhovna-rada-oligarchs-club-or-real-parliament/ [Accessed June 25th 2020].

Little, D. (1991). *Varieties of Social Explanation: An Introduction to the Philosophy of Social Science*. Boulder: Westview Press.

Little, D. (2016). *New Directions in the Philosophy of Social Science*. London, New York: Rowman & Littlefield.

Lough, J. (2021) *Ukraine's system of crony capitalism: The challenge of dismantling 'systema'*. Research Paper. Chatham House. Available: https://www.chathamhouse.org/2021/07/ukraines-system-crony-capitalism [Accessed September 9th 2022].

Lukes, S. (2013). "Power." Entry in: Kaldis, B. (ed.) *Encyclopedia of Philosophy and the Social Sciences*. SAGE. pp. 748-750.

Magelinski, T., Hou, J., Mylovanov, T. & Carley, K. M. (2019). Detecting Disruption: Identifying Structural Changes in the Verkhovna Rada. *Social, Cultural, and Behavioral Modelling*. Cham: Springer International Publishing. pp.194-203.

Magyar, B. & Madlovics, B. (2020). *The Anatomy of Post-Communist Regimes: A Conceptual Framework*. Central European University Press.

Markus, S. & Charnysh, V. (2017). The Flexible Few: Oligarchs and Wealth Defense in Developing Democracies. *Comparative Political Studies*, 50, 12, pp. 1,632-1,665. Available: https://bit.ly/2Wcuoye.

Marx, K. (1976). *Capital: A Critique of Political Economy. Volume One*. Introduced by Mandel, E; Fowkes, B. (trans.) London: Penguin Books in association with New Left Review.

Marx, K. (1994). *Selected Writings*. Simon, L. H. (ed.) Indianapolis/Cambridge: Hackett Publishing Company.

Matsiyevsky, Y. (2018). Revolution without regime change: The evidence from the post-Euromaidan Ukraine. *Communist and Post-Communist Studies*, 51, 4, pp. 349-359.

Matuszak, S. (2012). *The Oligarchic Democracy. The Influence of Business Groups on Ukrainian politics*. Warsaw, Ośrodek Studiów Wschodnich Im. Marka Karpia (OSW). Available: https://www.osw.waw.pl/en/publikacje/osw-studies/2012-10-16/oligarchic-democracy-influence-business-groups-ukrainian-politics [Accessed July 10th 2021].

Meyer, G. (2006). "Formal and informal politics: questions, concepts and subjects." In: Meyer, G. (ed.) *Formal institutions and informal politics in Central and Eastern Europe: Hungary, Poland, Russia and Ukraine*. Oplanden & Farmington Hills: Barbara Budrich Publishers.

References

Miklos, I. (2019a). *Reforms in Ukraine After Revolution of Dignity. What was done, why not more and what to do next.* Strategic Advisory Group for Support of Ukrainian Reforms/ SAGSUR. Available: https://ces.org.ua/wp-content/uploads/2019/07/SAGSUR-book_WEB_ed.pdf [Accessed July 1st 2021].

Miklos, I. (2019b). "Political economy of reforms: political system, governance and corruption." Chapter 1 in: Miklos, I. & Kukhta, P. (eds.) *Reforms in Ukraine After Revolution of Dignity. What was done, why not more and what to do next.* Strategic Advisory Group for Support of Ukrainian Reforms/ SAGSUR. pp. 10-33. Available: https://ces.org.ua/wp-content/uploads/2019/07/SAGSUR-book_WEB_ed.pdf [Accessed July 1st 2021].

Milanović, B. (2020). The history of global inequality studies. *globalinequality* [Online]. Available: http://glineq.blogspot.com/2020/11/the-history-of-global-inequality-studies.html [Accessed March 5th 2021].

Mills, C. W. (1956). *The Power Elite.* London, New York: Oxford University Press.

Minakov, M. (2019). Republic of Clans: The Evolution of the Ukrainian Political System. In: Magyar, B. (ed.) *Stubborn Structures: Reconceptualizing Post-Communist Regimes.* Central European University Press. pp. 217-245.

Minakov, M. & Rojansky, M. (2021). "Democracy in Ukraine." Chapter 9 in in: Minakov, M., Kasianov, G. & Rojansky, M. (eds.) *From 'the Ukraine' to 'Ukraine': A Contemporary History, 1991-2021.* pp. 321-357. Stuttgart: ibidem-Verlag.

Mohun, S. (1985). "Capital." Entry in: Bottomore, T., Harris, L., Kerenan, V. G. & Miliband, R. (eds.) *A Dictionary of Marxist Thought.* Oxford: Blackwell Reference.

NABU. (2016a). Detektyvy NABU zatrymaly shche odnoho uchasnyka skhemy rozkradannya hazu. Natsionalne Antykoruptsiyne Byuro Ukrayiny. Available: https://nabu.gov.ua/novyny/detektyvy-nabu-zatrymaly-shche-odnogo-uchasnyka-shemy-rozkradannya-gazu [Accessed August 25th 2021].

NABU. (2016b). Interpol may put Oleksandr Onyshchenko into International wanted list in October. National Anti-corruption Bureau of Ukraine. Available: https://nabu.gov.ua/en/novyny/interpol-may-put-oleksandr-onyshchenko-international-wanted-list-october [Accessed August 25th 2021].

NABU. (2017a). Holova DFS zatrymanyi. Bilya yoho palaty cherhuyut pratsivnyky NABU. Natsionalne Antykoruptsiyne Byuro Ukrayiny. Available: https://nabu.gov.ua/novyny/golova-dfs-zatrymanyy-bilya-yogo-palaty-cherguyut-pracivnyky-nabu [Accessed August 25th 2021].

NABU. (2017b). Spravu stosovno 8 uchasnykiv «hazovoyi skhemy» skerovano do sudu. Natsionalne Antykoruptsiyne Byuro Ukrayiny. Available: https://nabu.gov.ua/novyny/golova-dfs-zatrymanyy-bilya-yogo-palaty-cherguyut-pracivnyky-nabu [Accessed September 28th 2021].

NABU. (2017c). Rozsliduvannya roli holovy DFS u «hazoviy spravi» zavershene. Natsionalne Antykoruptsiyne Byuro Ukrayiny. Available: https://nabu.gov.ua/novyny/rozsliduvannya-roli-golovy-dfs-u-gazoviy-spravi-zavershene [Accessed September 28th 2021].

NABU. (2017d). The timeline of the case of the Head of State Fiscal Service of Ukraine. National Anti-Corruption Bureau of Ukraine. Available: https://nabu.gov.ua/en/novyny/timeline-case-head-state-fiscal-service-ukraine-updated-10112017 [Accessed September 28th 2021].

NABU. (2018a). «HAZOVA SPRAVA». Natsionalne Antykoruptsiyne Byuro Ukrayiny. Available: https://nabu.gov.ua/novyny/gazova-sprava [Accessed July 9th 2021].

NABU. (2018b). «Hazova sprava»: rozsliduvannya stosovno narodnoho deputata-orhanizatora skhemy zaversheno. Natsionalne Antykoruptsiyne Byuro Ukrayiny. Available: https://nabu.gov.ua/novyny/gazova-sprava-rozsliduvannya-stosovno-narodnogo-deputata-organizatora-shemy-zaversheno [Accessed July 8th 2021].

NABU. (2021). 196,8 mln hrn zbytkiv cherez nezakonnyy dozvil na vydobutok hazu: rozsliduvannya zaversheno. Available: https://nabu.gov.ua/novyny/1968-mln-grn-zbytkiv-cherez-nezakonnyy-dozvil-na-vydobutok-gazu-rozsliduvannya-zaversheno [Accessed March 13th 2022].

Naftogaz. (2018). Dynamika tsin na pryrodnyi haz dlya spozhyvachiv Ukrayiny [Online]. Available: C:\Users\VoloshynaL\AppData\Roaming\Softline\Megapolis2\Local Cache\38073308380_Динаміка_ціни_на сайт грудень_2013-2017 [Accessed September 19th 2021].

Naftogaz. (2020). VYDOBUVANNYA HAZU [Online]. Available: https://bit.ly/3tWO1ag [Accessed September 20th 2021; site inactive on December 12th 2022].

Naftogaz. (2021). Vykorystannya pryrodnoho hazu [Online]. Available: https://bit.ly/3nOf869 [Accessed September 9th 2021; site inactive on December 12th 2022].

References

Naftogaz Europe. (2014). Naftogaz Structure [Online]. Available: https://bit.ly/3AM8q45 [Accessed February 27th 2021; site inactive on December 12th 2022].

Naftogaz Research. (2017). Rozdribne postachannya hazu v ramkakh PSO: Manipulyatsiyi z obsyahamy ta subsydiyamy rehionalnymy hazopostachalnymy kompaniyamy. Naftogaz. Available: http://www.naftogaz.com/files/Information/170926_Report_re_RSCs_v2 -pdf_UA.pdf. [Accessed July 27th 2021].

National Bank of Ukraine (NBU). Daily official exchange rates. Available: https://bank.gov.ua/ua/markets/exchangerate-chart [Accessed November 9th 2018].

Noble, J. & Wildau, G. (2014). China: Fear of a deflationary spiral. *The Financial Times*. Available: https://www.ft.com/content/7a0e882e-700b-11e4-bc6a-00144feabdc0 [Accessed September 15th 2021].

Novokmet, F., Piketty, T. & Zucman, G. (2017). *From Soviets to Oligarchs: Inequality and Property in Russia 1905-2016*. Available: http://piketty.pse.ens.fr/files/NPZ2017WIDworld.pdf [Accessed September 23rd 2019].

O'Rourke, K., Bowles, S., Carlin, W., Stevens, M. (2017). "Technology, population and growth". Chapter 2 in *The CORE Team, The Economy*. Available: https://www.core-econ.org.

Olearchyk, R. (2015). Poroshenko ousts regional oligarch in Ukraine political shake-up. *The Financial Times*. Available: https://www.ft.com/content/c296e72a-d2cc-11e4-b7a8-00144feab7de [Accessed February 15th 2021].

Olearchyk, R. (2016). Ukraine's MPs forgo pay rise as public balks at scale of wealth. *The Financial Times*. Available: https://www.ft.com/content/210393c2-a02f-11e6-891e-abe238dee8e2 [Accessed September 30th 2019].

Olearchyk, R. (2017). Ukraine imposes cargo blockade on breakaway east: President's order comes after pro-Russian separatists seize steel and coal businesses. *The Financial Times*. Available: https://www.ft.com/content/276f3fd8-098c-11e7-ac5a-903b21361b43. [Accessed March 13th 2022].

Olesia, A. (2015). UKRAINIAN FUEL AND ENERGY SECTOR: DISTINCTIVE FEATURES. *Studies and Scientific Researches. Economics Edition* (University of Bacau), 21, Available: http://sceco.ub.ro/index.php/SCECO/article/download/302/281.

Orum, A. M. & Dale, J. G. (2009). *Political Sociology: Power and Participation in the Modern World*. 5th ed. New York: Oxford University Press.

Ostapchuk, D. (2016). The Power series, season 4: Verkhovna Rada under the Microscope-2. *VoxUkraine*. Available: https://voxukraine.org/longreads/coalition/article-en.html [Accessed June 6th 2020].

Parramore, L. S. (2015). Joseph Stiglitz: Thomas Piketty gets income inequality wrong. Salon. Available: https://www.salon.com/2015/01/02/joseph_stiglitz_thomas_piketty_gets_income_inequality_wrong_partner/ [Accessed March 22nd 2021].

Piketty, T. (2014). *Capital in the Twenty-First Century*. Goldhammer, A. (trans.). Cambridge, Massachusetts: The Belknap Press of Harvard University Press.

Pleines, H. (2016a). Oligarchs and Politics in Ukraine. *Demokratizatsiya*, 24, 1, pp. 105-127.

Pleines, H. (2016b). Dataset on Ukrainian oligarchs 2000-2016. Available at: http://www.forschungsstelle.uni-bremen.de/UserFiles/file/table-oligarchs-overview.xls [Accessed April 20th 2021].

Polanyi, K. (2001). *The Great Transformation: The Political and Economic Origins of Our Time*. Foreword: Stiglitz, J.E.; introduction: Block, F. 2nd Beacon Paperback ed. Boston, MA, Beacon Press.

Polityuk, P. (2016). Ukraine appoints Poroshenko ally with no legal experience as top prosecutor. Reuters. Available: https://www.reuters.com/article/us-ukraine-parliament-prosecutor-idUSKCN0Y311A.

Puglisi, R. (2003). The rise of the Ukrainian oligarchs. *Democratization*, 10, 3, pp. 99-123.

Razumkov Tsentr. (2017). Yak zminyuvalysya reytynhy politykiv i partiy v Ukrayini pislya vyboriv: infohrafika. Available: https://razumkov.org.ua/statti/yak-zminiuvalysia-reitynhy-politykiv-i-partii-v-ukraini-pislia-vyboriv-infohrafika [Accessed August 10th 2021].

Reytingi Fokusa. (2007). 100 samykh bogatykh lyudey Ukrainy [Online]. Focus.ua. Available: https://focus.ua/rating/archive/2007/ratings/580 [Accessed September 27th 2019].

Reytingi Fokusa. (2008). 130 samykh bogatykh lyudey Ukrainy [Online]. Focus.ua. Available: https://focus.ua/rating/archive/2008/ratings/17243 [Accessed September 27th 2019].

Reytingi Fokusa. (2009). 150 samykh bogatykh lyudey Ukrainy [Online]. Focus.ua. Available: https://focus.ua/rating/archive/2009/ratings/37752 [Accessed September 27th 2019].

Reytingi Fokusa. (2010). 200 samykh bogatykh lyudey Ukrainy [Online]. Focus.ua. Available: https://focus.ua/rating/archive/2010/ratings/110931 [Accessed September 27th 2019].

References

Reytingi Fokusa. (2011). 200 samykh bogatykh lyudey Ukrainy 2011 goda [Online]. Focus.ua. Available: https://focus.ua/rating/archive/2011/ratings/174865 [Accessed September 27th 2019].

Reytingi Fokusa. (2012). 200 samykh bogatykh lyudey Ukrainy 2012 goda [Online]. Focus.ua. Available: https://focus.ua/rating/archive/2012/225154 [Accessed September 27th 2019].

Reytingi Fokusa. (2013). 200 samykh bogatykh lyudey Ukrainy [Online]. Focus.ua. Available: https://focus.ua/rating/archive/2013/265322 [Accessed September 27th 2019].

Reytingi Fokusa. (2014). 100 samykh bogatykh lyudey Ukrainy 2013 goda [Online]. Focus.ua. Available: https://focus.ua/rating/archive/2014/303622 [Accessed September 27th 2019].

Reytingi Fokusa. (2015). 100 samykh bogatykh lyudey Ukrainy. Polnyi spisok [Online]. Focus.ua. Available: https://focus.ua/rating/archive/2015/328351 [Accessed September 27th 2019].

Reytingi Fokusa. (2016). 100 samykh bogatykh lyudey Ukrainy. Polnyi spisok [Online]. Focus.ua. Available: https://focus.ua/rating/archive/2016/350253 [Accessed September 27th 2019].

Reytingi Fokusa. (2017). 100 samykh bogatykh lyudey Ukrainy. Polnyi spisok [Online]. Focus.ua. Available: https://focus.ua/rating/archive/2017/372197 [Accessed September 27th 2019].

Reytingi Fokusa. (2018). 100 samykh bogatykh lyudey Ukrainy. Polnyi spisok [Online]. Focus.ua. Available: https://focus.ua/rating/archive/2018/396336 [Accessed September 27th 2019].

Roaf, J., Atoyan, R., Joshi, B., Krogulski, K. & IMF Staff Team. (2014). *25 Years of Transition: Post-Communist Europe and the IMF*. International Monetary Fund/IMF. Available: https://www.imf.org/external/region/bal/rr/2014/25_years_of_transition.pdf [Accessed July 10th 2021].

Roberts, K. (2011). *Class in Contemporary Britain*. 2nd ed. Basingstoke: Palgrave Macmillan.

Robinson, N. (2013). Economic and political hybridity: Patrimonial capitalism in the post-Soviet sphere. *Journal of Eurasian Studies*, vol 4, pp. 136-145.

Rojansky, M., Minakov, M. & Kasianov, H. V. (2021). *From 'the Ukraine' to 'Ukraine': A Contemporary History, 1991-2021*. Stuttgart: ibidem-Verlag.

Romanyuk, R. & Kravets, R. (2016a). Orhanizovani Partiyni Hrupy. Khto naspravdi keruye BPP. *Ukrayinska Pravda*. Available: https://www.pravda.com.ua/articles/2016/10/19/7124153/ [Accessed June 24th 2020].

Romanyuk, R. & Kravets, R. (2016b). Orhanizovani Partiyni Hrupy-2. Pyat stovpiv "Narodnoho frontu". *Ukrayinska Pravda*. Available: https://www.pravda.com.ua/articles/2016/11/1/7125375/ [Accessed June 24th 2020].

Romanyuk, R. & Kravets, R. (2016c). Orhanizovani Partiyni Hrupy-3. Samotnya "Samopomich". *Ukrayinska Pravda*. Available: https://www.pravda.com.ua/articles/2016/11/22/7127578/ [Accessed June 24th 2020].

Romanyuk, R. & Kravets, R. (2017a). Orhanizovani Partiyni Hrupy-4: "Vidrodzhennya" z Khomutynnikom i bez. *Ukrayinska Pravda*. Available: https://www.pravda.com.ua/articles/2017/09/22/7155980/ [Accessed June 24th 2020].

Romanyuk, R. & Kravets, R. (2017b). Orhanizovani Partiyni Hrupy-5: Zolota aktsiya "Voli narodu". *Ukrayinska Pravda*. Available: https://www.pravda.com.ua/articles/2017/10/3/7157083/ [Accessed June 24th 2020].

Romanyuk, R. & Kravets, R. (2017c). Orhanizovani Partiyni Hrupy-6: vid Tymoshenko i Lyovochkina do Akhmetova. *Ukrayinska Pravda*. Available: https://www.pravda.com.ua/articles/2017/10/11/7157940/ [Accessed June 24th 2020].

Romanyuk, R. & Kravets, R. (2018). Orhanizovani Partiyni Hrupy-7: Yak Lyovochkin i Akhmetov hotuyutsya do revanshu. *Ukrayinska Pravda*. Available: https://www.pravda.com.ua/articles/2018/07/12/7186058/ [Accessed June 24th 2020].

RosUkrEnergo. (2007). Official reports: Financial data and statements, 2005, 2006 [Online]. Available: https://web.archive.org/web/20070928230032/http://www.rosukrenergo.ch/eng/pub/business.html [Accessed September 30th 2021].

Rutherford, M. (1996). *Institutions in Economics: The Old and the New Institutionalism.* Historical Perspectives om Modern Economics. Cambridge University Press.

Sadowski, I. & Pohorila, N. (2017). Do Revolutions Bring Revolutionary Changes? Replacement in the Ranks of Ukraine's Parliament, 1990-2014. *International Journal of Sociology*, 48, 1, pp. 6-33.

Sakhno, Y. (2017). Geopolitical Orientations of the Residents of Ukraine. Kyiv International Institute of Sociology/KIIS. Available: https://www.kiis.com.ua/?lang=eng&cat=reports&id=720 [Accessed August 3rd 2021].

Savchenko, A. (2009). *Belarus: A Perpetual Borderland.* Leiden, Boston, Brill.

Sethi, R., Bowles, S., Carlin, W. & Stevens, M. (2017). "Rent-seeking, price-setting, and market dynamics". Unit 11 in *The CORE Team, The Economy*. Available: https://www.core-econ.org.

References

Shevel, O. (2015). The parliamentary elections in Ukraine, October 2014. *Election Studies*, 39, pp. 159-163.

Shorrocks, A., Davies, J. & Lluberas, R. (2017). *Global Wealth Databook 2017*. Credit Suisse Research Institute. Zurich.

Shorrocks, A., Davies, J. & Lluberas, R. (2018a). *Global Wealth Report 2018*. Credit Suisse Research Institute. Zurich. Available: https://www.credit-suisse.com/about-us-news/en/articles/news-and-expertise/global-wealth-report-2018-us-and-china-in-the-lead-201810.html [Accessed July 28th 2021].

Shorrocks, A., Davies, J. & Lluberas, R. (2018b). *Global Wealth Databook 2018*. Credit Suisse Research Institute. Zurich.

Shumska, S. S. (2012). Natsionalne Bahatstvo Ukrayiny u Vymiri Pokaznykiv SNR. *Finansy Ukrayiny*, 4, pp. 27-40.

Slidstvo. (2018). LYSTUVANNYA NARODNOHO DEPUTATA ONYSHCHENKA Z NAYBLYZHCHYM OTOCHENNYAM PREZYDENTA (POVNYI ARKHIV). Slidstvo. Available: https://www.slidstvo.info/news/whatsapp_onyshchenko/ [Accessed September 10th 2021].

Sowell, T. (1967). The 'Evolutionary' Economics of Thorstein Veblen. *Oxford Economic Papers*, 19, 2, pp. 177-198.

State Federal State Statistics Service/Rosstat. (2020). *Statistical Yearbook 2020*. Available: https://rosstat.gov.ru/storage/mediabank/Ejegodnik_2020.pdf [Accessed August 5th 2020].

State Statistical Service of Ukraine (SSSU). Economic statistics/Prices ["House price indices" towards the bottom of the page]. SSSU. Available: https://ukrstat.gov.ua/operativ/menu/menu_u/cit.htm [Accessed August 6th 2021].

State Statistical Service of Ukraine (SSSU). Naseleni punkty ta zhytlo > Zhytlovyi fond Ukrayiny. Available: https://ukrstat.gov.ua/druk/publicat/kat_u/publjitlo_u.htm [Accessed August 6th 2021].

State Statistical Service of Ukraine (SSSU). (2019a). Experimental balance of non-financial assets in 2017 and archive. SSSU. Available: https://ukrstat.gov.ua/operativ/operativ2011/vvp/balans/balans_u/balans_n_a_2017.htm [Accessed September 19th 2019].

State Statistical Service of Ukraine (SSSU). (2019b). Experimental balance sheets of financial assets and liabilities in 2017 and archive. Available: https://ukrstat.gov.ua/operativ/operativ2011/vvp/balans/balans_u/eksp_balans_2017.htm [Accessed September 19th 2019].

Stilwell, F. J. B. (2012). *Political Economy: The Contest of Economic Ideas*. 3rd ed. Australia & New Zealand: Oxford University Press.

Stilwell, F. J. B. (2019). *The Political Economy of Inequality.* Cambridge, UK: Polity Press.

Subramanian, C. (2019). Explainer: Biden, allies pushed out Ukrainian prosecutor because he didn't pursue corruption cases. USA TODAY. Available: https://eu.usatoday.com/story/news/politics/2019/10/03/what-really-happened-when-biden-forced-out-ukraines-top-prosecutor/3785620002/ [Accessed September 30th 2021].

Sukhov, O. (2016). New sordid details emerge from Yanukovych's ledger. *Kyiv Post.* Available: https://www.kyivpost.com/ukraine-politics/new-sordid-details-emerge-from-yanukovychs-ledger-421693.html [Accessed February 8th 2020].

Sukhov, O. (2018). TV show says it has evidence Poroshenko allies bought votes in parliament. *Kyiv Post.* Available: https://www.kyivpost.com/ukraine-politics/tv-show-says-evidence-poroshenko-allies-bought-votes-parliament.html [Accessed February 8th 2020].

Swain, A. & Mykhnenko, V. (2007). "The Ukrainian Donbas 'in transition'." In: Swain, A. (ed.) *Re-constructing the Post-Soviet Industrial Region: The Donbas in transition.* London, New York: Routledge. pp. 7-48.

The Central Election Commission of Ukraine. (2012, 2014). Election of people's deputies of Ukraine. Available: https://cvk.gov.ua/en/election-of-people-s-deputies-of-ukraine.html [Accessed September 9th 2021].

Tilly, C. (1992). *Coercion, capital, and European states, AD 990-1992.* Cambridge, Mass; Oxford: Blackwell.

Tkach, V. & Dalton, D. (2013). *The Political Outlook in Ukraine.* Dalton, D. (ed.) The Economist Intelligence Unit. Unpublished commercial report.

Tucker, M. (2016). Ukraine's fallen leader Viktor Yanukovych 'paid bribes of $2 billion' — or $1.4 million for every day he was president. *The Telegraph.* Available: https://www.telegraph.co.uk/news/2016/05/31/ukraines-fallen-leader-viktor-yanukovych-paid-bribes-of-2-billio/ [Accessed June 8th 2020].

Turley, G. & Luke, P. J. (2011). *Transition Economics: Two Decades On.* London: Routledge.

Ukrainian Crisis Media Centre. (2016). Party of Regions spent 66 million US dollars on bribes and paid articles in media over six months of 2012 — Serhiy Leshchenko, MP. UCMC press centre. Available: https://uacrisis.org/en/43610-sergij-leshhenko-2 [Accessed February 8th 2020].

References

Ukrayinskyi doshch. (2020). Yuliyi Volodymyrivni - dva po 30. Naytsikavishi fakty pro charivnu yuvilyarku. Available: https://ukrrain.com/yulii_volodimirivni_-_dva_po_30._najcikavishi_fakti_pro_charivnu_yuvilyarku.html [Accessed September 30th 2021].

Umland, A. (2017). Kyiv's leadership is on its way to reinvent Ukraine's patronalistic regime. openDemocracy. Available: https://www.opendemocracy.net/en/odr/kyiv-s-leadership-is-on-its-way-to-reinvent-ukraine-s-patronalistic-regime/ [Accessed 4th July 2021].

United Nations Development Programme (UNDP). Human Development Data Center. UNDP, *Human Development Reports*. Available: https://hdr.undp.org/data-center [Accessed July 24th 2021].

Unian. (2018). Ukraine initially expected invasion by 200,000-strong Russian army - Turchynov. Unian Information Agency. Available: https://www.unian.info/politics/10008878-ukraine-initially-expected-invasion-by-200-000-strong-russian-army-turchynov.html [Accessed February 4th 2021].

van den Berg, A. & Janoski, T. (2005). Conflict Theories in Political Sociology. In: Janoski, T., Alford, R. R., Hicks, A. M. & Schwartz, M. A. (eds.) *The Handbook of Political Sociology: States, Civil Societies and Globalization*. Cambridge: Cambridge University Press. pp. 72-95.

Veblen, T. (1909). The Limitations of Marginal Utility. *The Journal of political economy*, 17, 9, pp. 620-636.

Verkhovna Rada. ARKHIV ZA SKLYKANNYAMY. Verkhovna Rada. Available: http://static.rada.gov.ua/zakon/new/WR/index.htm [Accessed December 9th 2022]. This version of the archive is much less useable than the one that existed before the Russian invasion of February 2022.

Verkhovna Rada. (2010). *ZAKON UKRAYINY: Pro Rehlament Verkhovnoyi Rady Ukrayiny* [Online]. Verkhovna Rada of Ukraine. Available: https://zakon.rada.gov.ua/laws/show/1861-17#Text [Accessed December 9th 2022].

Wayne, L. (2016). A Ukrainian Kleptocrat Wants His Money and U.S. Asylum. *The New York Times*. Available: https://www.nytimes.com/2016/07/07/business/international/a-ukrainian-kleptocrat-wants-his-money-and-us-asylum.html.

Whitmore, S. (2004). *State-building in Ukraine: The Ukrainian Parliament, 1990-2003*. 1st ed. London: RoutledgeCurzon.

Whitmore, S. (2019). Disrupted Democracy in Ukraine? Protest, Performance and Contention in the Verkhovna Rada. *Europe-Asia Studies*, 71, 9, pp. 1474-1507.

Wilson, A. (2011) "Political technology": why is it alive and flourishing in the former USSR? openDemocracy. Available: https://www.opendemocracy.net/en/odr/political-technology-why-is-it-alive-and-flourishing-in-former-ussr/ [Accessed December 8th 2022].

Wilson, A. (2013). "Ukraine." In: Coleman, I. & Lawson-Remer, T. (eds.) *Pathways to Freedom: Political and Economic Lessons from Democratic Transitions*. London, UK: Council on Foreign Relations Press. pp. 181-200.

Wilson, A. (2014). *Ukraine Crisis: What it Means for the West*. New Haven, Connecticut; London, England: Yale University Press.

Wilson, A. (2015). *The Ukrainians: Unexpected Nation*. 4th ed. New Haven: Yale University Press.

Wilson, A. (2016). Survival of the richest: How oligarchs block reform in Ukraine. *Policy brief ECFR/160* [Online]. London, UK: European Council on Foreign Relations (ECFR). Available: https://ecfr.eu/publication/survival_of_the_richest_how_oligarchs_block_reform_in_ukraine6091/ [Accessed December 8th 2022].

Winters, J. A. (2011). *Oligarchy*. Cambridge: Cambridge University Press.

World Bank. (2013). *Doing Business 2014: Understanding Regulations for Small and Medium-Size Enterprises*. World Bank. Available: https://elibrary.worldbank.org/doi/abs/10.1596/978-0-8213-9984-2 [Accessed December 9th 2022].

World Bank. (2018). *The Changing Wealth of Nations 2018*: Country Tool. Second tab, Data & Resources. Available: https://bit.ly/3jzLEp5 [Accessed September 18th 2019]. Site since superseded by a newer version, available: https://datacatalog.worldbank.org/search/dataset/0042066 [Accessed December 12th 2021].

World Bank. (2020). *Doing Business: ARCHIVE: Methodology*. Available: https://archive.doingbusiness.org/en/methodology [Accessed December 9th 2022].

World Bank DataBank. GNI per capita, PPP (current international $) 2017. World Bank Group. Available: https://data.worldbank.org/indicator/NY.GNP.PCAP.PP.CD?view=map&year=2017 [Accessed June 17th 2021].

World Bank DataBank. *World Development Indicators*. World Bank Group. Available: https://databank.worldbank.org/source/world-development-indicators [Accessed July 24th 2021].

World Inequality Lab. World Inequality Database (WID). Available: https://wid.world/ [Accessed August 5th 2021].

REFERENCES

Yurchenko, Y. (2018). *Ukraine and the Empire of Capital: From Marketisation to Armed Conflict*. London: Pluto Press.

Zimmer, K. (2006). "Formal Institutions and Informal Politics in Ukraine." In: Meyer, G. (ed.) *Formal Institutions and Informal politics in Central and Eastern Europe: Hungary, Poland, Russia and Ukraine*. Oplanden & Farmington Hills: Barbara Budrich Publishers.

Zinets, N. & Polityuk, P. (2017). Ukraine makes two high-profile detentions in corruption case. Reuters. Available: https://www.reuters.com/article/us-ukraine-corruption-arrests-idUSKBN17N1AS [Accessed February 15th 2019].

Zucman, G. (2015). *The Hidden Wealth of Nations: The Scourge of Tax Havens*. Fagan, T. L. (trans.). Chicago: The University of Chicago Press.

SOVIET AND POST-SOVIET POLITICS AND SOCIETY
Edited by Dr. Andreas Umland | ISSN 1614-3515

1 Андреас Умланд (ред.) | Воплощение Европейской конвенции по правам человека в России. Философские, юридические и эмпирические исследования | ISBN 3-89821-387-0

2 Christian Wipperfürth | Russland – ein vertrauenswürdiger Partner? Grundlagen, Hintergründe und Praxis gegenwärtiger russischer Außenpolitik | Mit einem Vorwort von Heinz Timmermann | ISBN 3-89821-401-X

3 Manja Hussner | Die Übernahme internationalen Rechts in die russische und deutsche Rechtsordnung. Eine vergleichende Analyse zur Völkerrechtsfreundlichkeit der Verfassungen der Russländischen Föderation und der Bundesrepublik Deutschland | Mit einem Vorwort von Rainer Arnold | ISBN 3-89821-438-9

4 Matthew Tejada | Bulgaria's Democratic Consolidation and the Kozloduy Nuclear Power Plant (KNPP). The Unattainability of Closure | With a foreword by Richard J. Crampton | ISBN 3-89821-439-7

5 Марк Григорьевич Меерович | Квадратные метры, определяющие сознание. Государственная жилищная политика в СССР. 1921 – 1941 гг | ISBN 3-89821-474-5

6 Andrei P. Tsygankov, Pavel A.Tsygankov (Eds.) | New Directions in Russian International Studies | ISBN 3-89821-422-2

7 Марк Григорьевич Меерович | Как власть народ к труду приучала. Жилище в СССР – средство управления людьми. 1917 – 1941 гг. | С предисловием Елены Осокиной | ISBN 3-89821-495-8

8 David J. Galbreath | Nation-Building and Minority Politics in Post-Socialist States. Interests, Influence and Identities in Estonia and Latvia | With a foreword by David J. Smith | ISBN 3-89821-467-2

9 Алексей Юрьевич Безугольный | Народы Кавказа в Вооруженных силах СССР в годы Великой Отечественной войны 1941-1945 гг. | С предисловием Николая Бугая | ISBN 3-89821-475-3

10 Вячеслав Лихачев и Владимир Прибыловский (ред.) | Русское Национальное Единство, 1990-2000. В 2-х томах | ISBN 3-89821-523-7

11 Николай Бугай (ред.) | Народы стран Балтии в условиях сталинизма (1940-е – 1950-е годы). Документированная история | ISBN 3-89821-525-3

12 Ingmar Bredies (Hrsg.) | Zur Anatomie der Orange Revolution in der Ukraine. Wechsel des Elitenregimes oder Triumph des Parlamentarismus? | ISBN 3-89821-524-5

13 Anastasia V. Mitrofanova | The Politicization of Russian Orthodoxy. Actors and Ideas | With a foreword by William C. Gay | ISBN 3-89821-481-8

14 Nathan D. Larson | Alexander Solzhenitsyn and the Russo-Jewish Question | ISBN 3-89821-483-4

15 Guido Houben | Kulturpolitik und Ethnizität. Staatliche Kunstförderung im Russland der neunziger Jahre | Mit einem Vorwort von Gert Weisskirchen | ISBN 3-89821-542-3

16 Leonid Luks | Der russische „Sonderweg"? Aufsätze zur neuesten Geschichte Russlands im europäischen Kontext | ISBN 3-89821-496-6

17 Евгений Мороз | История «Мёртвой воды» – от страшной сказки к большой политике. Политическое неоязычество в постсоветской России | ISBN 3-89821-551-2

18 Александр Верховский и Галина Кожевникова (ред.) | Этническая и религиозная интолерантность в российских СМИ. Результаты мониторинга 2001-2004 гг. | ISBN 3-89821-569-5

19 Christian Ganzer | Sowjetisches Erbe und ukrainische Nation. Das Museum der Geschichte des Zaporoger Kosakentums auf der Insel Chortycja | Mit einem Vorwort von Frank Golczewski | ISBN 3-89821-504-0

20 Эльза-Баир Гучинова | Помнить нельзя забыть. Антропология депортационной травмы калмыков | С предисловием Кэролайн Хамфри | ISBN 3-89821-506-7

21 Юлия Лидерман | Мотивы «проверки» и «испытания» в постсоветской культуре. Советское прошлое в российском кинематографе 1990-х годов | С предисловием Евгения Марголита | ISBN 3-89821-511-3

22 Tanya Lokshina, Ray Thomas, Mary Mayer (Eds.) | The Imposition of a Fake Political Settlement in the Northern Caucasus. The 2003 Chechen Presidential Election | ISBN 3-89821-436-2

23 Timothy McCajor Hall, Rosie Read (Eds.) | Changes in the Heart of Europe. Recent Ethnographies of Czechs, Slovaks, Roma, and Sorbs | With an afterword by Zdeněk Salzmann | ISBN 3-89821-606-5

24 *Christian Autengruber* | Die politischen Parteien in Bulgarien und Rumänien. Eine vergleichende Analyse seit Beginn der 90er Jahre | Mit einem Vorwort von Dorothée de Nève | ISBN 3-89821-476-1

25 *Annette Freyberg-Inan with Radu Cristescu* | The Ghosts in Our Classrooms, or: John Dewey Meets Ceauşescu. The Promise and the Failures of Civic Education in Romania | ISBN 3-89821-416-8

26 *John B. Dunlop* | The 2002 Dubrovka and 2004 Beslan Hostage Crises. A Critique of Russian Counter-Terrorism | With a foreword by Donald N. Jensen | ISBN 3-89821-608-X

27 *Peter Koller* | Das touristische Potenzial von Kam''janec'–Podil's'kyj. Eine fremdenverkehrsgeographische Untersuchung der Zukunftsperspektiven und Maßnahmenplanung zur Destinationsentwicklung des „ukrainischen Rothenburg" | Mit einem Vorwort von Kristiane Klemm | ISBN 3-89821-640-3

28 *Françoise Daucé, Elisabeth Sieca-Kozlowski (Eds.)* | Dedovshchina in the Post-Soviet Military. Hazing of Russian Army Conscripts in a Comparative Perspective | With a foreword by Dale Herspring | ISBN 3-89821-616-0

29 *Florian Strasser* | Zivilgesellschaftliche Einflüsse auf die Orange Revolution. Die gewaltlose Massenbewegung und die ukrainische Wahlkrise 2004 | Mit einem Vorwort von Egbert Jahn | ISBN 3-89821-648-9

30 *Rebecca S. Katz* | The Georgian Regime Crisis of 2003-2004. A Case Study in Post-Soviet Media Representation of Politics, Crime and Corruption | ISBN 3-89821-413-3

31 *Vladimir Kantor* | Willkür oder Freiheit. Beiträge zur russischen Geschichtsphilosophie | Ediert von Dagmar Herrmann sowie mit einem Vorwort versehen von Leonid Luks | ISBN 3-89821-589-X

32 *Laura A. Victoir* | The Russian Land Estate Today. A Case Study of Cultural Politics in Post-Soviet Russia | With a foreword by Priscilla Roosevelt | ISBN 3-89821-426-5

33 *Ivan Katchanovski* | Cleft Countries. Regional Political Divisions and Cultures in Post-Soviet Ukraine and Moldova | With a foreword by Francis Fukuyama | ISBN 3-89821-558-X

34 *Florian Mühlfried* | Postsowjetische Feiern. Das Georgische Bankett im Wandel | Mit einem Vorwort von Kevin Tuite | ISBN 3-89821-601-2

35 *Roger Griffin, Werner Loh, Andreas Umland (Eds.)* | Fascism Past and Present, West and East. An International Debate on Concepts and Cases in the Comparative Study of the Extreme Right | With an afterword by Walter Laqueur | ISBN 3-89821-674-8

36 *Sebastian Schlegel* | Der „Weiße Archipel". Sowjetische Atomstädte 1945-1991 | Mit einem Geleitwort von Thomas Bohn | ISBN 3-89821-679-9

37 *Vyacheslav Likhachev* | Political Anti-Semitism in Post-Soviet Russia. Actors and Ideas in 1991-2003 | Edited and translated from Russian by Eugene Veklerov | ISBN 3-89821-529-6

38 *Josette Baer (Ed.)* | Preparing Liberty in Central Europe. Political Texts from the Spring of Nations 1848 to the Spring of Prague 1968 | With a foreword by Zdeněk V. David | ISBN 3-89821-546-6

39 *Михаил Лукьянов* | Российский консерватизм и реформа, 1907-1914 | С предисловием Марка Д. Стейнберга | ISBN 3-89821-503-2

40 *Nicola Melloni* | Market Without Economy. The 1998 Russian Financial Crisis | With a foreword by Eiji Furukawa | ISBN 3-89821-407-9

41 *Dmitrij Chmelnizki* | Die Architektur Stalins | Bd. 1: Studien zu Ideologie und Stil | Bd. 2: Bilddokumentation | Mit einem Vorwort von Bruno Flierl | ISBN 3-89821-515-6

42 *Katja Yafimava* | Post-Soviet Russian-Belarussian Relationships. The Role of Gas Transit Pipelines | With a foreword by Jonathan P. Stern | ISBN 3-89821-655-1

43 *Boris Chavkin* | Verflechtungen der deutschen und russischen Zeitgeschichte. Aufsätze und Archivfunde zu den Beziehungen Deutschlands und der Sowjetunion von 1917 bis 1991 | Ediert von Markus Edlinger sowie mit Vorwort versehen von Leonid Luks | ISBN 3-89821-756-6

44 *Anastasija Grynenko in Zusammenarbeit mit Claudia Dathe* | Die Terminologie des Gerichtswesens der Ukraine und Deutschlands im Vergleich. Eine übersetzungswissenschaftliche Analyse juristischer Fachbegriffe im Deutschen, Ukrainischen und Russischen | Mit einem Vorwort von Ulrich Hartmann | ISBN 3-89821-691-8

45 *Anton Burkov* | The Impact of the European Convention on Human Rights on Russian Law. Legislation and Application in 1996-2006 | With a foreword by Françoise Hampson | ISBN 978-3-89821-639-5

46 *Stina Torjesen, Indra Overland (Eds.)* | International Election Observers in Post-Soviet Azerbaijan. Geopolitical Pawns or Agents of Change? | ISBN 978-3-89821-743-9

47 *Taras Kuzio* | Ukraine – Crimea – Russia. Triangle of Conflict | ISBN 978-3-89821-761-3

48 *Claudia Šabić* | „Ich erinnere mich nicht, aber L'viv!" Zur Funktion kultureller Faktoren für die Institutionalisierung und Entwicklung einer ukrainischen Region | Mit einem Vorwort von Melanie Tatur | ISBN 978-3-89821-752-1

49 *Marlies Bilz* | Tatarstan in der Transformation. Nationaler Diskurs und Politische Praxis 1988-1994 | Mit einem Vorwort von Frank Golczewski | ISBN 978-3-89821-722-4

50 *Марлен Ларюэль (ред.)* | Современные интерпретации русского национализма | ISBN 978-3-89821-795-8

51 *Sonja Schüler* | Die ethnische Dimension der Armut. Roma im postsozialistischen Rumänien | Mit einem Vorwort von Anton Sterbling | ISBN 978-3-89821-776-7

52 *Галина Кожевникова* | Радикальный национализм в России и противодействие ему. Сборник докладов Центра «Сова» за 2004-2007 гг. | С предисловием Александра Верховского | ISBN 978-3-89821-721-7

53 *Галина Кожевникова и Владимир Прибыловский* | Российская власть в биографиях I. Высшие должностные лица РФ в 2004 г. | ISBN 978-3-89821-796-5

54 *Галина Кожевникова и Владимир Прибыловский* | Российская власть в биографиях II. Члены Правительства РФ в 2004 г. | ISBN 978-3-89821-797-2

55 *Галина Кожевникова и Владимир Прибыловский* | Российская власть в биографиях III. Руководители федеральных служб и агентств РФ в 2004 г.| ISBN 978-3-89821-798-9

56 *Ileana Petroniu* | Privatisierung in Transformationsökonomien. Determinanten der Restrukturierungs-Bereitschaft am Beispiel Polens, Rumäniens und der Ukraine | Mit einem Vorwort von Rainer W. Schäfer | ISBN 978-3-89821-790-3

57 *Christian Wipperfürth* | Russland und seine GUS-Nachbarn. Hintergründe, aktuelle Entwicklungen und Konflikte in einer ressourcenreichen Region| ISBN 978-3-89821-801-6

58 *Togzhan Kassenova* | From Antagonism to Partnership. The Uneasy Path of the U.S.-Russian Cooperative Threat Reduction | With a foreword by Christoph Bluth | ISBN 978-3-89821-707-1

59 *Alexander Höllwerth* | Das sakrale eurasische Imperium des Aleksandr Dugin. Eine Diskursanalyse zum postsowjetischen russischen Rechtsextremismus | Mit einem Vorwort von Dirk Uffelmann | ISBN 978-3-89821-813-9

60 *Олег Рябов* | «Россия-Матушка». Национализм, гендер и война в России XX века | С предисловием Елены Гощило | ISBN 978-3-89821-487-2

61 *Ivan Maistrenko* | Borot'bism. A Chapter in the History of the Ukrainian Revolution | With a new Introduction by Chris Ford | Translated by George S. N. Luckyj with the assistance of Ivan L. Rudnytsky | Second, Revised and Expanded Edition ISBN 978-3-8382-1107-7

62 *Maryna Romanets* | Anamorphosic Texts and Reconfigured Visions. Improvised Traditions in Contemporary Ukrainian and Irish Literature | ISBN 978-3-89821-576-3

63 *Paul D'Anieri and Taras Kuzio (Eds.)* | Aspects of the Orange Revolution I. Democratization and Elections in Post-Communist Ukraine | ISBN 978-3-89821-698-2

64 *Bohdan Harasymiw in collaboration with Oleh S. Ilnytzkyj (Eds.)* | Aspects of the Orange Revolution II. Information and Manipulation Strategies in the 2004 Ukrainian Presidential Elections | ISBN 978-3-89821-699-9

65 *Ingmar Bredies, Andreas Umland and Valentin Yakushik (Eds.)* | Aspects of the Orange Revolution III. The Context and Dynamics of the 2004 Ukrainian Presidential Elections | ISBN 978-3-89821-803-0

66 *Ingmar Bredies, Andreas Umland and Valentin Yakushik (Eds.)* | Aspects of the Orange Revolution IV. Foreign Assistance and Civic Action in the 2004 Ukrainian Presidential Elections | ISBN 978-3-89821-808-5

67 *Ingmar Bredies, Andreas Umland and Valentin Yakushik (Eds.)* | Aspects of the Orange Revolution V. Institutional Observation Reports on the 2004 Ukrainian Presidential Elections | ISBN 978-3-89821-809-2

68 *Taras Kuzio (Ed.)* | Aspects of the Orange Revolution VI. Post-Communist Democratic Revolutions in Comparative Perspective | ISBN 978-3-89821-820-7

69 *Tim Bohse* | Autoritarismus statt Selbstverwaltung. Die Transformation der kommunalen Politik in der Stadt Kaliningrad 1990-2005 | Mit einem Geleitwort von Stefan Troebst | ISBN 978-3-89821-782-8

70 *David Rupp* | Die Rußländische Föderation und die russischsprachige Minderheit in Lettland. Eine Fallstudie zur Anwaltspolitik Moskaus gegenüber den russophonen Minderheiten im „Nahen Ausland" von 1991 bis 2002 | Mit einem Vorwort von Helmut Wagner | ISBN 978-3-89821-778-1

71 *Taras Kuzio* | Theoretical and Comparative Perspectives on Nationalism. New Directions in Cross-Cultural and Post-Communist Studies | With a foreword by Paul Robert Magocsi | ISBN 978-3-89821-815-7

72 *Christine Teichmann* | Die Hochschultransformation im heutigen Osteuropa. Kontinuität und Wandel bei der Entwicklung des postkommunistischen Universitätswesens | Mit einem Vorwort von Oskar Anweiler | ISBN 978-3-89821-842-9

73 *Julia Kusznir* | Der politische Einfluss von Wirtschaftseliten in russischen Regionen. Eine Analyse am Beispiel der Erdöl- und Erdgasindustrie, 1992-2005 | Mit einem Vorwort von Wolfgang Eichwede | ISBN 978-3-89821-821-4

74 *Alena Vysotskaya* | Russland, Belarus und die EU-Osterweiterung. Zur Minderheitenfrage und zum Problem der Freizügigkeit des Personenverkehrs | Mit einem Vorwort von Katlijn Malfliet | ISBN 978-3-89821-822-1

75 *Heiko Pleines (Hrsg.)* | Corporate Governance in post-sozialistischen Volkswirtschaften | ISBN 978-3-89821-766-8

76 *Stefan Ihrig* | Wer sind die Moldawier? Rumänismus versus Moldowanismus in Historiographie und Schulbüchern der Republik Moldova, 1991-2006 | Mit einem Vorwort von Holm Sundhaussen | ISBN 978-3-89821-466-7

77 *Galina Kozhevnikova in collaboration with Alexander Verkhovsky and Eugene Veklerov* | Ultra-Nationalism and Hate Crimes in Contemporary Russia. The 2004-2006 Annual Reports of Moscow's SOVA Center | With a foreword by Stephen D. Shenfield | ISBN 978-3-89821-868-9

78 *Florian Küchler* | The Role of the European Union in Moldova's Transnistria Conflict | With a foreword by Christopher Hill | ISBN 978-3-89821-850-4

79 *Bernd Rechel* | The Long Way Back to Europe. Minority Protection in Bulgaria | With a foreword by Richard Crampton | ISBN 978-3-89821-863-4

80 *Peter W. Rodgers* | Nation, Region and History in Post-Communist Transitions. Identity Politics in Ukraine, 1991-2006 | With a foreword by Vera Tolz | ISBN 978-3-89821-903-7

81 *Stephanie Solywoda* | The Life and Work of Semen L. Frank. A Study of Russian Religious Philosophy | With a foreword by Philip Walters | ISBN 978-3-89821-457-5

82 *Vera Sokolova* | Cultural Politics of Ethnicity. Discourses on Roma in Communist Czechoslovakia | ISBN 978-3-89821-864-1

83 *Natalya Shevchik Ketenci* | Kazakhstani Enterprises in Transition. The Role of Historical Regional Development in Kazakhstan's Post-Soviet Economic Transformation | ISBN 978-3-89821-831-3

84 *Martin Malek, Anna Schor-Tschudnowskaja (Hgg.)* | Europa im Tschetschenienkrieg. Zwischen politischer Ohnmacht und Gleichgültigkeit | Mit einem Vorwort von Lipchan Basajewa | ISBN 978-3-89821-676-0

85 *Stefan Meister* | Das postsowjetische Universitätswesen zwischen nationalem und internationalem Wandel. Die Entwicklung der regionalen Hochschule in Russland als Gradmesser der Systemtransformation | Mit einem Vorwort von Joan DeBardeleben | ISBN 978-3-89821-891-7

86 *Konstantin Sheiko in collaboration with Stephen Brown* | Nationalist Imaginings of the Russian Past. Anatolii Fomenko and the Rise of Alternative History in Post-Communist Russia | With a foreword by Donald Ostrowski | ISBN 978-3-89821-915-0

87 *Sabine Jenni* | Wie stark ist das „Einige Russland"? Zur Parteibindung der Eliten und zum Wahlerfolg der Machtpartei im Dezember 2007 | Mit einem Vorwort von Klaus Armingeon | ISBN 978-3-89821-961-7

88 *Thomas Borén* | Meeting-Places of Transformation. Urban Identity, Spatial Representations and Local Politics in Post-Soviet St Petersburg | ISBN 978-3-89821-739-2

89 *Aygul Ashirova* | Stalinismus und Stalin-Kult in Zentralasien. Turkmenistan 1924-1953 | Mit einem Vorwort von Leonid Luks | ISBN 978-3-89821-987-7

90 *Leonid Luks* | Freiheit oder imperiale Größe? Essays zu einem russischen Dilemma | ISBN 978-3-8382-0011-8

91 *Christopher Gilley* | The 'Change of Signposts' in the Ukrainian Emigration. A Contribution to the History of Sovietophilism in the 1920s | With a foreword by Frank Golczewski | ISBN 978-3-89821-965-5

92 *Philipp Casula, Jeronim Perovic (Eds.)* | Identities and Politics During the Putin Presidency. The Discursive Foundations of Russia's Stability | With a foreword by Heiko Haumann | ISBN 978-3-8382-0015-6

93 *Marcel Viëtor* | Europa und die Frage nach seinen Grenzen im Osten. Zur Konstruktion ‚europäischer Identität' in Geschichte und Gegenwart | Mit einem Vorwort von Albrecht Lehmann | ISBN 978-3-8382-0045-3

94 *Ben Hellman, Andrei Rogachevskii* | Filming the Unfilmable. Casper Wrede's 'One Day in the Life of Ivan Denisovich' | Second, Revised and Expanded Edition | ISBN 978-3-8382-0044-6

95 *Eva Fuchslocher* | Vaterland, Sprache, Glaube. Orthodoxie und Nationenbildung am Beispiel Georgiens | Mit einem Vorwort von Christina von Braun | ISBN 978-3-89821-884-9

96 *Vladimir Kantor* | Das Westlertum und der Weg Russlands. Zur Entwicklung der russischen Literatur und Philosophie | Ediert von Dagmar Herrmann | Mit einem Beitrag von Nikolaus Lobkowicz | ISBN 978-3-8382-0102-3

97 *Kamran Musayev* | Die postsowjetische Transformation im Baltikum und Südkaukasus. Eine vergleichende Untersuchung der politischen Entwicklung Lettlands und Aserbaidschans 1985-2009 | Mit einem Vorwort von Leonid Luks | Ediert von Sandro Henschel | ISBN 978-3-8382-0103-0

98 *Tatiana Zhurzhenko* | Borderlands into Bordered Lands. Geopolitics of Identity in Post-Soviet Ukraine | With a foreword by Dieter Segert | ISBN 978-3-8382-0042-2

99 *Кирилл Галушко, Лидия Смола (ред.)* | Пределы падения – варианты украинского будущего. Аналитико-прогностические исследования | ISBN 978-3-8382-0148-1

100 *Michael Minkenberg (Ed.)* | Historical Legacies and the Radical Right in Post-Cold War Central and Eastern Europe | With an afterword by Sabrina P. Ramet | ISBN 978-3-8382-0124-5

101 *David-Emil Wickström* | Rocking St. Petersburg. Transcultural Flows and Identity Politics in the St. Petersburg Popular Music Scene | With a foreword by Yngvar B. Steinholt | Second, Revised and Expanded Edition | ISBN 978-3-8382-0100-9

102 *Eva Zabka* | Eine neue „Zeit der Wirren"? Der spät- und postsowjetische Systemwandel 1985-2000 im Spiegel russischer gesellschaftspolitischer Diskurse | Mit einem Vorwort von Margareta Mommsen | ISBN 978-3-8382-0161-0

103 *Ulrike Ziemer* | Ethnic Belonging, Gender and Cultural Practices. Youth Identitites in Contemporary Russia | With a foreword by Anoop Nayak | ISBN 978-3-8382-0152-8

104 *Ksenia Chepikova* | ‚Einiges Russland' - eine zweite KPdSU? Aspekte der Identitätskonstruktion einer postsowjetischen „Partei der Macht" | Mit einem Vorwort von Torsten Oppelland | ISBN 978-3-8382-0311-9

105 *Леонид Люкс* | Западничество или евразийство? Демократия или идеократия? Сборник статей об исторических дилеммах России | С предисловием Владимира Кантора | ISBN 978-3-8382-0211-2

106 *Anna Dost* | Das russische Verfassungsrecht auf dem Weg zum Föderalismus und zurück. Zum Konflikt von Rechtsnormen und -wirklichkeit in der Russländischen Föderation von 1991 bis 2009 | Mit einem Vorwort von Alexander Blankenagel | ISBN 978-3-8382-0292-1

107 *Philipp Herzog* | Sozialistische Völkerfreundschaft, nationaler Widerstand oder harmloser Zeitvertreib? Zur politischen Funktion der Volkskunst im sowjetischen Estland | Mit einem Vorwort von Andreas Kappeler | ISBN 978-3-8382-0216-7

108 *Marlène Laruelle (Ed.)* | Russian Nationalism, Foreign Policy, and Identity Debates in Putin's Russia. New Ideological Patterns after the Orange Revolution | ISBN 978-3-8382-0325-6

109 *Michail Logvinov* | Russlands Kampf gegen den internationalen Terrorismus. Eine kritische Bestandsaufnahme des Bekämpfungsansatzes | Mit einem Geleitwort von Hans-Henning Schröder und einem Vorwort von Eckhard Jesse | ISBN 978-3-8382-0329-4

110 *John B. Dunlop* | The Moscow Bombings of September 1999. Examinations of Russian Terrorist Attacks at the Onset of Vladimir Putin's Rule | Second, Revised and Expanded Edition | ISBN 978-3-8382-0388-1

111 *Андрей А. Ковалёв* | Свидетельство из-за кулис российской политики I. Можно ли делать добро из зла? (Воспоминания и размышления о последних советских и первых послесоветских годах) | With a foreword by Peter Reddaway | ISBN 978-3-8382-0302-7

112 *Андрей А. Ковалёв* | Свидетельство из-за кулис российской политики II. Угроза для себя и окружающих (Наблюдения и предостережения относительно происходящего после 2000 г.) | ISBN 978-3-8382-0303-4

113 *Bernd Kappenberg* | Zeichen setzen für Europa. Der Gebrauch europäischer lateinischer Sonderzeichen in der deutschen Öffentlichkeit | Mit einem Vorwort von Peter Schlobinski | ISBN 978-3-89821-749-1

114 *Ivo Mijnssen* | The Quest for an Ideal Youth in Putin's Russia I. Back to Our Future! History, Modernity, and Patriotism according to Nashi, 2005-2013 | With a foreword by Jeronim Perović | Second, Revised and Expanded Edition | ISBN 978-3-8382-0368-3

115 *Jussi Lassila* | The Quest for an Ideal Youth in Putin's Russia II. The Search for Distinctive Conformism in the Political Communication of Nashi, 2005-2009 | With a foreword by Kirill Postoutenko | Second, Revised and Expanded Edition | ISBN 978-3-8382-0415-4

116 *Valerio Trabandt* | Neue Nachbarn, gute Nachbarschaft? Die EU als internationaler Akteur am Beispiel ihrer Demokratieförderung in Belarus und der Ukraine 2004-2009 | Mit einem Vorwort von Jutta Joachim | ISBN 978-3-8382-0437-6

117 *Fabian Pfeiffer* | Estlands Außen- und Sicherheitspolitik I. Der estnische Atlantizismus nach der wiedererlangten Unabhängigkeit 1991-2004 | Mit einem Vorwort von Helmut Hubel | ISBN 978-3-8382-0127-6

118 *Jana Podßuweit* | Estlands Außen- und Sicherheitspolitik II. Handlungsoptionen eines Kleinstaates im Rahmen seiner EU-Mitgliedschaft (2004-2008) | Mit einem Vorwort von Helmut Hubel | ISBN 978-3-8382-0440-6

119 *Karin Pointner* | Estlands Außen- und Sicherheitspolitik III. Eine gedächtnispolitische Analyse estnischer Entwicklungskooperation 2006-2010 | Mit einem Vorwort von Karin Liebhart | ISBN 978-3-8382-0435-2

120 *Ruslana Vovk* | Die Offenheit der ukrainischen Verfassung für das Völkerrecht und die europäische Integration | Mit einem Vorwort von Alexander Blankenagel | ISBN 978-3-8382-0481-9

121 *Mykhaylo Banakh* | Die Relevanz der Zivilgesellschaft bei den postkommunistischen Transformationsprozessen in mittel- und osteuropäischen Ländern. Das Beispiel der spät- und postsowjetischen Ukraine 1986-2009 | Mit einem Vorwort von Gerhard Simon | ISBN 978-3-8382-0499-4

122 *Michael Moser* | Language Policy and the Discourse on Languages in Ukraine under President Viktor Yanukovych (25 February 2010–28 October 2012) | ISBN 978-3-8382-0497-0 (Paperback edition) | ISBN 978-3-8382-0507-6 (Hardcover edition)

123 *Nicole Krome* | Russischer Netzwerkkapitalismus Restrukturierungsprozesse in der Russischen Föderation am Beispiel des Luftfahrtunternehmens „Aviastar" | Mit einem Vorwort von Petra Stykow | ISBN 978-3-8382-0534-2

124 *David R. Marples* | 'Our Glorious Past'. Lukashenka's Belarus and the Great Patriotic War | ISBN 978-3-8382-0574-8 (Paperback edition) | ISBN 978-3-8382-0675-2 (Hardcover edition)

125 *Ulf Walther* | Russlands „neuer Adel". Die Macht des Geheimdienstes von Gorbatschow bis Putin | Mit einem Vorwort von Hans-Georg Wieck | ISBN 978-3-8382-0584-7

126 *Simon Geissbühler (Hrsg.)* | Kiew – Revolution 3.0. Der Euromaidan 2013/14 und die Zukunftsperspektiven der Ukraine | ISBN 978-3-8382-0581-6 (Paperback edition) | ISBN 978-3-8382-0681-3 (Hardcover edition)

127 *Andrey Makarychev* | Russia and the EU in a Multipolar World. Discourses, Identities, Norms | With a foreword by Klaus Segbers | ISBN 978-3-8382-0629-5

128 *Roland Scharff* | Kasachstan als postsowjetischer Wohlfahrtsstaat. Die Transformation des sozialen Schutzsystems | Mit einem Vorwort von Joachim Ahrens | ISBN 978-3-8382-0622-6

129 *Katja Grupp* | Bild Lücke Deutschland. Kaliningrader Studierende sprechen über Deutschland | Mit einem Vorwort von Martin Schulz | ISBN 978-3-8382-0552-6

130 *Konstantin Sheiko, Stephen Brown* | History as Therapy. Alternative History and Nationalist Imaginings in Russia, 1991-2014 | ISBN 978-3-8382-0665-3

131 *Elisa Kriza* | Alexander Solzhenitsyn: Cold War Icon, Gulag Author, Russian Nationalist? A Study of the Western Reception of his Literary Writings, Historical Interpretations, and Political Ideas | With a foreword by Andrei Rogatchevski | ISBN 978-3-8382-0589-2 (Paperback edition) | ISBN 978-3-8382-0690-5 (Hardcover edition)

132 *Serghei Golunov* | The Elephant in the Room. Corruption and Cheating in Russian Universities | ISBN 978-3-8382-0570-0

133 *Manja Hussner, Rainer Arnold (Hgg.)* | Verfassungsgerichtsbarkeit in Zentralasien I. Sammlung von Verfassungstexten | ISBN 978-3-8382-0595-3

134 *Nikolay Mitrokhin* | Die „Russische Partei". Die Bewegung der russischen Nationalisten in der UdSSR 1953-1985 | Aus dem Russischen übertragen von einem Übersetzerteam unter der Leitung von Larisa Schippel | ISBN 978-3-8382-0024-8

135 *Manja Hussner, Rainer Arnold (Hgg.)* | Verfassungsgerichtsbarkeit in Zentralasien II. Sammlung von Verfassungstexten | ISBN 978-3-8382-0597-7

136 *Manfred Zeller* | Das sowjetische Fieber. Fußballfans im poststalinistischen Vielvölkerreich | Mit einem Vorwort von Nikolaus Katzer | ISBN 978-3-8382-0757-5

137 *Kristin Schreiter* | Stellung und Entwicklungspotential zivilgesellschaftlicher Gruppen in Russland. Menschenrechtsorganisationen im Vergleich | ISBN 978-3-8382-0673-8

138 *David R. Marples, Frederick V. Mills (Eds.)* | Ukraine's Euromaidan. Analyses of a Civil Revolution | ISBN 978-3-8382-0660-8

139 *Bernd Kappenberg* | Setting Signs for Europe. Why Diacritics Matter for European Integration | With a foreword by Peter Schlobinski | ISBN 978-3-8382-0663-9

140 *René Lenz* | Internationalisierung, Kooperation und Transfer. Externe bildungspolitische Akteure in der Russischen Föderation | Mit einem Vorwort von Frank Ettrich | ISBN 978-3-8382-0751-3

141 *Juri Plusnin, Yana Zausaeva, Natalia Zhidkevich, Artemy Pozanenko* | Wandering Workers. Mores, Behavior, Way of Life, and Political Status of Domestic Russian Labor Migrants | Translated by Julia Kazantseva | ISBN 978-3-8382-0653-0

142 *David J. Smith (Eds.)* | Latvia – A Work in Progress? 100 Years of State- and Nation-Building | ISBN 978-3-8382-0648-6

143 *Инна Чувычкина (ред.)* | Экспортные нефте- и газопроводы на постсоветском пространстве. Анализ трубопроводной политики в свете теории международных отношений | ISBN 978-3-8382-0822-0

144 *Johann Zajaczkowski* | Russland – eine pragmatische Großmacht? Eine rollentheoretische Untersuchung russischer Außenpolitik am Beispiel der Zusammenarbeit mit den USA nach 9/11 und des Georgienkrieges von 2008 | Mit einem Vorwort von Siegfried Schieder | ISBN 978-3-8382-0837-4

145 *Boris Popivanov* | Changing Images of the Left in Bulgaria. The Challenge of Post-Communism in the Early 21st Century | ISBN 978-3-8382-0667-7

146 *Lenka Krátká* | A History of the Czechoslovak Ocean Shipping Company 1948-1989. How a Small, Landlocked Country Ran Maritime Business During the Cold War | ISBN 978-3-8382-0666-0

147 *Alexander Sergunin* | Explaining Russian Foreign Policy Behavior. Theory and Practice | ISBN 978-3-8382-0752-0

148 *Darya Malyutina* | Migrant Friendships in a Super-Diverse City. Russian-Speakers and their Social Relationships in London in the 21st Century | With a foreword by Claire Dwyer | ISBN 978-3-8382-0652-3

149 *Alexander Sergunin, Valery Konyshev* | Russia in the Arctic. Hard or Soft Power? | ISBN 978-3-8382-0753-7

150 *John J. Maresca* | Helsinki Revisited. A Key U.S. Negotiator's Memoirs on the Development of the CSCE into the OSCE | With a foreword by Hafiz Pashayev | ISBN 978-3-8382-0852-7

151 *Jardar Østbø* | The New Third Rome. Readings of a Russian Nationalist Myth | With a foreword by Pål Kolstø | ISBN 978-3-8382-0870-1

152 *Simon Kordonsky* | Socio-Economic Foundations of the Russian Post-Soviet Regime. The Resource-Based Economy and Estate-Based Social Structure of Contemporary Russia | With a foreword by Svetlana Barsukova | ISBN 978-3-8382-0775-9

153 *Duncan Leitch* | Assisting Reform in Post-Communist Ukraine 2000–2012. The Illusions of Donors and the Disillusion of Beneficiaries | With a foreword by Kataryna Wolczuk | ISBN 978-3-8382-0844-2

154 *Abel Polese* | Limits of a Post-Soviet State. How Informality Replaces, Renegotiates, and Reshapes Governance in Contemporary Ukraine | With a foreword by Colin Williams | ISBN 978-3-8382-0845-9

155 *Mikhail Suslov (Ed.)* | Digital Orthodoxy in the Post-Soviet World. The Russian Orthodox Church and Web 2.0 | With a foreword by Father Cyril Hovorun | ISBN 978-3-8382-0871-8

156 *Leonid Luks* | Zwei „Sonderwege"? Russisch-deutsche Parallelen und Kontraste (1917-2014). Vergleichende Essays | ISBN 978-3-8382-0823-7

157 *Vladimir V. Karacharovskiy, Ovsey I. Shkaratan, Gordey A. Yastrebov* | Towards a New Russian Work Culture. Can Western Companies and Expatriates Change Russian Society? | With a foreword by Elena N. Danilova | Translated by Julia Kazantseva | ISBN 978-3-8382-0902-9

158 *Edmund Griffiths* | Aleksandr Prokhanov and Post-Soviet Esotericism | ISBN 978-3-8382-0963-0

159 *Timm Beichelt, Susann Worschech (Eds.)* | Transnational Ukraine? Networks and Ties that Influence(d) Contemporary Ukraine | ISBN 978-3-8382-0944-9

160 *Mieste Hotopp-Riecke* | Die Tataren der Krim zwischen Assimilation und Selbstbehauptung. Der Aufbau des krimtatarischen Bildungswesens nach Deportation und Heimkehr (1990-2005) | Mit einem Vorwort von Swetlana Czerwonnaja | ISBN 978-3-89821-940-2

161 *Olga Bertelsen (Ed.)* | Revolution and War in Contemporary Ukraine. The Challenge of Change | ISBN 978-3-8382-1016-2

162 *Natalya Ryabinska* | Ukraine's Post-Communist Mass Media. Between Capture and Commercialization | With a foreword by Marta Dyczok | ISBN 978-3-8382-1011-7

163 *Alexandra Cotofana, James M. Nyce (Eds.)* | Religion and Magic in Socialist and Post-Socialist Contexts. Historic and Ethnographic Case Studies of Orthodoxy, Heterodoxy, and Alternative Spirituality | With a foreword by Patrick L. Michelson | ISBN 978-3-8382-0989-0

164 *Nozima Akhrarkhodjaeva* | The Instrumentalisation of Mass Media in Electoral Authoritarian Regimes. Evidence from Russia's Presidential Election Campaigns of 2000 and 2008 | ISBN 978-3-8382-1013-1

165 *Yulia Krasheninnikova* | Informal Healthcare in Contemporary Russia. Sociographic Essays on the Post-Soviet Infrastructure for Alternative Healing Practices | ISBN 978-3-8382-0970-8

166 *Peter Kaiser* | Das Schachbrett der Macht. Die Handlungsspielräume eines sowjetischen Funktionärs unter Stalin am Beispiel des Generalsekretärs des Komsomol Aleksandr Kosarev (1929-1938) | Mit einem Vorwort von Dietmar Neutatz | ISBN 978-3-8382-1052-0

167 *Oksana Kim* | The Effects and Implications of Kazakhstan's Adoption of International Financial Reporting Standards. A Resource Dependence Perspective | With a foreword by Svetlana Vlady | ISBN 978-3-8382-0987-6

168 *Anna Sanina* | Patriotic Education in Contemporary Russia. Sociological Studies in the Making of the Post-Soviet Citizen | With a foreword by Anna Oldfield | ISBN 978-3-8382-0993-7

169 *Rudolf Wolters* | Spezialist in Sibirien Faksimile der 1933 erschienenen ersten Ausgabe | Mit einem Vorwort von Dmitrij Chmelnizki | ISBN 978-3-8382-0515-1

170 *Michal Vít, Magdalena M. Baran (Eds.)* | Transregional versus National Perspectives on Contemporary Central European History. Studies on the Building of Nation-States and Their Cooperation in the 20th and 21st Century | With a foreword by Petr Vágner | ISBN 978-3-8382-1015-5

171 *Philip Gamaghelyan* | Conflict Resolution Beyond the International Relations Paradigm. Evolving Designs as a Transformative Practice in Nagorno-Karabakh and Syria | With a foreword by Susan Allen | ISBN 978-3-8382-1057-5

172 *Maria Shagina* | Joining a Prestigious Club. Cooperation with Europarties and Its Impact on Party Development in Georgia, Moldova, and Ukraine 2004–2015 | With a foreword by Kataryna Wolczuk | ISBN 978-3-8382-1084-1

173 *Alexandra Cotofana, James M. Nyce (Eds.)* | Religion and Magic in Socialist and Post-Socialist Contexts II. Baltic, Eastern European, and Post-USSR Case Studies | With a foreword by Anita Stasulane | ISBN 978-3-8382-0990-6

174 *Barbara Kunz* | Kind Words, Cruise Missiles, and Everything in Between. The Use of Power Resources in U.S. Policies towards Poland, Ukraine, and Belarus 1989–2008 | With a foreword by William Hill | ISBN 978-3-8382-1065-0

175 *Eduard Klein* | Bildungskorruption in Russland und der Ukraine. Eine komparative Analyse der Performanz staatlicher Antikorruptionsmaßnahmen im Hochschulsektor am Beispiel universitärer Aufnahmeprüfungen | Mit einem Vorwort von Heiko Pleines | ISBN 978-3-8382-0995-1

176 *Markus Soldner* | Politischer Kapitalismus im postsowjetischen Russland. Die politische, wirtschaftliche und mediale Transformation in den 1990er Jahren | Mit einem Vorwort von Wolfgang Ismayr | ISBN 978-3-8382-1222-7

177 *Anton Oleinik* | Building Ukraine from Within. A Sociological, Institutional, and Economic Analysis of a Nation-State in the Making | ISBN 978-3-8382-1150-3

178 *Peter Rollberg, Marlene Laruelle (Eds.)* | Mass Media in the Post-Soviet World. Market Forces, State Actors, and Political Manipulation in the Informational Environment after Communism | ISBN 978-3-8382-1116-9

179 *Mikhail Minakov* | Development and Dystopia. Studies in Post-Soviet Ukraine and Eastern Europe | With a foreword by Alexander Etkind | ISBN 978-3-8382-1112-1

180 *Aijan Sharshenova* | The European Union's Democracy Promotion in Central Asia. A Study of Political Interests, Influence, and Development in Kazakhstan and Kyrgyzstan in 2007–2013 | With a foreword by Gordon Crawford | ISBN 978-3-8382-1151-0

181 *Andrey Makarychev, Alexandra Yatsyk (Eds.)* | Boris Nemtsov and Russian Politics. Power and Resistance | With a foreword by Zhanna Nemtsova | ISBN 978-3-8382-1122-0

182 *Sophie Falsini* | The Euromaidan's Effect on Civil Society. Why and How Ukrainian Social Capital Increased after the Revolution of Dignity | With a foreword by Susann Worschech | ISBN 978-3-8382-1131-2

183 *Valentyna Romanova, Andreas Umland (Eds.)* | Ukraine's Decentralization. Challenges and Implications of the Local Governance Reform after the Euromaidan Revolution | ISBN 978-3-8382-1162-7

184 *Leonid Luks* | A Fateful Triangle. Essays on Contemporary Russian, German and Polish History | ISBN 978-3-8382-1143-5

185 *John B. Dunlop* | The February 2015 Assassination of Boris Nemtsov and the Flawed Trial of his Alleged Killers. An Exploration of Russia's "Crime of the 21st Century" | ISBN 978-3-8382-1188-6

186 *Vasile Rotaru* | Russia, the EU, and the Eastern Partnership. Building Bridges or Digging Trenches? | ISBN 978-3-8382-1134-3

187 *Marina Lebedeva* | Russian Studies of International Relations. From the Soviet Past to the Post-Cold-War Present | With a foreword by Andrei P. Tsygankov | ISBN 978-3-8382-0851-0

188 *Tomasz Stępniewski, George Soroka (Eds.)* | Ukraine after Maidan. Revisiting Domestic and Regional Security | ISBN 978-3-8382-1075-9

189 *Petar Cholakov* | Ethnic Entrepreneurs Unmasked. Political Institutions and Ethnic Conflicts in Contemporary Bulgaria | ISBN 978-3-8382-1189-3

190 *A. Salem, G. Hazeldine, D. Morgan (Eds.)* | Higher Education in Post-Communist States. Comparative and Sociological Perspectives | ISBN 978-3-8382-1183-1

191 *Igor Torbakov* | After Empire. Nationalist Imagination and Symbolic Politics in Russia and Eurasia in the Twentieth and Twenty-First Century | With a foreword by Serhii Plokhy | ISBN 978-3-8382-1217-3

192 *Aleksandr Burakovskiy* | Jewish-Ukrainian Relations in Late and Post-Soviet Ukraine. Articles, Lectures and Essays from 1986 to 2016 | ISBN 978-3-8382-1210-4

193 *Natalia Shapovalova, Olga Burlyuk (Eds.)* | Civil Society in Post-Euromaidan Ukraine. From Revolution to Consolidation | With a foreword by Richard Youngs | ISBN 978-3-8382-1216-6

194 *Franz Preissler* | Positionsverteidigung, Imperialismus oder Irredentismus? Russland und die „Russischsprachigen", 1991–2015 | ISBN 978-3-8382-1262-3

195 *Marian Madeła* | Der Reformprozess in der Ukraine 2014-2017. Eine Fallstudie zur Reform der öffentlichen Verwaltung | Mit einem Vorwort von Martin Malek | ISBN 978-3-8382-1266-1

196 *Anke Giesen* | „Wie kann denn der Sieger ein Verbrecher sein?" Eine diskursanalytische Untersuchung der russlandweiten Debatte über Konzept und Verstaatlichungsprozess der Lagergedenkstätte „Perm'-36" im Ural | ISBN 978-3-8382-1284-5

197 *Alla Leukavets* | The Integration Policies of Belarus and Ukraine vis-à-vis the EU and Russia. A Comparative Case Study Through the Prism of a Two-Level Game Approach | ISBN 978-3-8382-1247-0

198 *Oksana Kim* | The Development and Challenges of Russian Corporate Governance I. The Roles and Functions of Boards of Directors | With a foreword by Sheila M. Puffer | ISBN 978-3-8382-1287-6

199 *Thomas D. Grant* | International Law and the Post-Soviet Space I. Essays on Chechnya and the Baltic States | With a foreword by Stephen M. Schwebel | ISBN 978-3-8382-1279-1

200 *Thomas D. Grant* | International Law and the Post-Soviet Space II. Essays on Ukraine, Intervention, and Non-Proliferation | ISBN 978-3-8382-1280-7

201 *Slavomír Michálek, Michal Štefansky* | The Age of Fear. The Cold War and Its Influence on Czechoslovakia 1945–1968 | ISBN 978-3-8382-1285-2

202 *Iulia-Sabina Joja* | Romania's Strategic Culture 1990–2014. Continuity and Change in a Post-Communist Country's Evolution of National Interests and Security Policies | With a foreword by Heiko Biehl | ISBN 978-3-8382-1286-9

203 *Andrei Rogatchevski, Yngvar B. Steinholt, Arve Hansen, David-Emil Wickström* | War of Songs. Popular Music and Recent Russia-Ukraine Relations | With a foreword by Artemy Troitsky | ISBN 978-3-8382-1173-2

204 *Maria Lipman (Ed.)* | Russian Voices on Post-Crimea Russia. An Almanac of Counterpoint Essays from 2015–2018 | ISBN 978-3-8382-1251-7

205 *Ksenia Maksimovtsova* | Language Conflicts in Contemporary Estonia, Latvia, and Ukraine. A Comparative Exploration of Discourses in Post-Soviet Russian-Language Digital Media | With a foreword by Ammon Cheskin | ISBN 978-3-8382-1282-1

206 *Michal Vít* | The EU's Impact on Identity Formation in East-Central Europe between 2004 and 2013. Perceptions of the Nation and Europe in Political Parties of the Czech Republic, Poland, and Slovakia | With a foreword by Andrea Pető | ISBN 978-3-8382-1275-3

207 *Per A. Rudling* | Tarnished Heroes. The Organization of Ukrainian Nationalists in the Memory Politics of Post-Soviet Ukraine | ISBN 978-3-8382-0999-9

208 *Kaja Gadowska, Peter Solomon (Eds.)* | Legal Change in Post-Communist States. Progress, Reversions, Explanations | ISBN 978-3-8382-1312-5

209 *Paweł Kowal, Georges Mink, Iwona Reichardt (Eds.)* | Three Revolutions: Mobilization and Change in Contemporary Ukraine I. Theoretical Aspects and Analyses on Religion, Memory, and Identity | ISBN 978-3-8382-1321-7

210 *Paweł Kowal, Georges Mink, Adam Reichardt, Iwona Reichardt (Eds.)* | Three Revolutions: Mobilization and Change in Contemporary Ukraine II. An Oral History of the Revolution on Granite, Orange Revolution, and Revolution of Dignity | ISBN 978-3-8382-1323-1

211 *Li Bennich-Björkman, Sergiy Kurbatov (Eds.)* | When the Future Came. The Collapse of the USSR and the Emergence of National Memory in Post-Soviet History Textbooks | ISBN 978-3-8382-1335-4

212 *Olga R. Gulina* | Migration as a (Geo-)Political Challenge in the Post-Soviet Space. Border Regimes, Policy Choices, Visa Agendas | With a foreword by Nils Muižnieks | ISBN 978-3-8382-1338-5

213 *Sanna Turoma, Kaarina Aitamurto, Slobodanka Vladiv-Glover (Eds.)* | Religion, Expression, and Patriotism in Russia. Essays on Post-Soviet Society and the State. ISBN 978-3-8382-1346-0

214 *Vasif Huseynov* | Geopolitical Rivalries in the "Common Neighborhood". Russia's Conflict with the West, Soft Power, and Neoclassical Realism | With a foreword by Nicholas Ross Smith | ISBN 978-3-8382-1277-7

215 *Mikhail Suslov* | Geopolitical Imagination. Ideology and Utopia in Post-Soviet Russia | With a foreword by Mark Bassin | ISBN 978-3-8382-1361-3

216 *Alexander Etkind, Mikhail Minakov (Eds.)* | Ideology after Union. Political Doctrines, Discourses, and Debates in Post-Soviet Societies | ISBN 978-3-8382-1388-0

217 *Jakob Mischke, Oleksandr Zabirko (Hgg.)* | Protestbewegungen im langen Schatten des Kreml. Aufbruch und Resignation in Russland und der Ukraine | ISBN 978-3-8382-0926-5

218 *Oksana Huss* | How Corruption and Anti-Corruption Policies Sustain Hybrid Regimes. Strategies of Political Domination under Ukraine's Presidents in 1994-2014 | With a foreword by Tobias Debiel and Andrea Gawrich | ISBN 978-3-8382-1430-6

219 *Dmitry Travin, Vladimir Gel'man, Otar Marganiya* | The Russian Path. Ideas, Interests, Institutions, Illusions | With a foreword by Vladimir Ryzhkov | ISBN 978-3-8382-1421-4

220 *Gergana Dimova* | Political Uncertainty. A Comparative Exploration | With a foreword by Todor Yalamov and Rumena Filipova | ISBN 978-3-8382-1385-9

221 *Torben Waschke* | Russland in Transition. Geopolitik zwischen Raum, Identität und Machtinteressen | Mit einem Vorwort von Andreas Dittmann | ISBN 978-3-8382-1480-1

222 *Steven Jobbitt, Zsolt Bottlik, Marton Berki (Eds.)* | Power and Identity in the Post-Soviet Realm. Geographies of Ethnicity and Nationality after 1991 | ISBN 978-3-8382-1399-6

223 *Daria Buteiko* | Erinnerungsort. Ort des Gedenkens, der Erholung oder der Einkehr? Kommunismus-Erinnerung am Beispiel der Gedenkstätte Berliner Mauer sowie des Soloveckij-Klosters und -Museumsparks | ISBN 978-3-8382-1367-5

224 *Olga Bertelsen (Ed.)* | Russian Active Measures. Yesterday, Today, Tomorrow | With a foreword by Jan Goldman | ISBN 978-3-8382-1529-7

225 *David Mandel* | "Optimizing" Higher Education in Russia. University Teachers and their Union "Universitetskaya solidarnost'" | ISBN 978-3-8382-1519-8

226 *Mikhail Minakov, Gwendolyn Sasse, Daria Isachenko (Eds.)* | Post-Soviet Secessionism. Nation-Building and State-Failure after Communism | ISBN 978-3-8382-1538-9

227 *Jakob Hauter (Ed.)* | Civil War? Interstate War? Hybrid War? Dimensions and Interpretations of the Donbas Conflict in 2014–2020 | With a foreword by Andrew Wilson | ISBN 978-3-8382-1383-5

228 *Tima T. Moldogaziev, Gene A. Brewer, J. Edward Kellough (Eds.)* | Public Policy and Politics in Georgia. Lessons from Post-Soviet Transition | With a foreword by Dan Durning | ISBN 978-3-8382-1535-8

229 *Oxana Schmies (Ed.)* | NATO's Enlargement and Russia. A Strategic Challenge in the Past and Future | With a foreword by Vladimir Kara-Murza | ISBN 978-3-8382-1478-8

230 *Christopher Ford* | Ukapisme – Une Gauche perdue. Le marxisme anti-colonial dans la révolution ukrainienne 1917-1925 | Avec une préface de Vincent Présumey | ISBN 978-3-8382-0899-2

231 *Anna Kutkina* | Between Lenin and Bandera. Decommunization and Multivocality in Post-Euromaidan Ukraine | With a foreword by Juri Mykkänen | ISBN 978-3-8382-1506-8

232 *Lincoln E. Flake* | Defending the Faith. The Russian Orthodox Church and the Demise of Religious Pluralism | With a foreword by Peter Martland | ISBN 978-3-8382-1378-1

233 *Nikoloz Samkharadze* | Russia's Recognition of the Independence of Abkhazia and South Ossetia. Analysis of a Deviant Case in Moscow's Foreign Policy | With a foreword by Neil MacFarlane | ISBN 978-3-8382-1414-6

234 *Arve Hansen* | Urban Protest. A Spatial Perspective on Kyiv, Minsk, and Moscow | With a foreword by Julie Wilhelmsen | ISBN 978-3-8382-1495-5

235 *Eleonora Narvselius, Julie Fedor (Eds.)* | Diversity in the East-Central European Borderlands. Memories, Cityscapes, People | ISBN 978-3-8382-1523-5

236 *Regina Elsner* | The Russian Orthodox Church and Modernity. A Historical and Theological Investigation into Eastern Christianity between Unity and Plurality | With a foreword by Mikhail Suslov | ISBN 978-3-8382-1568-6

237 *Bo Petersson* | The Putin Predicament. Problems of Legitimacy and Succession in Russia | With a foreword by J. Paul Goode | ISBN 978-3-8382-1050-6

238 *Jonathan Otto Pohl* | The Years of Great Silence. The Deportation, Special Settlement, and Mobilization into the Labor Army of Ethnic Germans in the USSR, 1941–1955 | ISBN 978-3-8382-1630-7

239 *Mikhail Minakov (Ed.)* | Inventing Majorities. Ideological Creativity in Post-Soviet Societies | ISBN 978-3-8382-1641-6

240 *Robert M. Cutler* | Soviet and Post-Soviet Foreign Policies I. East-South Relations and the Political Economy of the Communist Bloc, 1971–1991 | With a foreword by Roger E. Kanet | ISBN 978-3-8382-1654-3

241　*Izabella Agardi* | On the Verge of History. Life Stories of Rural Women from Serbia, Romania, and Hungary, 1920–2020 | With a foreword by Andrea Pető | ISBN 978-3-8382-1602-7

242　*Sebastian Schäffer (Ed.)* | Ukraine in Central and Eastern Europe. Kyiv's Foreign Affairs and the International Relations of the Post-Communist Region | With a foreword by Pavlo Klimkin and Andreas Umland| ISBN 978-3-8382-1615-7

243　*Volodymyr Dubrovskyi, Kalman Mizsei, Mychailo Wynnyckyj (Eds.)* | Eight Years after the Revolution of Dignity. What Has Changed in Ukraine during 2013–2021? | With a foreword by Yaroslav Hrytsak | ISBN 978-3-8382-1560-0

244　*Rumena Filipova* | Constructing the Limits of Europe Identity and Foreign Policy in Poland, Bulgaria, and Russia since 1989 | With forewords by Harald Wydra and Gergana Yankova-Dimova | ISBN 978-3-8382-1649-2

245　*Oleksandra Keudel* | How Patronal Networks Shape Opportunities for Local Citizen Participation in a Hybrid Regime A Comparative Analysis of Five Cities in Ukraine | With a foreword by Sabine Kropp | ISBN 978-3-8382-1671-3

246　*Jan Claas Behrends, Thomas Lindenberger, Pavel Kolar (Eds.)* | Violence after Stalin Institutions, Practices, and Everyday Life in the Soviet Bloc 1953–1989 | ISBN 978-3-8382-1637-9

247　*Leonid Luks* | Macht und Ohnmacht der Utopien Essays zur Geschichte Russlands im 20. und 21. Jahrhundert | ISBN 978-3-8382-1677-5

248　*Iuliia Barshadska* | Brüssel zwischen Kyjiw und Moskau Das auswärtige Handeln der Europäischen Union im ukrainisch-russischen Konflikt 2014-2019 | Mit einem Vorwort von Olaf Leiße | ISBN 978-3-8382-1667-6

249　*Valentyna Romanova* | Decentralisation and Multilevel Elections in Ukraine Reform Dynamics and Party Politics in 2010–2021 | With a foreword by Kimitaka Matsuzato | ISBN 978-3-8382-1700-0

250　*Alexander Motyl* | National Questions. Theoretical Reflections on Nations and Nationalism in Eastern Europe | ISBN 978-3-8382-1675-1

251　*Marc Dietrich* | A Cosmopolitan Model for Peacebuilding. The Ukrainian Cases of Crimea and the Donbas | ISBN 978-3-8382-1687-4

252　*Eduard Baidaus* | An Unsettled Nation. State-Building, Identity, and Separatism in Post-Soviet Moldova | With forewords by John-Paul Himka and David R. Marples | ISBN 978-3-8382-1582-2

253　*Igor Okunev, Petr Oskolkov (Eds.)* | Transforming the Administrative Matryoshka. The Reform of Autonomous Okrugs in the Russian Federation, 2003–2008 | With a foreword by Vladimir Zorin | ISBN 978-3-8382-1721-5

254　*Winfried Schneider-Deters* | Ukraine's Fateful Years 2013–2019. Vol. I: The Popular Uprising in Winter 2013/2014 | ISBN 978-3-8382-1725-3

255　*Winfried Schneider-Deters* | Ukraine's Fateful Years 2013–2019. Vol. II: The Annexation of Crimea and the War in Donbas | ISBN 978-3-8382-1726-0

256　*Robert M. Cutler* | Soviet and Post-Soviet Russian Foreign Policies II. East-West Relations in Europe and the Political Economy of the Communist Bloc, 1971–1991 | With a foreword by Roger E. Kanet | ISBN 978-3-8382-1727-7

257　*Robert M. Cutler* | Soviet and Post-Soviet Russian Foreign Policies III. East-West Relations in Europe and Eurasia in the Post-Cold War Transition, 1991–2001 | With a foreword by Roger E. Kanet | ISBN 978-3-8382-1728-4

258　*Paweł Kowal, Iwona Reichardt, Kateryna Pryshchepa (Eds.)* | Three Revolutions: Mobilization and Change in Contemporary Ukraine III. Archival Records and Historical Sources on the 1990 Revolution on Granite | ISBN 978-3-8382-1376-2

259　*Mikhail Minakov (Ed.)* | Philosophy Unchained. Developments in Post-Soviet Philosophical Thought. | With a foreword by Christopher Donohue | ISBN 978-3-8382-1768-0

260　*David Dalton* | The Ukrainian Oligarchy After the Euromaidan. How Ukraine's Political Economy Regime Survived the Crisis | With a foreword by Andrew Wilson | ISBN 978-3-8382-1740-6

261　*Andreas Heinemann-Grüder (Ed.)* | Who are the Fighters? Irregular Armed Groups in the Russian-Ukrainian War in 2014–2015 | ISBN 978-3-8382-1777-2

262　*Taras Kuzio (Ed.)* | Russian Disinformation and Western Scholarship. Bias and Prejudice in Journalistic, Expert, and Academic Analyses of East European and Eurasian Affairs | ISBN 978-3-8382-1685-0

263　*Darius Furmonavicius* | LithuaniaTransforms the West. Lithuania's Liberation from Soviet Occupation and the Enlargement of NATO (1988–2022) | With a foreword by Vytautas Landsbergis | ISBN 978-3-8382-1779-3

264　*Dirk Dalberg* | Politisches Denken im tschechoslowakischen Dissens: Egon Bondy, Miroslav Kusý, Milan Šimečka und Petr Uhl. Gegenwartsbeschreibungen und Zukunftsvorstellungen (1968-1989) | ISBN 978-3-8382-1318-5

***ibidem**.eu*